Harrington on Modern Tournament Poker

How to Play No-Limit Hold 'em Multi-Table Tournaments

By
DAN HARRINGTON
1995 World Champion

BILL ROBERTIE

**A product of
Two Plus Two Publishing LLC**

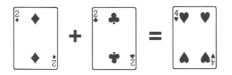

FIRST EDITION

FIRST PRINTING
May 2014

Printing and Binding
Creel Printing, Inc.
Las Vegas, Nevada

Printed in the United States of America

FSC
www.fsc.org
MIX
Paper from
responsible sources
FSC® C022441

Harrington on
Modern Tournament Poker
How to Play No-Limit
Hold 'em Multi-Table Tournaments

COPYRIGHT © 2014 Two Plus Two Publishing LLC

For information contact: **Two Plus Two Publishing LLC**
                             32 Commerce Center Drive
                             Suite H-89
                             Henderson, NV 89014

ISBN: 1-880685-56-6
ISBN13: 978-1-880685-56-3

*We can't change the cards we're dealt,
only how we play the hand.*

— Randy Pausch

Table of Contents

i

ii Table of Contents

iii Table of Contents

About Dan Harrington

Dan Harrington began playing poker professionally in 1982. On the circuit he is known as "Action Dan," an ironic reference to his solid but effective style. He has won several major no-limit hold 'em tournaments including the European Poker Championships (1995), the $2,500 No-Limit Hold 'em event at the 1995 World Series of Poker, and the Four Queens No-Limit Hold 'em Championship (1996).

Dan began his serious games-playing with chess, where he quickly became a master and one of the strongest players in the New England area. In 1972 he won the Massachusetts Chess Championship, ahead of most of the top players in the area. In 1976 he started playing backgammon, a game which he also quickly mastered. He was soon one of the top money players in the Boston area, and in 1981 he won the World Cup of Backgammon in Washington D.C., ahead of a field that included most of the world's top players.

He first played in the $10,000 No-Limit Hold 'em Championship Event of the World Series of Poker in 1987. He has played in the championship a total of 15 times and has reached the final table in four of those tournaments, an amazing record. Besides winning the World Championship in 1995, he finished sixth in 1987, third in 2003, and fourth in 2004. In 2006 he finished second at the Doyle Brunson North American Championships at the Bellagio, while in 2007 he won the Legends of Poker Tournament at the Bicycle Club. He is widely recognized as one of the greatest and most respected no-limit hold 'em players, as well as a feared opponent in both no-limit and limit hold 'em side games.

His first two poker books, *Harrington on Hold 'em, Volume I* and *Harrington on Hold 'em, Volume II* have become two of the best-selling poker books of all time. He lives in Santa Monica where he is a partner in Anchor Loans, a real estate business.

About Bill Robertie

Bill Robertie has spent his life playing and writing about chess, backgammon, and now poker. He began playing chess as a boy, inspired by Bobby Fischer's feats on the international chess scene. While attending Harvard as an undergraduate, he became a chess master and helped the Harvard chess team win several intercollegiate titles. After graduation he won a number of chess tournaments, including the United States Championship at speed chess in 1970. He also established a reputation at blindfold chess, giving exhibitions on as many as eight boards simultaneously.

In 1976 he switched from chess to backgammon, becoming one of the top players in the world. His major titles include the World Championship in Monte Carlo in 1983 and 1987, the Black & White Championship in Boston in 1979, the Las Vegas tournaments in 1980 and 2001, the Bahamas Pro-Am in 1993, the Istanbul World Open in 1994, and the New York Metropolitan Open in 2011 and 2013.

He has written several well-regarded backgammon books, the most noted of which are *Advanced Backgammon* (1991), a two-volume collection of 400 problems, and *Modern Backgammon* (2002), a new look at the underlying theory of the game. He has also written a set of three books for the beginning player: *Backgammon for Winners* (1994), *Backgammon for Serious Players* (1995), and *501 Essential Backgammon Problems* (1997).

From 1991 to 1998 he edited the magazine *Inside Backgammon* with Kent Goulding. He owns a publishing company, the Gammon Press (www.thegammonpress.com), and lives in Arlington, Massachusetts with his wife Patrice.

Introduction

In our two-part series *Harrington on Hold 'Em, Volumes I and II*, written in 2004 and 2005, Bill Robertie and I outlined the theory and practice of how to play in no-limit hold 'em tournaments. We explained how live and online tournaments were organized and structured. We showed how to evaluate preflop hands depending on your position at the table. We explained the basics of evaluating the flop and playing the flop, turn, and river. And, in what was probably the most important part of the books, we showed how your strategy needs to be adjusted based on your stack size and your 'M,' the ratio between your stack and the blinds and antes.

We believe our original books remain an excellent introduction to the world of no-limit hold 'em tournaments. But life moves on and times change. The enormous growth of interest in poker and poker tournaments led to an intense focus on the theory of tournament poker with the result being a reexamination of old theories and the introduction of many new ideas. The fundamentals of no-limit hold 'em did not change. But the game was revealed to have more depth than older players could have anticipated, and the result is that no-limit hold 'em has evolved over the last decade into a newer, tougher, faster game. And good players have had to evolve to keep up.

In *Modern Tournament Poker*, we're going to take a fresh look at the world of no-limit hold 'em tournaments. We'll explain how the game is played now, and what you'll have to do to be a successful tournament player in 2014 and beyond. While the fundamentals of no-limit hold 'em haven't changed, the tactics have. We'll introduce the sort of players you'll meet at today's tournaments and show how each style of play has weaknesses that can be exploited, as long as you understand what's happening.

No-limit hold 'em is a better game now than it was a decade ago. It's more exciting, it's got a faster pace, and it's more fun to play. If poker circa 2003 was like drifting down a lazy river, poker

1

circa 2014 is more like white water rafting. In this book, we'll show you how to negotiate your way in this new world.

Organization of the Book

"Part One: Understanding the Basis of NLH Tournament Poker" explains the basics of no-limit hold 'em tournaments. If you've never played no-limit hold 'em or hold 'em tournaments, or have only played a little but don't feel you have a real grasp of the game, this section is must reading. If you're a pretty experienced player, feel free to skip it.

"Part Two: Stacks, Blinds, Antes, and Ranges" focuses on the building blocks of tournament strategy: blinds, antes, stack sizes, and hand ranges. We'll show how to evaluate your stack size and the stack sizes of other players (at the table), and what effect this has on strategy. We'll talk about the Independent Chip Model (ICM) and how useful it is in various tournament situations. We'll also explain what a hand range is, and how to think about your opponent's plays in terms of the hand ranges they represent.

"Part Three: Playing Preflop" describes preflop play. Here we'll talk about selecting hands to play, how to play each type of hand, how to play on each street, how to size your bets, and how to make adjustments to your opponents. We'll also discuss the different styles of play you'll see at the table, how to exploit each style, and how to counter the kind of super-aggressive play you'll see in modern tournaments.

In "Part Four: Playing the Flop," we talk about play on the flop. Topics include how to properly size flop bets, whether or not to make a continuation bet, how to make and counter donk bets, and how to handle draws and monsters.

"Part Five: Playing the Turn" looks at the turn bet: Should you bet, check, bluff, or raise, and what to do when you bet and get raised?

In "Part Six: Playing the River," we move on to the river. How should you evaluate your hand at this point? What is thin value and when should you bet it? When should you bluff? And what do you do when your opponent takes the lead?

"Part Seven: The All-In Move," is all about all-ins. Topics include when to move all your chips in and when should you call if your opponent moves all-in first?

In "Part Eight: Playing Styles," we look at the key question of playing styles. We'll talk about the four basic styles you'll see in a modern tournament. We'll also talk about the modern loose-aggressive style, show why it's become the dominant style in today's poker tournaments, and give some ideas for how a fundamentally tight player can accommodate himself to the modern game.

Like many complex subjects, poker has its own elaborate terminology. We've included a Glossary after Part Eight, and there you'll find a basic explanation of all the words and expressions poker players use when they talk poker. Look there first if you run across a term that seems unfamiliar.

We the authors also want to express a few thank-you's. The terrific cover design is the work of Niko Bourassa-Wright who won The Cover Design Contest on www.twoplustwo.com and who posts there as "Reaper421."

We also need to thank Alan Berrelleza of Creel Printing for the graphics work throughout the book.

For the index, we need to thank Carol Roberts of Roberts Indexing Services. Her website is located at www.RobertsIndexing.com. And finally, we need to thank Mason Malmuth and David Sklansky for their comments on the manuscript as well as all the additional things they do relative to Two Plus Two.

Part One

Understanding the Basics of NLH Tournament Poker

Understanding the Basics of NLH Tournament Poker

Introduction

Before you can succeed in no-limit hold 'em tournaments, there are certain basic concepts you'll need to understand. If you're already an experienced player, or you've read *Harrington on Hold 'Em*, then you've probably already encountered these basic ideas and can move on to "Part Two: Stacks, Blinds, Antes, and Ranges."

If not, or if you need a quick review, then this section is for you (and a quick review never hurts). We'll also use the concepts explained here throughout the book, so make sure you're completely comfortable with them before moving on.

Some of the general ideas to be discussed like pot odds, implied odds, and types of bets, apply not just to hold 'em but to all forms of poker. And while you may have encountered many of these ideas before, their application to no-limit hold 'em may be slightly different than you've seen, so don't rush through these sections too quickly. These concepts do have a mathematical basis; however, the mathematics are not difficult. Success at no-limit hold 'em requires clear, logical thinking, not advanced mathematics.

Other ideas like tournament structures, escalating blinds, hand ranges, and flop textures, are unique to no-limit hold 'em tournament play, and understanding them is crucial. If these are unfamiliar ideas, pay close attention to the material here, as we'll be using it extensively in Parts Two through Eight.

Why No-Limit Hold 'em?

The poker variation known as no-limit hold 'em dates back to Texas in the 1950s and maybe as early as the 1920s. No one now remembers exactly how it originated, but by the early 1960s, it had replaced five-card stud and lowball as the preferred game of the big-time road gamblers.

Why did hold 'em elbow aside games like five-card stud and five-card draw? The answer has to do with an idea which is the basis of all poker games: the idea of *incomplete information*.

In all forms of poker, you're in possession of some information, but you're missing other information. In classic five-card draw, for instance, you know your own hand and all the bets that have been made at the table. But you know nothing about your opponent's hand except for how many cards he drew. That's a lot of missing information.

In five-card stud, however, you're at the other extreme. You know your own cards and you know about all the betting. You also know all of your opponent's cards save one: his hole card. That's a lot of known information, and only one piece of missing information.

So how much incomplete information makes the best game? The answer, it turns out, is not too much and not too little. With either too much or too little information, the best strategies tend to be simple and mechanical. Hold 'em exists at a sweet spot, where the two unknown cards (your opponent's hole cards) create a well-balanced and very complex game where proper strategy is anything but mechanical.

By the 1960s, hold 'em, especially the no-limit form, had become the most popular game among the big players. As they migrated to Las Vegas, they brought the game with them. In 1970, a bunch of the big players thought it would be fun to hold a tournament to pick the best of the bunch, and no-limit hold 'em was the natural choice for the game. Johnny Moss was proclaimed the best player, and the World Series of Poker was born.

The tournament grew in popularity every year after that, and gradually wealthy amateurs joined the crowd. The World Series settled at Binion's Horseshoe as its permanent location, but by the late 1970s and early 1980s, other casinos realized that there was money to be made running poker tournaments, so the number of tournaments increased slowly but steadily. This trend continued until 2003 when the combination of online poker, TV tournaments with hole card cameras, and an unexpected WSOP winner with a perfect name, Chris Moneymaker, caused the popularity of no-limit hold 'em to soar. The result was hundreds of tournaments around the world with gigantic prize funds, non-stop television exposure, and a steadily growing class of professional players.

While online poker tournaments were crippled by the government crackdown on PokerStars and Full Tilt Poker in April, 2011, live poker tournaments have retained their popularity. The largest tournament of all, the Main Event of the World Series of Poker, still draws between 6,500 and 7,000 participants every July, numbers only slightly below the peak of 8,800 in 2006, and still many times higher than the attendance pre-2003. Live tournament poker has become a fixture on the international gaming scene.

How No-Limit Hold 'em Tournaments are Structured

Live no-limit hold 'em tournaments are now held around the world. The greatest number are in the United States, but there are plenty in Europe, and in the last few years we've seen tours arise in Asia and South America. If you had the inclination and could afford the expenses, you could play live tournament poker nonstop from January to December. Tournaments are usually held in casinos or public card clubs like the Commerce and Bicycle Clubs in Los Angeles.

A tournament isn't just a single event lasting a few days. Most casinos will allot two to three weeks for a tournament. The 'main event' will usually have the largest entry fee and will take place in the last few days of the allotted time. But prior to that will be a long series of events with smaller entry fees that last only for a day or two, along with satellite events where the winner's prize is an entry fee to the main event. The majority of these tournaments will feature no-limit hold 'em, but some will be competitions in other forms of poker like limit hold 'em, Omaha, and lowball.

The biggest tournament in the world is still the World Series of Poker, held in Las Vegas over a period of six weeks in June and July. The Main Event occupies the last week of the tournament and attracts a crowd in excess of 6,000 players, some of whom pay their own way, while others win their entry in single-table and multi-table satellite tournaments. Despite inflation, the entry fee is the same $10,000 as in the first World Series tournament held back in 1971.

To enter a tournament, you show ID and pay your money at the cashier's window and receive in return both a receipt and a card that indicates the starting date and time, your table number, and your seat number. When the starting time arrives, you find your table, take your seat, and give your card to the dealer who verifies your ID and presents you with a stack of chips. When the starting time arrives, the dealer deals the first hand and you're off and running.

Rising Blinds and Antes

Tournament play is divided into levels (sometimes called rounds). The dealer will announce the blinds and antes at the start of each level which lasts for a set amount of time. It can be as little as 20 minutes in a small, fast tournament or satellite, and as much as two hours in a big event. At the end of a level, the blinds and antes increase and play starts at the new level. In addition, players generally get a short break every couple of hours, and a longer break at dinner time. Also, playing sessions can be long, so don't be surprised if play starts at noon and continues until the wee hours of the morning.

The distinctive feature of tournament play is the steadily rising blind levels. A tournament might start with blinds of 50 and 100, and if your starting stack was 20,000, blinds of 50 and 100 won't seem like much. But at the second level, blinds might be 75 and 150, and by the third level they might be 100 and 200. And by the sixth level, you might be looking at blinds of 200 and 400, with a 50-chip ante. At that point, each circuit of the table is costing you over a thousand chips, and if your stack hasn't increased from that 20,000 amount, there's a good chance it's going to start to shrink quickly.

Understanding the effect of the inexorably rising blind levels is the key to understanding poker tournament strategy. In cash games, where the blinds don't change and are small compared to the typical stack size, it's possible to be profitable with a conservative strategy that simply waits for good cards and then tries to play them well. (It's not an optimal strategy, but it should show a profit in weaker games.) In tournaments, however, this conservative approach won't make profits fast enough to stay ahead of the constant attrition of the rising blinds. Tournament play requires you to adopt a more aggressive approach.

The Bubble

As play continues and the blinds rise, the field starts to shrink. Most tournaments pay prizes to the final 10 percent of the field, and the first group of prizes are generally around twice the entry fee. As the prizes get closer, we reach a part of the tournament called "the bubble." Players with smallish stacks may have given up on the idea of winning, but they'd very much like to get their entry fee back and show a small profit for all the time and effort they've spent. Usually, they try to husband their chips and stay out of action with all but the best hands.

Meanwhile, the bigger stacks see their opportunity and relentlessly attack with all sorts of weak hands, picking up pots that the short stacks are afraid to contest. And by the time the bubble bursts and the survivors are in the money, the aggressive players have padded their stacks considerably, while the field is full of tiny stacks who have just managed to get in the money but have little chance for anything else.

After the Bubble

In the post-bubble phase, the tiny stacks start moving all-in with any reasonable hand, hoping for a few lucky double-ups to get back in contention. In this stage, another half of the field might get eliminated within a couple of hours.

Play then reverts to something approaching normal poker until a new bubble stage emerges as the field gets close to the final table. That's because prizes at the final table are large, and a position at the final table might bring with it some publicity and television exposure. Once again, the smallest stacks get conservative while the biggest stack try to attack and exploit the situation.

The Final Table and Heads-Up

Once the final table starts, stacks are typically fairly small relative to the blinds, and each step up the pay ladder represents a considerable increase in prize money. At this point, many hands are decided by an all-in move either preflop or on the flop. As the number of players at the table shrinks, the survivors find they need to play more and more hands to stay in contention. The tournament concludes with a heads-up battle between the last two survivors, followed by the crowning of a winner.

Table Structure

Most tournament play occurs at a full table, usually nine or ten players. As players are eliminated, seats will open up around the playing room. It's the organizer's job to keep track of the open seats, and once enough seats are open, an existing table will be broken and the players moved to fill in open seats. Only when the tournament is down to a few remaining tables will you find yourself sitting at a short-handed table (usually six or seven players) for any length of time.

Seat Names

In this book, we'll use certain conventions for naming seats at both full and short tables. We'll list the seats here in the order of action preflop.

At a Full 9-Handed Table

UTG	Under-the-Gun
UTG + 1	
MP	Middle Position
MP + 1	
HJ	Hijack
CO	Cutoff
BTN	Button
SB	Small Blind
BB	Big Blind

At a Short 6-Handed Table

UTG	Under-the-Gun
MP	Middle Position
CO	Cutoff
BTN	Button
SB	Small Blind
BB	Big Blind

The names at the short table are the same as the full table except that three positions have been dropped: UTG+1, MP+1, and Hijack. Throughout the book, we'll refer to seating positions using the names given above.

Position

Position is one of the key elements of no-limit hold 'em poker strategy. In its simplest sense, position just refers to the order in which players act in the hand. You have position on your opponent if you act after him. He has position if he acts after you. So why is this simple idea so important?

Early on in the movie *Wall Street*, Gordon Gekko gave young Bud Fox a piece of advice. He said, "The most valuable commodity I know is information." He was speaking about companies and stocks, but the same advice holds true for poker. It's also a game of information.

The more information you have about an opponent, the more closely his hand can be estimated, and the better your subsequent decisions will be. When having position, your opponent is always forced to act before you, thereby giving away information. But when he has position, you act first, giving him information. Consequently, with position, you should win more pots, and on average the pots won will be bigger. Without position, you should win fewer pots, and on average, they will be smaller.

In no-limit hold 'em, you want to have position on your opponents when playing a hand. Furthermore, if you're not going to have position later in the hand, you need some compensating advantage. That's why starting hand requirements are higher for early position than for later position. If you raise early and get called, your position is likely to be poor for the rest of the hand, so better cards are needed to balance your positional disadvantage. If instead when on the button and the hand is folded to you, a wide array of holdings can now be opened because you'll have position if the hand is played out. Stated another way, without position, every phase of poker is more difficult.

- It's harder to extract money with your strong hands because you have to announce your strength first, and your opponent makes his decision(s) with that knowledge.

- Draws are harder to play because in order to get a free card you first have to check and reveal weakness. Betting instead of checking, however, puts money in the pot when you may be the underdog, and allows the possibility of being raised off the hand.

- Bluffing is more difficult because you have to bluff in the dark, before your opponent has had a chance to check and show weakness.

As much as possible, play hands in position. When you're thinking about getting involved in a pot, and the decision doesn't seem crystal-clear, let your position be your guide. If you're likely to be in position after the flop, don't be afraid to get involved. If you're likely to be out of position, let the hand go and wait for a better opportunity.

Playing Styles

In general, we like to classify poker players along two axes: tight versus loose, and aggressive versus passive. Since these terms are used constantly, let's make sure we know exactly what we mean by them.

"Loose" and "tight" refer to how many hands a player is willing to play. A loose player likes action and doesn't want to spend his time sitting on the sidelines. He came to play poker, and you can't play much poker by folding almost all of your hands. So the loose player is willing to take a few chances and mix things up.

A tight player is interested in value. He doesn't want to get in a hand unless it's likely his holding is best, or there is a reasonable chance at drawing the best hand. The wild speculation will be left to others, and as far as he's concerned, the only thing better than being a favorite is being a *big* favorite.

A loose player might play anywhere from 25 to 50 percent of his hands — a lot of hands — and it makes him easy to spot since he seems to be in most pots.

A tight player doesn't play nearly that many hands. Depending on just how tight he really is, he might be involved in only 10 to 20 percent of the hands.

Because a tight player participates in so few hands, it might take awhile to spot them. That is, they're happy to keep throwing away mediocre hands until they spot something they really like.

So loose versus tight is the first axis of a poker player's style. The second axis is aggressive versus passive.

"Aggressive" and "passive" describe how a player will act once he gets into a pot. Aggressive players like to pressure their opponents by betting and raising, and if you're up against an aggressive player, he's constantly going to be trying to push you off your hand. A passive player, on the other hand, will be frequently checking and calling. He doesn't want to play a big pot unless he's sure he has the best hand. If he's not sure, the passive

17

player wants to keep the pot small and get to the river where he can see if he won the hand or not.

However, don't make the mistake of thinking that a passive player is easy to bluff. A lot of passive players really want to get to showdown and see if their hand is best. If they have something like a medium pair, they may stick around tenaciously.

With these two axes, we can create four broad categories of players as follows:

1.   Tight-aggressive

2.   Tight-passive

3.   Loose-aggressive

4.   Loose-passive

Loose-passive players will generally be the weakest opponents. They like to play lots of hands, but they'll only bet and raise with their best ones. This makes them easy to read: If they're raising, you only want to stick around with a strong hand. But they also like action, and if they hit a flop with a medium-strength hand like a pair, the loose-passive player will often stick around to see if the hand is good. They're an easy target because when you have a strong hand, you can extract a lot of money.

Loose-aggressive players can be dangerous. They'll play a lot of hands, see a lot of flops, and keep attacking with bets and raises. When they do hit a big hand, you won't know it and they can win a big pot. But most important, loose-aggressive players can be big winners if they can combine their aggression with good hand-reading and people-reading skills.

You won't have much to fear from a tight-passive player. He doesn't like losing money and he won't play anything but good hands, so you won't have much trouble figuring out where he stands. If he's in a pot, he has something. If he's betting, he has something pretty good. If he's raising, he has a monster. Watch what he's doing, play accordingly, and you'll do all right.

What about the last category, the tight-aggressive player? Because he's tight, he tends to play good hands. Because he's aggressive, he's usually attacking with those hands: betting when he's first to act, calling and sometimes raising when the pot has been opened in front of him. He's not in a lot of pots, but when there, he's putting maximum pressure on the other players.

In tournament play, you can be a winner with either a moderately tight style or a loose style. (Very tight won't work because the rising blinds and antes will slowly consume your stack.) However, it's hard to be a winner with a passive style. That's because a passive player only has one way to win a hand: He has to get to showdown and then show the best hand. An aggressive player has two ways to win: He can win by pushing his opponent out of the pot at some earlier stage, or he can win at showdown. Since players rarely have huge hands, winning by chasing your opponent out of the pot is a real option in most hands.

Passivity has another significant drawback. When you play passively, you allow your opponents to see more cards for free. If you're ahead in the hand but check, your opponent may check as well, then catch a free card that gives him the best hand. Had you bet, it might have forced him to fold, thus protecting your hand. Consequently, passive players tend to win fewer pots than aggressive players, and their wins tend to be smaller. That's why most successful players play some version of an aggressive style.

The Four Basic Principles of No-Limit Hold 'em

While there are lots of rules and generalizations for playing good poker, there are four simple rules that are more important than all the others, which I call the four basic principles. Once you understand these ideas, your game will be on a sound basis and we'll see them recur over and over again as other concepts and problems are explained. The four principles are stated here in their purest form.

Principle No.1: Strength

> In general you want to bet your strong hands, check or call with your hands of middling strength, and fold or bluff with your weak hands.

The idea that you'd want to bet your strong hands is fairly obvious. However, checking rather than betting with your middle strength hands is less obvious, but here's the main reason. A middle strength hand has value and could win the pot if you can get it to showdown. On the other hand, if you bet with one of these hands and your opponent folds a weak hand, you haven't gained much since it's likely you would have beaten that hand anyway. But if you bet and are raised, it's time to fold, and you may have had to lay down a hand that could have won at showdown.

As for your weak hands, folding most of them is clear. Choosing some of them as your bluffs is less clear until you look at the alternative. If you bluff with a worthless hand and get raised, it can be thrown away at no extra cost. But if you bluff instead with a hand of some value and get raised, it can still be thrown away, but now you've had to discard a hand that might have won at showdown.

Principle No. 2: Aggression

> In general, aggression (betting and raising) is better than passivity (checking and calling).

When you play passively, you're in essence trying to get to showdown with the hand you have. Put another way, playing passively produces only one way to win. You have to actually have the best hand at showdown.

On the other hand, playing aggressively produces two ways to win: You can push your opponent out of the pot at some point when he refuses to call your bet or raise, or you can win at showdown. Having two ways to win is better than having one way to win, so in general, aggressive play will win more pots.

We refer to the value we gain when we make our opponent give up as *folding equity*. All bets, even small ones, will have some folding equity, but checks and calls have none.

Principle No. 3: Betting

> In general, a good bet should do one of three things:
>
> 1. Force a better hand to fold.
>
> 2. Force a weaker hand to call.
>
> 3. Force drawing hands to put more money in the pot to see another card.

Although aggression is good, your bets still need to be made with some purpose in mind. A bet which forces a better hand to fold will win a pot that otherwise would have been lost. A bet which makes a weaker hand call builds a pot which you're favored to win. And if your opponent has a drawing hand, you don't want to let him have another card for free; betting charges him to see that card.

However, keep in mind that situations arise frequently on the turn and river where you have a hand that may be best, but the board is dangerous enough so that weaker hands will most likely fold to your bet, while better hands will call or raise. In this case, betting can't be profitable, and your goal is to reach showdown as cheaply as possible.

Principle No. 4: Deception

In general, you never want to do anything all of the time.

To win at poker, you can't allow your opponents to be sure about your hand. Playing in a rigid style allows them to get a clear line on your play, so it's important to make an effort to vary your play so you can't be easily read.

Also, the better your opponents, the more important this principle becomes. At weak tables where your opponents aren't paying attention, playing in a simple, straightforward manner may actually be close to optimal.

Opening Hand Ranges

Play has just started in a big tournament. You're sitting under-the-gun, and the action is on you. *With what hands are you happy opening the pot for a raise?* First, let's note that there is no simple answer to this question. What hands to play should be a function of your own style, how you perceive the other players at the table, and, perhaps more important, how they perceive you. While you might have a certain default set of hands that you're comfortable opening under-the-gun, be prepared to widen or narrow that set depending on what you've seen so far at this table. Let's start by taking a look at a typical hand range for both a tight player and a somewhat looser player, and then see how these players should adjust their range depending on circumstances.

A moderately tight player sitting under-the-gun might choose to open with only about 10 percent of his hands. Here's one such collection of starting hands:

- Pairs: AA down through 22
- Suited aces: AKs down through ATs
- Unsuited aces: AKo down through AJo
- KQs

(Note that we're referring to hands in an abbreviated form. AKs means 'ace-king suited.' AJo means 'ace-jack offsuit.' We'll use this method of abbreviation throughout in lists and in tables.)

This isn't the only possible collection of top-10 percent hands. Here's a slightly different one:

- Pairs: AA down through 66
- Suited aces: AKs down through A9s
- Unsuited aces: AKo down through AJo
- Suited kings: KQs down through KTs
- QJs, QTs, and JTs

23

These two sets have almost the same number of hands, but they play somewhat differently. The first set, which includes all pairs, has the advantage that it can make a credible threat on any kind of flop since it has the ability to flop a set no matter what cards are showing. It's also a hand range which is a little easier to play for beginners because its high card hands will usually make top pair or nothing at all instead of middle pair hands whose play requires more judgment.

The second set eliminates the low pair hands and replaces them with suited Broadway cards like king-jack suited and queen-ten suited. This group creates fewer sets on the flop, but more strong drawing hands as well as a lot of top pair and middle pair hands. The presence of more drawing hands, however, requires more post-flop skill than the first group.

A somewhat looser player might open with a wider range of hands under-the-gun. Here's an example of a range that might suit such a player, comprising about 17 percent of all hands:

- All pairs
- Suited aces: AKs down through A8s
- Unsuited aces: AKo down through ATo
- All suited Broadways: KQs, KJs, KTs, QJs, QTs, and JTs
- Offsuit Broadways: KQo, KJo, QJo, and JTo
- Suited connectors: T9s, 98s, 87s

So which of these three hand ranges is "correct" for opening under-the-gun? And which range is best for you?

A key concept in poker is that there are often no correct answers to certain kinds of questions. Under the right circumstances, any of these ranges (and others as well) could be considered "correct" in the sense that they might be the best hand range for a certain type of player at a certain type of table. Instead of trying to label one range as best, what we want to do is describe situations where one range is better than others.

For example, if you're a beginner in a small-stakes tournament, just getting started with no-limit hold 'em tournaments, we'd certainly recommend using the first range.

Compared to the other ranges, it has the great advantage of getting you involved in fewer hands and being much easier to play after the flop. And when the flop appears, you'll either have a strong hand like an overpair, top pair with a strong kicker, or a set, or you'll have nothing at all. Those are relatively easy situations for a beginner to play.

The third range, on the other hand, contains a lot more hands like lower Broadway cards (king-jack offsuit) and suited connectors. When you play these hands, you'll find yourself with more middle pairs and drawing hands after the flop, and handling these situations correctly requires much more experience and seasoned judgment, qualities not found in most beginners. This is a range for a player who's confident in his post-flop play.

In general, you should open with narrow, relatively strong ranges if you

1.   Are a beginner, or

2.   Lack confidence in your post-flop play.

But if you have confidence in your ability relative to your table, you can favor looser, somewhat more speculative opening ranges.

Your range should also be affected by other players at the table. If you've played long enough to see that they tend to be tight, consider loosening your opening ranges. The blinds will be easier to steal, the other players will be less likely to reraise preflop, and you'll encounter less resistance post-flop. But if the other players at the table are loose preflop, the opposite advice applies. Play tighter ranges, and try to enter fewer pots but with stronger hands.

Finally, be willing to adjust your range if the other players seem to be reacting to your current approach. If you've been loose and they now seem eager to play lots of pots, tighten up. If you've been tight and are now taking down a lot of pots without resistance, loosen up.

Opening from Later Positions

As you move around the table from under-the-gun to middle position, the cutoff seat, and the button, you can open raise with wider and wider hand ranges. The reason is twofold:

1. There are fewer players left to act behind you, so there's a better chance that no one has a hand they want to play.

2. There's a better chance that you will have position on any opponent after the flop.

When you open under-the-gun, for instance, there are eight players left to act who might have a hand they want to play. Of those eight, six would have position on you after the flop — everyone but the two blinds. But if you open from the cutoff seat, only three players remain to act, and only one of them (the button) can have position on you later in the hand.

While there are no exact rules for widening your ranges, a tight player who opens 10 percent of the time under-the-gun with the first range might reasonably expand his range like this:

1. Open 15 percent of his hands from middle position.

2. Open 22 percent of his hands from the cutoff seat.

3. Open 30 percent of his hands from the button.

Let's recall that our first range consisted of all pairs, suited aces down to ace-ten suited, unsuited aces down to ace-jack offsuit, and king-queen suited. Here's how he might add hands to create these new, wider ranges:

To open 15 percent from middle position, add:

• Suited Broadway cards: KJs, KTs, QJs, QTs, JTs

- Suited aces: A9s, A8s
- Offsuit aces: ATo
- Suited connectors: T9s, 98s
- Offsuit Broadways: KQo, KJo.

To open 22 percent from the cutoff seat, add to the 15 percent range:

- Suited aces: A7s, A6s, A5s
- Offsuit Broadways: KTo, QJo, QTo, JTo
- Suited connectors: 87s, 76s
- Offsuit aces: A9o, A8o.

To open 30 percent from the button, add to the 22 percent range:

- Suited aces: A4s, A3s, A2s
- Offsuit aces: A7o down through A2o
- Suited kings: K9s, K8s, K7s
- Q9s.

Opening from the small blind is a little different because although only one player is left to act (the big blind). He'll have position on you after the flop. So in this case, you can begin by opening with your button range, but if he calls frequently and uses his position well, consider changing to your cutoff range.

As before, these suggested ranges are for players using a tight style. If you're more comfortable with a looser style, start with the 17 percent range under-the-gun and increase your hand ranges proportionately.

Preflop Limping

When everyone has folded to you and it's your turn to act, you have a choice: either raise as described in the previous section, or just call the big blind. Calling in this way is better known as limping, and by limping, you enter the pot for the minimum amount of money possible. Usually, players who limp do so because they have a somewhat weak hand, like a small pair or suited connector; they'd like to see a flop, but don't think their hand is strong enough to raise. Furthermore, limping is commonplace in small-stakes tournaments or events with lots of inexperienced players; it becomes less and less common in bigger events.

The best advice to give about limping is — don't do it. If no one has entered the pot, and you have a playable hand, just raise. If you raise every time in this spot, you'll win more pots when your opponents don't have anything, and you'll project strength when called and actually see a flop. Your opponents won't be able to tell when you have a premium hand or when your holding is something like a suited connector, and as a result you'll be difficult to read and a more dangerous player.

Raising with strong hands and limping with weaker ones makes you exploitable. Your opponents who have position can raise your limps, a move known as the *isolation raise*. You'll then have to make a bad choice between folding your weak hand (thereby wasting the chips invested) or calling their raise, in which case you're out of position with a weak hand, having put as much money in the pot as if you'd raised to start.

Limping isn't an absurd play for very good players who can employ it occasionally as part of a balanced strategy involving some speculative hands and some strong hands. But if you're not in this category, simplify your game and minimize possible mistakes by raising when entering the pot.

Bet Sizing Preflop

In limit hold 'em, bets and raises are a fixed size, so sizing your bets isn't a problem. But in no-limit hold 'em, you can bet anything from the minimum bet to an all-in shove of your whole stack. With that kind of choice, bet sizing is a topic you really need to understand. So in this chapter, I'll talk about bet sizing preflop, and in a later chapter the problem of sizing your bets after the flop will be addressed.

Let's look at an example, You're in a no-limit hold 'em tournament, it's early in the event, and the blinds are at 100 and 200. You're under-the-gun (and first to act) with a good-sized stack of 21,000, and are holding the

That's a strong hand, much better than average, so you definitely want to play. *What are your choices?*

One option is just to call by matching the 200 bet of the big blind. As stated in the last section, that's a passive way of playing such a strong hand. Instead of trying to win the pot right now, you're waiting to see if you hit an ace or a king on the flop before putting any serious money to work. The problem with the play is that it allows other players to get into a growing pot cheaply by offering them good pot odds.

Instead of just calling, a better play is to raise since it takes control of the pot and makes an attempt to actually win the 300 that is already out there in the blinds. However, once you decide to raise, you still have a wide latitude in sizing your bet.

The minimum raise you can make is the size of the big blind. Here the big blind is 200, so a minimum raise would be from 200 to 400. That's a small raise, but unless somebody calls, it's enough for you to take down the pot. But if you want to raise a little more, so that your opponents have a harder time calling, there are a lot of choices.

The most you can bet in no-limit is your whole stack. This is called moving all-in, pushing, or shoving. It's a play that has its uses, but here it's just dumb. You would be risking all your chips (21,000) to win the 300 chips in the pot. While it's true that only a strong hand like aces or kings would call such a bet, if such a strong hand is out there, and there are still eight players left to act, then you'll be favored to get knocked out of the tournament. That's not a smart trade.

A better raise size is somewhere between 2.5 and 3.5 times the big blind. That's enough money to put some pressure on your opponent, without committing too much of your stack before you've actually seen the flop. With these blinds, that would be a bet between 500 and 700.

A good general rule is just to raise three times the big blind. You can make arguments for raising a little less or a little more depending on your exact position at the table, but three times the big blind is a solid amount that does the job without getting you in trouble.

Now take a look at a slightly different situation. The blinds are the same as before, the under-the-gun player raised to 600, you're on the button, and your hand is the

That's a huge hand — a pair of kings, and if you decide to reraise (also known as a 3-bet), how big should your raise be?

There are no hard and fast rules about reraising, and good players differ amongst themselves. Typical reraises, however, average about 2.5 times the previous raise. In this situation, that would mean a reraise to something like 1,500, give or take a little. When sizing your preflop raises, you're usually torn between two desires. If your holding is strong, you don't want to raise so much that your opponents all go away. That is, you'd like someone to stick around so that you win even more money later. On the other hand, it's usually best to raise enough to build a good-sized pot in case someone does call.

3-Betting
and 4-Betting Preflop

If an opponent open-raises in front of us and we have a hand worth playing, there are two choices: call or reraise. So under what circumstances is the reraise correct?

First, we need to learn some modern terminology. In no-limit hold 'em, the initial reraise is known as a 3-bet and a subsequent reraise is known as a 4-bet. It's a handy terminology because it lets us see just where each reraise fits into the betting order.

Example 1-1: We're playing in a live tournament with a substantial entry fee. We're in the third level and the blinds are now 150 and 300. The under-the-gun player folds, and the second player, with a stack of 17,000, raises to 850. That's a pretty standard raise size in today's play, a little less than three times the big blind. Play folds around to the button whose stack is 15,000 and he elects to 3-bet to 2,100. That's between two and three times the previous raise, which again is pretty standard in today's play.

The blinds fold and the action returns to the original raiser who now elects to 4-bet to 4,600. Once again, the amount is between two and three times the previous raise. However, notice that as the raises get larger, the amount of a new raise usually gets closer to twice the previous raise. The action is now on the button, who can fold, call, or 5-bet. But if his choice is to 5-bet, he needs to pay attention to his stack size which is 12,900 after the 3-bet.

A minimum 5-bet requires calling his opponent's 2,500 raise and raising at least another 2,500, making the bet 7,100 and leaving him with 7,900. If he makes that raise, almost half his stack will have gone into the pot. At that point, he's *pot-committed*, which just means that he's invested so much of his money that he's better off shoving in the rest than folding his hand after the flop.

In tournament play, where stacks are rarely very deep (a deep stack is usually considered to be more than 100 big blinds), pot commitment decisions can arise early in the hand. A good player will consider his stack size from the start of the hand, and plan his actions around that. A good rule of thumb is that if you're contemplating making a play that will get a third of your chips in the pot, moving all-in will be much better than raising and then folding to a reraise.

A Short History of 3-Betting

In the early years of no-limit hold 'em, where players were mostly tight and an opening raise often signaled a strong hand, 3-bets usually meant an extremely strong hand, while 4-bets and higher often meant a pair of kings or aces only. When online no-limit cash games and tournaments got started, a lot of players who were looking for action would open with a relatively wide range of hands. However, when they were 3-bet, they tended to tighten up and call or 4-bet only with their best hands. This approach created an exploitable situation.

For example, suppose you're on the button and the action is folded around to the player in the cutoff seat. He raises to three big blinds. From observation, you're pretty sure that he'll raise in this situation with about 20 percent of his hands. You're also sure that if you 3-bet, he'll call or 4-bet with only about 5 percent of his starting hands which is about 25 percent of the hands he originally raised with, (roughly AA down through TT, and AK and AQ, suited or not). And if this is the case, it becomes correct to 3-bet with any two cards! He'll fold 75 percent of the time, and even if you lose every hand where he doesn't fold, your expectation is positive. (We're assuming the blinds will fold behind you, which is mostly true.) Assuming your 3-bet is to nine big blinds, the calculation looks like this:

You win 4.5 big blinds 75 percent of the time, for a profit of 3.375 big blinds.

$$3.375 = (0.75)(4.5)$$

You lose your 3-bet 25 percent of the time, for a loss of 2.25 big blinds.

$$-2.25 = (0.25)(-9.0)$$

Thus, on average, you win 1.125 big blinds every time you make this move.

$$1.125 = 3.375 - 2.25$$

In the online cash games of 2005-2006, this insight led to a new approach to reraising, known as 'light 3-betting.' The idea was to exploit most players' tendencies to play only premium hands when 3-bet by raising with hands like suited connectors, small pairs, and medium Broadway cards, pocketing a solid profit when the opponent folded, while exploiting the disguised nature of the hand after the flop if the 3-bet was called.

Light 3-betting was soon followed by light 4-betting, which tried to exploit the strategy of light 3-betting by carrying the trend one step further. At first, these aggressive strategies were tried mostly in the high-stakes 6-max online cash games, but they gradually filtered down to the mid-stakes online cash games, and finally to the world of live and online tournaments.

The proper handling of 3-betting and 4-betting preflop is highly dependent on the kinds of opponents at your table. Light 3-betting is not hard to counter, but it requires a well thought-out open raising strategy. We'll have much more to say about these topics later in the book.

Flop:
Heads-Up or Multiway

Once the preflop betting is finished, the flop is dealt. At this point, you have most of the information you need to evaluate your hand.

Play on the flop depends heavily on the number of players left in the hand and the stack sizes of the players involved. When there are just two people left, you have what's called a heads-up flop. More players constitute a multiway flop. If all players involved have a deep stack (more than about 75 big blinds) then play tends to be more complex since everyone has some room to maneuver. If one or more of the players is short-stacked (less than about 20 big blinds), then the betting may end quickly with an all-in move by one of the players.

Most of the advice in this section is aimed at flops where everyone has a deep stack, which is typical of the early and middle stages of a tournament. Short stack play is very different, and we'll talk about that at length in "Bet Sizing on the Flop" starting on page 239 in "Part Four: Playing the Flop."

Heads-up pots give more scope for creative play because of the greater likelihood that both players have missed the flop. In a multiway pot, there's a bigger chance that someone has connected strongly with the flop and now has a good hand. Let's quickly consider each case and see how the number of players affects the play.

Heads-Up on the Flop

When you're heads-up on the flop, your play will be governed by several key factors. Let's look at them one at a time and see how they affect your strategy.

Key Factor No. 1: Aggressor. Whoever made the last (or only) raise preflop is considered to be the aggressor. He announced that he had the better hand, and unless his opponent connected with the flop in some way, he probably has the better hand post-flop. So if you were the aggressor, be prepared to bet on the flop. But if your opponent was the aggressor, he'll mostly be betting the flop, and you'll need to decide if your hand is worth playing.

Key Factor No. 2: Position. If you act after your opponent you have position. That's always advantageous because you get to see his action before responding. If he tries to be deceptive, perhaps by checking a strong hand, he has to pay a price. You may elect to check behind him, thereby getting a free card. So having position gives you an extra incentive to continue play beyond the flop. Your positional advantage may also give you an indication that your opponent is willing to give up on the hand.

Key Factor No. 3: Hand Strength. Much of your post-flop play is predicated on your hand strength. Let's take a look at hands of different strength and see how they should be handled.

1. **Monster hands** (quads, full houses, flushes, and straights). These hands are almost certainly best now and will most likely be best at showdown. The only disadvantage they have is that you may not be able to get action because a flop that connected with your hand this strongly may not have connected with your opponent at all. These holdings are well-suited for playing big pots, but your opponent may not cooperate.

2. **Very strong hands** (sets, two pair). These hands are likely to win and are worth betting on the flop and usually the turn as well. They can run into trouble on a later round if a drawing hand connects against them, but in the long run, they should win a lot of money.

3. **Strong hands** (overpairs and top pairs). These are your workhorse hands. They're usually worth a bet on the flop, and may win the pot at that point. For variety, you may elect to check the flop and bet the turn. These holdings, however, require a certain amount of caution. If you're betting and your opponent sticks around, it's often because he (a) can beat these hands, (b) is drawing to a really big hand, or (c) plans to bluff you off your hand later. Overpairs and top pairs are mostly good on the flop, but if you get to the river and haven't improved, and a lot of money is going in, you're probably beaten.

4. **Medium hands** (pairs below top pair). These are hands which may be best on the flop, but which are very vulnerable as the hand goes on and overcards appear on the board. Your main goal with medium pairs is to get to showdown cheaply and see if your hand is best. They play well against passive opponents, but much less well against active opponents.

5. **Drawing hands** (flush and straight draws, plus combination draws). Playing these hands well is crucial in no-limit hold 'em because they have the capability of winning your opponent's entire stack when he has a strong hand and your draw connects. In general, you'll have the odds to call a bet on the flop, but if you don't connect there, the odds may not be there to call on the turn.

6. **Nothing hands** (no pair, no draw). Your bluffing hands will come from this group. When playing well, you'll be able to win some of these hands, especially when your opponent also has nothing.

Multiway on the Flop

The nature of flop play changes dramatically when you face multiple opponents. Because more players are involved, hands at showdown will tend to be stronger than hands in a heads-up pot. The likelihood that you'll be facing stronger hands at showdown in turn affects how you play each type of hand on the flop.

Here's a quick summary of the changes you'll need to make in a multiway pot.

Change No. 1: With a very strong hand, you almost never want to slowplay. When you have a strong hand in a multiway pot, there's a better chance that someone else at the table has a drawing hand, or at least a hand that can call a bet. And if you have a strong hand and someone can call, you certainly want to bet.

Change No. 2: Medium strength hands may not be strong enough to bet. Medium strength hands like top pair, top kicker drop in value both because there is a better chance that someone already has a better hand, and because there is a better chance that someone else will improve to a stronger hand by showdown.

Change No. 3: With a drawing hand, you can accept smaller odds than usual to draw. With several opponents, there's a better chance that someone will have a hand that can call when you make your draw.

Change No. 4: If you're planning a bluff, circumstances must be better than usual to justify your move. The more players in the pot, the less chance that your bluff will chase everyone away.

Since more players create an incentive to bet big hands rather than slowplay, and an incentive to check or fold rather than bluff, we can summarize multiway play with a simple rule:

> The likelihood that a player's betting action represents his true strength is directly proportional to the number of players in the pot.

Types of Bets on the Flop

There are many different types of bets on the flop. We might have a strong hand and want to get more money in the pot as soon as possible, or a weak hand, but think the flop missed our opponent, or we can take it down with a well-timed bluff. We may want to bet because we took the lead preflop and don't want to show weakness. All these are valid reasons for betting the flop. In addition, there are some good reasons for *not* betting the flop which we need to consider.

Flop bets fall into a number of different groups. Let's look at each type of flop bet and see when and why we might want to make that kind of bet.

Value Bet

The simplest kind of flop bet is the *value bet*. After the flop comes, you have a hand which you think is probably best. Usually this will be top pair or better. So you bet, both to get more money in the pot and to discourage your opponents from drawing to beat you. If someone calls, you've built a pot with what is presumably the best hand. If everyone folds, the pot is yours.

Example 1-2. It's early in a tournament with 100 and 200 blinds, you have a good-sized stack of 25,000, and you're under-the-gun with the

You raise to 600 and get called by the button and the big blind, creating a pot of 1,900 chips.

The flop is the

giving you top pair with a good kicker. The big blind checks and it's your turn to act. You have a strong hand and right now have no reason to think anyone else has a better hand, so you make a value bet of 1,400, about two-thirds of the pot.. The button folds and the big blind calls, making the pot 4,700 as you go to the turn.

Your value bet accomplished three goals:

1. You built the pot with what is probably the best hand right now.

2. You eliminated one opponent.

3. You gained position on the last opponent for the rest of the hand.

Your opponent's call probably means one of four things:

1. He has a better hand but called rather than raised to trap you later in the hand.

2. He has a pair worse than yours, but he's not sure you actually have anything.

3. He has two hearts and he's drawing to make a heart flush.

4.   He has nothing but has decided to *float;* he's planning on taking the pot away with a bluff later.

The rest of the hand doesn't concern us right now. How it actually plays out depends on the turn and river cards, and the skill of the players.

Bluff

If you take the lead preflop but the flop doesn't help, you can elect to *bluff.* Flop bluffs are particularly effective if the flop might have helped a lot of your preflop raising hands. Here's a typical case.

Example 1-3. You're in the same tournament, a little later in the 100 and 200 blind level, pick up the T♥T♣ in middle position, and your stack is a still-healthy 23,000. The under-the-gun player folds, you raise to 600, and only the small blind calls. The pot becomes 1,400 chips.

The flop is the A♥J♠4♣ and the small blind checks. Although you missed the flop and there are two overcards to your tens, many of the hands with which you might have raised preflop contain an ace, and your opponent might easily believe this flop hit you. You bet 1,000 and the small blind folds.

Although your hand had some value and might actually have been best, this bet was actually a bluff. You represented that the ace on board had hit you, and your opponent folded.

Semi-Bluff

A *semi-bluff* is a bet (or raise) on the flop or turn with a drawing hand which is almost certainly not best now but which has outs to become the best hand. The combination of the bet plus the chance of improving to the best hand makes the semi-bluff profitable.[1]

Example 1-4. In the same tournament as before, the blinds are now 150 and 300 and your stack is a very healthy 31,000. You have the A♥K♥ under-the-gun, raise to 800, and only the button calls, so the pot is now 2,050 chips.

The flop comes the 9♥8♥4♣. You check, the button bets 1,200, and you raise to 2,800. Currently your holding is only ace-high which is probably not the best hand right now (although it might be). However, any of the nine remaining hearts give you a flush, and any of the six remaining aces or kings will give you a high pair which will likely be the best hand. Thus, there are nine sure outs (the hearts) and six likely outs (the remaining aces and kings). Notice that your raise may win the hand outright, and if he doesn't, you may still make the best hand. Semi-bluffs differ from true bluffs by having outs to a winning hand, whereas a true bluff usually has no outs (and there are no cards to come).

Continuation Bet

A *continuation bet* is a bet on the flop by the preflop aggressor. You raise preflop, get a caller, the flop comes, and now you bet again. This bet puts a lot of pressure on your opponent and it could be a value bet or a bluff, but in either case, if your opponent missed the flop or just has a small pair, he'll have difficulty continuing with the hand.

Continuation betting is a standard move in no-limit hold 'em. A typical good player will make a continuation bet between 60 and 70 percent of the time after raising preflop and only getting one or two callers.

---

[1] The semi-bluff was first quantified by David Sklansky in the 1970s. See his book *The Theory of Poker* for more discussion.

Donk Bet

A *donk bet* is a lead-off bet on the flop made by a player who didn't take the betting lead preflop. Donk bets are generally the mark of a weak and inexperienced player. If first to act post-flop and your hand is strong enough to bet, you would generally check to the preflop raiser, let him bet, and then raise, thereby getting more money in the pot.

Example 1-5. In the same tournament as before, the blinds are still 150 and 300 and your stack is 33,000. The under-the-gun player makes a standard opening raise to 850 and only you call in the big blind with the

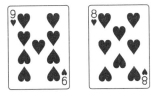

The pot is now 1,850 chips.
The flop comes the

giving you top pair with a weak kicker. The standard play would be to check and see what the preflop raiser does. Instead, you lead out for 1,200. The under-the-gun player folds.

Your donk bet informed the preflop raiser that you hit the flop and liked your hand. The preflop raiser probably had two high cards and decided (wisely) not to fight for the pot. Although you won, a little more money probably could have been made by checking and allowing the under-the-gun player to make a continuation bet.

Information Bet

An *information bet* is a bet made to get information about the strength of your hand by gauging your opponent's response. Players who bet this way often have a medium-strength hand and are trying to "see where they stand."

Betting like this used to be popular, but most good players now view such bets as mistakes. A better strategy is to usually check and gauge your strength by your opponent's play on the flop and the turn. Often, you will get the same information at less cost while keeping the pot small.

Understanding Flop Texture

A key element in playing the flop is understanding the significance of the *flop texture,* a term for describing the different characteristics of the flop. Are the cards of three different suits (a *rainbow flop*)? Are two suits represented (a *two-tone flop*)? Are all three cards of the same suit (a *monotone flop*)? Are the flop cards connected or are they widely separated? Is there a pair on board? All of these characteristics comprise the texture of the flop.

When the flop arrives, you can combine the flop texture with your knowledge of the preflop betting to answer some key questions:

● How good a hand do I have now?

● Given my opponent's preflop action, should the flop have helped him?

● Given what I did preflop, should my opponent think that this flop helped me?

Once these questions are answered, you can formulate a plan for betting the flop and later streets. If you now have a made hand (a high pair or better), mostly bet the flop for value. Your hand should be best, and you both want to start building the pot while discouraging your opponent from trying to catch a card that wins for him.

However, if you missed the flop, the decision is more difficult. If you were the aggressor preflop, is it best to make a continuation bet, or just check and try to see a turn card?

If you weren't the aggressor preflop, the same questions still have to be dealt with. For the most part, your opponent will be betting. Do you want to continue with the hand or should you just fold and cut your losses?

Let's take a look at some sample hands with different flop textures and see how they should be handled. Four examples are below.

Example 1-6. The dry flop. In a live tournament, the blinds are 100 and 200, your stack is 16,000, and you have the

in middle position. The first player folds, you raise to 550, and only the button calls. The pot is 1,400.

The flop is the

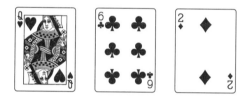

What do you do?

We call this sort of flop a *dry flop*. They have just one high card which is not an ace, three widely separated cards, and no two cards of the same suit. Notice that very few hands connect to a dry flop and no draws are possible. This means they are ideal flops for a continuation bet bluff from the preflop aggressor, and when players call preflop raises, they generally have one of four kinds of hands:

1. Medium to small pairs.

2. An ace with a medium to small kicker, often suited.

3. Medium suited connectors.

4.   Two medium suited cards, like the J♠9♠ or the 9♥7♥.

Very few of these hands will connect with a dry flop. No flush draws or straight draws are possible, and unless the caller started with a pair, he probably still doesn't have one. The caller may also suspect that you missed the flop as well, but since you probably started with a better hand, it's too difficult for him to play on after you bet.

Example 1-7. The wet flop. You're in a tournament with the same blind levels and stack as before. Under-the-gun, you pick up the A♠9♠. You're feeling loose and aggressive, raise to 600, and only the player in the cutoff seat calls. The pot is now 1,500 chips. The flop is the J♥T♥9♣. *What do you do?*

Here's the opposite of a dry flop: the *wet flop*. These flops connect strongly with many of the medium-card hands that a caller can be expected to have. If our caller's hand contained a queen, jack, ten, nine, or eight, he now has at least a pair or an open-ended straight draw, and he could easily have two pair, a set, or a made straight. In addition, the two hearts mean that about 20 percent of his suited hands now have a flush draw.[2]

Although you made bottom pair, the prudent play is to check. A bet won't chase away any of the hands that connected with this flop, and while you could take down the pot if he has a small pair, the chance isn't worth the investment.

You in fact bet 800. The cutoff raises to 2,000 and you fold.

Example 1-8. The paired flop. You're playing in a tournament with 200 and 400 blinds, your stack is 26,000, and you have the 6♥6♣ on the button. The first two players fold, the cutoff raises to 1,050, you call, and the blinds fold. The pot is now 2,700 chips.

---

[2] Note that it's not 25 percent since by having two suited cards on board your suited cards can only come from the eleven suited cards remaining in the deck, not thirteen which would be the case if there were none of your suit on board.

The flop is the 8♣8♥2♠. The cutoff bets 1,400. *What do you do?*

Paired flops share many of the characteristics of dry flops meaning that few hands connect with it. So if the cutoff didn't start with a pair, he probably doesn't have two pair now. In addition, he can't have a flush draw or a straight draw. Thus, your modest pair of sixes is likely to be the best hand.

Furthermore, if you probably have the best hand, your options are calling or raising. In this case, raising is the better choice. If your opponent has two high cards and is bluffing — the most likely scenario — a raise should win the hand. If you just call, many cards can arrive on the turn which you won't like to see. For instance, if you just call and an ace comes (on the turn) and your opponent bets, you won't know if the ace hit him or not, and you could be setting yourself up to lose a big pot if you guess wrong. You raise to 3,200 and the cutoff folds.

Example 1-9. The ace-high flop. You're early in a live tournament with blinds of 50 and 100 and a 25,000 stack. Under-the-gun, you pick up the

You raise to 300 and only the player in the small blind, who likes to play a lot of hands, calls. The pot is now 700 chips.

The flop is the

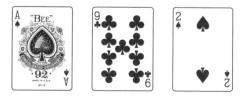

The small blind checks. *What should you do?*

Ace-high flops behave a little differently from other kinds of flops. Since the initial raiser often has a hand with a strong ace, these are natural flops for him to continue betting even if (as here) he actually has some other sort of hand. However, whether the flop is likely to connect with the caller depends heavily on what level of players are involved.

In weak games, many loose players call bets with weak aces and will therefore frequently connect with these flops. In general, weak players won't fold a pair or an ace preflop, so the aggressor has little chance of betting them off the hand. He can, however, win his opponent's whole stack if he has a better ace.

In stronger games, the caller rarely has an ace in this spot. Good players will often 3-bet with ace-king and sometimes ace-queen, while they'll usually fold aces with a medium or small kicker for fear of being dominated. In these games, the aggressor generally has a pretty risk-free continuation bet on these flops.

In this case, you know the small blind is loose and you're early in the tournament, so there's some chance that he has an ace. However, most of his possible hands don't have aces, so betting is a slightly better play than checking. You bet 450 and the small blind folds.

Bet Sizing on the
Flop and Later Streets

So the flop has arrived and now you want to bet. *How large a bet should you make?*

In general, when stacks are deep, typical flop bets range from a little less than half the pot to almost the full pot. When one of the players involved in the hand has a very short stack (up to about twice the existing pot) then an all-in move is common. The short stack will realize that any smaller bet will commit him to the pot, so he maximizes the chance his opponent will fold by moving all-in. The same logic applies in reverse. The player with the large stack will, if he wants to bet at all, simply put the smaller stack all-in.

In deep stack situations, deciding on a bet size hinges on several factors, including the strength of your hand, the flop texture, stack sizes, and any knowledge you may have about your opponents. Let's take a look at some typical bet sizes and the logic behind each one.

1. **Bets of less than half the pot.** Players make small bets for different reasons. Beginners will sometimes make the minimum bet possible because they want to bet but don't see any reason to bet more than the minimum. Other players will sometimes make a small bet for information ("to see where they stand"), although as we've seen, this is usually a bad reason for betting.

    However, there are two sensible reasons for a small bet. The first is as a blocking bet. You believe that your opponent will bet if you check, and your hand is good enough to call that bet. Rather than wait, you make a small bet first in the hope that your opponent will just call that bet, enabling you to see the next card at less cost. Blocking bets are more common on the turn and river, but they can occur on the flop.

The second reason for a small bet is to avoid committing too much of your stack to the hand. Late in a tournament, you will see many situations where all the stacks are relatively small. In that case, players will typically bet small amounts, making a move for the pot but leaving themselves an escape hatch (or the appearance of an escape hatch), in case they want to get out of the hand later.

2. **Half-pot bets.** In a deep stack situation, a half-pot bet is a typical size for a continuation bet on a dry flop. Since dry flops don't offer drawing chances, and since players who miss dry flops often don't continue with the hand, a half-pot bet is big enough to chase away the players who don't want to continue, while losing less when your opponent has connected with the flop. Half-pot bets offer a good risk-reward ratio since if your opponent folds more than one time in three, you will show a profit.

3. **Bets of two-thirds to three-quarters of the pot.** These are good bet sizes for value bets, designed to build the pot, or continuation bets on boards that are not so dry. For instance, a board like the 9♥8♠3♥ (with two cards of one suit) offers some drawing chances, so a larger bet cuts down on the odds being offered.

4. **Full pot bets.** Full pot bets are usually reserved for very wet flops where you have a hand and want to charge players for trying to draw. For example, suppose you have the

and the flop is the

While your holding is strong (top two pair), many hands could have a draw to beat you. So in this case, a pot-size bet charges them to play, while still not over committing you to the hand.

5. **More than the pot.** Betting more than the pot on the flop is an unusual move. Bets like this are usually driven by consideration of stack sizes rather than board texture. For instance, suppose the pot on the flop is 2,000 chips and you have only 3,200 left, while your opponent has much more. If you have a hand, the best bet size is usually all-in since a smaller bet leaves you committed to the pot anyway.

Whatever the situation, these are not fixed guidelines. You'll need to vary your bet sizes so your opponents can't deduce exactly what your bet means. However, in general, bets intended for a given purpose should average something like the amounts suggested here.

One final point: These suggestions are intended for flops where you're heads-up against a single opponent. If you intend to bet, and you're facing multiple opponents, you should plan on making a larger bet. That's because with multiple opponents there's a greater likelihood that someone has a made hand that can call (in which case, if you have a hand, you'd like to get more money in the pot), and also a greater chance that someone has a drawing hand (in which case you'd like to offer them incorrect odds.)

Small Ball

Small ball is a tournament style that's most associated with Daniel Negreanu, one of the most successful tournament players of the last decade. It's a style based on a few key ideas:

1. It's hard to hit the flop.

2. Most players won't continue in the hand when they have nothing.

3. You'd like to win the pot while risking the minimum.

4. You win big pots by trapping players with unexpected hands.

Small ball is a style that's been around for awhile, but it was explained and popularized by Negreanu in his book *Power Hold 'em Strategy*. It's a style designed for tournament play where the blinds and antes are steadily escalating, putting pressure on all the stacks at the table. The tight, conservative style favored by a lot of cash game players, based on waiting for "good" cards before getting involved, doesn't work as well in tournaments because good hands don't come around quickly enough to keep pace with the escalating blinds.

Small ball addresses this problem by looking more closely at the nature of hold 'em and crafting an approach that's specifically tailored to the requirements of tournament play. Small ball also blends a willingness to play a wider range of hands with generally smaller bet sizes. Let's look again at our key ideas from above and see why this approach might be effective.

Key Idea No. 1: In hold 'em, it's hard to hit the flop. When you play hold 'em, you start with two cards and it's hard to make a pair with just two cards. If you deal out starting hands at random, a little less than 6 percent will be pairs. Mostly, then, you'll be looking at two unpaired cards in your hand, and let's say you make a bet with your unpaired cards and manage to see a flop. Not counting draws, you'll only hit that flop about 30 percent of the time. Even if you start with ace-king, about 70 percent of flops will leave you with just an ace-high hand.

Key Idea No. 2: Most players won't continue after the flop with nothing. A few aggressive players will attempt to pull off big bluffs, but most players will quietly fold their tent when they completely miss a flop.

Key Idea No. 3: You'd like to win the pot with the minimum bet possible. When you do take a stab at a pot with a weak hand or a bluff, you're hoping that your opponent has nothing and will go away. In that case, it makes sense to put out the smallest bet that will get the job done. If your opponent has something and calls or raises, you're probably done with the hand, so a small bet will lose the fewest chips. If your opponent has already decided to fold to a bet, then a small bet is just as good as a big one.

Key Idea No. 4: You win big pots by trapping players with unexpected hands. Many players, especially beginners, get excited when they pick up a pair of aces. "This is it," they think. "I'll win somebody's whole stack!" But in fact, aces are a poor hand for stacking your opponent. Put another way, no matter what the flop looks like, if you can't at least beat an overpair like aces, you're not inclined to get all your chips in the middle.

The hands that can stack an opponent are the hidden, unexpected hands. For instance, suppose you hold a pair of queens and the board looks like this on the river:

- Flop: 9♥6♥2♣
- Turn: Q♦
- River: 5♠

If you had bet the flop and turn and your opponent called, and now he put you all-in when the 5♠ hit on the river, would you call? Most players would. The only hands that beat you are eight-seven or four-trey, and those are unlikely holdings. That is, it's more likely he has a smaller set, or perhaps two pair, or perhaps a bluff. But if he did call preflop with exactly eight-seven, your whole stack will be gone. That's the great strength of low connected cards. When playing them, you really do have a shot at stacking your opponent because your holding is so unexpected.

Putting all these ideas together, we can see the outline of the theory of small-ball tournament hold 'em. And assuming you have a deep stack, here's a quick summary of the basic approach:

1. Play a variety of hands preflop, including pairs, suited Broadway cards, and low suited and unsuited connectors.

2. Raise small preflop, usually about 2.5 big blinds.

3. Keep nibbling away on the flop with small continuation bets, usually half-pot or so.

4. Go away if your opponent shows real strength and you can't match it.

5. Don't get a lot of chips involved without a big hand.

Note, however, that small ball is a strategy that requires a deep stack. You start a tournament with a deep stack, and if your small ball approach works, you'll keep up with the blinds and antes and keep a deep stack.

What happens if you don't have a deep stack anymore? In that case, you revert to more normal play, abandoning the small pairs and low connectors. However, your bets and raises should remain on the small size since you don't want your opponents to notice that you've altered your basic style. And finally, small ball is a potent weapon in the hands of a good player who can use it to steal lots of small pots while staying out of trouble when his opponent actually has a hand.

Playing the Turn

By the time the turn comes, four of the five board cards have been dealt. You know a lot about your final hand, and if you've been paying attention to what your opponent has done, you probably have some good guesses about his hand.

The most important feature of the turn is that only one card remains to come. If you have the better hand now, you're usually a much bigger favorite than you were on the flop because your opponent has only one chance left to catch a card that wins. For the same reason, if you thought you were an underdog on the flop and didn't hit your hand, then you're usually a bigger underdog now.

The fact that the leader is usually in a better situation than before has some important implications for turn play. Let's look carefully at two of the most important:

1. **Value betting is stronger than before.** Let's say that after the flop, the pot was 1,000 chips, you have a high pair, and your opponent has a flush draw and both stacks are deep. With two cards to come, your high pair is about a 2-to-1 favorite over a flush draw with no other outs. You bet your complete stack of 800 and your opponent calls. Both actions are reasonable. You're a favorite, so you're happy to get more money in the pot, and he thinks his flush draw makes him a 2-to-1 underdog right now, and the pot is offering him 18-to-8 odds, or 2.25-to-1.

   Now suppose you had more than 800 but only bet 800 on the flop, and the turn card arrives and it doesn't help your hand or his. The pot is now 2,600 chips. With only one card to come, he's about a 4-to-1 underdog to hit his flush. While he should fold to a bet at this point (unless your bet is very small), any bet you make will have a much higher equity than before.

2. **Drawing hands are weaker than before.** From the above example, we can see that any drawing hand that hasn't connected by the turn will probably not get the odds it needs to continue. Even a half pot bet on the turn will be giving a drawing hand only 3-to-1 odds, whereas the odds of hitting a flush or an open-ended straight draw with no extra outs will be between 4- and 5-to-1. Therefore, to play a drawing hand, you would need to feel that it was likely that extra money could be won on the river (or that you think a bluff has a good chance of being successful on the river).

Betting the Turn

With these ideas in mind, let's look at several concrete reasons for betting on the turn.

Reason to Bet No. 1: For value with a strong enough hand. If you have a hand that's strong enough, you mostly want to bet to get more money in a pot you expect to win. The key words are "strong enough." How strong a hand has to be to qualify as strong enough depends on a number of factors. Let's take a look.

1. On the flop, a hand like an overpair, or top pair, top kicker, or top pair, good kicker will mostly be the best hand and is usually worth betting. Awkward situations can occur where the board is especially dangerous or several players are involved in the hand. For instance, if you hold the

are against three players, and the flop is the

you can't be very confident that your top pair, top kicker is in fact best. You might bet anyway just because it could be your best (or only) chance to win the hand, but if you get raised or otherwise run into resistance, you're unlikely to get more money involved on later streets.

2. As the hand develops and your opponent indicates that he's willing to get a lot of money committed, it becomes less and less likely that a hand like top pair, top kicker is in fact the best hand. By the river, a top pair type hand has become a hand of medium strength — good for catching bluffs, but somewhat dangerous for betting or raising.

　　You should make adjustments once you have some information about your opponent. Against a tight opponent, be extra cautious. Tight players don't play deep into the hand without a good holding to back them up. However, against a loose, passive player, bet more liberally. Loose passive players can go deep into the hand without anything better than bottom pair.

Reason to Bet No. 2: To build the pot if you checked the flop with a hand. You won't always bet when you have a hand on the flop. Sometimes you'll check to mix up your play — you don't want your opponent to know that if you check the flop he can bet with impunity and take the pot down. So check a few good hands on the flop. In addition, sometimes you won't bet the flop because, although you like your hand, it's a hand that's only good for winning a small pot. Checking here is a way to keep the pot small.

But if you have a hand, check the flop, and your opponent checks as well, then it's mostly best to bet the turn. At this point you need to start earning some money on the hand as well as preventing your opponent from hitting some random two pair that may beat you.

Reason to Bet No. 3: If the flop was checked around and you don't have a hand. If everyone checked, then it's likely that no one has much of a hand. This frequently means that even without a hand, betting the turn is now reasonable and may be your only chance of winning the pot.

Reason to Bet No. 4: Firing a second barrel if you made a continuation bet bluff on the flop and your opponent just called. A few years ago the idea of a "continuation bet" on the flop was new to many players. They would just fold if their opponent bet and they hadn't made a strong hand. But as continuation bets became understood, more players were willing to call a bet on the flop with a weak pair, a draw, or even nothing at all to see if they could win the hand later.

The counter-strategy to this approach is to fire a second bluff on the turn, known as "double barreling." This second bet shows a lot of strength and is correspondingly harder to call, and it's good strategy to double-barrel after some of your flop bluffs.

Reason to Bet No. 5: If you have a hand and your opponent is likely to have a draw. As we saw in the previous section, most draws will not have the odds required to call a bet on the turn with only one card to come. If you bet, you can either make these hands fold or force them to make a mistake by calling with incorrect pot odds.

Reason to Bet No. 6: Before the "cooler" comes. Another reason for betting into a potential drawing hand is that your opponent may not, in fact, have a drawing hand. Here's an example.

Suppose you have a moderately strong hand like top pair, good kicker. You bet the flop which has a couple of potential draws and your opponent calls implying he may have a drawing hand.

However, that's not the only reason he could have called. He may have a medium strength hand, and think that you are the one betting with a drawing hand. If this is the case, he probably wants to get to a showdown but is afraid you may hit your draw.

On the turn, a card comes which doesn't hit the draw. You could bet and your opponent will probably call again. But suppose you don't bet, worried that he may be trapping you or that the pot is getting too big.

Now comes a river card which seems to complete the draw. Again you won't bet for fear of being raised by a monster. But if you check, your opponent won't bet for the very same reason. At showdown, your hand will win, but you will have missed winning some extra money that you could have made with a bet on the turn.

We call the card that came on the river a "cooler." By creating a seemingly dangerous board, it froze the action. If you have a good hand and your opponent may or may not have a draw, the possibility of cooler cards gives you another reason to bet the turn.

Reason to Bet No. 7: To set up an all-in on the river. When holding a very strong hand, you'd like to win your opponent's entire stack if he has some sort of hand that he's willing to take to showdown. The way to set up an all-in bet on the river is to make a good bet on the turn. So try to bet enough on the turn so that the all-in river bet isn't much larger than the pot.

For instance, suppose you have made a concealed straight on the turn and your opponent has called your preflop and flop bets. Let's say the pot is now 24,000 chips and the effective stack is 100,000.[3] If you make a half-pot bet of 12,000 (to keep your opponent in the hand) and he calls, the pot will be 48,000 and the

---

[3] An effective stack is the lessor stack for both you and your opponent. Notice that this is all that can be bet since someone now must be all-in.

effective stack will now be 88,000. If you then push all-in on the river, it will be a massive overbet (compared to the pot) which may scare your opponent away.

However, if on the turn you make a pot-sized bet of 24,000 and your opponent called, the pot would be 72,000 chips on the river and your two stacks would be 76,000. Now an all-in move is essentially a pot-sized bet itself, and more likely to be called.

Checking the Turn

We've listed the reasons for betting the turn. What about checking the turn? When is that the best play? Let's take a look at some of the reasons for checking the turn.

Reason to Check No. 1: After a failed continuation bet. Double-barreling is an option, but not something to do to excess. If you have nothing and the board is unfavorable, it's often best to check and fold to a bet.

Reason to Check No. 2: As a trap. If you make a lot of continuation bets, occasionally check the turn with a strong made hand, particularly against an aggressive opponent. He will often bet to take the pot and you can then respond with a raise or a call. This play not only makes you more difficult to read and hence more dangerous, but garners at least one bet you might not otherwise have earned.

Reason to Check No. 3: To induce your opponent to bet or call. If you have a very strong hand by the turn, a bet by you threatens your opponent with the potential loss of his whole stack if he calls your turn bet and a subsequent river bet. As already mentioned, we call this the principle of *leverage*: You're leveraging a moderate turn bet into a threat against his whole stack. Checking the turn removes the threat to his stack, and may allow your opponent to call a bet on the river since his risk is then quantifiable and small.

Reason to Check No. 4: As a bluff catcher. A bluff catching hand is a hand with some showdown value, but which you don't want to bet. And if you bet, you're afraid stronger hands will call (or raise) but weaker hands will go away. So checking on the turn allows your opponent to bluff at the river with some of his weak hands, thinking the pot is up for grabs. You can then pick off those bluffs.

Playing the River

The river is the most important street in no-limit hold 'em. By the time you reach the river, you've seen the preflop, flop, and turn betting, and you've seen the entire board. You now have as much information as you will ever have. In addition, the bets are larger than on any other street, and all-in bets are not unusual.

The combination of large amounts of information combined with large bets means that a good player's edge is greater on the river than on any other street. Mastering river play is a key part of mastering no-limit hold 'em. And how you play the river largely depends on what sort of hand you have. Let's look at some categories of hands and see how they should be handled.

Hand Category No. 1: The nuts. Having the nuts on the river is a rare and happy situation, but you still need to play the hand correctly. The simple rule which governs this situation goes as follows:

> If you have the nuts on the river, you mostly want to push all-in.

This play may seem drastic, but the logic behind the move is actually easy to understand. If you make a normal-sized bet on the river, you'll get called some percentage of the time. If you push all-in, you'll get called less often, but when called, you'll win much more money. The extra money will more than compensate for the times your opponent folds when he would have called a smaller bet.

Under what circumstances don't you push all-in on the river? Since you need to vary your play, you can't always push with the nuts, and eventually, even feeble-minded opponents will figure out what you're up to. The best time to make a normal-sized bet is when your opponent has shown no real strength, but has indicated he has some kind of hand and he'd like to see a showdown. A typical case would be against a player who checks and calls a couple of bets when no obvious draw is present. This betting pattern indicates some sort of bluff-catcher like a medium pair or top pair, decent kicker. In this case, a big bet will probably chase him away, but a half-pot bet might make some money. So go with the smaller bet.

Hand Category No. 2: A very good hand which is not the nuts. To handle this situation, ask yourself a simple question: "If I make a good-sized bet, perhaps the size of the pot, and my opponent then puts me all-in, will I call?" If the answer is "yes," then treat this situation as though you had the nuts and play accordingly.

If your answer is "no" and you're actually going to fold to an all-in raise, then you must believe, from the previous betting action, that there's a decent chance that your opponent could have the nuts. In that case, try to get to showdown cheaply. You might make a small blocking bet or check with the idea of calling a modest bet by your opponent.

Hand Category No. 3: A good hand given the board and the betting. Here we're talking about hands that are not the second or third nuts, but are nonetheless "pretty good." Exactly what constitutes pretty good in a given situation can vary widely. If the board is paired, then quads and full houses are the nut hands, and straights and flushes could qualify as pretty good. On a non-paired board without three suited cards, straights are the nuts and sets are very strong, but a good two-pair hand qualifies as pretty good.

The classic (and very costly) mistake that many players make is to get cold feet with these hands and refuse to bet the river, thus turning them into bluff-catchers. And it's an easy mistake to make because with five different cards on board, all sorts of strong hands are possible. Your opponent could be trapping with some well-hidden straight, or he could have hit any of five different sets. The sheer number of possible very good hands makes betting with a hand like two pair difficult for the inexperienced player.

However, in general, pretty good hands are worth a good-sized value bet on the river. If you're having trouble making these bets, you need to be diligent about analyzing the hand thoroughly before making your river play. Consider how your opponent played the hand. Would he really have checked a set through two streets? Did he really call the flop and turn with a gutshot straight, only to hit on the river? Remember, that for the most part, people's actions reflect the strength of their hand. If it's unlikely that your opponent has your pretty good hand beaten, you should feel good about betting.

Also, keep in mind that on the river you either have the best hand or you don't. Therefore, a winning bet that elicits a call can double your overall profit on the hand. And over time, betting well on the river can be one of your biggest money-making skills.

Hand Category No. 4: A hand with some value. By the river, a hand with some value is typically a hand like top pair or even second or third pair, or depending on the board, it could be something much stronger, (like a good two pair hand). In any case, it's a hand that you believe might be best, but where you'd rather not put any more money in the pot if it's not necessary.

The ideal situation is to have a hand like this in position. In that case, if your opponent checks, you can check behind and see if your holding is best.

If he makes a small bet, you'll probably need to make what's known as a *crying call*. You're probably beaten, but his bet may be giving you pot odds of 5- or 6-to-1, and it's not necessary to win many of those bets to show a profit by calling.

If he makes a big bet, your odds won't be so good, and you'll need to make a tough decision. You'll need to call once in a while or your opponents will learn they can bluff you relentlessly. So your best strategy is to think back over the hand and ask yourself if he would have played a strong hand this way. If his story is consistent, just fold, and use the hands where his story is inconsistent to make your calls. Of course, sometimes you'll get tricked anyway, but this way your chance of picking off a few bluffs improves.

Hand Category No. 5: Nothing. When you have nothing on the river, your only options are to fold or bluff. Mostly, you're going to fold. However, you'll need to bluff some of the time so that your opponents won't be able to tell whether your river bet means a strong hand. Here are a few rules for bluffing on the river.

1. **Sometimes bluff with hands that have little or no showdown value.** If you bluff with nothing and your opponent raises, you can cheerfully throw your hand away.

2. **Sometimes bluff with weak to medium-strength hands that actually have showdown value.** This play is a little more complicated. When you bet the river with a hand like a medium or top pair, you run the risk that you may get raised and have to fold a hand that might actually be best. The flip side, however, is that your bet represents real strength and may get better hands (sometimes much better hands) to fold. If you can make this play occasionally, your river betting range isn't simply polarized between strong hands and bluffs, but now contains some medium-strength hands as well. Notice that you will now be more difficult to read and it should also be a little more likely that your monsters will get called.

3. **Don't bluff someone who's already shown a lot of strength.** They'll call even if they might not be happy.

4. **Don't bluff a calling station.**

5. **Don't bluff with an inconsistent story.** If you're representing a strong hand, think back to the turn and see if your action there was consistent with what you're representing now.

6. **Consider bluffing if the river is a scare card.** Good scare cards are cards which make a low or medium pair on board, or cards which seem to fill in a straight. The story you're

telling is that you had a medium hand or a draw and now hit the jackpot. One word of caution. Weak players often try to bluff when the third card of a suit hits on the river. Good players know that move and they'll figure you do as well.

7. **Be less inclined to bluff with a high card (like an ace) in your hand.** If you and your opponent were both drawing and you both missed, your high card may be good enough to win the pot.

Expectation
and Expected Value

In poker, all decisions have a value. We refer to this value as the "expected value," or "expectation" of the decision. (The shorthand term for expected value is just "EV.") In some cases, we can calculate this value directly, in other cases, we estimate the value by making educated guesses about our opponent's hand and what he might do in the future. In general, however, when making a decision in poker, we're trying to estimate or calculate the value of different courses of action, and picking the choice with the higher expected value.

Let's look at a concrete example and see this decision-making in action. Suppose we hold the

in a tournament where the blinds are 100 and 200. Preflop, one player raises to 700 and a second player calls. Our stack is 12,000, we elect to call as well, and everyone else folds. The pot is now 2,400 chips.

The flop comes the

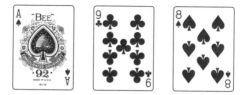

The first player now bets 2,000, a pretty sizeable bet. The second player folds and we call the 2,000 with our nut flush draw. (We have the K♠, and the A♠ is on the board, so if another spade comes our hand will be the best possible flush.) The pot is now 6,400 chips and we have 9,300.

The turn card is the 2♦ and we still have the flush draw with just one card to come. Our opponent now pushes all-in for his last 6,000. We don't believe he would make this move without a reasonably strong hand, at least top pair. *Should we call?*

To answer this question, let's calculate the expected value of calling and compare it to the expected value of folding. In this simple example, these numbers are actually easy to calculate. (In most real-life examples, we have to settle for educated guesses.) Let's see how it's done.

The expected value of folding is just zero. We put no more chips into the pot and just go away. Note that the 2,700 we've already put into the pot doesn't count here in any way. Those chips are already gone; they belong to the pot, not to us. We're only looking at new chips to risk, and folding costs us exactly nothing.

But suppose we call instead. The pot is currently 12,400 chips and we have to put in 6,000 more to see the river card. We're risking 6,000 to win the 12,400 that's out there. Our best guess is that hitting a king or a queen won't be enough to take down the pot. To win, we'll need to hit the flush. Right now there are nine remaining flush cards that we haven't seen out of a total of 46 remaining cards. So if we call, we think we'll hit the flush 9 times out of 46 (19.5 percent) and win,

$$0.195 = \frac{9}{46}$$

while we'll miss 37 times out of 46 (80.5 percent)

$$0.805 = \frac{37}{46}$$

and lose. (Another way of saying the same thing is that we have nine *outs*, where an out is a card that will turn a losing hand into a winner.)

Let's simplify by saying we'll win 20 percent of the time and lose 80 percent. In poker, there's mostly no need to make difficult calculations when a simple approximation will do just as well. This produces an expectation of -2,320.

$$-2,320 = (0.20)(12,400) + (0.80)(-6,000)$$

where
  0.20 is the probability of winning,
  12,400 is the size of the pot,
  0.80 is the probability of losing, and
  6,000 is the size of the bet required to call.

That is if we call, 2,320 is what we rate to lose on average.

In a single hand, of course, we'll never lose that amount. We'll either lose 6,000 or win 12,400. But if we were to set up this situation hundreds or thousands of times, our average loss would approach 2,320 per hand. In poker parlance, we would say that calling is 'negative EV,' and folding is the correct play.

Pot Odds

During a poker hand, we rarely try to make expected value calculations as in the previous section. Instead, we use a shortcut method based on *pot odds*.

Pot odds are just the size of the pot compared to the amount required to call a bet. In the previous example, the pot was 12,400 chips and we needed 6,000 to call the last bet, so our pot odds were 2.07-to-1.

$$2.07 = \frac{12,400}{6,000}$$

Big pot odds mean we're being well compensated if we hit our hand, and we can call as an underdog. Low pot odds mean the opposite.

At the table, to solve a problem like the previous example, we compare the pot odds being offered to the odds of making our hand. If the pot odds are bigger than the odds of making our hand, then it's profitable to call. If smaller, then we're not being offered enough odds and we should fold.

In the previous example, the odds of making our hand on the river were 4.1-to-1.

$$4.1 = \frac{37}{9}$$

where
    37 is the number of non-flush cards remaining, and
    9 is the number of flush cards remaining.

The pot odds are smaller than the odds of making our hand, so we should fold. In that case, the pot is just not offering us enough to justify our risk. That's the same conclusion we reached by doing an exact calculation of expected value, with much less work.

Expressed and Implied Odds

Let's look at this idea of pot odds a little more closely. Pot odds actually come in two varieties, *expressed* and *implied odds*. Expressed odds are the odds which occur when there is no more action in the hand. The odds you see are the only odds you're getting. If you have enough odds to call, you call, otherwise you fold. The example in the last section, where your opponent moved all-in on the turn and your call or fold would end the action, is an example of expressed odds.

Implied odds are a little different. Suppose you call a bet but the hand doesn't end. Another street or two is played where more betting can occur. You may be able to win more money later if you hit your hand, but you won't necessarily have to put any more money in the pot if you miss. Implied odds are an estimate of the real odds being offered, taking into account the money you may win later.

To see how implied odds work in practice, let's look at a tournament situation.

Example 1-10. It's the turn and you're holding the

The board is the

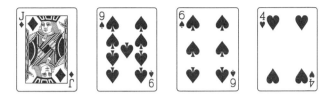

Right now the pot is 10,000 chips and you have another 20,000 in your stack. Your opponent, who has been leading the betting throughout the hand, bets 5,000 and he has another 40,000 left.

If you look just at the expressed odds, you have to either fold this hand or bluff at the pot by moving all-in. You can't just call because with only one card to come you're a 37-to-9, or a little more than 4-to-1, underdog, and you're only being offered 3-to-1 odds by the pot. (It's 15,000 after your opponent's bet, and you need 5,000 to call.)

However, the expressed odds don't tell the whole story. If you call, you still have 15,000 left in your stack, and your opponent has much more. If you hit the flush, you won't necessarily only win the 5,000 he just bet. You might win another 15,000 if he's willing to call a bet on the end.

The ability to win more money in the hand is the key idea behind implied odds. Calculating the odds of hitting the hand is fine, but it's important to also compare that to the total money you might win if you hit, not just the money that your opponent has bet thus far.

Estimating how much money can be won if you hit your hand is actually a tricky business. For instance, suppose your opponent's hand is the A♣J♣. Right now he's betting with top pair, top kicker, a good but not great hand. He might be betting because he thinks his hand is strong, but he might also be afraid that you have a hand like a couple of spades with a flush draw, or maybe something like the K♦Q♣ (with a straight draw), and he wants to charge you for drawing to your hand. Now suppose the river is the T♠. That's a scary card for him. Not only did the flush draw get there, but a straight draw got there as well!

Will he now bet the river with his top pair, top kicker? Most good players won't. If he checks and you bet, will he call? He'd probably call a small bet, but fold to a larger one. In this case, hitting our flush did win us some more money, but only a little more money.

You actually have more implied odds if he has a better hand! If your opponent has a set instead of just a pair, it will be much harder for him to lay his hand down to a river bet, and in that case you might make some real money. But during the hand you won't know exactly what sort of holding he has, so your estimate of what you can win will involve some intelligent guesswork.

One more factor that affects implied odds is exactly how easy it is to see that you might have a big hand. If you're drawing to a flush, for instance, it's clear when the third flush card hits the board that a flush is a possibility. Your opponent won't be sure you have the flush, but he'll be on his guard and he may be able to get away from his hand. But look what can happen when you're drawing to a straight.

Imagine your hand is the

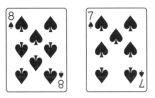

the board on the turn is the

and you called a bet on the turn. Notice your hand is a straight draw, and let's assume the expressed and implied pot odds were adequate to call and take another card. Now the river is the 6♥

The board now appears pretty innocuous because the straight is so well concealed. If your opponent has some kind of hand, it's likely he'll either bet again or call a bet on the river, even a sizeable bet. Because straights are harder to read than flushes, they generally have better implied odds. These are simple examples, but implied odds are a complex subject. Also, in many situations, it's easy to overestimate your implied odds. You may hit your hand and find that no more money goes in the pot because your opponents have nothing. You might also hit your hand and lose a lot of money when your opponent actually has a monster. Implied odds are real and you need to take them into account, but make conservative estimates. They're more likely to be correct.

Reverse Implied Odds

The concept of implied odds affects hands that are not strong now but can easily become strong on a later round. Small pairs, suited cards, and connected cards are hands that can improve to sets, flushes, and straights respectively. When these cards hit, they usually win the hand, and the extra money that goes in the pot mostly goes to them.

With reverse implied odds, the situation is turned around. Now we're looking at hands where we rate to lose money as play goes on and more money goes in the pot. Implied odds described situations where our hand took a sudden jump in value, as when we moved from a drawing hand to a made hand. Reverse implied odds describe situations where our hand steadily decreases in value, as our opponent is likely to improve to a strong hand while we aren't. Let's look at an example and see how this happens.

Example 1-11. In the early stages of a tournament, you're on the button with the

Your stack is 16,000 and the blinds are 100 and 200. The under-the-gun player, who has a few more chips than you, raises to 550, you call, and all other players fold. The pot is now 1,400 chips.

The flop is the

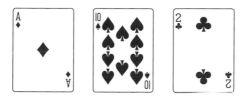

You've hit your ace and now have top pair. Your opponent leads out for 1,000 and you call.

You thought about raising with top pair because if the under-the-gun player has a pair of kings, queen, or jacks, you have him crushed. But there's some chance your opponent has a better ace, so you decide to be conservative and just call. You also figure you could be setting a trap since the under-the-gun player won't expect a hand as strong as a pair of aces to just be calling. You move 1,000 into the pot, leaving 13,000 in your stack. The pot is now 3,400 chips.

The turn is the J♠ which you're not happy to see arrive. You also recognize that if the under-the-gun player had a pair of jacks to start, he's now winning with a set. And if he had king-queen to start, his hand is now a straight. Still, there's plenty of other holdings he might have, so maybe things are still okay.

The under-the-gun player now bets 2,400, almost three-fourth's of the pot. You're a little worried that he seems so confident with an ace on board, but top pair is top pair, so you call again. The pot is now 8,200 chips and the effective stack is about 10,600.

The river is the Q♣ and the under-the-gun player bets 5,000, a development you don't like, but your hand is still top pair, and the pot is offering about 3-to-1 odds. Grudgingly, you make the call and your opponent shows you the

for a straight, and scoops the pot.

What went wrong? Quite a bit, actually. Let's step through the hand and see what really happened.

Your first problem was calling the raiser's initial preflop bet with the A♠9♠, a hand that's termed a 'weak ace.' The danger here is that the initial raiser's range includes lots of strong aces, as well as high or medium pairs — hands that range from aces down to eights or so. If the initial raiser has ace-queen, for instance, and you call with ace-nine, you're 'dominated.' That is, having an ace hit the board only appears to help you since it makes a pair of aces for both players. Now the strength of your hand is determined by your kicker, and since his kicker (a queen) beats your kicker (a nine), you're going to need to hit a nine to win (or perhaps make an unexpected hand like a straight with the nine).

So with a hand like ace-nine, you're often in a reverse implied odds situation. The longer the hand goes on, and the more money that goes in the pot, the less likely you are to win. The ace that hit the board was really a trap — it kept you in the hand because you had a pair of aces, but your opponent had aces with a better kicker, so you were always a big underdog. You couldn't really fold on the flop, but once he bet again on the turn, he was likely to have a better ace, and it was time to cut your losses.

The classic reverse implied odds hands are small aces because they're often dominated. You want to be careful with these hands, and if your opponent raises from early position preflop, it's often wise to just let them go. Other hands that suffer from reverse implied odds are weak Broadway hands like king-jack or queen-ten. Again, if you hit your hand on the flop and your opponent continues betting strongly, you might be dominated by something like ace-king or ace-queen. This doesn't mean that these hands are unplayable, but keep in mind that when playing one of these hands, you're playing them for straight possibilities as well as high card value.

Hand
Strength and Pot Size

One of our goals in no-limit hold 'em is to roughly match the strength of our hand with the size of the pot. We even have a shorthand expression to cover this situation: *big hand, big pot; small hand, small pot*. When we have a very strong hand, we want the pot to be as big as possible. When our hand is modest but still might be best, we want to keep the pot small and get to showdown.

The idea of correlating hand strength and pot size may seem obvious, but it's surprisingly difficult to implement in practice. When we have what may be the best hand, like top pair, top kicker on the flop, we have a lot of reasons to bet.

1.   We want to bet for value, (to get more money in the pot when our hand is best).

2.   We want to bet to force drawing hands to pay for the chance of beating us.

3.   We want to bet to balance the hands where we miss the flop and bluff with a continuation bet.

That's a lot of good reasons for betting. However, bets and pot sizes in no-limit hold 'em grow geometrically, so it's easy for bets that seem reasonable to quickly create pots that are out of line for the hand's strength. Take a look at this next example.

Example 1-12. You're in the early stages of a tournament and the blinds are 150 and 300. You're on the button with a stack size of 33,000 and the player in the cutoff directly on your right has a stack of 28,000. You've only been playing a short time and he seems to be a standard tight player who hasn't gotten out of line.

79

Your hand is the

The first two players fold and the player in the cutoff seat raises to 800. You have a reasonable hand and think he might be using his position to steal, so you reraise to 1,800. He calls and the blinds fold. The pot is now 4,050 chips and you have the best position.

The flop is the

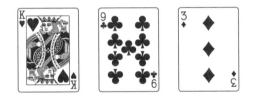

That's a good flop and your hand is now top pair with the second-best kicker. The cutoff checks and you bet 2,200 which is just over half the pot. With no draws available on this board, it seems likely you'll take the pot down right here, but your opponent calls. The pot is now 8,450 and the effective stack is 24,000.

The turn card is the 8♦. You still have top pair and your opponent checks again, not showing any strength. You decide to get rid of him for good and bet 7,000 but he raises all-in to 24,000.

The pot is now 39,450 chips and it costs 17,000 to call which is better than 2-to-1. And with top pair you decide you can't lay your hand down for that price. So you call and he shows you the

for middle set. The river is the A♥ and he takes the pot. You lose 28,000 and have only 5,000 left. You lost 85 percent of your stack in one hand. *What went wrong?* You didn't make any decisions that were ridiculous in themselves. In fact, even though at every decision point you made the most aggressive choice, each choice was plausible given what you knew at the time. However, each decision escalated the pot to the point where you got almost your whole stack involved with a hand (top pair, second kicker) that only warranted a small pot. That can happen in a game where bet sizes can grow so rapidly.

A better way of playing this hand was to check either the flop or, more likely, the turn. On the flop, you have a good top pair on a dry board (a board without any draws). If you have the best hand at this point, which is likely, your opponent has very few outs. If he holds, let's say, a pair of eights in his hand, only the last two eights are outs for him. If he holds ten-nine suited so that he has a pair of nines, he has five outs, the last three tens and the last two nines. If he holds king-jack, then only the last three jacks are outs. So checking the flop gives him few chances to catch up and keeps the pot small.

Betting the flop is all right, of course, but checking behind on the turn was definitely a better play. If your hand is still good, it's likely to be best at showdown, but betting the turn gives the hands that are beating you a chance at winning your whole stack, which is just what happened.

Checking the turn is what's known as a *pot control* move, deliberately limiting the size of the pot when your hand isn't strong enough to play a big pot.

So what hands are good enough to happily create a big pot? That's a difficult question which really depends on the opponent, the board, and the betting so far. But very generally, one-pair hands are small pot hands, while sets, straights, and flushes are big pot hands.

Pot Commitment

Closely related to the small hand, small pot / big hand, big pot concept is the idea of pot commitment. Basically, you are committed to the pot when the pot is large enough so that an all-in bet from your opponent will offer you such good pot odds that you are compelled to call given the hand you have and the hand you think your opponent may have. When pot commitment happens, you may elect to move all-in yourself to grab some amount of folding equity.

The example from the previous section is a textbook example of pot commitment. When your opponent moved all-in on the turn, the pot was so large that you were being offered better than 2-to-1 pot odds to call. Those were big odds, and you thought the chance that he was bluffing plus the chance that he might have had a hand like top pair, weak kicker plus the chance you could draw out if your holding was second best were worth taking a shot at that big payoff.

In no-limit hold 'em tournaments, pot commitment decisions arise constantly during the later rounds because so many players have stacks that are relatively small compared to the blind levels. Imagine that you're in a tournament at a nine-handed table, the blinds are 1,000 and 2,000, with a 300-chip ante, each, and your stack is only 22,000. If you pick up a pair of jacks, you're committed to the pot before the hand starts. If a player in front of you opens for 6,000, your best play by far is to move all-in. Your jacks are probably good, but if they're not, you won't be able to gather information fast enough to prevent getting all your money in the pot.

Part Two

Stacks, Blinds, Antes, and Ranges

Stacks, Blinds, Antes, and Ranges

Introduction

In Part One, we covered the basics of no-limit hold 'em and the mechanics of tournament play. At this point you should have some idea of how to evaluate hands preflop according to hand strength and position, how to evaluate the playing styles of your opponents, how to conduct a hand after the flop, and how to evaluate the odds you're being offered by the pot.

In Part Two, we're going to move on and explain some of the underlying theory of no-limit hold 'em tournaments. The key skill for a good tournament player is to understand the relationship between your stack, the size of the blinds and antes, and your opponent's stack. This relationship drives all of the decisions you'll make at a tournament table. It can be understood in a couple of different ways, and we'll explain what those ways are and how you can pick one that best suits your own situation.

After we've covered the stack-blind relationship, we'll take a look at ICM, the Independent Chip Model, and discuss some of its strengths and limitations. Finally, we'll introduce the idea of ranges and explain why it's better to think about your opponent's hand as consisting of a set of possible hands, rather than try to puzzle out his exact holding.

Stacks, Blinds, and Antes

We'll start our discussion of tournament strategy by looking at stacks and blinds, and the relationship between the two of them. As we'll see, the relationship between your stack and the blinds (and antes, if there are any) is the key idea that will drive the play of a hand.

If you play a lot of no-limit hold 'em cash games, you've probably become accustomed to playing with a certain level of blinds and a big stack of chips. Cash games begin with a fixed blind structure. For example, a "$2-$5 game" in a casino simply means that the small blind is $2 and the big blind is $5, and those blinds will remain constant no matter how long you play.

When buying into a game, you determine how big your stack will be. A standard cash game in a Vegas casino will have a range of possible buy-ins, with a usual minimum of 40 big blinds, and a maximum that might be as high as 150 or 200 big blinds. Many players entering the game will buy in for 100 big blinds, which would be $500 in a $2-$5 game.

The key feature of a cash game, however, is that if your stack dips, you can pull more money out of your pocket and buy more chips. If you lose a big pot and your stack dips from $500 to $100, you can buy another $400 worth of chips and get your starting stack back for the next hand.

Some players will leave the game when their stack gets decimated, while others will buy back. Only a handful will elect to keep playing with a tiny stack. The effect is to create a game where most stacks are deep, in the 75 to 150 big blind range, and sometimes more.

Tournament play is different in three ways:

1. The blinds are constantly rising.

2. Antes enter the picture after a few levels, accelerating the growth of the pots.

3.   Players can't add more chips. (We're ignoring rebuy tournaments for the moment. In rebuy events players can rebuy during the first few levels of play, but rebuys represent only a small percentage of the major live events.)

The effect of these changes creates a completely different playing environment. By the time you're a few levels into the tournament, some players will have huge stacks, some will have tiny stacks, and many will be muddling along with a little more or less than their starting stack. The steadily increasing blinds and the introduction of antes means that the cost of playing a round gets larger and larger as time passes. Players must accumulate chips or die trying.

Measuring Stack Sizes

By itself, your stack size really doesn't mean much. If you started a tournament with a stack of 20,000 and you've built that stack to 200,000, it's easy to sit back and say "I'm doing great!" However, what's important is the relationship between your stack and the relentlessly increasing blinds and antes. Once you understand that relationship, how comfortable (or uncomfortable) a position you're in will become clear, how you stand in relation to the other players, what sort of hands are necessary to play and most important, how you should play them. The relationship between your stack and the blinds and antes is the single most important relationship in tournament poker. Let's look at a couple of quick examples.

Example 2-1. You've just sat down at your table for the start of the Main Event in the World Series of Poker. The dealer pushes over a stack of 30,000. In the first level of play, which lasts two hours, the starting blinds will be 50 for the small blind and 100 for the big blind. *What's the ratio between your stack and the sum of the blinds?*

With no antes in the mix, the blinds total 150 chips. Dividing your 30,000 stack by 150 gives a ratio of 200. Your stack is 200 times the blinds at this point. That's a very deep stack.

Example 2-2. You've been playing in the Main Event all day. It's now 10:30 pm and you're about to start level 5, the last level of the day. You've grown your stack to 45,000, a 50 percent increase over the starting stack. But in level 5, the blinds have risen to 200 and 400, and a 50-chip ante is now required. You're at a full table of nine players. *What's the ratio between your stack and the blinds and antes in this situation?*

This problem is a little more difficult, and note that with antes in the mix, we need to know the number of players at the table to calculate the starting pot. The sum of the blinds is 600. Nine players are anteing 50 each, so the antes amount to 450. The sum of the blinds and antes is 1,050 chips.

Dividing our stack of 45,000 by 1,050 might seem to be a chore, but it doesn't have to be if we use a trick or two. Note that 1,050 is almost the same as 1,000, and dividing 45,000 by 1,000 is easy: the answer is 45. We can get a little closer if we realize that 1,050 is a little bigger than 1,000, and dividing by a slighter bigger number gives us a slightly smaller answer. Let's estimate the answer to be 43. That's fine for our purposes. We don't need an exact answer at the table, just a ballpark answer. (If you're interested, the exact answer is 42.8.)

Magriel's M

The ratio of a stack to the blinds and antes is such an important concept that it deserves its own name. In the poker world we call this ratio 'M.' It's named after the mathematician and backgammon genius Paul Magriel who first codified the idea about a decade ago.

Keeping M in mind helps clarify our ideas about how to play at different stages of the tournament. When M is big, greater than 70 or so, all our options are available. We can be aggressive, play speculative hands, and pull off elaborate bluffs when the situation seems right. We can also lay back, play tight, and wait for solid hands if that seems a better choice.

As the blinds rise and M shrinks, certain types of plays lose their effectiveness and our options get constrained. As the process continues and M gets even smaller, we start thinking more and more about pot commitment and all-in moves. With a very small M, say 5 or less, our universe shrinks to just one play: move all-in before the flop.

As an introduction to the usefulness of M, let's imagine we pick up a small pair, say a pair of fours, and look at how we might play this hand at different stages of the tournament.

Example 2-3. It's early in a big tournament and we have our starting stack of 30,000. The blinds are 100 and 200, so our M is a very healthy 100. We're sitting on the button and we look down to see the

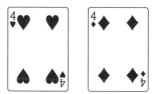

The first two players fold, but the third player opens for 550, a standard raise to almost three times the big blind. The players in the hijack and cutoff seats both call, all three players have stacks similar to ours, and all seem thus far to be solid, competent players. *What should we do?*

The best play under the circumstances is to just call the bet. To see why, let's assume the big blind also calls (reasonable with any playable hand since he'll be getting huge pot odds) and we play a five-way pot. The pot will be 2,850 chips (don't forget the small blind's contribution) and we'll have put in 550, so we'll be getting almost 5-to-1 odds. Our game plan is pretty simple: play the hand if we hit a set on the flop, and give up if we don't.

The key to the hand is the implied odds we're getting. We're about a 7-to-1 underdog to catch a four on the flop, and we didn't quite get those odds in the preflop betting. But if we do hit our set, we should be able to win at least one or two more good-sized bets, and there's even a chance that we can win someone's whole stack. Since those stacks are very large right now, that chance represents a huge payoff on a small investment. (Our call of 550 was less than 2 percent of our stack.)

Now let's change the parameters a bit and see what happens.

Example 2-4. We're in the same tournament as before, but we've progressed a few levels. Blinds are now 200 and 400 and the antes won't come into play until the next level. Our stack has grown to 60,000, so our M is still a healthy 100. As before, we've picked up a pair of fours on the button. The player in second position, with 9,000 and an M of 15, opens for 1,000 in third position. He's been loose and aggressive, and just lost a big pot which cost him most of his stack. *Should we call as well?*

The answer is no. However, we do have two other options:

1. **Option No. 1 is to simply fold.** The problem is not our stack, which is certainly big enough for a speculative play. The problem is the opener's stack. Because it's so small, the implied odds needed are not there, so we don't expect to win enough money when a four flops. If we call and miss the flop, our lost will mostly be the 1,000 we put in the pot, but if our set comes in, our gain is capped at 9,000 (assuming the blinds don't get involved), and we don't know how often we'll even get that. Folding is a solid, prudent choice.

2. **Option No. 2 is to raise to 9,000, putting him all-in.** If he's a loose player playing a lot of speculative hands, this might be the best play. We'll have a lot of fold equity and be a slight favorite whenever he calls with two high cards. We're only in bad shape if he calls with a higher pair, but a loose

player won't be holding that hand all that often. Putting him all-in is a reasonable alternative to just folding.

Example 2-5. The tournament continues and blinds are now 1,000 and 2,000, with a 200-chip ante, and the table is 9-handed, so the pot is 4,800 chips to start. Some bad luck has whittled our once-proud stack down to 25,000. We have a pair of fours in fourth position. The first three players fold to us. *What should we do?*

Here's yet another application of M. With the blinds and antes now totaling 4,800 chips, our stack gives us an M of just 5, and with an M this small, we can't make a normal raise of 5,000 to 6,000 since that represents a big portion of our meager stack. The best play is to move all-in with our 25,000, generating maximum fold equity.

When we push, sometimes we'll pick up the pot and increase our M from 5 to 6. Sometimes we'll get called by a player with two high cards and we'll be a favorite to more than double up, raising our M to about 11. And sometimes we'll get called by a higher pair and probably bust out right here. But when your M is very low, you don't have the option of sitting around and waiting for legitimately big hands. You have to consider how strong your hand is and how many players are left to act, and then move in when your hand seems good enough.

Remember that with a pair of fours, there are just ten hands in the deck that are actually beating you — fives through aces. There is less than a 5 percent chance that any single player holds one of those hands right now, and with five players left to act, you're about 75 percent to hold the best hand at this point. That's easily good enough to take decisive action when your situation is getting desperate.

Big Blinds and M

Besides M, there's another method for evaluating your stack size at any point in the tournament. Instead of comparing your stack to the sum of the blinds and antes, just divide your stack by the amount of the big blind itself.

Doing the calculation using big blinds is easier since you don't need to add up the blinds and antes. For instance, suppose at an eight-player table your stack is 100,000 chips and the blinds are 2,000 and 4,000, with a 500-chip ante. To see the size of your stack in big blinds, just divide 100,000 by 4,000 to get 25. That's a quick and simple calculation, and calculating your M takes longer. The sum of the blinds is 6,000, while the eight antes add another 4,000. The sum of the blinds and antes is therefore 10,000 chips, so your M in this case is exactly 10.

Although the numbers are different, they're describing the same situation, so you need to use different scales. In this example, whatever action you would think is proper with an M of 10 is the same action you should take with a big blind count of 25. If you want to use a certain strategy when your M is between 20 and 30, use the same strategy if your big blind count is between 50 and 75.

There are a couple of simple conversion methods that allow you to translate M into big blinds or vice-versa. Which method you use depends on whether antes are in play or not.

- If antes are in play, multiply M by 2.5 to get a rough equivalent in big blinds. Multiply big blinds by 40 percent to get a roughly equivalent M. These methods work because in most cases the antes are equivalent to one extra big blind. For example, an M of 20 is about equivalent to 50 big blinds when antes are involved.

- If antes are not in play, multiply M by 1.5 to get an equivalent in big blinds. Multiply big blinds by 0.67 or ⅔ to get an equivalent in M. For example, with no antes, an M of 40 is equivalent to 60 big blinds.

M or Big Blinds: Which is Better?

When you play, feel free to use whichever measure you want, but each one has certain advantages and disadvantages. The great advantage of using the big blind count in a live event is its simplicity. You already know the big blind at any stage of the tournament, and your stack is sitting right there in front of you. So just do a quick estimate of your stack, divide it by the size of the big blind, and there's your answer. As long as you have a knowledge of what needs to be done for each range of stack to blinds, you'll be all right.

If you play online and are multi-tabling several events at once, you really have to use the big blind method. Decisions are coming at you so quickly from the various tables that it's necessary to have an answer almost instantly, and using big blinds is much quicker because you don't have to deal with the antes.

The great advantage of M is its accuracy. Taking antes into account gives you a truer picture of the usefulness of your stack than does the big blind method.

Playing Different Stack Sizes

In cash games, players tend to have certain well-defined styles. Some are aggressive, and they like to be betting and raising, always in control and driving the action. Others see themselves as solid and in control. They like to wait for good preflop hands — high cards and pairs — before investing their money. Whatever their particular style, most players tend to stick to that style and play it consistently throughout a session.

In tournament play, however, we need to let the situation at the table, in particular our stack size, govern our style. If your stack demands aggressive play, then be aggressive. If it demands solid play, then be solid. Play in accordance with the requirements of your stack, and you should be consistently successful. Ignore your stack and pay the price.

"All right," you say, "my stack is important. But just how does my stack tell me what to do?"

For the answer to that question, let's consider three different stack sizes and see how we would plan to play our hand in each case.

Playing a Deep Stack

We'll start by looking at how to play a deep stack. For our purposes, let's say a deep stack is anything bigger than an M of 40, or bigger than 60 big blinds if no antes are in play or 100 if antes have started. The rule here is simple: If you have a big stack, try to be aggressive. When your stack is big, you pose a threat to all the smaller stacks at the table. You can eliminate them, but they can't eliminate you. Players with medium-to-small stacks are reluctant to get in a pot with a big stack if they have a marginal hand and since your big stack is a real weapon, use it to try to pick up as many easy pots as possible.

Tight players with a big stack often waste the opportunities that the stack presents. Since they know they're in no danger of running out of chips anytime soon, they'll sit back and wait for the big hands that they feel most comfortable playing. The problem here is that big hands don't come around often enough, and even when one finally arrives, there's no guarantee you'll win a big pot with it. Don't fall into this trap. Let your big stack work for you and try to build an even bigger one.

And to play aggressively with a big stack, don't restrict yourself to just the big pairs and Broadway cards. You can also play speculative hands like small pairs, hoping to flop a set, or hands like suited connectors or suited one-gappers, hoping to flop a straight draw or a flush draw. When you make a good drawing hand, try to semi-bluff aggressively. Your bet may win the pot, and if it doesn't, you might hit your hand and win a huge pot on the end.

Playing a Small Stack

Now suppose you have a small stack, let's say with an M of 7 or less, equivalent to about 17 big blinds when antes are in play. In this situation, we're also looking to be aggressive, but our aggression now takes a different form because we'll be blinded out of the tournament pretty soon if we try to play a normal game. Therefore, we're looking to take a pretty good hand and get all our chips in the center of the table. If we lose, we're out. But if we play tight we're out pretty soon anyway, so there's no great loss when that happens. However, if we can double up, we're back to a somewhat comfortable stack and we're not desperate any longer.

What kinds of hands do we want to play here? In this case we're looking for hands that are either top pair right now, or can make top pair on the flop. We're certainly happy to play a pair of tens or better, and if necessary, we'll get all-in with smaller pairs as well. We're also happy to push a couple of high cards like ace-king, ace-queen, ace-jack, and king queen. If they hit the flop they make a high pair, which is good enough for our purposes. But hands like suited connectors or various middling cards should be avoided. Lacking any high card strength, these holdings can hit the flop and still lose.

When you don't have a small stack but your opponent does, remember that he's likely to be pushing with a lot of different hands. Furthermore, you won't necessarily need a premium hand to call his push, and since the pot may be offering attractive odds, any decent hand might be enough.

Playing a Medium Stack

Is tournament play all about aggression? No. There is a time when it's best to be a little more conservative, and it occurs when your chip stack is in a middle range between deep and small. You don't have to be desperate, but you often can't get enough implied odds to justify gambling with the speculative hands. So in this middle range, start to phase out the small pairs and suited connectors and start to concentrate on medium pairs, high pairs, and Broadway cards.

Playing Your Opponents

While stack size is a key factor in planning the hand, you'll always need to combine that factor with a knowledge of your opponent and how he plays. Is he weak? If he's weak, in what way is he weak? Does he call down to the end with a pair, or is he constantly bluffing with nothing? Does he play too many hands or not enough? Does he seem competent and confident? If you think he's strong, can you put him on a style? Is his chip stack growing or shrinking? The answers to these questions will determine who you avoid and who you target, and how you play against them.

When you're starting the tournament and have a deep stack, your first job is to spot the weak players at the table, and do it quickly. Why quickly? There are two simple reasons:

1. It's much easier to win money from weak players than strong ones.

2. Weak players may not be around very long.

After you identify the weak players, try to play pots in position against them. In the long run, those should be profitable pots.

Evaluating
Tournament Formats

A decade ago, before the start of the big poker boom, poker tournaments had a relatively small number of formats. There were big multi-table tournaments with a variety of possible entry fees, and satellite tournaments with smaller entry fees, where the players could win an entry into the big events. If you played in a tournament, you'd be sitting at a full table of nine, ten, or sometimes even eleven players.

The poker boom and the growth of online poker changed all that. Online poker rooms were quick to experiment with lots of new formats. Some didn't make the grade, but many became popular and eventually migrated from the online scene to the live poker scene.

No-limit hold 'em tournaments now come in a great variety of formats. While good play is always rewarded, strong players prefer some formats to others. So if you're planning on concentrating on tournament play, it's important to know what formats to seek out and which ones to avoid. Let's take a look at some of the different possible formats and see which favor skillful play the most and which the least.

The Multi-Table Tournament

The mainstay of tournament poker is the big multi-table tournament. The largest and most famous of these is the Main Event of the World Series of Poker, with over 6,000 players and a $10,000 entry fee. Hundreds of other tournaments take place around the world each year, with smaller fields and entry fees ranging from a few hundred dollars to $50,000 or more. In fact, in the run-up to the Main Event at the World Series of Poker, 2012 saw the first event with a million-dollar entry fee. (Antonio Esfandiari took down the $18,000,000 first prize.)

Evaluating a multi-table tournament (usually abbreviated to 'MTT') requires looking at a few parameters. Here are the most important:

1. How deep is the starting stack?

2. How long are the levels?

3. How fast do the blinds and antes increase?

4. How many players sit at a table?

5. How skewed is the prize structure?

6. How big is the rake?

Let's look at each parameter in turn.

Parameter No. 1: How deep is the starting stack? In most multi-table tournaments, your entry fee buys you a set number of chips, called your starting stack. In the Main Event of the World Series, your starting stack is 30,000. If you lose your whole stack, you're out of the tournament. Typical starting stacks are in the 10,000 to 20,000 range.

Bigger starting stacks allow for more deep-stack play, and favor the better players. Some smaller tournaments have an entry fee which buys a certain number of chips and usually another 'add-on' fee which is typically small but which buys more chips. For example, a local tournament might have a $120 entry fee which buys a stack of 10,000, and an 'add-on' fee of $10 which buys another 2,000. The add-on fee in this case is a great deal and should always be taken.

An exception to the starting stack rule is the rebuy tournament which also can include an add-on that allows you to rebuy chips if your stack dips below a certain point within a specified period of time. For example, an online rebuy and add-on event with a $100 entry fee might work as follows:

1. Your $100 entry fee gets you a starting stack of 1,500. At any time during the first hour, if your stack is at 1,500 or less, you can rebuy another 1,500 for another $100.

2. After one hour, you can pay an add-on of another $100 and get an additional 2,000.

In this tournament, you might buy-in for $100, then immediately exercise another buy-in and begin with 3,000. If at the end of an hour your stack has increased to 5,000, you can add-on for another $100 and bring your stack up to 7,000 for the rest of the tournament.

Rebuy and add-on events have very high equity for good players because there's so much dead money in the prize pool by the end of the rebuy period. Many players buy-in for the minimum, then drop out when they are eliminated. Others move all-in over and over again with weak hands, hoping to double up quickly knowing they can buy back when something goes wrong. However, chips are chips, and if you make a lot of foolish moves you're just handing equity to your opponents. Therefore, the right way to play a rebuy and add-on event is to play sensibly in the early stages, while remembering that many players are pushing all their chips in with weak hands. Be aware that you don't need a monster hand to call these players; a strong hand is enough.

If you're able to play online, the small-stake rebuy and add-on events are an excellent way to get started in tournament play. But be aware that it's always in your interest to rebuy for the maximum amount, so you should assume that the effective entry fee is three to four times larger than the posted entry fee. That is, a tournament with a $20 entry fee and $20 rebuys and add-on will, on average, cost you $60 to $80 to play.

Parameter No. 2: How long are the levels? Tournaments are organized in the form of levels which is just a period of time when the blinds and antes are set at a certain amount, and they remain at that amount for the entire level. Once a level ends and a new level starts, the blinds and/or antes increase. In a live tournament, levels last between 20 minutes and two hours. The pace is slow because cards have to be dealt and collected, so you might play 30 to 40 hands per hour. In online tournaments, levels vary between five and 30 minutes, but the pace is faster, with as many as 60 to 80 hands being dealt per hour.

Longer levels favor the better player since they allow more hands to be played in deep stack situations. (The shallower the stack, the fewer decisions that can be made before one player or the other is all-in.)

Parameter No. 3: How fast do the blinds and antes increase?
If the blinds and antes double every level, you're quickly going to move from deep-stack poker to short-stack poker no matter how big your starting stack might have been. If the blinds and antes are increasing slowly, say by 20 to 25 percent per round, then the tournament will stay in the deep-stack phase longer and the opportunities for skill will be greater.

As an example, here's the blind and ante structure for the first few levels of the Main Event at the World Series:

Blind and Ante Structure at the WSOP

Level	Blinds	Ante
1	50/100	
2	100/200	
3	150/300	
4	150/300	25
5	200/400	25
6	250/500	50
7	300/600	50

As you can see, there's a doubling of the blinds from Round 1 to Round 2, but after that the rate of increase slows down quite a bit. And by the time we're moving from Round 6 to Round 7, the total of the blinds and antes increases from 1,200 chips to 1,350 chips, an increase of only about 15 percent. That sort of modest increase from round to round prolongs the period of deep-stack play and increases the edge for the better players.

By contrast, in small buy-in single day events, the blinds and antes might be increasing by 50 percent or more every round, quickly plunging the players into short stack play. Short stack play does have its own strategy and requires skill, but the results of these tournaments are much random than those of slower-paced events.

Parameter No. 4: How many players sit at a table? For a long time, poker tournaments were only played with full tables, with nine, ten, or even eleven players present. More players at live tables meant fewer dealers, and hence a lower cost for the operator.

Once online poker took hold, sites were free to experiment with smaller tables since a tournament with more small tables cost no more to operate than one with fewer full tables. Heads-up tournaments were the first to catch on, using a knock-out format like tennis. Shortly afterwards, the online sites began to run events with six-player and four-player tables. As these formats became popular, live events began to feature them as well, despite the added dealer cost. The World Series of Poker now features several events with short tables.

For a good player, short tables offer higher equity than full tables. Many beginners and weaker players have a reasonable idea of opening hand requirements at full tables. Most will have a basic tight style, which, while not optimal, is not a terrible way to play. At short tables, however, everyone needs to loosen their game, play more hands, and play them aggressively. For an experienced player, this shouldn't be a problem, but weaker players will have a lot of difficulty adapting.

Parameter No. 5: How skewed is the prize structure? Most large tournaments pay out prize money once the field is reduced to 10 percent of its starting size. A tournament that starts with 200 players will typically pay money to the last 20 or so.

However, even tournaments that pay the same number of players can have a very different prize structure. Take a look at these payout structures for two tournaments which each pays ten places:

Payout Structures for Two
Tournaments that Pay Ten Places

Place	Tournament A	Tournament B
1st	40%	25%
2nd	25%	20%
3rd	15%	15%
4th	8%	10%
5th	5%	7%
6th	2%	6%
7th	2%	5%
8th	1%	4%
9th	1%	4%
10th	1%	4%
Total	**100%**	**100%**

The payout structure for Tournament A is heavily skewed toward the top three places, which together gobble up 80 percent of the prize money. Places 4 through 10 share the last 20 percent, with places 8, 9, and 10 just getting their entry fee back.

The payout structure for Tournament B is much more evenly distributed. The first three places now get only 60 percent of the total money, while the players who finish in spots 8 through 10 quadruple their initial investment.

Note that neither of the structures is more "fair" than the other. Both pay out all the money they're supposed to, but the different payout structures necessitate different playing strategies. In Tournament A, the best strategy is to take risks early to build up a big stack with the aim of eventually finishing in one of the first three spots. In Tournament B, an optimal strategy is to be a little more risk-averse. You should play a little tighter in this case with the aim of first getting into the money. Which payout structure favors the better player? In this case, it's the top-heavy structure in Tournament A. Weaker players will tend to play too conservatively in the early stages and will miss opportunities to build a stack. A tight style which tries to finish in the money is relatively better suited to the payouts in Tournament B.

Parameter No. 6: How big is the rake? The rake is simply the portion of the entry fee that goes to the organizer instead of into the prize fund. Sometimes casinos or cardrooms will state the rake clearly. For example, a casino might announce an event with a "$530 buy-in, $70 entry fee." In this case a player has to pay $600 to play, of which $530 goes to the prize pool and $70 will be kept by the house. The rake in this case is 70/600, or 11.7 percent.

$$0.117 = \frac{70}{600}$$

Another casino might announce a tournament with a $1,000 buy-in, but give no indication as to what percentage was being kept by the house. In this case, you might need to ask some questions and do a little arithmetic before entering.

Tournaments with big entry fees tend to have lower rakes than smaller events. Here's a chart that shows the approximate range of rakes for tournaments with different buy-ins:

Approximate Rake Structure
at Large Casinos and Card Rooms

Buy-In	Rake Range
> $3,000	3% to 6%
$1,000 to $3,000	7% to 9%
$500 to $1,000	10% to 12%
< $500	13% to 20%

Small casinos and local card rooms can have much higher rakes, sometimes up to 35 percent. And obviously, the lower the rake the better.

In online tournaments rakes tend to be much lower since the sites have very little overhead. Most small-stake online tournaments have rakes in the 10 percent range. In high-stakes online events, the rakes will be even lower, but rarely below 5 percent.

The Single-Table Tournament

On the other side of the poker tournament spectrum is the single-table tournament, or 'Sit 'n Go' as it's usually called. (Sit 'n Go is often abbreviated to 'SNG.') These are just tournaments of a single table with no set starting time. Once nine or ten players sign up, the tournament gets underway. Online, a large site might have Sit 'n Go's running constantly, especially when the entry fees are small. In a live casino, players looking for a Sit 'n Go might have to wait awhile for enough players to show up.

The typical nine or ten-player Sit 'n Go pays prizes to the final three players, usually divided 50 percent to first, 30 percent to second, and 20 percent to third.

At first glance you might think that a sit-and-go is just an abbreviated form of a multi-table tournament, with the same general strategy: take chances early, build a big stack, and go for first place. But actually it's not. Poker tournament strategy is determined in part by the prize structure, and there are significant differences between the prize structures of the two types of events:

1. In an MTT, about 10 percent of the players finish in the money. In a SNG, 30 percent finish in the money.

2. In an MTT, just getting in the money earns only a tiny percentage of the prize fund. In a SNG, getting in the money earns 20 percent of the prize fund.

3. In the MTT prize schedule we called 'Tournament A' a few pages back, 10 percent of the prize money was given out as soon as the players reached the money. That is, with 10 players left and tenth place paying 1 percent, all ten players were guaranteed at least a 1 percent prize. In a SNG, 60 percent of the prize money is given out once the last three players are determined. (All three are guaranteed at least 20 percent.)

The effect of these changes to the prize structure is that simply finishing in the money is relatively a much higher priority in a SNG than in an MTT. As a result, early play should be relatively cautious, with the idea of preserving chips until there are only four or five players left. Once you reach the money bubble, aggression is handsomely rewarded. It now becomes difficult to call an all-in bet without a premium hand as you're risking your already good chance of cashing to gain a slightly higher chance at first and second. The edge therefore goes to the player who makes the all-in move, not the player who has to call him.

In this book, we'll be focusing on multi-table tournaments. Reader who want an excellent introduction to sit-and-go strategy should consult Colin Moshman's book *Sit 'n Go Strategy*, available from Two Plus Two.

Multi-Table Sit 'n Go's

It's also possible to run a tournament which blends the MTT format with the SNG format by collecting entry fees until you have enough players to run an MTT event with a fixed number of starting tables. In the online world, multi-table SNGs with 45, 90, or 180 players are common at various buy-in levels. A tournament like this offers a lot more play than a single table SNG, but doesn't take nearly as long to run as a full-scale multi-table event with hundreds of players. As with big MTTs, a multi-table Sit 'n Go will usually pay prizes to 10 percent of the field, with the bulk of the money concentrated in the first three places.

If you live in an area where online poker is legal, the multi-table SNG offers a great way to get practice in the intricacies of tournament poker for a cheap price and a fixed and manageable commitment of time.

Satellite Tournaments

The other tournament structure that's common is the satellite tournament which is designed to qualify players for a larger event with an entry fee that might be out of reach for a lot of players. For instance, at the World Series of Poker, the days before the start of the main event are filled with satellites designed to give winning players the $10,000 entry fee needed for the tournament. A single table qualifier would have 10 players each paying a $1,050 entry fee. The winner gets a direct entry to the main event, while the extra $500 collected goes to the house.

The single table satellite is just an extreme version of the prize structure described earlier as 'Tournament A.' Now all the money goes to first, and the other positions are worthless. And the proper strategy is to play aggressively early to build a big stack, and then use the big stack in the middle stages to squeeze chips out of players who are playing too tight.

There are also super satellites, which are multi-table events starting at a specific time and qualifying as many players as possible. For instance, the organizers might run a $300 super satellite starting at 10:00 am; if 400 players show up, the prize pool would be $120,000, enough to give a free entry to the top 12 qualifiers. In this type of event, play continues until only 12 players remain, at which point all 12 qualify no matter what their relative chip stacks might be.

The super satellites are an extreme version of the prize structure we called 'Tournament B.' Once you get in the money, all the prizes are the same. The idea here is to play a normally aggressive game in the early stages. As you build a good stack, look to pressure players who seem naturally tight, who have a medium stack, and who aren't yet desperate but who would be in bad shape if they lost a big pot. Once you have a stack that's big enough to qualify, you become ultra-conservative and just play to maintain your position. As the bubble approaches, it's not unusual to see the big stacks simply shut down completely. If you're sure to qualify in any event, you have no reason even to play aces preflop!

The ICM Idea
and Its Limitations

One of the first theoretical approaches for unlocking the secrets of proper tournament play was a method known as the Independent Chip Model, or ICM for short. The Independent Chip Model gives an approach for calculating your equity in a tournament based upon the prize structure, your chip stack, and the chip stacks of other players. By using the Independent Chip Model, you can figure out how much risk is appropriate to take at key stages of the tournament, such as around the bubble or at the final table.[4]

Let's start by talking about what at first seems to be a simple idea: How much is a chip worth?

In cash games, this is a straightforward, almost trivial question. Chips in a cash game have a fixed value — the value printed on the chip. But in tournaments, chips don't have a fixed value. Their value actually fluctuates a lot depending on stack sizes, the prize distribution, and at what stage the tournament is at. This statement comes as a surprise to most tournament newcomers, but it's quite true. Let's look at a couple of examples and see why this is the case.

Imagine that you walked into a poker room in Las Vegas and sat down at a $10-$20 no-limit cash game. The runner comes by and asks how many chips you want. You say $2,000, pay him, and he brings $2,000 in chips. You're ready to start playing.

Now a stranger at the rail tells you that he wants to buy your seat and chip stack, but he won't pay more than a fair price.

---

[4] Even though he didn't use the name Independent Chip Model, the first person to describe the ICM and apply it to poker tournaments was Mason Malmuth in his book *Gambling Theory and Other Topics,* first published in 1987.

What's that price? Well, it's just $2,000. There's no reason for him to pay more, and there's no reason for you to sell for less. The value of your chips hasn't changed. If you play for five hours and still have a $2,000 stack, the value is exactly the same as at the beginning: $2,000.

Now let's imagine you decide to play in a tournament instead of a cash game. You grab $2,000, run down to your local casino, and plunk down your entry fee. So do 499 other people, and the tournament starts off with 500 entries at $2,000 apiece. Your friendly casino doesn't charge a rake, so the total purse is a cool $1,000,000. As is customary, a total of 50 players, just 10 percent of the field will be paid. Each player sits down and is given a stack of 2,000. Right now, each of your chips is worth their face value. If, before the tournament starts, a stranger offers to buy your seat, the fair price is just $2,000, as in the cash game.

Hours pass, excitement happens, hopes are dashed, and eventually the field is whittled down to just two players, you and one other lucky fellow. As it happens, the two of you have identical stacks, 500,000 each. You're competing for a first prize of $300,000 and a second prize of $150,000. The other $550,000 of prize money has been paid out to places 3 through 50.

Question: *What is each of your chips worth now?*
Answer: This is easy to figure out, but the result might be surprising. Since the chip stacks are the same, you and your opponent have an equal chance at first and second place. Your equity in the tournament is therefore halfway between first prize and second prize, or $225,000 each. Since you have 500,000 and an equity of $225,000, your chips are worth 45 cents on the dollar, which is $225,000 divided by 500,000.

So you started the tournament with chips worth their face value, and after a great run, on the verge of winning the event, your chips are worth only 45 cents on the dollar.

Question: *What happened to the missing equity?*
  Answer: It was gobbled up by all the other players who took a chunk out of the prize fund. To see this even more clearly, look at what happens if you now win the tournament. Despite having accumulated all 1,000,000 in chips, your prize is only $300,000. Notice that each chip is now worth only 30 cents on the dollar

Question: *What does this mean?*
  Answer: As you go further and further in the event, your chips keep dropping in value because equity is being siphoned off by the other prize winners.

The prize structure of the tournament determines how much the chip values drop as the players get closer and closer to first prize. In the extreme case where all the prize money goes to first place (as in a winner-take-all satellite qualifier), there is no loss of equity as play proceeds. At the end, one player will have both all the chips and all the prize money. The more even the prize distribution (as in Tournament B in our previous discussion), the more the chip values are reduced as play proceeds.

The Independent Chip Model is a good way of attacking a certain class of tournament problems: those where making the right play hinges on a knowledge of the players' equity for different stack sizes. Using stack sizes and the prize structure as inputs, the model can calculate, for instance, whether moving all-in or calling an all-in move is a good play. The model also gives clues as to whether your situation calls for aggressive or conservative play.

Using ICM

Solving problems using ICM requires making a key assumption:

> The probability of winning the tournament is directly proportional to the players' current chip stacks.

This assumption just says that if, at a given point in the tournament, Player A has 20,000 and Player B has 10,000, A's chance of winning the tournament must be exactly twice that of Player B.

Let's start with a simple example and see how the ICM method works.

Example 2-6. Suppose there are two players left in a 10-player Sit 'n Go. Player A has 8,000, Player B has 2,000, first prize is $100, and second prize is $60. The players want to settle right now. *What's a fair settlement?*

From our first assumption, Player A will take first place 80 percent of the time, and he'll finish second 20 percent of the time. So he's entitled to $92.

$$\$92 = (0.80)(\$100) + (0.20)(\$60)$$

where
0.80 is A's probability of winning,
$100 is first prize,
0.20 is A's probability of finishing second, and
$60 is second prize.

Player B's calculation is just the opposite and he's entitled to $68.

$$\$68 = (0.20)(\$100) + (0.80)(\$60)$$

The settlement amounts are closer together than you might first suppose, but that's because the players are already guaranteed $60 apiece, and they're only fighting over the $40 difference between first and second place.

That was a simple one. Let's add a third player to the mix and see what happens.

Example 2-7. The bubble bursts in a Sit 'n Go and three players now remain. The prizes are $100, $60, and $40. The stack sizes are

Player	Stack Size
A	6,000 chips
B	3,000 chips
C	1,000 chips

If the players want to settle, *what's the fair settlement in this case?*

The Independent Chip Model can solve this problem, but the solution gets much more complex as we add more players. We'll explain the method for getting to the solution, after which we'll give the answers without spending a lot of time crunching the numbers. Once you understand the method, and if you wish, you can solve problems like this on your own.

We'll start by looking at the $100 first prize and calculating what share of that prize belongs to each player. This is pretty easy. Player A has 60 percent of the chips outstanding, so he's entitled to 60 percent of first prize, or $60. Players B and C get 30 percent and 10 percent respectively. So our first prize breakdown looks like this:

Share of First Prize

Player A	$60
Player B	$30
Player C	$10

Now we're ready for the hard part. We still need to allot shares of second and third prize among the players. We do this by considering three separate cases.

Case No. 1: Player A wins first prize. This occurs 60 percent of the time. Players B and C are now contending for second and third. Since Player B has 75 percent of the total number of chips shared by B and C, he gets 75 percent of second prize and 25 percent of third prize. Player C's numbers are reversed.

Case No. 2: Player B wins first prize. This occurs 30 percent of the time and if Player B wins first prize, Players A and C are competing for second and third. Player A has a huge 6,000 to 1,000 advantage. Therefore, he finishes second $\frac{6}{7}$ or 85.7 percent of the time, and C will finish second $\frac{1}{7}$ or 14.3 percent of the time.

Case No. 3: Player C wins first prize. This occurs 10 percent of the time making it the most unlikely, with A and B battling for second and third. Since A has a 2-to-1 chip advantage over B, he wins second ⅔ or 66.7 percent of the time, while B finishes second ⅓ or 33.3 percent of the time.

When we put all this information together, we can see how often each player finishes first, second, and third:

Each Player's Chance of Finishing First, Second, or Third

Player	First	Second	Third
A	60.0%	32.4%	7.6%
B	30.0%	48.3%	21.7%
C	10.0%	19.3%	70.7%

The chart makes sense. All the rows add to 100 percent showing that each player must finish somewhere, and all the columns add to 100 percent, showing that someone must finish in each place. In addition, each player has the highest probability of finishing in the place corresponding to the order of his chip stack.

If we combine these probabilities with the $100/$60/$40 prize structure, we get an equity for each player. The next table shows the resulting equities compared to their current stack size.

Equity and Current
Stack for Each Player

Player	Current Stack	Equity
A	6,000	$82.48
B	3,000	$67.66
C	1,000	$49.66

This last table is surprising to most players, so take a careful look at the different equities. Although the chip stacks are widely disparate, the equities are fairly close together. Player A has twice as many chips as Player B, but his equity is only 22 percent bigger. And although he has six times as many chips as Player C, his equity is just 65 percent bigger.

These numbers help explain why just surviving the bubble and getting into the money is a crucial strategy in tournaments, like your basic Sit'n Go event, with a fairly flat prize structure. Finishing in third place gets you a big chunk of the prize money, so you need to be very careful about making a play that can get you eliminated.

If we change the format of the tournament to a winner-take-all event ($200 to first place), then the equity of the player's changes dramatically.

Equity and Current Stack for Each Player in a Winner-Take-All Format

	Current Stack	Equity
Player A	6,000 chips	$120
Player B	3,000 chips	$60
Player C	1,000 chips	$20

Now finishing third gets you zero money, and the equity of C's short stack is very small. This helps explain why taking risks early to accumulate a big stack is a better strategy for the typical big MTT when the prizes are heavily weighted toward the top few places.

Strengths of the ICM Method

The Independent Chip Model allows you to make equity calculations when only a small number of players remain in an event and the stacks and prize amounts are known. That's very useful since those calculations lead to strategies and plays that aren't obvious at first glance. The model also has weaknesses when we try to apply these conclusions to the early stages of larger tournaments.

One obvious strength of the ICM method is in making fair settlements when only a few players remain in a tournament. An even more important application lies in figuring out proper playing strategies in these situations. Let's look at an example of bubble play and see the power of ICM at its fullest.

Example 2-8. A ten-player Sit 'n Go tournament has been reduced to just four players. The prizes are $50 first, $30 second, and $20 third. Right now the blinds are 100 and 200. The four remaining players are seated as follows:

Position	Player	Stack Size
Under-the-Gun	A	5,000
Button	B	2,000
Small Blind	C	1,500
Big Blind	D	5,000

We're in a pretty typical situation near the end of a Sit 'n Go. We're on the bubble. The next player eliminated goes home with nothing, while the remaining three will cash.

Right now Players A and D are in great shape with the biggest stacks. Players B and C are gasping for breath, on the verge of elimination.

Let's imagine you're Player D, sitting in the big blind. You look down at your cards and see the

You're tied for the chip lead and just picked up a pair of queens, the third-best hand possible. Sweet!

Now Player A, with the same stack as yours, pushes all his chips in the middle. Players B and C quickly fold. Not so sweet! *What do you do?*

In a cash game with just four players, your hand is much too strong to fold. At first glance, that should be the case here as well. Surely a pair of queens is good enough for a call, considering that Player A must have a pretty wide range of hands here. *Or is it?*

Here's the problem. If we call and win, we eliminate Player A and get into the money. With what would then be a 10,000 stack, our chance of finishing first has risen. But if we fold, we're very likely to get into the money, and our chance of finishing first is pretty good as well.

However, if we call and lose, we're out of the money, and that's a very big deal given our current great situation.. The fact that we're eliminated if we lose raises a question — we can't be certain that calling is the right play. To solve the problem, we have to know how our equity will change if (a) we fold, (b) we call and win, or (c) we call and lose.

Let's start by looking at our equity before the hand was dealt. As before, we won't go through the calculations in detail — they're cumbersome — but instead we'll use the same methods as before and just give the results.

Equities Before
the Hand was Dealt

Player	Chips	Equity
A	5,000	$33.26
B	2,000	$18.77
C	1,500	$14.71
You	5,000	$33.26

This table should make sense. You and Player A have the highest equities, and Players B and C are trailing behind with their short stacks. The equities add up to $100, the sum of the prizes.

Now let's see how the equities change if you call and win, eliminating Player A.

Equities After
Calling and Winning

Player	Chips	Equity
You	10,000	$44.44
B	2,000	$28.86
C	1,500	$26.70

Notice what just happened. Player A went away and his $33 equity was absorbed by you and the other two players. *Did most of that equity go to you?* Most players would assume that it did since you doubled your stack and now easily dominate Players B and C. But in fact that's not what happened. Take a look at how much equity each player gained and lost as we moved from the first chart to the second.

Changes in
Equity After the Hand

Player	Before	After	Change
A	$33.26	$0.00	-$33.26
B	$18.77	$28.86	+$10.09
C	$14.71	$26.70	+$11.99
You	$33.26	$44.44	+$11.18

Your equity increased, but only from $33 and change to $44 and change, about one-third of Player A's loss. Player B did almost as well as you, but Player C was the biggest gainer of all, picking up almost $12 in equity while he sat out the hand and took no risk!

Players B and C were the biggest percentage gainers. They're now in the money and assured of at least $20 apiece, with a small chance for one of the top two prizes. Before the hand, they were the players most likely to go home with nothing. You did all the work and risked losing everything, but your gain when you won was relatively modest.

Viewed in this light, it's clear that calling or folding with a pair of queens isn't such an obvious question after all. You're taking a big risk for a relatively small gain. Instead of just shoving your chips in the pot, you need to spend a little time thinking about just what hands he might have and how you're doing against that range.

We'll start by figuring out what your winning chances in the hand need to be in order to justify a call. This turns out to be pretty easy. Your potential loss is $33.26, and your potential gain is just $11.18. In order to call, your winning chances need to be 74.8 percent.

$$0.748 = \frac{\$33.26}{\$33.26 + \$11.18}$$

where
$33.26 is your potential loss, and
$11.18 is your potential gain.

Therefore, your queens need to be almost a 75 percent favorite in the hand to profitably call. In poker, that's a big number. If he has a lower pair, you're about 80 percent to win, so you're all right. But if he has ace-king, for instance, you're only a 57-to-43 favorite, not nearly enough.

There are applications which, given your hand and an estimate of your opponent's range of hands, can calculate exactly what your winning chances are. Let's create some sample ranges and see how our queens are doing.

If your opponent is fairly tight and understands how equities change around the bubble, he might be pushing with a range that looks like this:

- Pairs: 88 or better
- AT, AJ, AQ, and AK, suited or unsuited
- KQ, suited or unsuited

That's a pretty tight range, representing only about 9 percent of all possible hands. Against that range, your queens are a 64-to-36 favorite — almost but not quite 2-to-1. However, it's far short of the 3-to-1 favorite you need to call.

Suppose instead you think your opponent is pretty loose and doesn't really understand the mathematics of this bubble play stuff. In that case, maybe he has a range that looks like this:

- All pairs: 22 through AA
- All aces, suited or unsuited
- KQ, KJ or QJ, suited or unsuited

That's a big range, including almost one-quarter of his possible starting hands. Your queens are a solid favorite against all but two hands (aces and kings) in this range, and yet overall you're almost exactly a 70-to-30 favorite, a substantial favorite, but still not nearly enough to call while battling 3-to-1 odds.

How wide would his range have to be to justify a call on your part? Amazingly, if you knew he was shoving with half the deck, the top 50 percent of all hands, your call would be a break-even proposition. Anything less and you need to fold. Against the reasonable ranges we considered earlier, only aces and kings are good enough to call.

Being able to solve endgame problems like this is one of the important strengths of the Independent Chip Model. Without it, these problems would be difficult to attack.

Weaknesses
of the ICM Method

Like all models, ICM doesn't just have strengths. It also has weaknesses. Let's take a look at three of them.

Weakness No. 1: The model doesn't take playing strength into account. The ICM calculations in the problems above all assumed that the remaining players at the table were the same strength.

Generally, this is never the case. Once in a while you might see a table where all the players are playing at approximately the same level, but mostly there will be wide difference in both style and playing ability. Clearly, any stack in the hands of a better player has a higher equity than the same stack in the hands of a weak player. We can't really say much more than this, so using ICM to estimate proper strategy at a table of actual players is a matter of guesswork. We can get an answer for an abstract table of theoretically equal players, but that's all.

Weakness No. 2: The model doesn't take table position into account. If you have a small to medium stack, and an aggressive big stack is sitting on your left with position on you, your equity is less than if the roles were reversed. As before, we can't use ICM to take this factor into account.

Weakness No. 3: The model assumes that all stacks are equally likely to gain or lose chips in the upcoming hands. ICM incorporates a sort of 'random walk' hypothesis. When we say that a stack's chance of winning the tournament is directly proportional to its percentage of the available chips, we're assuming that the stacks are moving up or down in small random movements over the course of the tournament. If we imagine two stacks, one with 10,000 and the other with 2,000, we're really assuming that each stack has the same chance of gaining or losing x number of chips in the next hand where x is a number that's a lot smaller than the stack size.

The problem with this assumption is that it's false. Big stacks have more weapons at their disposal, and as a result they have an easier time accumulating chips than medium or small stacks. A basic idea of tournament play is that, as much as possible, you should avoid confrontations with big stacks and concentrate your energy on the medium and small stacks. It's good advice: The small stacks have to be careful because they're always on the verge of elimination, and the medium stacks have to be careful they don't lose a showdown and drop down to the world of the small stacks. But if players are trying to avoid butting heads with the big stacks, it follows that the big stacks have a notable advantage accumulating chips.

How important is this factor? It's impossible to exactly quantify, but players experienced in large multi-table tournaments understand that once you get a big stack, you can use it to bully the table. The equity of a big stack must therefore be somewhat larger than the raw stack would indicate, and the equity of a small stack must be somewhat smaller.

Like most theories, ICM has its strengths and weaknesses. It's very useful when indicating optimal strategies for bubble situations and short tables. However, when a tournament has a long way to go, this model overstates the chances of small stacks and understates the value of big stacks. Keep these points in mind and you'll be able to evaluate ICM predictions properly.

Ranges

Ranges are a relatively new concept to most poker players.[5] If you played in a tournament ten years ago, you wouldn't have heard the term used. But now, you'll hear the term everywhere, and it's rare to listen to the discussion of a hand without the idea of "range" popping up. "What was his range?" "Did you think he was playing a tight or loose range?" "Was his range balanced or polarized?" Without some understanding of ranges and what to do with them, it's hard to grasp much of modern poker.

What is a Range?

The basic idea of ranges is pretty simple. A *range* is just the set of all hands with which a player might have take a particular action. If there are a lot of possible hands that a player might be holding, we say he has a *wide* range. If we think he would only have made a play with a few hands, then we'll say he has a *narrow* range.

We can also refer to ranges as percentages. For instance, saying "I put my opponent on a 10 percent range," means we think he would have made his play only with the top 10 percent of his hands. A "50 percent range" means he might have made a play with half the hands in the deck.

---

[5] They were first discussed by David Sklansky almost 20 years ago. See "An Essential Hold 'em Concept" starting on page 224 of his book *Fighting Fuzzy Thinking in Poker, Gaming, & Life — Expanded Edition.*

The Old Way: "Putting Your Opponent on a Hand"

Talking about hands in terms of possible ranges has replaced the old approach, which was "putting your opponent on a hand." The idea was to watch your opponent's actions and, based on what you had seen, try to figure out exactly what hand he had. If you'd been hanging around tournaments a decade ago, you might have heard comments like "When he bet on the end I put him on ace-king, but he showed up with a set of eights and beat my two pair! Why can't I ever catch a break?"

The problem with putting your opponent on a hand is that you usually don't collect information fast enough to actually do it. Let's look at a concrete situation and see why this doesn't work.

Example 2-9. You're playing in a big multi-table tournament nearing the end of the first day. You've spent the whole day at the same table, have been paying close attention, and have picked up a lot of information about the other players.

Blinds are now 150 and 300 with a 25-chip ante. The table is full (nine players) so the starting pot is 675 chips. The first two players fold but the third player opens the pot with a raise to 850. He has about 40,000 left after his bet, making him one of the top two stacks at the table. He seems competent, and his play is tight but not excessively so. You also know he's capable of bluffing because an hour ago he got caught making a river bluff and had to show his hand.

The next two players fold and the action is on you in the cutoff seat. Right now your stack is 32,000, just a bit ahead of where you started the day. You haven't held a lot of cards, so you think your image at the table is tighter than your actual style.

You look down and see the

With position on the raiser, you're happy to call with this hand, so you slide 850 into the pot. You figure your tight image might help you win a few pots even when your suited connectors don't connect. The button and the blinds fold. The pot is now 2,375 chips.

The flop is the

giving you middle pair. Your opponent in third position bets 1,400. You call because your pair may well be best and there is still a possibility for a runner-runner straight. And, of course, you have position. The pot is now 5,175 chips.

The turn is the T♥. Your opponent bets again, this time 3,000. *What do you do?* Can you put your opponent on a hand at this point?

You still have a pair, but the appearance of another overcard has downgraded it to third pair. Your chance for a straight is also gone. However, it's still possible that your pair is the best hand. *Should you call, fold, or turn your hand into a bluff and raise?*

If you're trying to put your opponent on a hand, you've run into a problem. Some information about his hand is available. He raised in third position and you don't think he's a wild man, so he probably started with something decent. Let's list a few possibilities:

1. He could have a pair, but maybe not one of the lowest pairs.

2. He could have a good ace, perhaps ace-king down through ace-ten.

3. He might have a lower suited ace, perhaps as low as ace-eight suited.

4. He might have two Broadway cards, suited or unsuited.

For a moderately tight player, these are the most likely raising hands from third position. There are a variety of other hands that he might play once in a while, like the small pairs and medium suited connectors, but this list represents the main possibilities.

If we think he could have started with these hands, does his bet on the flop allow us to eliminate any hands from consideration? The answer, actually, is no. If he had a value hand after the flop, like an overpair or top pair, he probably bet it for value. If he had a medium pair, anything from jacks down through eights, he would have bet that on the assumption that we probably didn't call with a queen in our hand, and therefore he's still ahead. But even if he missed the flop, he might have stuck in a continuation bet to try to take the hand down right there since it's likely we missed the flop as well. So in fact, his bet on the flop doesn't tell us much of anything. He could have bet any of his possible starting hands, either for value or as a well-considered continuation bet bluff.

Now we call on the flop. *What does our call mean from his point of view?*

When we call on the flop, we're indicating some interest in the hand. Perhaps we have a small pair and think he might have nothing. But we might have a flush draw, and be calling to see if we can hit our flush. Or our holding might also be nothing but we're *floating* (calling with nothing) to see if we can steal the pot with a later show of strength.

On the turn, the T♥ comes. That's a good card from our opponent's point of view. If we had a flush draw, it was no help.

If our hand was a low pair, the ten was another overcard and we should be ready to give up. We're only happy if our holding was already a strong hand, like a set or a pair of queens.

Now our opponent bets again. This bet still doesn't tell us much of anything. If he has a strong hand, he's still betting for value. If his hand was something like ace-jack, he's betting because we probably don't have anything, and his bet is likely to win the hand. "Putting him on a hand" isn't working because we still don't have any information that lets us narrow down his possibilities very much. All of his starting hands could have made all the plays we've seen.

Thinking in terms of his range of hands, and how the various hands in his starting range are doing is a better way to look at what's been happening.

1. If he started with a medium-to-high pair, he's still beating us and we're a huge underdog to outdraw him on the river.

2. If he started with a good ace, he's beating us if he had ace-queen or ace-ten. We're ahead of ace-king and ace-jack.

3. If he started with a weaker suited ace, we're ahead unless he had specifically ace-seven. It's also possible he has a flush draw.

4. If he started with a couple of Broadway cards (kings, queens, jacks, and tens), he's beating us unless he has specifically king-jack.

When we look at his range of hands this way, it's clear that we're not doing well. Most of his hands are ahead of us, and when he's ahead we have little chance of drawing out on the river. When we're ahead we're in good shape, but if he makes a big bet on the river, we won't know where we stand and it will be difficult for us to call. Therefore, folding right now is our best choice.

Thinking about an opponent's hands in terms of ranges is much more useful than trying to put him on a hand. By seeing how we're doing against the different groups that make up his range and combining that information with the pot odds, we can usually make a good decision without a lot of guesswork.

Preflop: Wide Ranges and Narrow Ranges

There are a number of different ways of describing preflop ranges. The most common is 'wide' or 'narrow.' A wide range includes a lot of hands while a narrow range includes only a few hands, and aggressive players tend to have wide ranges. They like to be in action, and to be in action you have to be willing to bet and raise with lots of different hands.

Tight players have narrow ranges. They want to have solid values when they enter a pot, so they're restricted to playing relatively few hands, even in position.

Let's look at some typical ranges for different types of players and positions. We'll start with some tight ranges.

A tight player in early position will likely have a very narrow range, probably around 5 percent of his possible hands. Here's what a 5 percent range actually looks like:

- Top pairs: AA down through TT
- The top suited aces: AKs down through AJs
- The top unsuited aces: AKo, AQo

That's a very tight range. A slightly looser player in early position might be willing to play a 10 percent range. Here's what that range looks like:

- Big and medium pairs: AA down through 77
- The big suited aces: AKs down through ATs
- The top unsuited aces: AKo down through AJo
- Suited Broadway cards: KQs, KJs, KTs, QJs, QTs, JTs
- Unsuited Broadway cards: KQo only

To create the 10 percent range we kept all the hands from the 5 percent range and added some medium pairs, all the suited Broadway cards, and a couple of offsuit Broadway hands.

This isn't the only possible way to expand a 5 percent range to a 10 percent range. While this 10 percent range contains as many high hands as possible, it has no hands at all with low cards. If your opponents can deduce that you're playing this sort of range, they'll know that a flop like the

or the

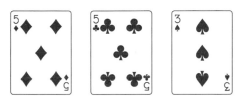

will miss your hand unless you started with a high pair. That's a problem since a moderate number of flops contain only low cards.

You can create a 10 percent range in a different way that avoids this problem. Take a look at the next range:

- All pairs: AA down through 22
- The big suited aces: AKs down through ATs
- The top unsuited aces: AKo, AQo
- Suited Broadway cards: KQs, QJs
- Unsuited Broadway cards: KQo only

What we did here was to eliminate some of the weaker Broadway cards and replace them with the low pairs from sixes down to deuces. As a result, anyone who had watched us carefully would notice that we could occasionally pop up with a set on a board of low cards. This slight change means we could have a monster hand on any flop, which in turn gives us more latitude in our betting, and making us difficult to read and therefore much more dangerous.

Suppose we're playing a relatively loose and aggressive opponent, and we think he might raise preflop with about 25 percent of his hands. *What does a 25 percent range look like?* Here's one possible solution:

- All pairs: AA down through 22
- Suited aces: AKs down through A6s
- Unsuited aces: AKo down through A8o
- All suited Broadway cards: KQs, KJs, KTs, QJs, QTs, JTs
- All unsuited Broadway cards: KQo, KJo, KTo, QJo, QTo, JTo
- All suited connectors: T9s down through 54s
- Medium unsuited connectors: T9o, 98o
- Suited one-gappers: J9s down through 75s

Playing a wide opening range has both an upside and a downside. The upside is that you get to play a lot of hands, and almost any flop could possibly hit your hand pretty hard. This makes you a dangerous player at the table, especially when you're willing to push the action with a lot of betting and raising. (Which is exactly what most loose-aggressive players do.)

The downside, however, is that most of your big range will miss any particular flop. If your opponent actually has a hand after the flop, he's a solid favorite to have you beaten! This is an important point to know when playing loose players, so let's take a closer look at just what we mean.

Suppose you're on the button and your hand is the

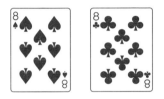

The first three players fold and the fourth player opens the pot for a standard raise. You've been playing at this table since the start of the day and have pegged this player as loose and aggressive. You estimate that he could open the pot with the range we just described — 25 percent of all his hands. The action folds around and you call with your pair of eights. That's a good call. His range consists of 351 possible hands, and right now your pair of eights is ahead of all but 36 of them. (The only hands beating you right now are the six higher pairs, aces down through nines, and there are six ways to draw any particular pair.) You could also 3-bet in this situation, but decide you want to play a smaller pot in position with your eights.

The blinds fold and it's a heads-up pot between you and Mr. Loose-Aggressive. The flop comes the

and your opponent bets a little over half the pot. *Assuming he would make a continuation bet with his entire range, how likely is it that you still have the best hand?*

Actually, it's pretty likely that your eights are still best. If he held a higher pair to start, he's still ahead. If he held a pair of sevens or deuces, he just made a set. And if he held ace-king or a Broadway combination with a king, he moved in front with top pair. Those combinations total 87 hands, only about one-quarter of the possible hands in his range. So if you're correct that he would have bet his whole range on this flop (a reasonable assumption since he would think the flop probably missed you for the same reasons), then you have an easy call.[6] Compare this example with what would happen if we were playing a tight player with the 5 percent range we looked at earlier. If we were holding a pair of eights and that flop came, we'd be in big trouble. His 5 percent range consisted of high pairs, ace-king, ace-queen, and ace-jack suited. The high pairs are all beating us, and now the ace-king combinations are beating us as well. We're only ahead against the ace-queen and ace-jack combinations. In all, about two-thirds of his hands now have us beaten, and even with the pot odds we're getting, we still should lay our hand down.

The conclusion of this example is very important for tournament play. You're going to run into a lot of good loose-aggressive players who play wide ranges. When you actually make a hand against a player like that, even a modest hand like middle pair, you can't be in a hurry to lay it down. You'll usually be ahead of his range and getting pot odds as well, so be prepared to call some bets and see what happens.

Balanced, Unbalanced, and Polarized Ranges

A range isn't just a concept restricted to preflop betting. Players also have ranges when they make postflop bets and raises. However, after the flop, we describe ranges in a slightly different

---

[6] When you're analyzing a problem like this at home, you need to recognize that the arrival of the three flop cards has changed the number of card combinations that he can hold. For instance, there were six possible combination of cards that gave him a pair of sevens preflop: 7♠7♥, 7♠7♦, 7♠7♣, 7♥7♦, 7♥7♣, and 7♦7♣. Once the 7♥ arrives on the flop, he now has only three ways to hold a pair of sevens: 7♠7♦, 7♠7♣, and 7♣7♦. The same is true for other hands in his range that contains a king, seven, or deuce.

way with terms like balanced, unbalanced, and polarized. Before we talk about what these terms mean, let's talk a little about hand strength after the flop.

Post-flop, we usually think about a hand as belonging to one of three broad categories:

1. **Very strong.** This is a hand that's well above average given the board and the betting action so far. It's not necessarily the nuts, but it's a hand that has a high probability of being the best right now.

2. **Medium strength.** This is a hand that has some value and can beat a bluff or a weak made hand. It's a hand that you'd like to take to showdown, but not a hand that makes you want to build a big pot.

3. **Air/bluff.** This is a hand with no value except as a possible bluffing hand.

Let's look at a couple of quick examples to get a better idea of just what kinds of hands might constitute 'very strong.'

Example 2-10. The player in second position raises preflop and gets called by the big blind. The flop is the Q♥9♦4♠. A very strong hand on this board would be a set or top pair with an excellent kicker — either ace-queen or king-queen. Two pair would be very strong but it's very unlikely for either player to have two pair.

A medium strength hand would be any hand with a pair that's weaker than the hands we just mentioned. A pair of nines, a pair of fours, or a hand like queens with a ten kicker would all qualify. All of those hands might be best, but none of them wants to play a big pot.

Any hand without a pair constitutes 'air' and is, at this point, only good for a bluff.

Example 2-11. Here's a more complex example. The stacks are deep and the table is full. Preflop, the under-the-gun player raises. All fold to the button who 3-bets. The blinds fold and the initial raiser calls. The flop is the A♦Q♦J♠. The initial raiser checks and the button bets. The initial raiser raises, the button calls, and the turn is the J♦. Before the turn betting takes place, *what constitutes a very strong hand in this situation?*

Not only is the board dangerous, with potential flushes, full houses, quads, and a Royal flush, but the betting action indicates that both players are happy with their hands despite the obvious strength shown by their opponents.

A very strong hand on this board would be either the nuts (a Royal flush), the second nuts (four jacks), or the better full houses. The third nuts right now are a pair of aces for the best possible full house, followed by a pair of queens, followed by ace-jack or queen-jack.

The medium-strength hands are the flushes and the weakest full houses. Anyone holding these hands would be happy to get to showdown on the river without getting any more money involved. Holdings lower than a flush are just air at this point.

So when we want to evaluate a hand after the flop, we're interested not only in its absolute strength, but also in the betting action that accompanies the hand. When the betting action is restrained, a medium pair might start to look good, and a hand with air might still take down the pot with a well-timed bluff. When the betting action is intense, as in our last example, something like trip jacks might be essentially worthless, and the chance of running any sort of successful bluff will be slim to none.

Now let's define the three terms we mentioned earlier for post-flop ranges: balanced, unbalanced, and polarized.

- A **balanced range** is just a set of hands that includes hands of all different strengths: some very strong, some medium strength, and some air. Against a player who is known to bet or raise a balanced range, you'll have a hard time putting him on an exact hand.

● An **unbalanced range** is just the opposite. It's a range that leaves out some groups of hands altogether. Weak-tight players typically have extremely unbalanced ranges. When they bet or raise a lot, their range consists entirely of very strong hands. Medium-strength hands and air are entirely missing.

● A **polarized range** is a particular type of unbalanced range. It's a range that's missing the medium strength hands, leaving the very strong hands and bluffs.

Balanced and unbalanced ranges are a crucial concept in cash games where the stacks are almost always deep and players have plenty of time to observe their opponents and collect data about their tendencies. And learning to balance your range in a proper way is a key skill in a tough cash game. For example, a player who won't make a big bet on the river without a very strong hand is easy to exploit: When he bets the river, just fold unless you have a very strong hand as well.

In tournaments, balancing your range is sometimes important and sometimes not. The early stages of a tournament play somewhat like a cash game because the stacks are deep. They're unlike a cash game in that the players rarely know anything about each other, at least to start, and there is a wide mix of abilities, from world-class players to those who are almost beginners. At this stage, range balancing is less important than just playing good, exploitative poker and trying to win money from the weak players in the simplest way possible.

In the middle stages of the tournament, the situation changes in a number of ways:

1.   Most of the weak players have either been eliminated or have been reduced to small stacks.

2. There are still many good-sized stacks, with Ms in the 25 to 60 range.

3. Players may have acquired some solid information on several of their opponents.

Assuming you have a decent-sized stack, balancing your range is important at this stage of the tournament. Blinds are rising steadily and you need to continue accumulating chips. Waiting for strong hands doesn't allow you to do this fast enough, so you need to play more hands and attempt more bluffs. Since your opponents will be doing the same, it's important to keep medium-strength hands in your mix to pick off some of these bluffs.

In the late stages of the tournament, there will be lots of short stacks around and plenty of all-in moves. Range balancing once again becomes less important. Now the focus moves to value betting questions. How strong a hand do I need to shove all my chips given my stack size and the number of opponents left? How strong a hand do I need to call a shove under the same circumstances? These are range-based questions, but now the bluffing hands are almost out of the picture, and the issue is what sort of hand constitutes a strong-enough value hand?

Now let's look at a few hands where balancing your range comes into play.

Example 2-12. You're in a live tournament on the second level of the first day. Blinds are 50 and 100, and you have 22,000, a little more than your starting stack. The players at your table have stacks ranging from 12,000 to 32,000.

So far you've played a tight, conservative game. Most of your gains came from one big hand where you showed down a set.

Under-the-gun, you pick up the T♥9♥. *What's your play?*

Raise to 300. Many tight players have an unbalanced range in early position, playing only high pairs and the very best aces. Playing this way makes you easy to read and reduces your chance to win a big hand from early position. By balancing your range with some middle suited connectors and a few low pairs, you make yourself much more dangerous. If an ace hits, you can credibly represent it, but if middle cards arrive and connect well with your hand, you can still bet out. And your bet will likely be interpreted by the table as a continuation bet by a couple of high cards that missed the flop.

Example 2-13. You're in a big live tournament, on the third level of the first day. The blinds are 100 and 200, and there are not yet any antes. You're in the big blind with 24,000 and pick up the

Everyone folds to the button (16,000) who raises to 450. The small blind folds and now it's your turn. You haven't seen a lot of action from the button and think he's tight. However, you're not sure if he's a weak player or not.

This is an easy call. The button's range is very wide, so your pair is probably the best hand now. In addition, you're getting pot odds of 750-to-250, or exactly 3-to-1. Any reasonable hand getting 3-to-1 odds is worth a call, and your holding is more than reasonable.

If your call is so easy, should you 3-bet? It's not a terrible play, but you won't be happy if your opponent 4 bets, and if he simply calls your 3-bet, you'll be playing a big pot out of position, facing either a higher pair or two overcards to your sixes. Furthermore, at this stage of the tournament where many players still have lots of chips, the idea is not to play huge pots out of position where you don't know what's happening. Put another way, you want to extract money from weaker players when it's likely you have the best hand, so just calling is the prudent play.

You call, the pot is now 1,000 chips, and the flop is the

You don't like the two overcards, but know that this disconnected, dry flop has missed a lot of the button's range. You check.

Your opponent also checks. That's a good sign since an aggressive player would have bet almost his entire range on this flop. But it's also likely this flop missed your wide range as well.

It's also possible that your opponent might be trapping with a big hand, but it's more likely that he simply missed the flop and decided to check, or has a flush draw and decided not to semi-bluff. Thus right now, you believe your hand is best.

The turn is the 8♦. That's a harmless card for you since he already had you beaten if he had an eight in his hand. And if you were ahead on the flop, that's still the case.

The right play here is to bet, and a good bet would be a little over half the pot, say 600 to 650. Furthermore, a bet here actually serves many purposes, so let's quickly list them.

1. **Value bet.** Your analysis of the hand on the flop indicates that you probably have the best hand right now. If that's true, a bet will be profitable.

2. **Blocking bet.** If you check, your opponent may well decide you have nothing and bet his entire range. (We've classified your opponent as a tight player, but even a tight player could bluff here.) You'll have to call that bet, but you've put yourself in an awkward position on the river — out of position with a weakish hand and not knowing where you stand. By betting, you're blocking his potential steal and giving yourself a chance to win the hand right now.

3. **Protection bet.** He may well have two overcards to your sixes or a flush draw. Those hands are all a big underdog to beat you, but if you don't bet they may get a free shot. Therefore, betting either forces him to fold or charges your opponent to draw at bad odds.

4. **Range balancing.** Many players will bet the turn or the river with a very polarized range. They'll bet strong hands for value, like a pair of kings with a good kicker in this example. If they have nothing, they may check or they may bluff because it's the only way for them to win the pot. But with a medium-strength hand like our pair of sixes, they'll check in the hope of getting to a cheap showdown and seeing if their hand is in fact best.

   Playing with a polarized range like this makes sense, but it has a vulnerability. Suppose you only want to bet strong hands and air. Strong hands are hard to come by, but air is pretty easy, so you'll have air a lot of the time. If your opponent knows that your range is polarized this way, he also knows that you'll have air a good chunk of the time. (If you're a loose-aggressive player, this will be even more true.) In this case, he can feel good about calling with hands like an ace with a decent kicker. These will be good enough to beat all your bluffs, although they'll lose to your genuine value hands.

   Therefore, by moving some of your medium and small pairs into your betting range, you can counter his plan. Now you have more hands in the mix that can beat his ace-x type hands, so he can't be sure any longer that calling with them will show a profit.

   However, this plan comes with some small costs. Sometimes when betting with a small pair, your opponent will raise with one of his bluffing hands! Now, in this case, you'll probably fold and lose a pot you might have won had you checked your pair and then called his bet. In another case, you'll lose some money if he calls with a hand that wants to reach a cheap showdown, like the medium pairs that are beating your small pair. However, these sequences are long shots, and you'll recover your losses on the occasions when he bluff-raises one of your genuinely strong hands.

Back to our example. You bet 650 and he folds.

Range balancing is an important concept, but it's easily overdone. It's an essential tool in any sort of ongoing cash game with a small, consistent group of players. Most home game are like this, as well as high-stakes games in casinos or online. And if you play in these games with unbalanced and polarized ranges, you'll slowly be ground down as the other players learn what hands make up your range in certain spots.

Range balancing is of minor importance in tournament situations where either the players don't have much familiarity with each other, or where Ms are low and you can quickly become pot-committed. In the first case, you're mostly playing straightforward exploitative poker, and in the second case, you're looking for hands and situations that are good enough for an all-in move.

Here's an example of a range balancing blunder in a tournament hand.

Example 2-14. You're in the second level of a major live tournament. Blinds are 100 and 200, all fold to the cutoff with about 28,000, and he raises to 450. In the three hours you've been playing, you know he's an aggressive player willing to get involved in a lot of hands. But he tends to raise small, regardless of his holding. In addition, he appears to be a strong player with an understanding of tournament strategy.

You're on the button with 32,000 and have also been pretty active, although mostly in hands where the cutoff player hasn't been involved. Your hand is the 9♠9♣ and you elect to 3-bet to 1,100 with a medium pair. Since he opened from late position and is aggressive, it's likely that his range is wide and he may throw most of it away. The blinds fold.

He now 4-bets to 3,100. *What's your play?*

You elect to 5-bet to 7,000. Your reasoning is that while your hand is not strong enough to 5-bet for value, you can't just 5-bet with aces or kings. Therefore, in order to balance your range, you need to be 5-betting with some other hands as well, and a pair of nines certainly has some value. Since he's an aggressive player, you expect that this move will make him lay down a lot of his range, and even if he calls, you're only an underdog against the five top pairs.

Is there anything wrong with this thinking? Well, quite a lot, actually. Your 3-bet with the pair of nines was an aggressive but reasonable play given your opponent's level of activity. Calling was, of course, perfectly sound as well, and would be the preferred play against most opponents. However, after his 4-bet, you need to throw your hand away. This is not a situation where you should be looking to make a range balancing play which may cost you your whole stack. In the early part of the tournament, your job is to win money from the weak players at the table in a series of small, controlled pots. If you get your whole stack involved at this stage, you need to have a hand that's close to the nuts.

Also notice that right now, all we know for certain is that we have a hand that's at best a coin flip in an all-in situation. If our opponent is a good player, as we suspect, it's likely he understands the point we just made and his range for the 4-bet is probably very strong, something like aces through queens and ace-king. So unless we flop a set, our hand does very poorly against that range. (We're a little less than a 2-to-1 underdog.)

In tournaments, any hand where we're likely to get our whole stack involved is a poor candidate for range balancing. These situations usually arise in the later stages of a tournament when stacks are short. However, they can arrive at any stage, especially when the hand gets raised and reraised preflop. So don't catch yourself in overly fancy thinking. Recognize that in these situations your opponent's range is likely to be very unbalanced toward the strong end, and play accordingly.

A Range of Ranges

Under certain circumstances, you may not have enough information to put your opponent on a well-defined range. You might, however, have enough information to say that he has one of two or three possible ranges; you just don't know which one. In this case, we can't put him on a range, but we can put him on a *range of ranges*.

In situations like this, you want to do some quick estimating: Try to guess the percentage of time he has each possible range, and then estimate your winning chances against each of those ranges. Combine the two pieces of information and compare the result to your pot odds. You'll be making a quick-and-dirty approximation, but the result will be faster and better than trying to figure out exactly what range your opponent has.

Here's an example that shows when this approach comes into play.

Example 2-15. You're in the middle of the first day at a live tournament. Blinds are 200 and 400, with a 50-chip ante. There are eight players at your table, so the starting pot is 1,000 chips.

You've done well so far and your stack is 68,000. You pick up the A♥K♥ in second position and raise to 1,200. Everyone folds to the button who just lost a big hand when his aces were cracked by a weak player's ace-jack. His stack is 21,000 and he moves all-in. The blinds fold and the action is on you.

The pot is now 23,200 chips, you need to put in 19,800 to call his shove, and the pot is offering you 1.17-to-1; better than even money, but not by much. You need about 46 percent winning chances to profitably call.

There are two possible interpretations of your opponent's huge bet:

1. **He's on tilt.** After his brutal beat, he picked up some sort of reasonable hand and just shoved his chips in the pot.

2. **He just picked up a premium hand** and realizes that shoving all-in will be seen as a tilting play and probably get called.

    You're new at the table and don't know your opponent well enough to know which of these scenarios is actually the case. Each interpretation implies a completely different range. In Case No. 1, his range is something like the top 10 to 15 percent of all hands, minus a pair of aces or a pair of kings (and maybe queens) which are so strong that he would try to play them normally. In Case No. 2, his range consists of aces, kings, queens, and maybe ace-king.

    So we have two totally different possible ranges, and only one is right. If we're facing the first range, we're about a 60-to-40 favorite. If we're facing the second range, we're about a 60-to-40 underdog. *How should we proceed?*

    In a case like this, we're just going to make an educated guess as to how likely he is to have each range. He just lost a bad beat, and now he's shoving all his chips. I think there's a much better chance that he's on tilt and picked up a decent hand than that he just hit a very unlikely top-2 percent hand. It's not certain, it's just much more likely. Let's say that we think the breakdown looks like this:

1. 80 percent of the time he's on tilt with the wide range.

2. 20 percent of the time he's setting a trap with the narrow range.

    If we go with those numbers, our average winning chances are 56 percent.

$$0.56 = (0.80)(0.60) + (0.20)(0.40)$$

where
  0.80 is the probability he's on tilt,
  0.60 is the probability our hand wins when he's on tilt,

0.20 is the probability he picked up a premium hand, and 0.40 is the probability our hand wins when he picked up a premium hand.

That estimate makes us an overall favorite in the hand, and we're getting 1.17-to-1 odds besides. Easy call.

The range of ranges approach is very useful in cases where we think our opponent could be using one of two or three strategies, but we don't know enough about him to say which strategy is in play. By making some rough estimates of what he could be doing and what our chances are in each case, we can make a pretty good decision in a murky situation.

Part Three

Playing Preflop

Playing Preflop

Introduction

In the last section we looked at some of the deeper strategic ideas in no-limit tournament play: understanding the importance of the ratio of your stack to the blinds, seeing how ICM informs some of our tournament decisions, and using ranges to get a clearer idea of where we stand in the hand.

Now we'll move on to the question of how to play on the various streets, and we'll start in this part with preflop play which focuses on two main questions:

1. What hands do you want to play given your stack size, your position, and what, if anything, you know about your opponents' tendencies?

2. How much do you want to bet?

We'll cover the different hand types one by one, starting with the premium pairs and moving down the list through weaker pairs, strong and weak aces, Broadway cards, suited connectors and one-gappers. Each hand type presents some characteristic problems, and we'll discuss those with plenty of examples.

These categories comprise more than 30 percent of all possible hands. And even if you consider yourself a loose-aggressive player, you don't need to play many more hands than this except in specific, very favorable situations such as when the hand is folded to you on the button, or you're getting great odds in the big blind.

Bet sizing used to be pretty straightforward: If you want to raise, raise to three times the big blind. In the modern game, however, smaller raises have become more common. There are advantages and disadvantages to different raise sizes, and that's where we'll start this chapter.

Bet Sizing Preflop

Let's imagine you're playing in a live tournament and it's still early in the event. The blinds are 100 and 200. Your stack is a healthy 22,000, up slightly from your starting stack. Most of the other players have similar stacks, some a little larger and some a little smaller. You're in fourth position and the action is folded around to you. You look down and see a pair of jacks. You certainly want to open with a raise. *But how big should your raise be?*

The minimum you can raise is 400, twice the big blind. If you want to make a pot-sized raise, you would put in 700, (200 to call the big blind, creating a pot of 500 chips, and then another 500 for a raise, making a total of 700.) You could bet some in-between amount, like 500 (2.5 times the big blind), or 600 (three times the big blind). You could also bet an amount even larger than a pot-sized raise, like 800 (four times the big blind.) *Is there a right amount to raise, or is it just a matter of style?*

Let's state at the beginning that there is no "correct" preflop raise size. Even so, raise sizing isn't just a matter of style. Each of the raises we just mentioned has some advantages and some disadvantages. Let's take a look at these raise sizes and see what they have to offer.

Raise Size No. 1: The big 4x raise to 800. (In poker slang, we call a raise to four big blinds a 4x raise.) Raising to four big blinds is an unusual play. You're investing a lot of chips and offering poor odds to the other players at the table. Someone not in the blinds is now looking at an 1,100 chip pot, needing to put in 800 to call; he's getting 1,100-to-800, or 1.375-to-1 odds. The big blind is doing a little better, getting 1,100-to-600, or almost 2-to-1. A raise this big or bigger is a shutout raise, designed to keep players with speculative hands from entering the pot, and hoping to take the pot down right now.

A shutout raise often means the raiser has one of four hands: JJ, TT, 99, or 88. When playing weaker players, this deduction is about 80 percent accurate. That's because the weaker player figures his hand is the best right now, but he's afraid of getting a couple of overcards on the flop and not knowing where he stands. So the idea is to stick in a big raise now and take down the pot at this point in time.

Against a strong player, you'll need to be much more cautious. Good players understand how these bets will be interpreted and will sometimes make them with premium pairs. I've done it myself and it's a powerful weapon.

Big raises will in general take down more pots, but at a cost. A player who makes this move has a range that's pretty well defined, so a good counter-strategy is to just call in position with a lot of hands containing an ace, king, or queen. If a flop comes that looks dangerous to a middle-pair hand, you can frequently take the pot away on the turn.

Example 3-1. You're on the button with the

The blinds are 200 and 400, and your stack is 40,000. A player in middle position with a stack of about 35,000 raises to 1,600. You should call. You have one overcard and possibly two to his likely range, plus a very good idea of his hand. Since you're getting odds and are in position, go ahead and play.

You call, making the pot 3,800 chips. The blinds fold and the flop is the

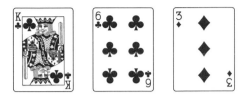

It missed you, but if your opponent has what you think, he's nervous about the overcard on board.

He bets 1,600. The big preflop raise combined with the small flop bet reinforces your theory. Again, you should call, representing that you like the flop. As for your opponent, he probably won't be happy. You call and the pot is now 7,000 chips

The turn is Q♥. You still haven't made anything but an inside straight draw. But if your estimate of his range is correct, your opponent's now very unhappy.

He checks, another piece of evidence that you're on the right track. Time to pounce. You bet 3,500 and your opponent folds.

Raise Size No. 2: The pot-sized raise to 700. This is a common raise size in online cash games, partly because the online sites usually provide a button for pot-sized bets. In tournaments, it's an unusual bet size, not quite big enough to aggressively chase people away, but not small enough to be economical.

Raise Size No. 3: The 3x raise to 600. For a long time the 3x raise was the standard raise size in tournament play. It was large enough so it didn't offer excessively attractive odds to players in later position (1.5-to-1) or the big blind (2.25-to-1), but small enough to be less than a pot-sized bet.

In current tournament play, the 3x bet is the standard only in the early stages of tournaments when the stacks are deep. As the tournament evolves, raises typically start to drop into the 2.5x or 2.25x range. There are a couple of reasons for this:

1. **The rise of the 3-bet.** As 3-bets and light 3-bets became more common in tournaments, players wanted to limit their

exposure and keep a little more control over the pot size. Over the course of a tournament, reducing the raise size slightly to 2.5x saves a lot of chips on hands that eventually fold to a 3-bet and also encourage smaller pots on the future rounds.

2. **The ignorance of the masses.** Smaller raises should encourage more players to get involved in the pot because of the better pot odds being offered. But in fact, many players don't make this adjustment, and the 2.5x raise wins just about as many uncontested pots as the 3x raise.

Raise Size No. 4: The 2.5x raise to 500. This is now the standard opening raise size in the middle stages of tournaments where most stacks have between 50 and 150 big blinds (or an M between 20 and 60). Its two advantages are that it loses less chips when you fold your hand to a 3-bet, and it's just about as likely to win the pot as a larger raise.

Its main disadvantage are the good pot odds it offers: 8-to-5 or 1.6-to-1 to a player in later position, and 8-to-3 or 2.67-to-1 to the big blind.

Raise Size No. 5: The 2x min-raise to 400. The preflop min-raise used to be a rare event in poker tournaments. Now it's commonplace, especially in the later stages of tournament where the blinds and antes are large compared to the average stack.

The old idea was that a min-raise was too dangerous because it offered extremely good odds for speculative hands to come in and take a shot at the pot. For example, suppose we're late in a tournament and the blinds are 2,000 and 4,000, with a 500-chip ante and a table of eight players. A player in early position makes a min-raise to 8,000. Take a look at the pot odds being offered to the remaining players at the table:

1. A player in late position needs to call 8,000 to see a pot of 18,000. His odds are 18-to-8 or 2.25-to-1. In addition, he'll have position on the original raiser after the flop.

2. The small blind won't have position, but he only has to call 6,000 to get in. His odds are 18-to-6 or exactly 3-to-1.

3. The big blind also won't have position, but he only has to call 4,000. His pot odds are 18-to-4, or 4.5-to-1.

These are big odds, and if someone does call, the odds for the remaining players get bigger yet. *So why is the min-raise popular?* There are several good reasons.

1. **The small raise helps control the pot size and avoid early pot commitment.** As Ms get small in the later stages of a tournament, large preflop bets may not leave you with a lot of room to maneuver. A smaller bet costs less if you have to give up to a reraise. It also gives you a better chance to call a raise and see a flop without getting yourself pot-committed.

   Let's look at a quick example to see the effect of a 2x raise compared to a 3x raise. Suppose the blinds are 2,000 and 4,000, with a 500-chip ante and there are eight players at the table, the same as the example above and it's folded to you in middle position. You have a pair of tens and a stack of 140,000.

   Suppose you make a min-raise to 8,000 and the button, with a stack of 220,000 chips, reraises to 16,000. The blinds fold and you call. Here's how you stand before the flop:

   - Current pot: 42,000
   - Effective stack: 124,000
   - Amount invested: 16,000

   You've invested a little over 10 percent of your starting stack, and the pot is only about a third of your remaining stack.

   Now let's look at the same scenario, but this time you raise to three big blinds, and the reraise is also three times. Your raise is to 12,000 and his reraise is to 36,000. If you now call and see a flop, the situation looks like this:

- Current pot: 82,000
- Effective stack: 104,000
- Amount invested: 36,000

The larger betting has doubled the pot which is now almost as big as your remaining stack, and you've invested about a quarter of your starting stack to this point.

In the second scenario with the 3x raises, any action on the flop will end up with you all-in and playing for your tournament life. In light of that, you're probably better off just moving all-in with your tens preflop and getting some fold equity rather than waiting and trying to figure out what to do if overcards appear on the flop.

Getting all your money in with a pair of tens and an M of 14 (35 big blinds) isn't really a bad result. The min-raise, however, left you with more choices. You could make an easy call if you wanted. You could also reraise to 32,000, giving yourself a chance to win the pot right there, while still being able to fold to an all-in. Modern aggressive players like having choices, and small raises and bets give them more options.

2. **Attack more pots for the same investment.** If you're an aggressive player who likes to make a move at a lot of pots, the min-raise offers a cheap way to do so. You could attack three pots for an investment of six big blinds. Using a 3x raise only allows you to attack two pots for the same investment. For an active player at a table where most players aren't reacting to the difference in raise size, the min-raise becomes a great bargain.

3. **Save money when you're forced out by a 3-bet.** With 3-betting more common in tournaments than before, aggressive raises now require a clear plan for dealing with 3-bets. If you raise with the intention of folding to a 3-bet, a min-raise will save you an entire big blind over a 3x raise. Over time, those

saved blinds will start to amount to a significant amount of chips.

4. **Adjusting odds when you face a possible all-in shove from a short stack.** After you pass the midpoint of a tournament, you'll start to see a lot of short-stacked players at your table with 30 or fewer big blinds, or Ms less than 12. Stacks of that size are sometimes called 'restealing stacks' because they're big enough to put real pressure on the initial raiser with an all-in move, but not so big that the all-in is a monstrous overbet. If you have several short-stacked players behind you and are contemplating a raise, consider your raise size carefully. A large raise on your part may force you to call if one of the short stacks moves all-in. A small raise, on the other hand, will leave you facing worse odds after an all-in and may allow you to make an easy fold. This is a common situation, so let's look at a couple of examples and see just what's going on.

Example 3-2. You're about two-thirds of the way through a medium-sized live tournament. Right now you're at an eight-handed table, and the blinds are 2,000 and 4,000, with a 500-chip ante producing a starting pot of 10,000 chips. You have 180,000, representing 45 big blinds or an M of 18.

In this hand, you'll be fourth to act and behind you are two short stacks. The player directly to your left has 80,000, with an M of 8 (20 big blinds), and the player to his left has 50,000, with an M of 5 (12.5 big blinds). The player on your left with 80,000 seems inexperienced, but the player with the smaller stack is a tournament veteran who just lost a big pot to get to this situation. The blinds both have stacks a bit larger than yours and seem to be experienced players.

The first three players fold and you look down at your hand and see the

It's a speculative hand, but you're comfortable raising with this hand at this table with just four players left to act. *What raise size should you choose?*

Your only real concern here is a shove from either of the small stacks on your left. If they elect to call, you're happy to just play the hand. You also don't mind a call from the blinds, and if either of the blinds decides to 3-bet, you'll just fold.

However, an all-in from either of the small stacks is a trickier situation. You'll need to consider what the pot odds are and what their ranges might be, and how you're doing against those ranges. But if your raise is properly sized, you can avoid a tough decision and give yourself an easy and clear choice.

Let's start by supposing that everyone folds to our raise except the smallest stack, who moves all-in. Here are the pot odds we'll be offered for each of three possible raise sizes on our part: a 3x raise, a 2.5x raise, and a 2x raise:

If we raise to 12,000 (3x) and he moves all-in for 50,000, the pot is 72,000 and we need to call 38,000. Our pot odds are 72-to-38, or about 1.9-to-1 and we need to win 34.5 percent of the time to break even.

If we raise to 10,000 (2.5x) and he moves all-in for 50,000, the pot is 70,000 and we need to call 40,000. Our pot odds are 70-to-40 or about 1.75-to-1 and we need to win 36 percent of the time to break even.

If we raise to 8,000 (2x) and he moves all-in for 50,000, the pot is 68,000 and we need to call 42,000. Our pot odds are

68-to-42 or about 1.6-to-1 and we need to win 38.5 percent of the time to break even.

The key point to notice is that as our initial raise becomes smaller, the pot becomes smaller and the amount we have to call becomes larger, so we're being offered progressively worse pot odds on the all-in. A big raise on our part has the effect of pricing us in when he shoves, while a small raise results in worse pot odds and gives more room to fold.

So what should we do against this player when he shoves? Since we think he's an experienced player, he should be shoving here with a wide range. It's a great situation for a short stack, and he should be good enough to take advantage of it. Hand simulation software tells us if his range is 30 percent of his hands, our jack-nine suited is a little better than 40 percent against that range. If his range is 40 percent of all hands, we're almost 43 percent to win. Clearly, we can call his all-in with any of our opening raise sizes. That's good, because it means we don't need to worry about the short stack. However we choose to play the hand, we'll just call his all-in.

But what about the larger stack? He presents some different problems. Here's how our three possible raise sizes do against an all-in from the 80,000 stack.

If we raise to 12,000 (3x) and he moves all-in for 80,000, the pot is 102,000 and we need to call 68,000. Our pot odds are 102-to-68 or about 1.5-to-1 and we need to win 40 percent of the time to break even.

If we raise to 10,000 (2.5x) and he moves all-in for 80,000, the pot is 100,000 and we need to call 70,000. Our pot odds are 100-to-70 or about 1.4-to-1 and we need to win 41.3 percent of the time to break even.

If we raise to 8,000 (2x) and he moves all-in for 80,000, the pot is 98,000 and we need to call 72,000. Our pot odds are 98-to-72 or about 1.36-to-1 and we need to win 42.4 percent of the time to break even.

Notice that his larger raise gives us worse pot odds in every case. As we would expect, we need a better hand to call his all-in than was the case with the raise from the shorter stack. His range, however, presents an additional problem. We assessed the short stack as an experienced player, who would probably know that he could shove with a wide range because of his small M. But we assessed the player with 80,000 as inexperienced, which usually means he'll only be shoving with a tighter range.

Against tighter ranges, our jack-nine suited isn't doing so well. It's only 34 percent to win against a 10 percent range and 37 percent to win against a 20 percent range. Even if we thought he could be shoving with 30 percent of his hands, we'd only be about 40 percent to win, which is exactly what we need if we're raising three times the big blind.

Conclusion: We're going to fold our jack-nine suited against an all-in from the bigger stack, although it's a closer call if we started with a big raise. Making a min-raise and folding to a shove has the double merit of losing less money and giving an easier decision, one where we're less tempted to go wrong. Since our raise size didn't matter against an all-in from the shortest stack, the min-raise is the best play here.[7]

5.   **The min-raise is almost as effective in winning the pot as a larger raise.** Of all the reasons for making small raises instead of large raises, this is the most compelling. When you make an initial raise in the middle to late stages of a

---

[7] By the way, if you found the depth of this analysis intimidating, don't worry. This is not the sort of analysis you're going to perform at the table. Try to work on situations like this at home where you have plenty of time, learn what you can learn, and use your conclusions to make better plays in tournament situations.

tournament, you're just about as likely to take down the pot with a min-raise as with a larger one. At first glance, this shouldn't be happening. We've already described the great pot odds that a min-raise offers to the remaining players at the table, especially when antes are in play. A min-raise offers about 4.5-to-1 odds to the big blind, and about 2.25-to-1 to the players between you and the button (who will also have position on you after the flop.) Those are huge odds, and you might expect lots of callers when you make a min-raise. But, as an empirical fact, players don't call as much as the odds would indicate.

Why not? There are different theories, but here's mine. As we get to the middle and late stages of a tournament, players who don't have a huge stack (which is most of the field) are aware that any hand they play could lead to a situation where they'll have to put their tournament life on the line. As a result, players who aren't hardened tournament veterans stop asking "Am I getting the right pot odds to play here?" and start asking "Is this a hand where I'm happy to risk getting knocked out?" and "How many more chips do I have to put in the pot?"

Since even a min-raise requires putting a lot of chips in the pot when the blinds get big, players lose sight of the pot odds and focus purely on their cards. Once you make that mistake, your cards rarely look good. It's too easy to just say "This situation isn't good — I'll surely see a better one later," and the cards go into the muck.

Experienced players don't fall into this trap. Gus Hansen is famous for playing almost anything in the big blind when he's getting long odds, but he's not the only one. Getting 4-to-1 odds (or better) is a very big deal, and when your improbable hand hits the flop hard, you can add big implied odds as well. Being able to take big odds in crucial situations is a major reason why successful players seem to get lucky so often.

Bet Sizing Summary

Let's reduce our bet sizing discussion to a few simple rules that you can take to the table.

Rule No. 1: In the early part of the tournament, when stacks are deep and pot commitment isn't an issue, use raise sizes in the range of 2.5x to 3x. Using bigger raises reduces the pot odds you're giving at a time when your opponents are inclined to see pots and speculate.

Rule No. 2: Later in the tournament, when lots of players have small stacks, reduce your raise size to something in the range of 2x to 2.5x. Recently, raises of 2.2x have become something of the norm here. Raising slightly more than the bare minimum seems to convince players that you're more serious about the hand.

Rule No. 3: Vary your bet size according to the stage of the tournament, not according to your hand strength or hand type. Varying your bet size according to your hand type is a classic mistake and one that your opponents will spot quickly.

Rule No. 4: Observe your table carefully, especially just after a blind increase. Usually you'll see that a certain opening raise size quickly becomes the new standard. If that raise size fits within your raising range, adopt it. By using the table standard, you won't call any extra attention to yourself, which is good.

Rule No. 5: Watch how each player handles their big blind. In particular, you're looking to see which players defend their big blinds vigorously. Once you've spotted them, plan on raising a little more when you're going to be the opening raiser with a good hand and they're in the big blind. The change doesn't need to be excessive. If the table standard is a 2.5x opening raise and you're up against a big blind defender on this hand, make your opening raise 3x.

Playing Different Hand Types Preflop

Different preflop holdings present different problems. In this chapter,we're going to talk about the different hand types and what the options are for preflop play. It's not a simple question because how you play hands depends on your stack size, on the image you've presented to the table, your position at the table, and what the other players have been doing.

However, before we talk about the different hand types, we need to talk a bit about limping, or entering the pot with a call rather than a raise. *Should we ever limp into a pot, and if so, when?*

In ancient times (pre-2004) limping was commonly seen in tournament play. Since then, it has become increasingly rare, and many modern players never limp in an unopened pot. They raise if they want to play, and otherwise fold.

There are a couple of good arguments for always opening the pot with a raise:

1. Raising gives you the chance of winning the pot right there; you can't win the pot if you limp.

2. Raising makes the problem of balancing your range much easier. If you always raise, and raise with a variety of hands from each position, your range will be balanced. If you sometimes raise and sometimes limp, you have to balance two sets of ranges. This sounds easy but can be hard to do in practice.

It's certainly true that inexperienced players should never limp. Newcomers to tournaments tend to make the common blunder of limping with hands like suited connectors and small pairs, hoping to hit a big hand on a cheap flop. This habit makes them easy to read and exploit (with a big raise). If you fall into this category, you can improve your results quickly by never limping — either raise or fold.

For veteran players, the question is a little more difficult. Limping, in general, will create smaller pots and more post-flop play. If you happen to be particularly strong at post-flop play, then limping into a few pots may add a little extra dimension to your game. Whether this 'extra dimension' can compensate for the possible loss of some pots you might have won just by betting is, however, a debatable point. For the large majority of players, adopting a simple rule of never limping can't be a bad strategy. In discussing how to play the different types of hands, we'll assume you're a player who has decided that open limping is not an option.

Playing the Big Pairs (AA, KK, and QQ)

These are the premium hands and you're delighted to get them. They're not hard to play preflop, but there are a few subtleties you'll need to watch for, especially with queens.

If the pot has not been opened, or there's a limper in front of you, raise with all three of these hands. If the pot is unopened, use your standard opening raise for that phase of the tournament. If there are one or more limpers, raise an extra big blind for each limper.

Example 3-3: It's early in a big tournament and most stacks are deep. The blinds are 50 and 100. A player who seems tight and conservative limps for 100 under-the-gun, and the players in fourth and fifth position also limp. You're on the button with the

Your normal opening raise would be 300 at this stage, but with three limpers, raise to 600. If one of the limpers should then come over the top, you have a new problem, but it's not a problem you have to address right now. The most likely result of your raise is that you'll take down a nice little pot.

Suppose there's already been a raise in front of you? With aces and kings, this isn't a problem. You simply make a 3-bet, and in the event the initial raiser (or someone else at the table) sticks in a 4-bet, you raise again until your whole stack is in the center of the table.

Should you ever lay down kings to a series of raises? Years ago, when play was generally more conservative, I argued that you should not. If you pick up kings at a full table, there's about a 5 percent chance that someone else at the table will pick up aces. Although you would occasionally be right by laying down your kings to a 4-bet or 5-bet, it's much more likely that your opponent is raising with ace-king or queens or jacks, or even something weaker. In the long run, laying down your kings was a money-losing play.

Nowadays, there are many more aggressive players at the table, and when two aggressive players butt heads, it's not terribly unusual to see them get all-in with ace-queen against jacks, even when the stacks are deep. If it was wrong to fold kings in the old days, it's even more wrong now.

Non-Standard Plays with Aces and Kings

There are a couple of non-standard preflop plays with aces and kings that are worth mentioning. The first is limping in early position with the intention of reraising after someone raises you. This play once had a little bite, but it's been around so long that everyone knows it. With 3-betting so common, you'll make more money with your premium hands by just raising and reraising after someone 3-bets you.

There's a different play, however, which I like a lot. You have aces or kings in late position. Someone in front of you raises. Instead of a normal reraise to 2.5x or 3x, you reraise to a little more than 4x!

This move almost screams "Scared money!" It's a raise typically made by someone with a medium to low pair who doesn't want to throw their hand away, but who also doesn't want to take a flop and try to play facing overcards. They're hoping their big raise will chase the leader of the hand and they can scoop the pot quickly. Good players with deep stacks know they can either reraise again and take the pot right now or call and reevaluate after the flop knowing their opponent probably has a hand from a pair of eights up through a pair of jacks.

A play like this can get a lot of money in the pot quickly while leaving you with a disguised and powerful hand. Don't try it if the table knows you to be a good player as it won't have the desired effect. But if you're an unknown, give it a try and see what happens.

Playing Queens

Queens presents some problems compared to kings. Take a look at the differences:

1. It's now dominated by more hands — aces and kings, instead of just aces).

2. It's only a small favorite against ace-king, instead of a large favorite.

3. There are fewer hands that it can dominate.

As a result, queens isn't really a hand where you want to get all your chips in the middle when the table has deep stacks. However, that doesn't mean you have to be excessively cautious. Let's look at a few examples and see how queens should be handled in different situations.

Example 3-4. It's early in a big tournament. The blinds are 100 and 200 and you're on the button with a stack of 27,000 and an M of 90 (135 big blinds). You pick up the Q♣Q♦ and have a neutral image so far, neither particularly aggressive or excessively cautious.

After three folds, the player in fourth position raises to 550. He's been very aggressive so far and has a stack of 36,000 with an M of 120 (180 big blinds). The players in seats four through six all fold.

A pair of queens here is a strong hand and well ahead of his range, so a 3-bet to something like 1,300 is a perfectly good play and should be your standard move in this situation. An alternative play is to just call, which has the merit of being very deceptive. Also, you don't want to fall into the habit of calling just with hands like low pairs or suited connectors, and by putting some very strong hands into your calling range, you make yourself a more dangerous opponent. So calling here about 20 percent of the time should diversify your ranges nicely.

All right. Let's suppose you 3-bet to 1,300. The small blind folds but the big blind, a tight older player with a stack of 22,000, 4-bets to 3,500 and the original raiser now 5-bets to 7,000. *What's your play now?*

At this point, you have to put your tail between your legs and go away. It's likely that the tight player's range is AA, KK, and AK (suited or unsuited), and you're only about 40 percent against that range. The aggressive player's range is harder to estimate, but it might be very tight here given the action he's already seen. Getting all your chips in the middle as a substantial underdog early in the tournament is precisely the play you don't want to make. That's because the early part of a tournament is a time to chip up by playing aggressively and taking small risks when there are lots of weaker players to exploit. Getting all your money in here will get you knocked out of the tournament most of the time, and the fact that you'll occasionally triple up isn't worth it. Fold.

Example 3-5. You're in the late middle stages of a live event. It's a full table of nine players. The blinds are 1,000 and 2,000, with a 200-chip ante, so the starting pot is 4,800 chips and the standard raise at the table in this level has been in the 4,400 to 4,800 range. You're third to act and have the

You've been at the table for about an hour and a run of bad cards has prevented you from playing a lot of pots, so the table probably thinks you're tight. Your stack is 72,000, so your M is 15 (36 big blinds). The other players at the table have stacks ranging from 20,000 (M = 4) to 200,000 (M = 42).

With your relatively small stack, a pair of queens is a hand you won't be able to lay down. Because of your stack size, your opponents will think you're playing with a fairly wide range despite the fact that you haven't played many hands, so their ranges against you will be a little wider than normal. There's no way you'll be able to accumulate enough information about their hand strength before you're pot-committed, so your job is to play in such a way that you get all your chips in the pot.

The first two players fold and now it's your turn. Obviously, you have to raise, and a good raise size would be 5,000. It's a little bigger than the 4,800 that has become the table standard, but not so large that it looks like you're trying to get all your chips involved.

You raise to 5,000. All fold to a somewhat tight player on the button who calls. The small blind then folds and the big blind, an aggressive player with the big stack of 200,000 makes a 3-bet to 13,000. The pot is now 25,800 chips.

This sequence is almost ideal for you. The tight player on the button almost certainly has a worse hand. His most likely holding is a medium to low pair or a couple of Broadway cards. The big blind has a real hand, but his range is fairly wide and contains many hands you're beating.

Therefore, you want to raise. A normal-sized 4-bet would be in the range of 30,000 to 33,000, more than twice but less than three times his 3-bet. Anything in that range, however, would be almost half your stack, effectively committing you to the pot. So under those circumstances, it's best to move all-in. Given your strong hand and your small stack, that's a great result for you whether your opponents call or fold.

You move all-in. The button folds but the big blind calls and shows the A♦Q♦. Your queens hold up to win the hand, and your stack grows to just over 150,000.

Playing the Medium Pairs (JJ, TT, 99, and 88)

Slightly lower than the premium hands are the middle pairs — jacks down through eights. (Some writers put sevens in this category, but I think of them as having more of the characteristics of the low pair hands.)

The changes brought about by the prevalence of the super-aggressive style have had a big effect on how these hands must be played. In the old days of a decade ago, players would raise with these hands preflop in the hope of taking down a small pot right there. But if you raised with a pair of tens and got reraised, you had a real problem. Back then, the reraising range for a typical player was very tight: AA, KK, and AK for sure, and maybe QQ. Reraising with jacks and ace-queen made you a very aggressive player, and reraising with anything else made you a certifiable wild man, if not an outright lunatic. Your tens were in big trouble against those tight ranges, and many players would fold them preflop.

Now that's all changed. The rise of the super-aggressive player with his wide 3-betting range and the decline of the ultra-tight style means that in contested pots these hands are much stronger than they used to be, and I now like to think of them as 'sub-premium' hands rather than as mere 'middle pairs.'

Let's look at how to play these hands in a few different preflop scenarios:

Scnnario No. 1: The pot is unopened, or was opened by one or two limpers. Since I don't advocate limping into pots with good hands, you should raise with all the middle pairs if no one has entered the pot, or if players have only limped. If limpers have already entered the pot, you should make a slightly bigger raise. Here's a quick example:

Example 3-6: It's the third level of a major tournament with the blinds at 150 and 300, and no antes as yet. You're sitting in the big blind and your stack is 38,000, an above-average number. You pick up the

The somewhat tight player in second position, with a stack of 27,000, limps for 300. A very aggressive player in fifth position, who just suffered a big loss and now has 14,000, calls, everyone else folds, and the action is on you. The pot is now 1,050 chips.

You have a great hand and should certainly raise. The only question is exactly how much. The common rule of thumb with deep stacks is to raise three times the big blind plus an extra big blind for each limper. Here that formula would indicate a raise to 1,500. (Since you're in the big blind and you already have 300 in the pot, you would need to put in an additional 1,200 to make that raise.) If I'll be out of position after the flop, it's my preference to bump the pot a little bit more, so in this case I'd raise to 1,650 or so. The exact amount isn't crucial, but with two players already showing interest, you want to charge them a healthy amount to play.

A different sort of bet sizing problem can arise late in a tournament when there are a lot of short stacks at the table.

Example 3-7. You're playing in the big weekly event at your local casino. It's late in the day and two tables remain with eight players each. Blinds are 3,000 and 6,000, with a 600-chip ante. The starting pot is 13,800 chips. The stacks at your table look like this:

Position	Stack	M	Big Blinds
UTG	450,000	33	75
UTG+1	190,000	14	32
MP	1,200,000	86	200
Hijack (You)	700,000	50	117
Cutoff	60,000	4	10
Button	90,000	6	15
SB	110,000	8	18
BB	100,000	7	17

The typical raise size at this level has been 14,000. The three players in front of you fold. You look down and see the 8♠ 8♥. *What's your play?*

In the later stages of tournaments, it's important to keep a careful eye on the stack sizes of the players to your immediate left. Since they will always act after you, your raise size may be influenced by their stack sizes and how you think they might react to your move.

In this case, the four players after you all have small stacks, and if you make a normal raise to something like 14,000 to 15,000, and they want to play their hands, their most likely move will be to shove all-in. Given their stack sizes and probable wide range, you'll be compelled to call their shove. If that's the case, you're better off raising an amount that's enough to put each player all-in, thereby getting the most possible fold equity from the hand. You should raise to anything over 110,000, letting each of the players know that they have to risk their tournament life to call you, and they won't have fold equity on their side.

If one or two of the players after you had bigger stacks, don't bother with this play. In that case, just make your normal raise and see what happens.

Scenario No. 2: The pot was opened with a raise and you will have position post-flop. Now let's consider what happens when there is a raise in front of you and your position is late, so you'll have position on the raiser after the flop.

Let's first note that your choices are calling and 3-betting. You could only consider folding if the original raiser were some kind of super-nit in early position who you knew was raising only with the top 3 to 4 percent of his hands. There aren't many of these players left anymore, so let's assume you're dealing with an opponent whose range is somewhere between a little tight and super-aggressive. Your medium pair is a good hand, so don't fold.

If the stacks are deep and the raise came from early position, and you don't have much specific information about your opponent, plan on mostly just calling with your medium pairs. Calling here has a number of merits:

1. It prevents a 4-bet which could be awkward for your hand, especially if the 4-bet is coming from a moderately tight or unknown player.

2. It keeps all your opponent's weak hands in the mix.

3. It controls the pot size.

4. After the flop, you'll be in position with a hand that should be easy to play.

If the stacks are deep but the raise came from middle or late position, then you should 3-bet sometimes and call sometimes. Two good situations for 3-betting are:

1. **Your opponent is weak-tight.** He'll open with a fair number of hands but fold all but his best to a 3-bet, and a 3-bet here is very profitable because you win many small pots immediately and usually have a pretty clear idea where you stand if you get called or 4-bet.

2. **Your opponent is super-aggressive.** Many players are uncomfortable playing super-aggressive players, and make the blunder of holding back and waiting for a monster hand so they can pounce. Not surprisingly, the super-aggressive players know about this strategy, and it doesn't work well. Attacking with medium pairs is part of a better and balanced approach. You're mostly well ahead of the super-aggressive player's range, and you're marking yourself as a player to be avoided when there are easier targets at the table.

Now let's look at a couple of examples.

Example 3-8. It's early in a major tournament, the blinds are 50 and 100, and you've played one round at the table. You have 29,850 chips (M = 199), almost your starting stack, are on the button, and pick up the T♥T♠.

The player in third position opens with a raise to 300. His stack is about the same as yours, and you don't know anything about him except that he raised once and won the blinds. The hand is then folded to you. *What's your play?*

You can't fold a hand as strong as a pair of tens, so your choices are calling and 3-betting. Now I can't say 3-betting is actually a mistake, but it's a play I don't like when my knowledge about the table is lacking. If I 3-bet and my unknown opponent 4-bets, I've maneuvered myself into a position where it's not clear what to do, and any play I make could be a big mistake.

Therefore, calling is a more appealing choice. I avoid the 4-bet, reveal little about my hand, risk a minimal amount of money, and get to see the flop in position. The combination of the flop and my opponent's follow-up will leave me knowing a lot more about my situation. So just call and play the hand after the flop.

Example 3-9. You're many hours into a major live tournament and you've been at the same eight handed table all day. The blinds are 2,000 and 4,000, with a 400-chip ante making the starting pot 9,200 chips. Your stack is 368,000 with an M of about 40 (92 big blinds) and you're on the button with the T♥T♦.

A very aggressive player in second position, with a stack of about 90,000 raises to 8,800 (2.4x). He's been very active all day, but hasn't been able to accumulate a big stack of chips, and now his M is around 10 (23 big blinds). *What do you do?*

Although your hand and position are the same as in the previous example, your action should be different. Since you know this player is aggressive, it's safe to assume that your tens are well ahead of his opening range, and given that his stack is short, there's no reason to play the hand slowly. Therefore, you should 3-bet, and the only question is how to size your raise to create the best chance of getting his whole stack involved.

Specifically, moving all-in is reasonable given his stack size, but a better play is to 3-bet to something in the range of 20,000 to 25,000. This gives him the chance to come over the top with an all-in 4-bet which might appear to have some fold equity. You'll then call, of course.

When making plays like this, make sure you're clear in your mind about why this is the play to make and what you intend to do if raised. On many occasions, I've seen players bet to induce a raise or an all-in, but then go into the tank after the all-in comes and finally decide to fold on the theory that their opponent must really be stronger than they thought! When you lay out a plan for the hand, follow through with it, and don't panic when your opponent actually does what is expected.

If you call with a medium pair against an aggressive player, be aware that's you'll need to play well after the flop to justify your call. Hitting a set (on the flop) would be nice, but that's only going to happen about one time in eight. So it's important to win some hands where you miss the flop entirely.

Here's a typical example.

Example 3-10. It's late in the first day of a live tournament. The blinds are now 1,200 and 2,400, with a 200-chip ante producing a starting pot of 5,400 chips. You're in the cutoff seat with the

and your stack is about 180,000, giving you an M of 33 (75 big blinds).

An aggressive player in second position with a stack of 160,000 raises to 5,200, the next three players fold, you call, and the button and blinds fold. The pot is now 15,800 chips.

The flop comes the

and the aggressive player bets 8,000. *What do you do?*

Clearly, you must at least call. An aggressive player can raise preflop with a wide range that includes hands like pairs, Broadway cards, suited and unsuited aces, and suited connectors. And depending on just how aggressive he is and how the table has been playing, there may even be more hands in the mix as well.

Furthermore, in order to play this style, an aggressive player has to keep attacking. So it's likely he would have made a continuation bet with essentially his entire range, and only a small part of that range includes higher pairs than yours or hands with a king, so you're still well ahead of his range. In addition, the pot is offering 3-to-1 odds, so there's no doubt you can at least call.

What about raising? If you feel you're mostly ahead of this player (on this flop), then raising should be a real consideration, but is it a good play?

The upside of raising is clear. If you raise and your opponent folds, you take down the pot right now, guaranteeing that you won't lose when he gets lucky and hits a card on the turn or river to beat you. The raise-fold sequence won't gain a lot of equity because he's almost always folding hands where you're ahead right now and where his chances of outdrawing you are pretty small. But when raising makes him lay down his hand, you will have gained something.

Raising, however, has a couple of downsides. The first is when he reraises. Now you're in a difficult situation. If he's an aggressive player, his reraises will come from two groups: hands where he has you crushed and hands where he's bluffing with air. Thus your position will be awkward because you'll need to guess what he's doing, and if your guess is wrong, you'll be making a big mistake.

A second downside of raising shows up when we look at the stacks and the pot size. Suppose you raise to 20,000 and the aggressive player calls. Going to the turn the pot is 55,800 chips, his stack is 134,800, and your stack is 154,800. Notice that his stack, the effective stack, is now slightly more than twice the pot. Also notice that a bet on the turn from either of you should be in the range of 30,000 to 35,000, and unless that bet wins the pot, both of you will be pot-committed.

These arguments make the case for just calling pretty strong. Calling keeps the pot small and enhances the value of your position while avoiding lines where you could make a big, expensive mistake. Now raising isn't a clear mistake, but it has the potential to put you in situations that are difficult to play.

You actually call, making the pot 31,800 chips and the turn is the 6♣. That's another good card for your hand, and unless he had a pair of sixes or something like eight-seven suited, his hand didn't improve. So if you were ahead on the flop, you're probably still ahead.

He bets 14,000. *What do you do?*

Again, you must at least call. You're investing a fair amount of money with second pair, but when your opponent is very aggressive, you have to be willing to make calls with medium-strength hands because they'll often be good. And right now the pot is 45,800, and a call costs you 14,000, so you're getting better than 3-to-1 pot odds.

Since it's still likely your hand is probably best, you can consider raising. However, the arguments against raising are even stronger than on the flop.

Raising will fold out a lot of the hands you beat, like smaller pairs and air. But those hands have little chance of drawing out on the river, so you don't gain much. Again, the problem comes when your opponent reraises, which because of his stack size and the pot size, will be an all-in reraise. (If you raise to something like 34,000, a call would leave him with a stack of about 112,000 and a pot of about 100,000 chips. Therefore, the only sensible raise at this point would be all-in.)

Now you'll have a really tough decision. His move will most likely consist of very strong hands and air, and if you fold the best hand, about a quarter of your stack on a hand you should have comfortably won will be lost. But if you call and he has the nuts, almost 90 percent of your stack will be gone and a quick exit will be near. Either way, it's a bad result given that you started with a solid hand in position.

You call, the pot is now 59,800 chips, and the river is the 2♠. Your opponent checks and you check behind for all the reasons we discussed above. He shows the A♥9♥ and your tens take the pot.

This wasn't a particularly difficult hand to play, and the purpose of including the example was threefold:

1. Medium pairs can't be played as fit-or-fold in a heads up pot. You have to be prepared to play after the flop, and an aggressive opponent can force you to invest a fair amount of your stack defending the hand.

2. When considering raising after the flop, keep a careful eye on the pot and stack sizes. Pot-commitment problems can arise quickly.

3. Beware of plays that can force you to make very tough decisions later.

Scenario No. 3: The pot was opened with a raise and you will be out of position post-flop. This scenario mostly covers situations where you pick up a medium pair in the blinds and the hand gets raised in front of you. Compared to the case where you are in position, being out of position creates some interesting choices and makes the hands more difficult to play. Let's see why.

The first point to notice is that when you're in the blinds with a middle pair, you not only have a good hand, but you're being offered a cheap price to get involved. Barring some very unusual preflop action, you're going to play the hand. But whether you call or raise is the interesting question.

There are some solid arguments for just calling, especially when stacks are deep:

1. You keep the pot small when you're out of position.

2. Your hand is well-disguised if you hit something good.

3. You avoid the difficult decision that may come if you 3-bet and get 4-bet in return.

There are also some very good arguments for 3-betting:

1. Your hand plays better preflop than postflop when you may be facing overcards, so take it down now.

2. You'll be out of position postflop, so take it down now.

These are all good arguments which is why this particular choice is usually difficult. In practice, I like to call sometimes and 3-bet sometimes, and I'll let the situation at the table dictate my decision. Here's a list of the factors to take into consideration:

1. **Stack sizes.** Deep stacks are an argument for calling. The deeper the stacks, the less I want to create a big pot with my medium pair. Short stacks, however, argue for playing the hand fast. If my M is in the 10 to 12 range or lower (25 to 30 big blinds or less), my standard play will be an all-in 3 bet after an opening raise.

2. **My opponent's image.** A tight image for my opponent is an argument for calling. I'll have to fold to a 4-bet from a tight player, and that will happen more often since his range is narrow to start. Calling allows me to see a flop, which is important since a tight player should have a little more trouble releasing his hand if he has a big pair and I hit a set. A loose image for my opponent is an argument for 3-betting.

3. **My image.** If my image is tight, I'm more likely to 3-bet since my opponent should often fold. If my image is loose, I'm more likely to call. Both actions go against my established image which creates the most profitable situations.

4. **Table strength.** If the table is generally weak, I want to call. At a weak table, the key idea is not to take actions that might be marginally correct but can get you busted out when things go awry. Your goal is to stick around and slowly win money from the weak players while they are alive. At a generally strong table, I'm more inclined to 3-bet since it's important to take advantage of every marginal edge.

5.   **Tie-breaker.** In a totally marginal situation, I'll break ties in favor of calling. That's because I'm happy to play the hand post-flop and don't need to try and settle the hand immediately.

However, notice one crucial point. If you decide to 3-bet with any of the middle pairs, it's impoirtant to know how you're going to respond to a 4-bet, either from the original raiser or from someone else at the table. In any event, this is good practice, but it's not as important if you have a premium pair that you're willing to take all the way, or if you have something like a suited connector that you can just fold. It's worth a lot to see a flop with middle pairs, so before you jeopardize that by raising, make sure you've decided on a response in case your opponent fires back.

Now let's look at a couple of examples and see how to analyze these situations.

Example 3-11. You're three levels deep in a big live tournament. The blinds are 150 and 300, and your stack is 27,000 for an M of 60 (90 big blinds). The player in second position, who arrived at the table a few hands ago, raises to 850. The player in the cutoff, who has been pretty tight through the first few hours, now 3-bets to 2,200. The button and the small blind fold and you're in the big blind with the T♠T♦. *What's your play?*

You should fold, and it's an easy decision. An unknown player raises from early position and a known tight player then 3-bets. The unknown player could be raising with a wide range, but you don't know that. The tight player certainly has a narrow range. At best you have a coin flip, and at worst you're crushed. Let it go. You don't need to play every hand where you're dealt a medium pair.

Sometimes you'll see a player call with his pair in this spot, hoping to flop a set and double up. It's a bad play for a couple of reasons. First is that his stack is too small compared to the amount he has to call. Right now the big blind has 27,000 in his stack, and he has to call 1,900 to stay in the hand. The ratio of his stack to his call is 27,000-to-1,900, or just over 14-to-1. The odds that he hits his set are about 7.5-to-1, and when the set flops, he won't always stack his opponents. Consequently, most good players like to see a potential payoff of between 20- to 25-to-1 before calling for set value. The other problem with calling is that a call won't necessarily close the action. If you call and the original raiser 4-bets to something like 5,000, you'll either have to fold or call with even worse odds.

Example 3-12. You're in the second level of a live tournament. Blinds are now 100 and 200, you're in the small blind with a stack of 32,000 and an M of 107 (160 big blinds), and pick up a pair of tens. The action folds to the cutoff who raises to 600. He's been aggressive and loose, and doesn't seem particularly good. The button folds, the action is on you, your image is tight, and the table has a fair share of weak players. *What do you do?*

This is a tough play. The deep stacks and the generally weak table both argue for a call. His image (loose-aggressive) and your image (tight) both argue for a 3-bet. Even though I generally like breaking ties in favor of calling, in this case my preference is to 3-bet. You've got a strong hand against an opponent who, based on what you've seen so far, may do something foolish. That means there's a reasonable chance to collect a lot of chips on this hand, and you need to take some chances early in a tournament to build a stack, and this looks like a good spot to take some of those chances. Raise to 1,400 and see what happens.

However, before 3-betting, you need to be clear in your mind how to respond to a 4-bet on his part. So let's suppose you 3-bet to 1,400, the big blind folds, and your loose-aggressive opponent 4-bets to 3,300. *Now what?*

You can't fold this hand against this player, but here I think a call is better than a raise. If you 5-bet, you'll be pot-committed given your knowledge of your opponent and the strength of your hand. But getting all your money in the middle with a pair of tens when sitting at a weak table isn't the right idea. A call lets you see the flop and make a better judgment on just how far to go with the hand. Just make sure to figure all this out before making your 3-

bet. That is, anticipating possible sequences and understanding what you'll do in each case is a key part of preflop play, and it's a routine that too many players lack.

Scenario No. 4: The pot was opened with a raise and a 3-bet. This is a situation that causes trouble for a lot of players. You're sitting in late position or the blinds with a pair of jacks. Someone opens for a raise from early position and you're deciding just how to play your hand. But before the action gets to you, one of the intervening players sticks in a 3-bet! *Now what?*

In the old days, this play would be pretty easy. The first guy raised from early position, so he probably has a narrow range of strong cards. The second guy reraised, so his range must be really narrow, perhaps as narrow as just AA, KK and AK (a 2 percent range), or if he was a little loose perhaps you could add QQ to the mix (a 2.5 percent range). Either way, your jacks are crushed. You have a 40 percent chance against the 2 percent range and a 36 percent chance against the wider range. (Note that the wider range has more hands that dominate you.) Not good odds for getting all your money in, and calling to flop a set is even less appealing. Therefore, folding your jacks was the best play against the tight players of yesteryear.

Nowadays it's a little different. There are still tight players at the table, but there are also super-aggressive players with 3-betting ranges as wide as 12 to 15 percent, including hands like small pairs, suited connectors, and suited aces besides the premium hands. With this mix, folding medium pairs after a raise and a 3-bet isn't automatic. With deep stacks, you'll still be mostly folding. With shorter stacks, there'll be plenty of situations where 4-betting or moving all in is a perfectly good play. However, each situation has to be evaluated separately, taking into account what you know about your opponents, your own image, and the stack sizes. Let's look at a couple of examples and see what's going on.

Example 3-13. You're in the third level of a live tournament. The blinds are 150 and 300, your stack is 22,500 for an M of 50 (75 big blinds), you're in the big blind, and pick up the T♥T♦.

The player in second position, who has seemed tight so far and has 26,000 in front of him, raises to 900. Players three, four and five all fold, but the player in the cutoff seat, with about 30,000, 3-bets to 2,500, and in the action so far, he has been at least as tight as the initial raiser. The button and the small blind fold and the action is on you. *What's your play?*

You were happy to pick up a nice pair, but unhappy to see the action. If only the tight player in position two was in the pot, you'd have no trouble making the call. His likely range is something like most pairs and the better Broadway cards, and you can play against that range. However, the reraise from the second player is a problem. You're flipping against part of his range and dominated by the rest.

In this case, you just have to fold. Raising is out of the question; you'd be pot-committing yourself in a situation where you're likely dominated by one opponent and possibly both. Calling doesn't work either. You're calling another 2,200 in the hope of flopping a set, a 7.5-to-1 shot. But the stacks aren't nearly big enough to justify this call; most players want to see stacks about 20 to 25 times the size of the amount they have to call to justify the pot odds when drawing for a set. In addition, your call wouldn't end the hand because the player in second position can still reraise. You hate to wait a long time for a nice pair and then fold it, but remember that patience is a big part of being a good poker player.

If I had a pair of jacks instead of the tens, I'd call and play the hand. Jacks is just too strong to lay down. I'd would also call with the tens if on the button instead of in the big blind. Even though my pot odds would be a little worse, the advantage of having position throughout the hand would more than compensate. As for a pair smaller than tens, with or without position, they would be instantly folded.

Example 3-14. It's the second day of a big live tournament. The blinds are 500 and 1,000, with a 100 chip ante. The table is nine-handed and the starting pot is 2,400 chips. You have the J♣J♠ in the big blind and a stack of 180,000 (M = 75, 180 big blinds).

The action folds to the player in third position who's been aggressive and has played well. But he just lost most of his chips in an unlucky showdown and now has 5,200 left (M = 2.2). He moves all-in.

The action now folds around to the button, another aggressive, strong player. His stack is 120,000 or so (M = 50, 120 big blinds), and he raises to 13,000. The small blind folds and now it's your turn. *What do you do?*

As in the previous example, you have a good medium pair and there's been a raise and a 3-bet in front of you. But the similarity ends there. The initial raiser has a tiny stack and needs to make a move quickly. His range could be anywhere from 40 to 70 percent of his hands, and being a good player, the button knows this, and also should have a wide range. His 3-bet is likely a shutout move, designed to keep the blinds from entering the pot with medium-strength hands. He wants the pot for himself.

Compared to the button's range, you have a monster hand. Therefore, your play here is to 4-bet to something like 35,000. The initial raiser is now irrelevant, and the only opponent you care about is the button.

However, before you announce your action, it's important to be clear in your mind about what you'll do if he 5-bets. Since your 4-bet was to 30 percent of his stack, he's pot-committed if he keeps going in the hand, so his choices will be to fold or to 5-bet all-in. This means that you need to know how to respond to that 5-bet.

Under normal circumstances, you shouldn't like the idea of getting all-in with deep stacks and just a pair of jacks. Here, however, it's the right play. The 3-bettor knew the original raiser's range was very wide, so he could 3-bet with a wide range himself. You know this and thus can 4-bet him with a wide range (for 4-betting). But the 3-bettor also knows you knew, so a 5-bet from him could again represent a wide range. But what you know that he doesn't is that your 4-bet came from a hand near the top of your wide range. And so you have to call because your hand rates to be solidly better than what he has.

Scenario No. 5: You opened the pot with a raise and get 3-bet. The variation where you start out raising and then get 3-bet is tricky to play. You have five possible responses: folding, calling, 4-betting with the intention of folding, 4-betting with the intention of moving all-in, and moving all-in directly. Let's look at each move in turn and see when they might be most effective.

1. **Folding.** This might have been a play in the era of tight players and tight tables where a reraise meant a monster hand. But at today's tables, with their wide ranges and aggressive 3-betting, it's an almost impossible choice. To justify folding, you'd need to be in a situation where you had a tight image, the 3-bettor had a tight image, and the stacks were small to medium so your implied odds were questionable. Of the five choices, this will usually be the second-worst.

2. **Calling.** Calling is the standard play and often the best choice. You don't give away much information, you avoid being taken off the hand, and by keeping the pot small, you generate the best possible implied odds for hitting a set.

3. **4-betting with the intention of folding if raised.** In most cases, this will be the worst choice available. The exception is against a player where you're fairly certain his 3-betting range is wide but his calling or raising range against a 4-bet is very tight. There are players who fit this profile, but you'll rarely develop enough information in tournament situations to identify them. So calling and preserving the equity of your middle pair is almost always a better option.

4. **4-betting with the intention of pushing if raised or calling if pushed upon.** This is a move when the effective stack produces an M between about 12 and 22 (30 to 50 big blinds). In this area, ranges are wide and your middle pair is too strong to fold.

5. **Moving all-in.** This is the play when you or your opponent have an M between about 7 and 12 (16 to 30 big blinds). As before, your middle pair is too good to fold, but now the effective stack is short enough that moving all-in generates more fold equity than 4-betting.

Example 3-15. It's early in a one-day live tournament that began with fairly short stacks. Right now the blinds are 200 and 400, with a 50-chip ante producing a starting pot of 1,050 chips. Your stack is 11,000, with an M of 10. The table was aggressive to start and has continued that way throughout the day.

You pick up the 9♥9♦ in third position and raise to 900. The player in fifth position, who's been pretty active, raises to 2,200. The remaining players fold around to you. *What's your play?*

Your hand is too strong to throw away with a short M, and your stack is an ideal size to move all-in since a 4-bet commits more than 40 percent of your chips. Therefore, move all-in and hope to double up. If you do, your stack will be big enough to get out of the 'move all-in or fold' mode and you can start playing real poker again.

Example 3-16. You're in the second day of a live tournament. Blinds are 1,000 and 2,000, with a 200-chip ante. The table is 8-handed so the starting pot is 4,600 chips, and the table has been generally aggressive, with a lot of 3-betting. Your stack is 70,000, with an M of 15 (35 big blinds), and you're in the cutoff seat with the T♠T♣.

The first four players fold, you raise to 5,000, the button and small blind fold, but the big blind 3-bets to 12,000. His stack was about the same as yours, 70,000, and up to now he's been as aggressive as anyone else at the table. *What do you do?*

The first point to notice is that you can't consider folding. It's an aggressive table, he's an aggressive player, and your raising range from the cutoff is wide, so his 3-betting range should be loose. Also, your hand is near the top of your range, and probably doing well against his 3-betting range. In addition, your M is relatively low and you've picked up a big hand. Hence, we can eliminate both folding and 4-bet/folding from your possible actions. This reduces us to three choices: calling, 4-bet/calling, and moving all-in. Let's consider each one.

1. **Moving all-in.** Not a terrible play at this stage of the tournament, but it's a little too much for your stack size. Such a big bet will fold out most of his range, but his calling hands will either be dominating a pair of tens or in a coin flip against you. If his 3-betting range was huge, this play could be very profitable because you'd be making him fold a lot of hands. But you can't be sure of that here, so moving all-in looks a little too big.

2. **4-betting.** A good 4-bet here would be to about 26,000, and that's a reasonable play. Your intention would be to call if he puts you all-in, and the 4-bet will fold out some of the weak hands in his range. But it still looks small enough that he may feel you've left yourself some room to fold. And in this case, he may push with some hands you're doing well against.

3. **Calling.** This quiet play lets you postpone the all-in decision until you see the flop. Since a good chunk of his 3-betting range are ace-high hands, your intention would be to let the pot go if an ace or two overcards hit, but be prepared to get all the chips in if the flop has just one non-ace overcard or no overcards at all. Calling has the additional merit of keeping all the hands you beat in play, which could result in your opponent making a big mistake after the flop.

Playing the Small Pairs (77 down through 22)

Below the premium pairs and the middle pairs lie the six small pairs: sevens down through deuces. These hands occupy an odd little niche all their own. Before the flop, a small pair is likely to be the best hand at the table. You're only dealt a pair once in 17 hands, so if you pick up a small pair under-the-gun at a nine-handed table, you're a favorite to have the best hand at that point. However, once the flop arrives, the value of a small pair either soars or plummets. If you hit a set, (about 7.5-to-1 against) you have a monster hand. If not, you'll probably be facing some number of overcards and now hold a bluffing hand with very few outs.

The strength of small pairs depends heavily on the stack sizes at the table. With deep stacks, small pairs are powerful because they're getting the implied odds they need to play for a set. With very short stacks, small pairs are good because you can push all-in and be a favorite against any hand that calls with two unpaired cards.

But if the table is mostly medium stacks, small pairs can be difficult to play. With Ms between eight and twenty (roughly 20 to 50 big blinds when antes are present), small pairs don't get the implied odds they need to play for a set, but moving all-in is awkward because the stacks are too large. In this range, small pairs often have to be discarded.

One last advantage to small pairs is that they provide an easy way to loosen your raising ranges without running into a lot of difficult situations post-flop. For instance, suppose you're a tight player and are accustomed to opening under-the-gun with this range:

- Pairs, aces down through tens, ace-king and ace-queen

That's a range of only 62 hand combinations which is a little less than 5 percent of all hands, and since this is a very tight range, once the table gets a good look at you, don't expect much action when you open in first position. Now suppose you do open and get called, and a flop comes the

Your opponent now knows that you either have an overpair or just ace-high, and both are about equally likely. This means it won't be hard to play against you.

A simple cure for this sort of problem is to expand your early position raising range to include all pairs as well as ace-king and ace-queen. A range of all pairs, ace-king and ace-queen includes 110 hand combination, or a little more than 8 percent of all hands. While that may not sound like a big change, your opponents won't be able to read you as well, and you can now pose a credible threat on any flop. So when the set comes on a flop like the one above, your opponents should be caught by surprise and you can win a big pot.

Now let's look more closely at how to play the small pairs preflop. We'll consider four different scenarios:

Scenario No. 1: The pot is unopened or was opened by one or two limpers. When the stacks are deep and the pot is unopened, playing small pairs is pretty straightforward. Just raise from any position. Your goal is to win in one of three ways:

1. **Having everyone fold preflop.** If your image is tight and you're in early position, you'll often get credit for a big hand.

2. **By flopping a set.** The deep stacks give you the implied odds you need for this scenario and sometimes the pot you win will be huge.

3. **By representing an ace or king.** If one of these cards flops, you may be able to win a small pot by betting aggressively, representing the hand that your opponents were afraid you had.

The last variation is important for making the play profitable. If you choose to raise with small pairs, you can't just play fit-or-fold. Your opponents are expecting you to show up with big cards, so use that fact to your advantage.

If you are sitting behind limpers at a deep-stack table, there's no need to overplay your hand. Just limp behind and keep your implied odds as large as possible. If an aggressive player acting after you does raise, just call. Now you're playing to hit a set, and the implied odds you get should justify the play.

If your stack is short, with an M of less than 6 (or less than 14 big blinds with antes in play), then your optimal play with a small pair is usually to move all-in. You'll have some fold equity, and if called, you'll often be a small favorite. Any pair is a great hand when you have a short stack.

With a stack that's small but still too large for moving all-in (M between 7 and 12, or 17 to 30 big blinds with antes in play) your situation is difficult. If you raise a normal amount, someone may move all-in and you'll either have to fold or call with no fold equity and no implied odds. So when this is the case, I'll fold a small pair in early or middle position, but raise in late position, especially if the players behind me have been passive in defending their blinds.

Example 3-17. It's late in the first level of a big live tournament. The blinds are 50 and 100, and you're on the button with 22,500 and an M of 150 (225 big blinds).

The player in third position with about 19,000 limps for 100. He's been limping a lot through this level and seems weak. The player in the cutoff also calls for 100, you look down and see the 6♦6♣, and limp as well. The small blind folds but the big blind, a very aggressive player, raises to 500. The player in third position calls another 400. The player in the cutoff seat folds. *What do you do?*

Call. The pot is now 1,250 chips and it costs you just 400 to call, so your expressed odds are better than 3-to-1. If you hit your set on the flop, your implied odds are enormous with an aggressive player in control and leading off, followed by a weak player who might do anything. To accumulate big stacks in tournaments you have to look for early situations where you can accumulate a lot of chips. This is a good one, so stay in the hand and hope to flop a six. If you miss, you're done with the hand.

Example 3-18. You're in the second day of a major tournament. Blinds are 1,500 and 3,000, with a 300-chip ante producing a starting pot of 7,200 chips. You have 210,000 with an M of 29 (70 big blinds), are on the button, your hand is the 4♠4♣, and the action is folded to you.

You look to your left and check the stacks on the players in the blinds. The small blind has about 35,000 with an M of about 5. The big blind has a little over 45,000, with an M of about 6. The table in general has been active, but these players have been a little tighter than average. *What's your play?*

Raise to about 45,000, enough to put either blind all-in. Ideally, you'd like to pick up the pot, and mostly that's what will happen. If not, you don't mind a coin flip for less than one-quarter of your stack; it's very unlikely that either player has a higher pair.

A normal-sized raise would allow either player to move all-in and put you in a difficult spot with no fold equity. You want to avoid this variation if possible, so just put them all-in instead.

Scenario No. 2: The pot was opened with a raise. You have a small pair and someone in front of you opens with a raise. Here your play depends on your stack size and what you know about your opponent. In addition, position on the raiser isn't as important as it was with the middle pairs because you'll have a clear idea of where you stand after the flop. If the set comes, you have a monster, and if it doesn't, you'll probably be giving up on the hand. Let's look at some different stack sizes and see how they affect your play.

If stacks are deep, just call because you have the implied odds to try to flop a set. On the other hand, three-betting is more problematic since you risk being bet off the hand if your opponent comes back with a 4-bet and you have to fold. Notice that this is not a result you want if your hand has the potential to flop a monster. So calling a raise when the stacks are deep is simple and good.

When your stack is small, with your M in the range of 6 to 12 (15 to 30 big blinds when antes are present), you're in a perfect spot to move all-in over a raise. That's because your stack size is big enough so that your opponent needs a good hand to call, and you'll pick up a lot of fold equity. And if he calls with two higher cards, you're a slight favorite to double up, and if he calls with a higher pair, you can always get lucky.

With a small (but not tiny) stack (an M of 5 or less), just fold. Now your stack is so small that your opponent is priced into a call if you reraise, so your fold equity is gone, and that's not what you're looking for, so let the hand go.

The most difficult situations occur when your M is in the 12 to 25 range (30 to 60 big blinds when antes are present). Here the stacks are not big enough to give you the implied odds you need to flop a set. Remember, when putting money in the pot with a small pair, I like to think that there's a good chance to win at least 20 to 25 times that much if my set flops and my opponent is willing to come along. And the reason my potential win needs to be this big is to cover the 7.5-to-1 odds of hitting a set, plus the chance that I won't win any more money when the set comes, plus the chance that the set comes and my hand still loses. So when calling a raise with an M in this range, this payoff won't be there, so I'm letting the hand go.

Example 3-19. It's late in a big live tournament, and there are eight players left at the table. The blinds 10,000 and 20,000, with a 2,500 chip ante producing a starting pot of 50,000 chips. You're in the cutoff seat with the 4♦4♥, a stack of 1,400,000, and an M of 28 (70 big blinds).

The player in second position raises to 50,000. He's been playing at your table for a few hours, has been very aggressive, and before the raise had about 800,000, so his M was 16 (40 big blinds). The next two players fold, you have an aggressive image, but not as aggressive as the raiser, and the button and the blinds all have stacks in the one million to two million chip range. *What do you do?* You should fold. You can't call because his stack is not big enough to give you the implied odds needed to hit your set. You'd have to put in 50,000 to have a chance of winning his 800,000 plus the 50,000 already in the pot. That's a 17-to-1 ratio, less than what I like to see when trying to hit a set. In addition, there are three players still to act, anyone of whom could raise if you call, forcing you to fold.

Moving all-in would be a play if his stack were smaller, perhaps about 400,000 with an M of 8. Here, it's too big a bet. He's not committed to the pot, so he can fold all his weak hands and only call with higher pairs that dominate you or high-card hands where you're only a tiny favorite. Therefore, folding is the prudent choice.

Scenario No. 3: The pot was opened with a raise and a 3-bet. The stack sizes don't matter much here. When you have a small pair and two players in front of you have shown strength, just fold. Each additional show of strength creates the possibility of a hand that contains a higher pair and has you dominated. Remember also that the more chips you have to invest to call, the more you need to win to justify making the call.

Scenario No. 4: You open with a raise and get 3-bet. With deep stacks, just call and play the hand. That's because if stacks are deep, you're still getting the implied odds you need to draw to your set even after calling.

With medium stacks, carefully evaluate the raise and the size of both stacks. As long as the effective stack is 20 to 25 times or more the amount of your call, then you're getting the price you need and can play. If the ratio is smaller than this, let the hand go.

When stacks are small, tend to fold. Your ideal situation with short stacks and a small pair is to get maximum fold equity by moving all-in on an unopened pot. And once someone else shows real interest, you should be folding your weaker hands and looking for a better spot to move in.

Example 3-20. It's early in a big live tournament. Blinds are 100 and 200 and you're in second position with a stack of 26,000 and an M of 87 (130 big blinds). The under-the-gun player folds, you look down at the 6♦6♣ and raise to 600.

The action folds to the player in the cutoff seat with a stack of about 28,000 and an M of 93 (140 big blinds) who, so far, has been aggressive, but not wild. He 3-bets to 1,400 and the button and blinds fold. *What do you do?*

You should call. The stacks are deep with both you and your opponent having an M above 70. Right now, the pot is 2,300 chips and it costs 800 to call, so you're getting direct odds on your call of almost 3-to-1. In addition, the effective stack, after you call, is your remaining stack of 24,600. The ratio between that effective stack and the chips required to call the bet is 24,600-to-800, or almost 31-to-1. That's well above the 20/25-to-1 threshold I like to see when calling with a small pair for set value.

The fact that your opponent is aggressive is a neutral factor here. His aggression means that if you hit your set, a flop continuation bet is likely. However, if you call or raise that bet, you may not see any more action. That's because since aggressive players play a lot of hands, they have to be able to sniff out dangerous situations and shut down when necessary. A tight player who doesn't see many flops is more likely to walk the plank with an overpair.

Your call also allows you to play with a pretty well disguised hand. Not everyone will call a 3-bet with a low pair, so if the flop comes with a six and a couple of small cards, your set will be well hidden.

Playing Ace-King and Ace-Queen

We've now covered all the pairs, so let's begin to look at the groups of hands that aren't paired. The first group consists of just two hands: ace-king and ace-queen. These are the best of the unpaired hands. Ace-king is obviously stronger than ace-queen, but the two hands play similarly, so let's take a look at some of their characteristics.

If you hold ace-king and the stacks are fairly short, so you can get all the money in preflop, you're in good shape. You're only a big underdog against two hands, aces and kings. Otherwise, you're somewhere between a solid favorite and a slight underdog. Here's a list of the winning chances for ace-king against some possible opposing hands. (The numbers are given as ranges because the exact chances depend on whether hands are suited and whether the suits overlap or not.)

Ace-King Winning Results

Hand Against	Winning Percentage (%)
AA	8 to 12
KK	30 to 34
A Lower Pair	About 45
A Weaker Ace	70 to 74
A Weaker King	About 75
Two Lower Cards	60 to 65

If you hold ace-king and don't get all the money in preflop, the picture changes. Ace-king is a reverse implied odds hand; it tends to win small pots and lose bigger ones. When ace-king connects with the flop, it mostly makes top pair, top kicker. That's a nice hand and is often best, but your opponent won't be inclined to put a lot of money in if he can't beat that hand or isn't drawing to a hand that can beat it. As a result, when you make top pair with ace-king and your flop bet gets called, you're frequently in a tough spot. Does he have a set or two pair? Is he drawing? Is he floating? Even if you miss the flop your ace-high hand may be best, but if your opponent doesn't go away, it can be a difficult hand to play all the way to the river.

However, none of this means that ace-king is bad. In fact, it's a good hand, but it does take some skill to play well. In contrast, a small pair is easy to play well. If you connect with the flop you have a huge hand, and your 'problem' is how to extract the most money from your opponent.

Ace-queen is similar to ace-king, only less so. Ace-king was an underdog against six possible card combinations: three pairs of aces and three pairs of kings. (If you hold ace-king, there are only three aces and three kings out against you, hence fewer possible pairs.) In contrast, ace-queen is an underdog against 24 possible card combinations: three pairs of aces, six pairs of kings, three pairs of queens, and twelve possible ace-king combinations. That's four times as many hands that can dominate you. Ace-queen is still a good hand, but when you run into resistance, you're more likely to be in trouble.

Now let's talk about how to play ace-king and ace-queen preflop. We'll consider four scenarios:

Scenario No. 1: The pot is unopened, or was opened by one or two limpers. If the stacks are deep, just make a normal raise, and if a limper or two has come into the pot, raise an extra big blind for each limper. Ace-king and ace-queen are strong hands and there's no reason to shy from building a pot.

With a medium stack (M in the range from 20 to 60), you'll play the same way. Just make the normal raise for your table and see what happens. Attack the limpers in the same way as with a large stack.

With a small stack (M less than 20 or less than 50 big blinds), play gets a little trickier. The problem isn't avoiding pot-commitment; with strong hands like these, you certainly want to get all your chips in the middle. The problem is figuring out the best way to play so the chance of getting all-in preflop is maximized. You'll need to pay close attention to the players yet to act, their tendencies, and their stack sizes. Let's look at a couple of examples.

Example 3-21. It's fairly late in a live tournament. About 20 percent of the field remains and 10 percent get paid, so you're still quite a ways from the bubble. The table is 8-handed, blinds are now 3,000 and 6,000, with a 600-chip ante producing a starting pot of 13,800 chips, you're in second position with a stack of 54,000 (the shortest stack at the table), and your M is above 4 (9 big blinds). You hold the A♣Q♦. The standard opening raise at the table has been 2.5 big blinds for quite a while. The first player folds. *What do you do?*

With an M under 5 you should move all-in. A normal-sized raise here would be in the range of 14,000 to 18,000. A raise of that size would consume about 30 percent of your stack, so if you raised and then folded, your M would be down to 3, and an M that small doesn't have much fold equity on subsequent bets. Remember, with a small stack and a strong hand, you're committed to the pot. So get your money in and see what happens.

There is also an argument for just making a normal-sized raise in this case. By raising to, say, 15,000, you're left with a stack of 39,000. Someone behind you might see the opportunity to make a perfectly-sized 3-bet by putting you all-in, and since you're going to call anyway, you will then call. Notice that all the money has now gone in the pot while giving your opponent the impression that his bet had some fold equity.

But there's a problem with this argument. If the players at the table have any skill at all, they'll realize that your normal-sized raise with a very small stack is in fact a pot-committing bet, and will suspect that you likely have a strong hand while an all-in move could be more or less anything. So the larger the bet is more likely to get action than the smaller one.

Example 3-22. The situation at the table is exactly the same as in the previous example except your stack is 80,000 (M is 6, 13 big blinds). *What do you do in this case?*

With an M in the 5 to 7 range, you can make a normal raise without being pot-committed, or you can shove. The normal raise is now less suspicious than before, while the shove is a big raise. In this range, it's my opinion that you should do whatever you've been doing over the last couple of orbits. Specifically, if raising to 2.5 big blinds has been your strategy, then do it again. If you've been shoving, then shove. By keeping your raise in line with the pattern you've established, it should minimize the chance that you'll arouse undo suspicion. And if you bet 15,000 and get raised, then, of course, it's time to move all-in.

Example 3-23. It's late in the first day of a live tournament. Blinds are 300 and 600, with a 75-chip ante. With nine players at the table, the starting pot is 1,575 chips.

Things haven't gone well for you in the latest level and your stack is down to 16,000, with an M of just over 10 (26 big blinds). Your image is aggressive and probably a little desperate. Most players at the table are also aggressive and seem pretty competent. You have the A♥K♥ in third position and the first two players fold. *What's your plan?*

A stack in this range (M between about 10 and 15) is perfect for a 4-bet all-in. Since you act first, you should make a normal raise in the range of 1,500 to 1,800 and let the previous action at the table determine the exact sizing. If someone 3-bets, then move all-in when the action comes back around to you. Their 3-bet will probably be in the range of 4,000 to 5,000, so your 4-bet to 16,000 should get a fair amount of fold equity without being a monstrous overbet.

Even with a stack of 24,000 and an M of 15, your all-in 4-bet is still only about five to six times the size of their 3-bet. Also, as the bet gets larger, more fold equity will be generated, but you'll face a stronger range when called. In addition, notice that these two factors roughly balance out making the all-in 4-bet a strong play across the entire range of Ms.

A play that you'll sometimes see from Ms in the 10 to 15 range is to limp with ace-king in early position. The idea is to hope for another limper or two to join in, followed by a big raise from someone looking to take the pot away. However, I'm not a fan of this play although it's worth trying once in a while for variety. A limp from a player with a short stack always sets off alarm bells around the table and the hoped-for raise often never comes, leaving you with a strong hand and a small pot. Put another way, with a small stack and a strong hand, don't overthink the situation. When you make a normal raise, your opponents will give you credit for a wide range and they'll frequently come after you and that's what you want.

Scenario No. 2: The pot was opened with a raise. If you have ace-king or ace-queen and the pot has been raised in front of you, your choices are normally calling or 3-betting. (With a strong hand and position, folding is off the table.) What choice you make depends on a lot of factors: stack size and position are important, of course, but some other considerations will impact your play as well. Here's a list of six factors to take into account, and how they should affect your decision.

1. **Stack size.** If you have a short stack with an M of 15 or less, the best play is just to move all-in. You have a strong hand, you'll pick up a lot of fold equity, and if called, the hand will go through the river which is important for extracting full value from your hand.

   If the stacks are deep with Ms greater than 60, you should mostly 3-bet, although calling is a reasonable play in some circumstances. This decision should hinge on some other factors like the strength and style of your opponents and the speed of the structure, which we'll discuss below.

   With medium sized stacks and Ms between about 15 and 60, you should mostly raise with ace-king and call with ace-queen. Even at the low end of this range, your stack is still too big for an all-in move, but normal 3-bets create a relatively big pot for a hand that's still just ace-high. And as with the deep stacks, weigh all the other factors before deciding on your play here.

2. **Position.** If your opponent raised from early position, you want to call more and 3-bet less. His opening range is likely to be narrow, so your 3-bet won't make him fold as often as you would like. Against middle position raisers, 3-bet more and call less, and against late position raisers, you should almost always 3-bet with ace-king and ace-queen. Call only occasionally to balance your range.

If you have position against the original raiser after the flop, tend to 3-bet more and call less. By taking the lead in the hand, you increase the chance of getting a free card later on, which is especially useful. If you will be out of position after the flop, tend to call. The call will disguise your hand and give you a better chance of making money on an ace-high or king-high flop.

The number of players still to act behind you shouldn't affect your decision much. This is surprising to many players since it might seem that you should be more cautious with several players left to act. However, the combination of a raise and your 3-bet looks very strong, and most opponents will fold hands, like medium and small pairs, that are ahead of you, which they would consider good enough to play when you just call. This helps to compensate for the extra chance that some player wakes up with a genuinely big hand.

3. **Strength of Opponents.** If your opponents are weak or tight, you'll always want to 3-bet and give them a chance to make some big mistakes. Against strong but not especially loose opponents, tend to call more and 3-bet less. But against super-aggressive opponents, you need to 3-bet. You're certainly far ahead of their initial raising range, and also likely to be ahead of their 4-betting range as well.

4. **Your image.** If your image is tight, 3-bet less and call more. Tight players have tight 3-betting ranges, so when you 3-bet with ace-king, your opponents will put you on just the sort of hand you actually have. And if you then hit the flop, don't expect much action unless you're beaten. So calling with ace-king and ace-queen will convey much less information.

The opposite thinking applies when your image is loose. Now 3-bet more and call less. Your opponents will believe your 3-betting range is wide and are less likely to give you credit for a hand at the very top of your range.

5. **Speed of structure.** If the tournament has a fast structure (with the blinds going up rapidly) you should tend to 3-bet more and call less. That's because it's important to gamble more to accumulate chips, and this is an ideal spot for that purpose. If the tournament has a slow structure, call more and 3-bet less.

6. **Tournament status.** At any stage of the tournament where players are particularly afraid to be knocked out, such as the bubble, the final table, and the last hand of the day, 3-bet more and call less.

Example 3-24. It's the middle of the first day in a big live tournament. The structure is slow, with each level lasting an hour and a half. Blinds are 150 and 300. The players at your table seem to range from competent to very strong. The one weak player you had spotted was eliminated a few hands ago and replaced by a known world-class player.

The under-the-gun player with about 30,000 raises to 800. The next player folds and the action is on you with 27,000 and an M of almost 60 (90 big blinds), in third position. So far, you haven't played a lot of hands and your image is tight, the players yet to act have stacks that are roughly similar to yours, except for a very aggressive player who has about 50,000, and your hand is the A♥K♥. *What's your play?*

We're clearly not folding ace-king suited; our play is to either 3-bet or call. Let's run through our checklist of factors and see if they favor one play over the other.

1. **Stack size.** We're deep enough so that 3-betting to something in the range of 2,000 to 2,200 is both strong and non-committing. In a choice between an aggressive play (3-betting) and a passive play (calling), we favor aggression, so the stack size points to 3-betting.

2. **Position.** Our opponent raised from the earliest possible position, so his range tends to be strong and tight, arguing for

a call. But a 3-bet from us with several players left to act will look very strong. So position doesn't strongly favor either play.

3.   **Strength of opponents.** The strong table argues for a call.

4.   **Your image.** Your image is tight, so a 3-bet indicates the type of hand you actually hold. Image argues for a call.

5.   **Speed of structure.** The slow structure favors calling over 3-betting.

6.   **Tournament status.** You're not in a special situation where anyone feels pressured to fold, so this is an argument for a call.

Running through our list of inputs shows one pointing to a 3-bet, one neutral, and four pointing to a call. Therefore, your default play should be calling. On the other hand, if I knew something about this specific opponent that made me think 3-betting was unusually likely to win the pot, or that my opponent had clearly defined post-flop problems, then 3-betting would be my strategy. But lacking this, you should mostly be calling here.

Example 3-25. You're in a live tournament in the middle of the second day and the bubble is still a few levels away. The tournament structure is about average, neither particularly slow or fast. Right now the blinds are 2,000 and 4,000, with a 400-chip ante. The table is eight-handed producing a starting pot of 9,200 chips.

You're in the cutoff seat with a stack of 250,000 (M = 27, 62 big blinds), your hand is the A♠Q♣ and the player in second position, with a stack a little smaller than yours, raises to 9,000. He's a good player, with about an average amount of aggression. Everyone folds to you, your image is on the tight side, and you haven't played many pots in the last hour and a half. The players behind you are competent to good. *What do you do?*

In the tight-poker era of a decade ago, folding wouldn't have been considered unusual. Your hand would have been a tossup against his likely opening range, and there were still three players to act behind you. But I would have called back then, but it would be a speculative call.

In modern poker, you can't fold here; hand ranges are just too wide. Let's run through our checklist once more and see if we prefer 3-betting or calling.

1. **Stack size.** We're nowhere close to being deep-stacked, and while not short yet, we're getting there. On the other hand, a 3-bet would be to about 25,000 chips, about 10 percent of our stack. That's not committing, but it's a big chunk of chips to venture with ace-queen offsuit. So stack size argues for a call.

2. **Position.** Late position is good, and argues for a 3-bet.

3. **Strength of opponents.** Our opponent is at least competent, and so are the players behind us if they choose to get involved. There is no obvious weak target in sight, so this is an argument for calling.

4. **Your image.** We have a tight image, and that argues for a call.

5. **Speed of structure.** An average structure doesn't point in one direction or the other.

6. **Tournament status.** We're not at any crucial stage, so this is not an argument for 3-betting.

Only our position is really pointing to a 3-bet; the rest of our indicators are either neutral or point to a call. Let's call and formulate a plan on the flop.

Example 3-26. You're in a live tournament, towards the next-to-last level of the first day. The structure is slow, with blinds now at

200 and 400, and a 50-chip ante. There are nine players at your table producing a starting pot of 1,050 chips. It's a tough table, with generally strong and aggressive opponents. You haven't done particularly well and your stack is down to 12,500, a little more than half your starting stack. In addition, you've only shown down strong hands and your image is pretty tight.

The first two players fold and the player in third position, an apparently good player who has been solid throughout, and has about 32,000 left in his stack, raises to 1,100. All fold to you in the small blind and your hand is the A♥K♠. *What do you do?*

Most of the features of the hand point towards a call. You'll be out of position after the flop, your image is tight, your opponent's image is tight and he plays well, the structure is slow, and there's plenty of time left in the day. However, your stack is short and a short stack will dominate all other playing factors.

Specifically, if you call, your hand will be difficult to play when you miss the flop. But if you make a normal 3-bet to about 3,000, a quarter of your stack will be invested in the hand. And while you technically won't be pot-committed, if your opponent puts you all-in, investing a quarter of your stack and then folding isn't an appealing prospect.

Therefore, the best play is to move all-in right now. You get the maximum fold equity from your hand, your positional disadvantage is eliminated, you can't make an error after the flop, and you'll be able to see all five cards on the board. The shorter your stack gets, the less all the other features of position matter in your decision.

Scenario No. 3: The pot was opened with a raise and a 3-bet. You're in late position at the table and you look down and see ace-king. You're feeling pretty good about playing this hand. A player in early position raises, a couple of people fold and now another player 3-bets. After a couple of more folds the action is on you. *How does your ace-king look now?*

The answer to this question depends on the relative stacks of the three players involved (you and the two raisers) and on what, if anything, you know about your opponents. If all three stacks are deep and neither of your opponents are crazy-aggressive, then this is a bad spot and you should mostly fold. Now this may seem unduly conservative, but let's look at the other two choices and see where they lead.

If stacks are deep you really don't want to get all your money in preflop with ace-king. In the worst case, you're up against aces which have you crushed, or kings which put you in bad shape. In the best case, your opponent turns over queens or jacks and you're only a slight underdog. (Remember, we stipulated that your opponents were not known to be crazy-aggressive.) If you 4-bet with the idea of calling an all-in or moving all-in yourself over a 5-bet, you'll end up in this scenario. If you 4-bet with the idea of folding to a 5-bet, you've turned your hand into a bluff. Either way, 4-betting isn't appetizing.

Calling, however, raises other problems. Calling and folding to a 4-bet from the original raiser is unappealing. If you call and the original raiser doesn't 4-bet, he'll likely call given the great pot odds he's getting with what was presumably a good hand. Now you're in a three-way pot with decent pot odds and position. That might sound good, but the specter of reverse implied odds now begins to make itself felt.

Suppose, for example, that the original raiser has the

and the 3-bettor has the

The flop comes the

You have the best hand with top pair, top kicker. But how much money can now be made? Probably not much. Neither the jacks nor the queens has any incentive to invest more money since they're in a three-way pot with two opponents who showed preflop strength, and now an ace has hit the board. With the two low cards on board they can't even credibly represent a set or two pair, so it's likely both will fold to the first bet.

Here's a slightly different flop:

Your first opponent has hit his set. Now you can get all the action you want, but you're a huge underdog. The big reverse implied odds inherent with hands like ace-king and ace-queen makes getting involved in big multi-way pots a bad idea when stacks are deep.

On the other hand, when either of the first two raisers has a short stack, the picture is completely different. Take a look at this example.

Example 3-27. It's early in the third day of a major live tournament. Blinds are 15,000 and 30,000, with a 4,000-chip ante. The table has nine players producing a starting pot of 81,000 chips. You're on the button with a stack of 2.4 million, your M is 30 (80 big blinds), and while there are a couple of moderately tight players, the table is generally loose-aggressive, with a lot of 3-betting going on, your image is about average for the table. The first three players fold and the player in fourth position, with a stack of 330,000 and an M of 4 (11 big blinds), moves all-in. The player right behind him, who is somewhat looser and more aggressive than you, and has a stack of about 2.2 million chips (M = 27), raises to 750,000. The cutoff folds and now it's your turn with the A♣K♣. *What's your play?*

Again, we have a raise and a reraise, but because the first raiser has a short stack, the situation is completely different from our deep-stack problems. The original raiser, with an M of only five, is getting desperate, and while we think he has some sort of decent hand, his range is probably wide, likely to include all pairs and most high card combinations.

The 3-bettor surely knows this, so his range will also be wide. Since we also think he's loose and aggressive, his range may actually be as wide as the original raiser. The most likely point of his 3-bet is just to try and shut out the players behind him and get heads-up against the original raiser where he expects to be some sort of favorite.

So our ace-king suited is well ahead of both player's ranges, and our proper play is to move all-in. There's some chance that this action will make the 3-bettor fold, and we'll be left against the original raiser with a ton of dead money in the pot. If not, we'll at least be all-in in a situation where we dominate one opponent and have a coin flip against the other, a pretty good outcome at this stage of the tournament.

Scenario No. 4: You open with a raise and get 3-bet. This is the most interesting and complex preflop scenario with ace-king or ace-queen. You make a normal opening raise, someone behind you sticks in a 3-bet, and the action folds back around to you. You actually have six possible plays, and while a couple of these are pretty rare, the other four all have merit in various circumstances.

They are:

1. Fold.
2. Call
3. 4-bet all-in
4. 4-bet and fold to a 5-bet
5. 4-bet and call a 5-bet
6. 4-bet and move all-in after a 5 bet.

A couple of these are plays that you would hardly ever make. Play No. 4, 4-betting and folding to a raise, simply turns your hand into a bluff. And if you want to bluff, you should be bluffing with hands that have little intrinsic value rather than ace-king or ace-queen which have solid value. Play No. 5, 4-betting and calling a raise, gives you a chance to take down the hand right away, but otherwise puts you in a worse position than just calling right now since you'll be involved in a much bigger pot with a hand that's only about 30 percent to improve on the flop, and when it improves, it may not improve to the best hand.

The other plays are all reasonable in the right circumstances. Let's consider them one at a time.

Play No. 1, folding, is unusual but can be correct. In order to fold, I'd be looking for a situation like this:

1. **Deep stacks.** You can't fold a premium hand against a move from a short stack because their likely range is too wide. Also, for the same reason, you can't fold a premium hand if your own stack is short.

2. **A known tight opponent.** If he's tight, his 3-bet is probably representing a narrow range. If it's narrow enough, even your premium ace may be too big an underdog to call.

3. **A tight image of your own.** If your image is loose, even a tight player may be willing to fool around with a less than

premium hand. But if your image is tight, he probably has something good.

4.   **A small or minimum 3-bet.** A 3-bet that's only about twice the size of your original raise is a big red flag, more often than not pointing to a very strong hand.

5.   **A huge 3-bet.** A very big raise leaves you with bad pot odds to call. Now you're reduced to guessing whether the play is a trap or a bluff. If you're in good shape in the tournament, don't take the chance of crippling yourself if you guess wrong.

6.   **Ace-queen.** In unfavorable situations, I'm much more likely to fold ace-queen than ace-king.

If all or most of these factors are present, I'd be willing to consider a fold. But remember, this is still an unusual play, especially with ace-king.

Play No. 2, calling, is the default play in most deep-stack situations. Your hand is too good to fold, but not good enough to embark on a raising sequence that might get your whole stack committed with an ace-high hand. Calling is a low-variance play which is good when you have a lot of chips, and to give an example, Johnny Chan has practically made a career out of just calling raises with hands like ace-king and ace-queen.

Play No. 3, moving all-in, is the standard play when the effective stack is short, with an M of about 15 or less. Moving in generates maximum fold equity and ensures that you see all five board cards.

Play No. 6, 4-betting with the idea of moving all-in after a 5-bet, is another unusual variation. I'd consider this play under the following conditions:

1.   **Deep stacks.** The stacks have to be deep for this play to be possible, but I also want a stack that's substantially bigger

than my opponent's. Don't make this play if it can cost you the tournament.

2.   **A known super-aggressive opponent.** I'm looking for someone who's shown that he can get a lot of chips involved with a less than premium hand. A player who's been pushing the table around, playing a lot of hands, and making his opponents lay down is a prime candidate. In addition, someone who's steaming after a bad beat is also a possible target.

3.   **A loose image on my part.** When you're tight, people play tight ranges against you. If you've been very active lately, your opponents might not credit you with a big hand.

Put all this together and the 4-bet is a possible play. If in doubt, just call.

Example 3-28. It's late in the second day of a major live tournament. Blinds are 5,000 and 10,000, with a 1,200 chip ante producing a starting pot is 25,800 chips. Your stack is 340,000, with an M of 13 (34 big blinds), you've played a few hands lately, so your image is probably a little on the loose side, your stack is the second-shortest at the table, and your opponents are a random mix of loose and tight players.

You're in third position, hold the A♦Q♥, the first two players fold, and you make the standard raise to 25,000. The action folds around to the small blind, a somewhat active player with a stack of about 1 million. He 3-bets to 70,000, the big blind folds, and the action is on you. *What do you do?*

With your short stack, this is the time to just move all-in. You'd be a little happier if you held ace-king rather than ace-queen, and the situation would be a little better if your opponent were loose and more likely to call with a dominated hand. However, on the good side, your image is a little loose, so your opponent may decide that you're making a desperation move.

But these are all minor points because there is no good plan B. Your hand is too strong to fold given your small stack, and calling leaves you with a very tough decision when you miss the flop. Finally, any raise smaller than all-in commits you to the pot anyway. So move your chips to the middle and see what happens.

Example 3-29. It's late in the first day of a live tournament. You've been doing well so far, but your table just broke and you've been moved to a new table, and are in the middle of the second round of the table..

The blinds are 400 and 800, with a 100-chip ante producing a starting pot of 2,100 chips, and your stack is 98,000, so your M is 47 (122 big blinds). You pick up the A♣K♦ in fourth position, make the opening raise to 2,000, and everyone folds to the big blind who 3-bets to 4,800. His stack seems to be about 110,000, a little bigger than yours and you've seen him play a couple of hands aggressively in the first orbit. (You've played only one pot so far and folded on the turn when your draw missed.) *What's your play?*

Neither you nor your opponent have an established tight image, so folding ace-king isn't on the table. The choice therefore comes down to calling or 4-betting (to something like 11,000) with the intent of moving all-in if he 5-bets. The 4-bet play, however, really requires that your opponent be very aggressive (so that his range is very wide), and you at least have a loose image (so that he thinks your range is wide). He may in fact be very aggressive, but you haven't been at the table long enough to be sure, and you also haven't been at the table long enough for him to have any sure opinion about you. So without solid evidence, 4-betting is just asking for trouble. Therefore, it's best to go for the default play of calling, and you'll then be able to see the flop and evaluate his action before making a decision on how to play the rest of the hand.

Playing the Weak Aces

Our next group of hands consists of what I call the weak aces, namely ace-jack through ace-deuce, suited or unsuited. Up until now, we've been looking at hands that you really wanted to open preflop, almost regardless of the stack sizes, position, or composition of the table. For the hands we'll discuss in the rest of the chapter, that's no longer true. Stack sizes, position, table composition, and image all have a lot to do with whether weaker hands are playable or not.

The problem with weak aces is that they're dominated by better aces. If, for instance, you open a hand with the A♣9♣, and your opponent calls with the A♦Q♦, you're about a 70-to-30 underdog before the flop is dealt. And that's the good news.

The bad news comes when an ace flops. For example, if you two are heads-up and the flop is the

you've hit your top pair and are now a whopping 86-to-14 underdog! If you play these hands carelessly, it's easy to get a lot of money in the pot with little chance of winning.

There is one point in favor of the weak ace that needs to be mentioned. With an ace in your hand, only three aces remain in the deck, so the chance that one of your opponents holds an ace (especially a good ace) is reduced. But you don't want to weigh this factor too highly because the cost of running into a better ace can be high.

The reality of playing weak aces is that unless you hit a really big hand like two pair, trips, or a straight, you're probably not going to showdown even if an ace hits the board, especially if the stacks are deep. If the flop comes and you just have a pair of aces with a weak kicker, you're fighting huge reverse implied odds: the more money that goes in the pot, the bigger the chance you're dominated by a better ace.

Another way of looking at the problem is to ask yourself just what good the ace in your hand is really doing for you. For instance, consider the following thought experiment. You're seated at a table in middle position in a tournament with mostly deep stacks and are against opponents of average competence and aggressiveness. Just before you pick up your cards, a voice whispers in your ear that your hand can be ace-six suited or eight-six suited, your choice. *Which do you choose?*

Beginners will pick ace-six almost every time (unless they suspect a trap or want to be contrary). And why not? Ace-six will beat eight-six in a matchup against most ranges. But let's take a closer look and see what happens with the two hands in some common situations.

Suppose you raise with the A♦6♦ and get a call behind you. The flop comes the

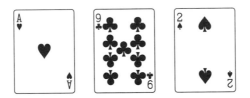

(with no cards of your suit) giving you a pair of aces. Your opponent, who (let's say) started with a low pair, sees the ace on board along with your bet and reasonably folds. That's a good result for you.

But suppose you started with the 8♦6♦ instead. The same flop comes and you bet again. This time you don't have anything but you're representing the ace. Again your opponent folds. The two different hands produce exactly the same result because your opponent is reacting to the flop and your betting, not to the cards hidden in your hand.

Now let's change the problem slightly. Again you raise preflop from middle position, get a call behind you and the flop is the A♥9♣2♠.

Again you bet, but this time your opponent raises. *Now what?* If you started with eight-six suited, you have an easy play: just fold. If you started with ace-six suited, your choice is more difficult. Are you willing to put in a chunk of money on the possibility that he's bluffing? Or do you just fold? If he has what he's representing (a better ace than yours or a set), you could lose a big part of your stack on this hand. Therefore, the prudent play is to fold against most opponents, but it can be a tough play to make in the heat of battle, especially if you haven't seen a good hand for some time.

A similar problem arises if he just calls your flop bet. If you started with eight-six, you're basically done with the hand. You have nothing and he says he has something, so let this hand go and prepare for the next one. But if you started with ace-six, there's another problem. *How far are you willing to go?*

Hitting two pair or trips on the flop is a different story. Now you have a genuinely strong hand and should be willing to get involved with it. But your chance of hitting one of these hands is just as good whether you started with ace-six or eight-six. In fact, hitting two pair with eight-six offers some advantages. Here's an example.

Suppose you started with the A♦6♦ and the flop comes the

Anyone holding a pair between kings and sevens won't like calling your flop bet with the ace on board. And while you may get a flop call, if you keep betting on the turn, it's unlikely to get any more money. However, suppose you hold the 8♦6♦ and the flop comes the

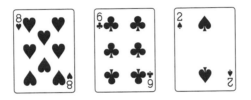

Now you're in a much better position to make some money from someone with an overpair to the board.

And as a final point, eight-six suited offers one upside that ace-six suited can't match. It has the ability to make a well-concealed straight on an innocuous board.

The conclusion from all this is that if you're trying to construct a range of non-premium hands to play in certain situations, weak aces have less to offer than you might think. Because of the strong reverse implied odds and the possibility of domination, you don't want to take these hands, if they only improve to one pair, to showdown in a big pot. But if that's true, you might as well put some other hands in your range and just represent an ace if one falls on the flop.

However, under the right circumstances, these hands are playable. Let's again look at some of the common preflop situations and see how we want to handle the weak aces.

Situation No. 1: The pot is unopened, or was opened by one or two limpers. Unlike the previous hand types, there are no hard and fast rules for playing the weak aces. The decision is affected by the stack sizes, the composition of the table, your image, the big blind's style, and the status of the tournament. In the abstract, I like to fold all the weak aces in early position, open with the better hands like ace-jack and ace-ten in middle position, and make a move at the pot with any ace from the cutoff or button. But the other factors mentioned will have a big effect on my decision in any particular hand, and here's a quick summary of the key factors and how you should weigh them.

1. **Suited or unsuited.** Obviously, suited is better. Not only will it wind up with the winning hand more often, it will also

more often make a monster hand that may win you a large pot, plus it will frequently flop a big draw which gives you semi-steal possibilities.

2. **Drawing to a wheel straight.** The small aces, ace-deuce through ace-five, can all flop a straight or a draw to a straight. Again, being able to make a disguised big hand compensates to some extent for the reverse implied odds inherent in these holdings.

3. **Stack size.** When you have a small stack, M less than 10 or so, and you're looking to move all-in, these hands are useful. Preflop, the ace gives you a shot at having the best hand while reducing the number of aces outstanding. With medium and deep stacks, the reverse implied odds feature forces you to be careful.

4. **Who's behind you?** If the players behind you are weak and aren't short-stacked, there is a strong incentive to play these hands. Someone who is weak and tight can be bluffed out of many hands on the flop or turn while a player who is weak and loose may pay off when you hit your ace and he makes a lower pair. With good players still to act, you will mostly want to fold.

5. **Stack size behind you.** If several players behind you have stacks with Ms ranging from 6 to 15, be aware that they have good restealing stacks and may be looking to move all-in over your raise. Therefore, you should figure out your response in advance before raising the pot.

6. **Your image.** If your image is tight, these hands are more playable because you'll fold out more opponents and get credit for a bigger hand when betting after the flop. With a loose image, your opponents will correctly read you for weaker hands.

7. **Tournament status.** On the bubble or in other situations where players are folding more, these become good hands. You're more likely to win the pot preflop, which is exactly your preference. But when called, you can put your opponent on a strong ace or a good pair and play accordingly.

8. **The big blind.** You can play more weak aces against a tight big blind because he'll often let you have the pot. On the other hand, if the big blind is an aggressive player who likes to defend, folding is better.

Situation No. 2: The pot was opened with a raise. From the previous discussion, you might think that weak aces are an easy fold against an opponent who opens with a raise. If he's a tight player, that's true. But if he's loose-aggressive and your image is tight, the weak aces make good 3-bet bluffing hands. And if his raising range is wide, he'll be folding a large portion of it to your (presumably) tight 3-betting range. But if he 4-bets, you can comfortably fold. The most awkward situation occurs when he calls, but calling ranges against a 3-bet tend to be tight, even for a loose-aggressive player, so this variation doesn't happen often. And finally, using weak aces as your 3-bet bluffing holdings gives you plenty of hands to balance your 3-betting range while preserving hands like medium pairs and suited connectors as possible calling hands.

Scenario No. 3: The pot was opened with a raise and a 3-bet. This one is easy: just fold. Unless the raise and the 3-bet are all-in moves from short stacks, you've got no business in this pot.

Scenario No. 4: You open with a raise and get 3-bet. As in the previous case, you're mostly going to fold. There are, however, a couple of exceptions. If the stacks are very deep, you can occasionally 4-bet as a bluff, folding to a 5-bet. Your ace reduces the probability that he has aces or ace-king, which helps your chances a little bit. The second exception occurs when either your stack or your opponent's is very short, in which case moving all-in is probably correct.

Example 3-30. It's the middle of the first day at a live tournament. The blinds are 200 and 400, with a 50 chip ante producing a starting pot of 1,050 chips. You're in the hijack seat with a stack of 45,000, well above the table average, and your M is 43 (112 big blinds).

The first four players fold and you look down to see the A♠5♠. Here's your quick impression of the four players behind you:

1. **Cutoff.** 35,000, seems to be a good player, tight and aggressive.

2. **Button.** 16,000, M = 15, weakest player at the table, loose and calls too much.

3. **Small Blind.** 22,000, M = 21, definitely weak-tight.

4. **Big Blind.** 34,000, strong, aggressive player who has shown down good hands, definitely likes to defend his big blind with anything playable.

You haven't played a lot of hands but have had good luck when you did get involved, and your image is definitely tight. *What's your play?*

Raise to about 1,000 to 1,100. There are factors for and against raising here, but the preponderance of the evidence is in favor of an aggressive play. Your cards are suited and could make a small straight, which is good. You have two weak players behind you, which is very good. Your image is tight, so you'll get credit for a stronger hand than you have. And only one player, the button, has a stack in the restealing range, but he's weak and calls too much, so a resteal move is unlikely.

The main argument against a raise here is the big blind who's both a good player and inclined to defend his blind. But a good player won't defend every blind, and you can't play only premium hands against such a player anyway. Thus, it's a reasonably good situation overall, and that's what you're looking for, so stick in a raise and see what happens.

Example 3-31. You're in a small daily tournament at a Las Vegas casino. Only 18 players of the original 100 remain at two tables. The blinds are 2,000 and 4,000, with a 500-chip ante, and the starting pot is 10,500 chips.

The first four players fold to you in the hijack position. Your hand is the A♣8♣, your stack is 280,000 with an M of 27 (70 big blinds), and the four players yet to act look like this:

1. **Cutoff.** 100,000, M = 10. A weak-tight player who's been getting whittled down in the last few rounds. He's clearly focused on somehow making the money.

2. **Button.** 85,000, M = 8. An aggressive player who's been up and down over the course of the day. He likes to 3-bet, although the only hand you remember where he 3-bet and got to showdown was a pair of queens.

3. **Small Blind.** 50,000, M = 5. A moderately tight and competent player before his stack got short. In the last two rounds, he's made two all-in moves, each time taking down the blinds without opposition.

4. **Big Blind.** 160,000, M = 15. A tight player who has shown no particular inclination to defend his big blind without a strong hand.

You've been aggressive over the last hour, using your big stack and a good run of cards to take down lots of pots without resistance. *What's your play?*

You should make a normal raise to about 10,000 or 11,000. Although at the beginning of this section we listed a lot of factors that should go into the decision to play a weak ace, there are times when a single factor dominates, and that's the case here. The bubble is approaching and that knowledge will affect all but the most seasoned competitors. You've been doing the right thing, using your big stack to attack the table and pick up blinds. Are the other players aware of what you're doing? Yes. Will they now take a stand and fight back? Some will, most won't. Players who simply want to cash won't jeopardize their chance with a less-than-premium hand, and some won't put their money in with anything less than aces. Under the circumstances, your hand is pretty good, so raise and see if you can pick up another unwanted pot.

However, before you raise, it's a good idea to decide how you will respond to a 3-bet or an all-in move from the remaining players. Making that decision *before* raising will help avoid a foolish error later. Let's look at each player and see what you should do.

1. **Cutoff.** If this guy raises, you have to fold. He's weak-tight and is trying to fold his way into the money. If he 3-bets, there's a good chance you're looking at aces or kings.

2. **Button.** If he raises, it will be all-in because a normal 3-bet would commit more than a third of his dwindling stack. He's aggressive and his stack is short, and after he moves all-in, you'll be getting about 1.4-to-1 against his wide range. Call.

3. **Small blind.** He will push if he stays in the hand and you'll be getting big odds, about 1.75-to-1 to call. And even though he's tight, it seems he understands that he has to push his chips in if he has something, so his range should be fairly wide.

4. **Big blind.** This guy has a stack that's big enough to coast into the money, and he hasn't shown any great willingness to defend his blind. If he 3-bets, he has a pretty good hand. In addition, his range will be wider than the cutoff's range, but it won't be so wide that your A♣8♣ is worth much. Fold.

Example 3-32. It's the second day of a major tournament and you've been playing for a few hours. The blinds are 1,500 and 3,000, with a 300-chip ante producing a starting pot of 7,200 chips. There are several aggressive players at the table and your image is moderately tight.

You're in the small blind with a stack of 240,000 and an M of 33 (80 big blinds). There are three folds to the player in fourth position who's been consistently aggressive for several hours, opening a lot of pots and tossing in the occasional 3- and 4-bet. His stack is 320,000 and his M is 44. He has the biggest stack at the table and you have the third largest. He raises to 7,400, the next three players fold, and now it's your turn, with the A♥6♦. *What do you do?*

Your hand isn't good enough to call, so you could of course fold. But this is a good opportunity to make a 3-bet bluff. Raise to about 18,000 or 19,000, and you'll fold if he decides to 4-bet. But otherwise ,your bluff has a good chance of success. Remember, your image is somewhat tight, so he should give you credit for a much stronger hand than an ace-six, and since he seems to be loose and aggressive, his raising range should be wide, containing lots of hands that's he willing to fold to a raise from a tight player.

There are two other points in favor of this move. First, your risk-reward ratio is good because antes are present. After his initial raise, the pot contains 14,600, and you're risking 18,000 or so to steal it. You only have to win the pot about 55 percent of the time right here to break even. Second, if he does call, his calling range shouldn't contain many aces. Notice that the ace you hold serves as a blocker, so it's less likely he started with an ace-x hand, and if he did hold an ace-x, he's likely to fold for fear of domination. Most of his calling range will be medium pairs, and hitting an ace on the flop will probably give you the best hand. All in all, this is a good hand and a good spot for a 3-bet bluff.

Playing the Broadway Hands (KQ, KJ, KT, QJ, QT, and JT)

A Broadway hand is a no-pair hand with two cards ten or above, but lacking an ace. Like the weak aces of the previous section, these hands have a serious problem with reverse implied odds. If you see a flop hit top pair, it's difficult to know where you stand when you meet sustained opposition. The more money that goes in the pot, the less likely your hand is good, and when flopping a single pair, these hands are notoriously hard to play post-flop. As compensation, they can be very strong when you flop a straight draw, a flush draw, or a combination draw.

Broadway cards have an additional problem compared to weak aces: They can't chase away as many of the hands that dominate them. Let's say you're in middle position with the A♠5♠, the early position players fold, and you elect to raise. Many of the hands that dominate your holding, like ace-six, ace-seven, ace-eight, and ace-nine will be folded since these hands are also weak aces and most players will let them go. But if you're in the same position with the K♥J♥ and raise, the hands that dominate you are ace-king, ace-jack, and king-queen, and you're more likely to face a call from them than from the medium aces.

Despite these drawbacks, the Broadway hands have their uses and you'll play them frequently. Just remember that these hands have to be played cautiously post-flop when you hit a single high pair. Now let's go through our set of preflop situations and see how we want to handle the Broadway cards.

Situation No. 1: The pot is unopened, or was opened by one or two limpers. The guidelines that we gave in the last section for the weak aces apply well to the Broadway cards. When the stacks are deep, fold all these hands from early position. (I'll make an exception for king-queen suited and get frisky with it, but the reverse implied odds are too big to make me excited about the other hands in this group.) In middle position with deep stacks, I'll open with the suited connectors (king-queen, queen-jack, and jack-ten) and play the other hands if I like the look of the players behind me and think there's a good chance to pick up the blinds. With deep stacks and late position, I'll open with all these hands. When the stacks aren't especially deep, the table and tournament situation will determine which hands to play and which ones to throw away (as was the situation with the weak aces). Here's a quick summary of the kinds of issues I'll be thinking about:

1. **Suited or unsuited.** Obviously suited cards are a plus, but unlike the weak aces, I won't be drawing at the nut flush, just the second or third-nut flush. But that's still pretty good. Also, the Broadway cards have a much better chance of flopping a straight draw, either open-ended or gut shot. This provides a little compensation for the reverse implied odds since there will be hands where my opponent has me dominated but I'm drawing to a straight.

2. **Stack size.** With short stacks (M less than 10 to 12), these hands are usually good enough to get all your money in, either with an immediate push or with an all-in 3-bet. But with medium or deep stacks, these hands should be played carefully post-flop because of the reverse implied odds with a single high pair.

3. **Who's behind you?** As with the weak aces, your table will have much to do with your decision to play. And at a weak table, these hands can be cheerfully played. But at a strong table, you'll mostly throw them away.

4. **Stack sizes yet to act.** With very short stacks behind you (M less than about 7), raise and call if they move all-in. Their range should be wide enough that you'll be getting the right pot odds to call. With moderately short stacks (M between 8 and 14) their all-in ranges will be more narrow and your pot odds will be less, so it might be best to fold when they 3-bet.

And when there are a mix of short stacks yet to act, you need to assess the stacks carefully.

5. **Tournament status.** When the bubble is approaching and you have a good-sized stack, these holdings (along with the weak aces) are your bread and butter hands. Raise relentlessly as long as people won't stand up to you. The same logic applies to other tournament situations where people are less inclined to play a hand, like the last hand before a break.

6. **The big blind.** As with the weak aces, a passive player who won't defend his big blind makes you much more inclined to play.

Situation No. 2: The pot was opened with a raise. Some of the most interesting preflop situations occur when you have a Broadway hand and the pot has been opened in front of you by a single raiser. You'll find yourself in this situation many times during the course of a long tournament session, and how you handle yourself will go a long way towards determining whether you end the day with a big or a short stack.

Before we get started, let's note that not all Broadway cards are created equal. I like to think of them as comprising three separate subgroups:

1. The strongest Broadways: KQs, QJs, JTs.

2. The medium Broadways: KJs, KTs, QTs.

3. The weakest Broadways: all the unsuited hands.

The strongest hands are suited connectors combined with some high card strength. The medium hands still have suited power but are a little less likely to flop a straight or straight draw. The unsuited hands are the poor stepchildren of the group. When I'm playing Broadway cards, I'm conscious of where my hand falls in this hierarchy and are only looking to play the strongest hands unless all other factors are favorable. That is, I'm ready to dump the weakest hands unless every other factor screams "Play!" Having categorized the Broadways, let's now look at our choices. If the pot is opened in front of you, these hands can be played in five different ways. As for which option you choose, as with the weak aces, depends on a lot of factors, and here are the five different ways.

1. **Folding** is never an unreasonable choice. Remember, these are not premium hands and you don't have to fight over every pot to be a player. Therefore, I'll fold to a raise from a tight opponent no matter what his position because tight players typically have ranges consisting mostly of the very hands that dominate Broadway cards. An if the raiser is in early position, I'll fold unless he is very loose. But if the raiser is in middle or late position, (unless he's extremely tight), my plan is to play.

   In general, I'm not folding the Broadways against very aggressive players; their ranges are wide enough that my hand should be profitable in position. If in the big blind, I'm again at least calling. The improved pot odds should compensate for the disadvantage of being out of position.

2. **Calling** is my default option and it's my strategy most of the time. In the big blind, I like to call because of the good pot odds. In position, I like to call because — I'm in position! But the small blind is the one spot where great pot odds or good position is not available, and that's where I'll tend to let these hands go rather than call.

   The 3-bet/4-bet revolution of the last few years has turned flat calling into an underutilized option by many players who see it as "too passive" for the modern game. In fact, calling is a powerful option. It lets you see flops at a cheap price with the advantage of either good pot odds or position, and before letting the pot grow to a size where pot commitment starts to become a problem.

3.   **3-betting with the intent of folding to a 4-bet** was a good move with the weak aces, but I don't think it's a great option with these hands. There are two problems:

   A.   If you make this play (a 3-bet bluff) with both weak aces and Broadway cards, you're 3-bet bluffing too much. That's because there aren't enough premium hands in your 3-betting range to compensate for the huge number of 3-bet bluffs you'll be making. Admittedly, in a tournament setting, your opponents will have less time to form an opinion on your 3-betting range, so this particular problem isn't as big a mistake as it would be in a cash game. But, there is another issue.

   B.   These hands play pretty well after the flop, so we don't want to turn them into bluffs before the flop. This point might surprise many players who are so used to thinking of Broadway cards as "trouble hands" that's it's difficult to appreciate that they could play well after the flop. But Broadway cards are only a problem when they flop top pair with no other outs and the opponent won't go away. Often, however, they'll flop flush draws, straight draws, and various kinds of combination draws, and with these flops, they're good hands, not the type you want to waste on a bluff.

   A 3-bet bluff should only be an occasional move with the Broadway hands, usually aimed at an opponent who has demonstrated both a wide opening range and a narrow range for calling a 3-bet. Of course, you'll need to have been at a table for a few hours before you can make that judgment.

4.   **3-betting with the intent of calling a 4-bet.** This play should hardly ever be an option with the Broadway hands. You're better off calling right away and just playing a small pot than creating a big pot.

5. **3-betting with the intent of raising a 4-bet.** Again, this is the wrong idea. These are not big-pot hands. Wait until you see a flop before you plan to commit a lot of chips.

Situation No. 3: The pot was opened with a raise and a 3-bet. As with the weak aces, you should just fold. The only exception would come when both raises were from short stacks with very wide ranges, in which case the pot odds would probably justify a call.

Situation No. 4: You open with a raise and get 3-bet. When you raise with the Broadway hands, you're not hoping for a 3-bet. Ideally, the goal is to take down the pot right there or face just one caller. But when against a 3-bet, you'll need to exercise some caution. Here are a few guidelines:

1. **If the 3-bet is from a known tight player, or an unknown player, just fold.** As stated earlier, you don't need to contest every pot or win every hand. A tight player will have a 3-betting range that includes most of the hands that dominate you, and not much else. An unknown player will have those hands in his range as well. Yes, he may have some others, but since he's an unknown, you won't be able to make a good estimate, and there's no need to play guessing games for a big pot. Just give up and move on.

2. **If the 3-bet is from a known aggressive player who can 3-bet with a wide range, call with position and decent pot odds, otherwise fold.** Let's say you raised from middle position with the Q♠J♠ and an aggressive player on the button 3-bets. Even if his 3-betting range is as big as 20 percent (roughly all pairs, high aces, Broadway cards, and suited connectors), your queen-jack suited is only 45 percent against that range. Even king-queen suited, the best of the bunch, is only a tiny favorite. But if you have position on your side, you can make a case for calling, but folding is perfectly reasonable.

3. **If the 3-bet is an all-in move from a short stack, call.** Here position isn't an issue. His range should be wide and you'll be getting good pot odds. And under these circumstances, any reasonable estimate of his range will give you a call.

Example 3-33. You're deep into the third day of a major tournament. Blinds are 10,000 and 20,000, with a 2,000-chip ante producing a starting pot of 48,000 chips. You're in the big blind with 220,000 after posting your blind and ante, and your M is now 5 (12 big blinds).

The first two players fold, and Player 3 moves all-in for his last 180,000. He recently arrived at the table with a small stack and you don't know much about him. After three more folds, the button, with a stack of 800,000 and an M of about 17, also moves all-in. You've been playing with the button all day and he's an active player with what seems to be a good understanding of the game. The small blind folds and you have the K♠Q♠. *What should you do?*

With an M of 5 you were looking for some action, and here it is. In fact, it might be a little more than you were looking for! Our hand isn't bad, but two players have moved all-in and one of them has us comfortably covered.

Let's start by calculating our pot odds and seeing what they tell us. The starting pot was 48,000 and Player 3 added another 180,000. The button moved all-in, but only the amount equal to our stack counts toward the pot (the rest will be returned to him), so he added another 240,000, making a grand total of 468,000 on the table.

$$468,000 = 48,000 + 180,000 + 240,000$$

We need 240,000 to call, so we're getting pot odds of approximately 1.95-to-1. So to call a bet with those odds, we need to be at least 34 percent to win.

$$0.34 = \frac{1}{1.95 + 1}$$

[Note: We're ignoring here the fact that there's a main pot and a side pot. If we play, the main pot will be a three-way pot with 568,000 chips, while the side pot will contain 160,000 chips and be heads-up between us and the button. If you'll be contesting both pots, lumping them together is much easier than trying to consider them separately, and in most cases will give the same answer. Over the table, you're always on the lookout for handy shortcuts that can minimize your labor.]

So is it reasonable to think that we can win this hand 34 percent of the time? Let's start by looking at Player 3's range. His M is between 3 and 4, and he'll be hitting the blinds very shortly. If he understands short-stack play, he should be willing to move all-in with a very wide range.

The button seems to be a sharp player, so he probably understands this. In addition, his all-in move with a good-sized stack looks like an attempt to shut out any marginal calling hand which likely indicates that he'd like someone with a hand like yours to fold. Thus, this provides you with a good incentive to call.

A quick analysis like this indicates that calling should be a good play. Away from the table we can run this situation through one of the hand simulators, giving Player 3 a very wide range while giving the button a generous range but not including hands like aces, king, and queens where he would probably raise a little less hoping to entice someone else into the pot. And under those assumptions, you'd be more than 40 percent to win, indicating that a call is clearly right.

If everyone in the hand had deep stacks, you would have laid down king-queen suited very quickly after a raise and a 3-bet. However, in short stack situations, high card hands are strong and usually merit a call.

Example 3-34. You're late in the second day of a major tournament. Blinds are 6,000 and 12,000 with a 1,500-chip ante. There are eight players left at your table producing a starting pot of 30,000 chips. You're on the button with 520,000 in your stack and an M of 17 (43 big blinds). You've had a run of good cards in the last hour and built your stack from the smallest at the table to about the middle of the pack. Your image is certainly loose and aggressive, especially since you haven't had to show down many hands.

Three players fold and the player in the hijack seat, with a stack of about 330,000 and an M of 11 (27 big blinds), raises to 27,000. He's an older player who has been somewhat loose and aggressive, but not a crazy man. He also seems to have a pretty good understanding of the aggressiveness required for short-stack play. The cutoff folds and the action is on you with the K♥Q♥. The blinds seem to be average players and the small blind has about the same stack as you, and the big blind has you easily covered with about a million chips. *What do you do?*

1. **Folding** shouldn't be an option. Your opponent has a short stack and there's every reason to think his opening range is pretty wide. You have a good hand which should be ahead of a substantial chunk of his range, and you have position. So folding can't be right.

2. **3-betting and then folding to a push** also can't be right. Let's say you 3-bet to 70,000. Since your image is aggressive, your opponent may credit you with a wide range and also push aggressively. You'll win some hands when he folds, but it's not clear this play will show a profit.

3. **3-betting and calling a push** is a high-variance way of playing this particular hand. It will show a profit, but it doesn't look like the best choice.

4. **Calling** is simple and good, and you get to see a cheap flop where your position can work for you. Of course, there's

some risk that one of the blinds will come over the top with a squeeze play, but neither blind is especially aggressive and every play will have some drawback.

Example 3-35. It's the first level of a big tournament. Blinds are 50 and 100 and you have 30,200, very close to your starting stack. You're in second position with the Q♥J♣. The player under-the-gun folds. Your initial impression is that the table is mostly tight with a number of older players. You've won one hand so far, but don't think you've developed an image as yet. *What do you do?*

Fold. The only aspect of this situation that's favorable for you is the presence of a few tight players. On the other side of the coin, you're in early position with a weak hand and deep stacks. The reverse implied odds inherent with the Broadway hands will be in play. If you had this hand in the cutoff or the button and no one was yet in the pot, you could play. However, in early position, a fold is routine and correct.

Playing the Medium Suited Connectors (T9s, 98s, 87s, and 76s) and the Suited One-Gappers (J9s, T8s, 97s, 86s, and 75s)

Unlike the last few groups we've looked at, the medium suited connectors and suited one-gappers aren't troubled by reverse implied odds. When these hands flop top pair, it's always with a weak kicker, so they are easy hands to lay down when you only have a pair and encounter strength.

You play these hands to flop a straight or flush draw (or in rare cases a made straight or flush). And when the draw comes (especially a straight draw), it can be played strongly. If you have a tight image, your opponents will rarely give you credit for making a semi-bluff move. Instead, they'll mostly assume you're working with a high pair or a set.

Some players might be surprised to find the suited one-gappers included here with the suited connectors, but there are some good reasons to lump the two together. The primary reason is that the two groups of hands are almost identical in strength! This fact surprises many players since the suited connectors have more ways to make a straight than two cards separated by a gap, so they assume that the suited connectors must be stronger. But hand simulation software tells a different story. Look at the winning chances for some suited connectors and suited one-gappers against an identical 20 percent range consisting of pairs, aces, and Broadway cards:

Hand	Winning Percentage	Difference Percentage
T9s	37.6	0.8
T8s	36.8	
98s	38.2	1.2
97s	37.0	
87s	38.0	1.0
86s	37.0	

Notice that the average difference is only 1 percent in favor of the suited connector over the suited one-gapper. And that's much less than the typical 3 percent difference between two suited cards and two unsuited cards of the same ranks.

(The careful observer will note that ten-nine suited is doing worse than either nine-eight suited or eight-seven suited in the examples above. That's because the 20 percent opposing range includes several Broadway hands containing a ten, but almost no hands containing nines or eights.)

It's also good that the suited connectors and suited one-gappers are almost equivalent in strength because it provides us with a bigger group of hands to use. There are only 16 medium suited connectors out of 1,326 possible starting hands, just a bit more than 1 percent. That's only as many hands as the number of ace-king combinations in the deck, and since we're going to use these hands to balance some of our opening ranges, a bigger group is more useful.

Now let's take a look at how we should handle these hands in some typical preflop situations.

Situation No. 1: The pot is unopened or was opened by one or two limpers. In general, you can open with these hands from any position. To a tight player, this might seem very aggressive, but it's really just good poker. The suited connectors and suited one-gappers are ideal range-balancing hands, especially if you've created a tight image at the table. In addition, they're easy to play after the flop if you hit a strong hand or a draw, and if you miss but an ace or a king flops, you can bet and represent ace-king, the hand that everyone expects a tight player to have. But if you miss and can't represent anything, just let the hand go. Remember, as already stated, you don't need to win every hand to play strong poker.

If there is a limper in front of you, just limp behind. The strength of these types of hands is good implied odds in cheap pots against multiple opponents, and this situation is a great chance to get involved at a cheap price. Raising a limper to isolate him isn't a terrible play, but I'd rather do that with my various high card hands.

Also, keep in mind that if you limp after a limper or two, there's a decent chance of a raise by someone behind you, especially if it's an aggressive table. In that case, be prepared to call, especially when the stacks are deep. Limping with the idea of folding to a raise is a bad maneuver, and limping with no idea of how you'll respond to a raise is even worse. As compensation for being raised, you'll usually be getting decent pot odds, and you're demonstrating that when your money goes in the pot, you're prepared for a fight.

Raising suited connectors and similar hands from early position might look like a modern aggressive play, but in fact it has a long pedigree. The first player I saw to utilize this move on a regular basis was Jack Keller (World Series of Poker Winner in 1984). He began making the move in the early 1990s, when accepted wisdom was to raise only premium hands from early position. Eventually other good players realized the obvious advantages of the move and began to incorporate it into their repertoire as well.

Situation No. 2: The pot was opened with a raise. The default play here is to call. If you'll be in position after the flop, go ahead and call because you have a decent hand, some pot odds, and position. If you're in the big blind, position will be poor but you'll have good pot odds. In the small blind, neither good pot odds or position will be available, and I tend to fold these hands in this situation.

However, calling isn't mandatory. You can fold, and a lot of factors come into play that influence this decision. Let's take a quick look at some of them.

1. **How many players are behind you?** The more players to act, the more likely you are to face a squeeze play preflop, and the less likely you are to have position post-flop. Consequently, I'm happy to call a raise from the button or the cutoff, but more likely to fold from early or middle position.

2. **Is the raiser loose or tight?** This question doesn't play as big a role as you might think. If the raiser is tight, your implied odds go up since he's more likely to have high cards or a big pair and less likely to give up when you hit your hand. But loose players will have a lot of weak hands in their range, and they're more likely to miss any particular flop.

3. **What's your image?** A tight image is ideal for calling because you won't get credit for having these hands in your range. Loose players are assumed to be playing these hands, so there's less surprise value.

4. **How many short stacks are behind you?** Calling with these hands is really a deep-stack play. You're relying on good implied odds and a disguised hand to win the occasional monster pot. Short stacks behind you will have wide ranges for making a move and a strong incentive for making a play. Stacks with Ms between 8 and 14 are particularly bad because they're looking for a chance to move all-in over a raiser, and you can get caught in the middle.

5. **Are there aggressive players with deep stacks left to act?** A deep-stacked aggressive player will be looking for a perfect chance to squeeze, and you just gave it to him. The presence of one such player wouldn't stop me from calling, but a second aggressive player would motivate me to look for a better spot.

Is 3-betting ever an option? Yes, but it's certainly not my favorite play with these hands and it's not necessary for balancing your range. As we've seen before, there are better hands for that purpose, particularly hands that don't play well post-flop. These medium suited cards are great post-flop hands, so you don't really want to get blown off them preflop by giving your opponent a chance to make a big 4-bet.

However, there's one situation in particular where 3-betting is so strong that I would do it even with these great implied odds hands. It occurs when the raiser is moderately short-stacked, with an M in the 14 to 18 range (roughly 20 to 27 big blinds if no antes are in play, and about 35 to 45 big blinds when antes are present). Now a 3-bet puts the initial raiser in an awkward position. A 4-bet commits him to the pot, but a call leaves him out of position post-flop with a stack that's about twice the pot, so that a bet post-flop also commits him to the pot.

In this situation, your 3-bet gives you tremendous leverage over his entire stack. That's always a good situation, so I'd 3-bet here even with hands that are normally perfect calling hands.

Situation No. 3: The pot was opened with a raise and a 3-bet.
No mystery here. We're playing these hands for good implied odds, not for butting heads in a big pot. Even with short stacks all around, you need to fold these holdings once two or more people start showing strength.

Situation No. 4: You open with a raise and get 3-bet. Opening with medium suited cards and getting 3-bet isn't an ideal scenario. If the action folds back to me, my default play will be to call. But I'll tend to fold in two specific situations:

1. My stack is short enough so that playing post-flop (especially out of position) will be difficult and my implied odds will be too small. An M under 30 would qualify.

2. The 3-bettor is a known aggressive player. That's because these opponents play wide ranges but will abandon much of their range when they miss the flop and encounter resistance, thus cutting down my implied odds.

Part of the reason for calling is to show the other players at the table that it's hard to chase me off a hand preflop. Once it becomes clear to the table that you're willing to fight for hands when you put money in the pot, players, even the aggressive ones, will tend to avoid playing back at you in marginal situations, and in the long run, that's to your advantage.

Example 3-36. It's early in a big tournament and stacks are still relatively deep. The blinds are 50 and 100, and your stack is 31,000 for an M of 207 (310 big blinds), you're in the hijack seat at a nine-player table, and your hand is the 8♠7♠.

The player in second position limps for 100. He's been tight and conservative, and you assume his limping hands are low pairs and suited connectors. The next two players fold and now it's your turn. You limp as well.

The cutoff, button, and small blind all fold but the big blind raises to 450. He's a young player who's played an above-average number of pots so far and he's usually raising making it appear he'll be one of the most aggressive players at the table. The player in second position folds. *What do you do?*

Call. You're being offered nice odds to play. The pot was 150 to start and another 550 have gone in, for a total of 700 chips. It will cost you 350 to play, so you're being offered 2-to-1 odds. Combine that with your position and a hand that plays easily post-flop, and you have a pretty clear call.

Three-betting is out of line given the situation. You're not looking to build a monster pot preflop with an eight-high hand.

Given the pot odds, folding is only reasonable if you think that you're a weak post-flop player and won't be able to win any pots unless you flop a big hand or a big draw. On the other hand, it's important to develop your post-flop skills sometime; if not now, when? You've got a nice big stack, so gamble a little and maybe you'll learn something.

Example 3-37. You're well into the second day of a major tournament. The blinds are now 1,000 and 2,000, with a 200-chip ante producing a starting pot of 4,600 chips at this eight-player table. After two folds, the player in third position raises to 4,800. His stack is about 150,000, giving him an M of 32 (75 big blinds), and you think he's perhaps a little tighter than average.

The hijack folds and the action moves to you in the cutoff seat. Your stack is now 120,000, with an M of 26 (60 big blinds), your image is about average for the table, and your hand is the T♣8♣.

You look at the players yet to act.The button and the two blinds have stacks of 190,000, 60,000, and 50,000, with Ms of 40, 12, and 10 respectively. In addition, the button has been very aggressive, while the players in the blinds have been tighter than average. *What do you do?*

If no one else could enter the pot and this was purely a confrontation between you and the player in Seat 3, a call would be reasonable. The stacks are deep and he's a little tight, producing good implied odds if you hit your hand on the flop. You also have position meaning some hands should be winnable where you miss the flop entirely.

However, the players behind you are a problem. The blinds might be a little tight, but with Ms of 12 and 10 (30 and 25 big blinds), they have perfect stacks for moving all-in. The button presents a threat from a different direction: he's got a big stack and position, and is aggressive, so he's in a nice position to execute a squeeze play. Taken together, this is more trouble than you need with a marginal hand. Just fold.

Example 3-38. It's the middle of the afternoon of a small live tournament at your local casino. The blinds are now 120 and 240, with a 25-chip ante. It's a nine-player table producing a starting pot of 585 chips. You've been struggling and your stack is down to 6,200 after posting the blind, your M is 11, and your image is loose and aggressive.

The player in third position (14,000, tight, somewhat aggressive) raises to 600, the cutoff seat (11,000, tight and passive) calls, and the button and small blind fold. You're in the big blind with the 8♦6♦. *What's your play?*

The pot was 585 chips to start and another 1,200 just went in, so it's now 1,785 chips and it costs 360 to call. That's odds of almost 5-to-1. And while it's true that you'll be out of position against two players after the flop, both have you easily covered, and your stack is too small for good implied odds, the correct play is to call. That's because your hand could develop into something, it will be easy to play, and the pot odds are huge. Now I wouldn't call with total trash, but two suited cards close together with those kind of odds are good enough.

Playing Other Hands

The hands we've examined so far — pairs, aces, Broadway cards and the medium suited connectors and one-gappers — comprise about 30 percent of all the possible starting hands. With that many hands to choose from, there's no real need in normal situations to play hands that are weaker. Furthermore, even though you'll often be folding some of these good hands because of the betting action, there are still plenty of hands to play, and over time your image will be that of a player who's somewhat loose and very aggressive.

In situations where most of the players at the table are much less willing to get involved in hands, the rules change and you can profitably play almost any two cards. Typical examples include

1. **The money bubble** when players are shutting down to try and get in the money.

2. **The last few hands of the day** when players want to survive to play another day.

3. **The last hand before a bathroom or dinner break** when everyone wants to beat the crowd out of the room.

4. **The television bubble** where players are trying to make sure they qualify to appear on a television broadcast.

At any of these times, your cards don't much matter. If the action is folded to you, open the pot. Your fold equity is so high you should show a profit even if your strategy is to give up whenever you're 3-bet.

Part Four

Playing the Flop

Playing the Flop

Introduction

As players have gotten looser and more aggressive, fewer and fewer hands are decided in the preflop betting; many hands will see a flop and later streets as well. Furthermore, flop betting is now a big subject, and in this chapter we'll focus on some topics that are key to tournament play.

1. **Bet sizing.** *If you bet the flop, how big should your bet be?* As with preflop betting, the modern tendency is to slightly smaller bets.

2. **Continuation betting.** A continuation bet is just a bet from the player who took the lead preflop. Ten years ago, a continuation bet had a good chance of ending the hand. Today, players understand that a continuation bet doesn't necessarily mean anything, so they've become a little less common and are more often called. In this chapter, we'll discuss the best and worst times to make a continuation bet, and how to respond.

3. **Donk betting.** A donk bet is just a lead bet from the player who wasn't the aggressor preflop. These bets used to be the mark of a bad player (hence the name), but now they're recognized as a potential weapon. We'll talk about when to make them and how to respond.

4. **Monster hands and drawing hands.** These two categories of hands share a common characteristic: big profit potential. However, maximizing that potential requires some skill, and we'll talk about what to do and what not to do.

Bet Sizing on the Flop

So the flop has arrived and now you want to bet. *How large a bet should you make?*

In general, when stacks are deep, typical flop bets range from a little less than half the pot to almost the full pot. When one of the players involved in the hand has a very short stack (up to about twice the existing pot), then an all-in move is common. The short stack will realize that any smaller bet will commit him to the pot, so he maximizes the chance his opponent will fold by moving all-in. The same logic applies in reverse, so the player with the large stack will, if he wants to bet at all, simply put the smaller stack all-in.

In deep stack situations, deciding on a bet size hinges on several factors, including the strength of your hand, the flop texture, stack sizes, and any knowledge you may have about your opponents. Let's take a look at some typical bet sizes and the logic behind each one.

1. **Full pot bets.** These bets are usually reserved for situations where the stacks are deep and the flop is very wet; you have a hand, but you need to charge players for trying to make their draw. For example, suppose you have the

and the flop is the

You have a strong holding (top two pair), but many hands could have a draw to beat you. So in this case, a pot-size bet charges them to play while still not committing you to the hand.

2. **Bets of two-thirds to three-quarters of the pot.** These are good bet sizes for value bets designed to build the pot, or continuation bets on boards that are not so dry. For instance, a board like the 9♣8♥3♥ offers some drawing chances, so a larger bet cuts down on the odds being offered.

3. **Half-pot bets.** In a deep stack situation, a half-pot bet is a typical size for a continuation bet on a dry flop. Since dry flops don't offer drawing chances, and since players who miss dry flops often don't continue with the hand, a half-pot bet is big enough to chase away the players who don't want to play on, while losing less when your opponent has connected with the flop and wants to raise. In addition, half-pot bets offer a good risk-reward ratio since if your opponent folds more than one time in three, you will show a profit.

4. **Bets of less than half the pot.** Players make small bets for different reasons. Beginners will sometimes make the minimum bet possible because they want to bet but don't see any reason to bet more than the minimum. Others will sometimes make a small bet for information — "to see where they stand" — although as we've already seen, this is usually a bad reason for betting.

There are two sensible reasons for a small bet. The first is as a blocking bet. You believe that your opponent will bet if it get's checked to him, and your hand is good enough to call that bet. Rather than wait, however, you make a small bet first, in the hope that your opponent will just call that bet, enabling you to see the next card at less cost. Blocking bets are more common on the turn and river, but they can occur on the flop.

The second reason for a small bet is to avoid committing too much of your stack to the hand. Late in a tournament, you'll see many situations where all the stacks are relatively small. And in this case, players will typically bet small amounts, making a move for the pot but leaving themselves an escape hatch, or the appearance of an escape hatch, in case they want to get out of the hand later.

In today's tournaments, small bets on the flop or later streets are becoming more and more common, especially once the deep-stack phase of the tournament has passed. Modern players are increasingly adopting the view that the upsides of a small bet, conserving chips for use later and avoiding premature pot-commitment decisions, outweigh the downside of giving your opponent slightly better pot odds.

Howard Lederer was actually the first player who succinctly explained the advantage of small post-flop bets about a decade ago. He pointed out that small bets work better than you might think not because players are afraid of the small bet, but because they're afraid of the *leverage* of the small bet. Someone who calls a small bet now with some sort of minimal value hand has to worry about calling a series of larger bets down the road, and it's that fear that causes people to fold even though the immediate pot odds might seem to warrant a call.

My own view is that small bets aren't a more "correct" way to play, but rather a tool like other poker tools. At a table where players are inclined to fold to small bets, then bet small. At a table where players will take the odds offered by a small bet, bet one-half to two-thirds the pot. What you've actually seen at the table should always be a key determinant of your play.

Whatever the situation, these are not fixed guidelines. You'll need to vary your bet sizes so your opponents can't deduce exactly what your bet means. However, in general, bets intended for a given purpose should average something like the amounts suggested here.

One final point: these suggestions are intended for flops where you're heads-up against a single opponent. If you intend to bet and you're facing multiple opponents, you should plan on making a larger bet. With multiple opponents, there's a greater likelihood that someone has a made hand that can call you (in which case, if you have a hand, you'd like to get more money in the pot) and also a greater chance that someone has a drawing hand against you (in which case, you'd like to cut down on their odds.)

Interpreting Your Opponent's Bet Sizing

The previous section should give you a good idea of what your opponent's flop bets mean in normal situations. However, in some other cases, your opponents will make unusual bets and raises that can give you a pretty reliable tell on the sort of hand they have. Here are a couple of examples.

1. **The overbet.** You'll usually see overbets (bets larger than the pot) in multi-way pots with a draw-heavy board. A weak player has some sort of made hand (typically two pair or bottom set) but he's terrified of the draws and wants to take the pot down now, so he bets something like 150 percent of the pot.

    This is an easy move to spot but a hard move to do anything about. Unless you have the nuts or a strong combination draw, you have to let the hand go. The problem is that you don't have any implied odds in this situation. He's afraid of the draws, and if you have a draw and call, and your draw hits, it's difficult to get any more money out of him. Yes, it's hard to fold when it's likely you know exactly what's happening, but this is a case where you must.

2. **The small pot-committed raise.** You're heads-up post-flop against a relatively short-stacked opponent who seems not particularly strong or tricky. You hit top pair, top kicker on the flop and make a normal continuation bet. He makes a small raise which offers you great pot odds but leaves him obviously pot-committed. *Now what?*

   This play almost always means a very strong hand — at the very least an overpair, and sometimes a set or two pair. Moving all-in over your bet would have given him more fold equity, but he didn't do it because he probably wants you to call.

   Therefore, for the most part, you'll need to fold. A top pair, top kicker hand is usually about 3 percent to win against a set, about 20 percent against an overpair, and about 25 percent against two lower pair. These aren't good odds, so unless his stack size is unusually small, it's best to be done with the hand.

Bet Sizing Against Short Stacks

When you have a big stack and are at a table with many short stacks, you're in a good situation. There should be many opportunities to steal blinds, antes, and pots, both preflop and post-flop. Your biggest problem both preflop and post-flop will be getting your bet sizing right when you want to play the hand. So when your opponent's stacks are short, you'll need to think carefully about your bet size and how the hand is likely to play before you move chips in the pot. Here are some guidelines:

Guideline No. 1: If you're thinking about making a bet which doesn't put your opponent all-in, be sure to answer the question "What will I do if he then moves all-in?" Short stacks really have only one weapon, and that's the all-in move, and when they move all-in, you'll be offered certain pot odds. So make sure you know if you're going to call or fold if they push all their chips in response to your bet. And if you decide to call, ask yourself if putting them all-in isn't a better play.

Guideline No. 2: Don't give your opponent the perfect all-in. A perfect all-in is a bet that's anywhere from a little less than the pot to about twice the size of the pot. With a perfect all-in, he's not making a huge, inefficient overbet which allows you to either comfortably fold or call if you think the situation warrants. He's also not making a tiny raise which offers such good odds that you can't refuse them. Instead, your opponent will be making a bet which puts you under real pressure and where deciding what the right response is will be difficult.

Guideline No. 3: When in doubt, just move all-in yourself. If you have a real hand and a big stack, and your opponent is short stacked, the right play is to often move all-in. You pick up the maximum fold equity which helps compensate for the times when he has a better hand, and also gives him the chance to make a big mistake while taking the pressure off your own shoulders.

Example 4-1. In the later stages of a tournament, the blinds are 2,000 and 4,000, with a 400-chip ante producing a starting pot of 9,600 chips. You're in the hijack seat, the first four players fold, your hand is the

and you have a stack of 400,000 (M = 42), the largest of the remaining players. You raise to 10,000, get called by the button, a competent player with a 110,000 stack (M = 11), and the blinds fold. The pot is now 29,600 chips.

The flop is the

giving you top pair with a good but not great kicker, plus a gutshot straight draw. A normal continuation bet here would be in the range of 15,000 to 20,000, a little over half the pot. But before you make this bet, it's important to look at his stack size and see what his options are.

There's no problem, of course, if he folds. But suppose you bet 15,000 and he doesn't fold. The pot will now be 59,600 and he'll have 85,000 left. A competent player should realize that just calling leaves him essentially pot-committed. In addition, a player whose starting M was 11 can't like the idea of putting a quarter of his chips in the pot only to fold later in the hand. Therefore, if he has some kind of hand and decides to keep playing, his best strategy is to move all-in.

So if his last 100,000 does go to the center, the pot will be 144,600 and you'll have to put up another 85,000 to call. That's pot odds of 1.7-to-1, and I would call in this spot, but it's not a no-brainer. That's because his bet has put you in a tough spot where automatically calling is wrong even though you're getting great odds.

To avoid giving your opponent this option, just move all-in on the flop. You have a reasonable hand and would likely decide to call his all-in move, so you may as well take away that option while giving yourself maximum fold equity. Remember, as stacks get short, it's best to always consider your opponent's possible responses to any move you make.

Continuation Bets

The most common type of bet on the flop is the continuation bet, also known as a *c-bet*, which is just a bet made by the preflop raiser. A continuation bet represents strength. That is, the preflop raiser said he had a good hand by taking the lead preflop, and now his bet says he's still happy with his hand and is ready to invest more money. The bet *continues* his show of strength from before the flop, hence the name.

The initial raiser has a lot of reasons to want to bet on the flop. If he has a strong made hand, he's making a value bet, trying to build a pot. If he flopped a draw, he's semi-bluffing and giving himself multiple ways to win the hand. If he doesn't have anything, he's making a cheap bluff. And notice that all these types of hands have valid reasons to bet the flop, which is why continuation bets are strong, powerful, and common.

A short history of the continuation bet is in order. *Harrington on Hold 'Em, Volume I* introduced the term to the public, but it had already been in common use among strong players for years. The power of the continuation bet was a big advantage for experienced players in the 20 years prior to the poker boom of 2003-2004. Weaker players in that era tended to bet the flop when they connected, or when their preflop pair still looked good. If they missed the flop, they tended to check, and this tendency gave the good players a steady edge as they were big favorites to win the pots where neither player flopped anything.

But by 2005, continuation bets were well known, and everyone was making them. In most pots, the preflop aggressor could be counted on to toss out a bet. But since most flops miss most hands, the majority of these bets were bluffs or semi-bluffs, and a counter-strategy to overuse of the continuation bets appeared. It became known as *floating*, which is where players would just call the flop bet to see what would happen on the turn. And weak players with weak hands would tend to shut down when their continuation bet didn't work, and their opponents could then pick up the pot with a turn bet.

In today's game, the continuation bet has settled into a more stable equilibrium. There are still plenty of c-bets, just not quite as many as a few years back. Specifically, very aggressive players might c-bet 80 to 85 percent of the time, while more conservative players might hold the number down to 60 to 65 percent. In addition, everyone recognizes the need to check with some good hands, so that a check doesn't simply mean "Take the pot if you want." So in general, c-bets represent a slightly stronger range of hands than a few years back, but players still recognize that a well-timed c-bet is the cheapest bluff available, and a great way to take down a share of the many pots where no one has anything.

When to Make a Continuation Bet

A good continuation bet isn't made at random. It depends on your hand and the texture of the flop, but also on a number of other factors — how many opponents you have, your position, your image, your opponent's image, stack sizes, and the stage of the tournament. In some cases, all the factors align and you know you want to bet. In other cases, the situation is particularly unfavorable and the best strategy is to check. And of course there are some difficult decisions where there are arguments on both sides. Let's look at some of the key factors involved and how they affect your decision.

The Flop

When deciding whether to c-bet or not, the flop is the most crucial piece of the puzzle. Once it arrives, you want to ask yourself three key questions.

Question No. 1: What kind of hand do I have? Depending on the flop, your hand can fall into one of several categories:

1. **A monster — A set on up to full houses and four of a kind.** If you have a monster, other considerations fade away and the only real question becomes whether you want to c-bet and build a pot or check and allow your opponent to try and catch up.

2. **A very strong hand — overpairs and two pair hands.** You can certainly value bet with these, but you'll occasionally check to make sure that your checking range contains some good hands.

3. **Top pair — top pair, top kicker to top pair, weak kicker.** You can c-bet for value or you can check to control the pot size and perhaps make a delayed c-bet on the turn. These hands are good for winning small pots. But if your opponent hangs around and the pot starts to get large, there's a good chance that they have something that can beat top pair.

4. **Medium and small pairs.** The default strategy with these hands is to check and keep the pot small. Medium and small pairs have some value, and it's a real problem if you c-bet and get raised.

5. **Strong draws — draws to flushes, open-ended straights, and some combination of the two.** A semi-bluff c-bet with these hands is very strong, giving you multiple ways to win.

6. **Weak draws — two overcards to the board, an overcard plus a gutshot straight draw, or a backdoor flush draw.** They're typically hard to play because they have some value, and you'd rather not be bet off the hand; but the easiest way to win is to make a c-bet and hope your opponent goes away.

7. **Air — hands that completely miss the flop and leave you with nothing but hope.** Your only way to win is a bluff, and depending on the flop, a bluff might have a good chance of success.

Question No. 2: Is the flop likely to have helped my opponent given the preflop action? Here you have to consider how your opponent's image interacts with the flop. If you raised preflop and your opponent called, you can usually narrow his range considerably. Players tend to 3-bet with high pairs and strong aces, so you can tentatively eliminate them. They also don't tend to call with nothing, so you can eliminate most of the air from their range. This leaves pairs from queens or jacks on down, medium aces, and various Broadway and connecting cards. The non-pairs will tend to be suited in the case of a tight player, but loose aggressive players will use lots of unsuited cards to build their wider ranges.

Let's take a look at a few sample flops and see how they would interact with a typical calling range.

Flop No. 1.

This is your basic dry flop with one high card, two low cards, and three different suits. No strong draws are possible and only a couple of calling hands made top pair: KQ and KJ. Weaker kings would probably have folded, and ace-king would probably have 3-bet. Your opponent could also have a set of sevens or deuces, but he has essentially zero chance of holding two pair.

This is one of the worst possible flops for the preflop caller. If you c-bet and get a call, you're probably facing a pair of sevens (if he initially called with hands like A7, 87, or 76) or a medium pocket pair in the range of jacks through eights. It's also just barely possible that a pocket pair lower than sevens would call, but that's a stretch, and someone who calls here with something like a pair of fours is planning to take the pot away with a move on the turn.

Flop No. 2.

Here's a paired flop that's almost as dry as the previous one. Straight draws are out, but a heart flush draw is now possible. If you c-bet this flop and get a call, you're likely up against one of three hands: a nine, a medium pocket pair in the range of jacks through fives, or a flush draw.

Flop No. 3.

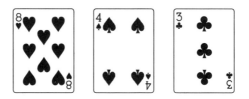

Low flops do occur, and here's a typical example. Your plan should be to c-bet almost all low flops since the preflop caller misses with almost his entire range. But if he calls your c-bet, you can reliably put him on an eight or a pocket pair.

Notice that if you open preflop with something like a pair of fours and now have a small set, your c-bet is especially effective. Anyone with a medium pocket pair will assume he probably has the better hand and should come along for this bet, and probably for another bet on the turn as well.

Flop No. 4.

This is a surprising poor flop for the preflop caller despite the presence of the T♣, and it's almost always worth a c-bet. A big chunk of the caller's range consists of pairs below tens and various suited connecting cards, and that chunk has not only missed but now faces two overcards, making for a pretty easy fold. But if the raiser leads out and gets called, he could be facing a pair of kings, a pair of tens, or a club flush draw. There are also some big hands lurking about: the defender could have a set of tens or treys, or two pair if he initially called with king-ten and might be trying to trap with any of them (if he didn't straightforwardly raise).

Flop No. 5.

This is the typical nightmarish wet flop. It squarely hits the sweet spot of the caller's range with the possibility of flushes, straights, sets, two pair, and all sorts of draws.

How bad is this? Well, if you raised preflop with a pair of aces, got called by a good player in position with an average calling range, and then saw this flop hit, you're about a 5-to-4 dog already! If you consider that you're out of position as well, it's hard to suggest a really great line of attack. However, as a general rule, bet (and raise) strongly if you connect well with this flop. If you've missed entirely, give up. There will be easier and less dangerous places to accumulate chips. If you have something like a single overpair, make your normal c-bet, but be prepared to let the hand go if you encounter resistance.

Question No. 3: Given what my opponent thinks about my range, does the flop appear to have helped me? Now you're asking how your perceived image interacts with the flop. If you're the preflop raiser, it's important to look at the flop through the eyes of the caller and try to see what he sees. If you're a tight player and raised from early position, the caller expects your range to consist of medium to high pairs, high aces, and perhaps some high Broadway cards like king-queen suited. Therefore, he'll be reluctant to call when the flop appears to hit that range.

If you're a normally tight player but included low pairs and suited connectors into your early position raising range (as good strategy dictates), you've got some extra leverage on the flop. If you have a low pair and a couple of high cards appear, consider betting as though you were holding ace-king and be completely convincing. On the other hand, if you're holding a pair of fives and the flop is the 6♦5♣2♠, your c-bet will look more like a bluff and probably get some action, especially if your opponent holds a medium pair.

Loose-aggressive players are in a somewhat different situation. Because they have wide ranges, no particular flop is guaranteed to hit them. However, no particular flop is guaranteed to miss them either. And to a good player, this means that any made hand or draw is worth a call when a loose-aggressive player c-bets. Weak players, however, tend to be intimidated by aggression and are looking for a big hand so they can call (or raise) with confidence. That is, they'll lay down a fair number of playable hands to c-bets while they wait for that monster to show up.

Let's look at a couple of sample flops and see how they should appear to the early-position raiser facing a competent caller:

Flop No. 6.

In the old days, when opening ranges in most positions were tight, c-betting this flop just meant you hit your ace-king, ace-queen, or ace-jack and now had a pair of aces. The normal betting action on the flop was c-bet and fold.

Since those days, several changes have occurred. First, ranges are wider, so the preflop caller won't assume that this flop necessarily connected with the raiser's hand. Second, continuation betting, especially on an ace-high board, is now commonplace and widely understood, so the preflop caller usually recognizes that a c-bet here is often a bluff. And third, preflop callers often understand that calling on this board also represents a pair of aces, after which play devolves into a guessing game of "Who's got the ace?"

So what's the conclusion for the preflop raiser? If he actually has an ace, he can c-bet with the expectation of making a little more money than in the past. If he encounters resistance, he's not necessarily facing a strong hand anymore, just a hand that doesn't yet believe he has what he says he has.

Lacking an ace, the original raiser should still mostly bet. Failing to do so will be interpreted as giving up on the hand, and will probably prompt a bet from the original caller. The bet will sometimes take the hand down, but will often be met with a call which simply means "I don't believe you unless you're willing to bet the turn as well."

Flop No. 7.

To the preflop caller, this flop can't look especially scary. The jack only hits a few hands in the raiser's range and the low cards are unlikely to play a role. This means that if the preflop caller has something like a pair of sevens or eights, he'll be calling a flop bet essentially all the time.

However, the preflop raiser can comfortably bet this flop with virtually his whole range. The reason isn't the strength of the flop itself but the presence of many scare cards on the turn. If the flop action is bet and call, the arrival of an ace, king, queen, or ten on the turn poses some serious problems for the caller. All of these cards could reasonably hit the preflop raiser's range, and continuing on with a medium to low pair suddenly looks dangerous.

Notice the contrast between this flop and the K♥6♣3♦ flop. On the latter, only an ace is a real scare card, and on the jack-high flop, there are plenty of scare cards. However, continuation betting is strong on both flops, albeit for slightly different reasons.

How Many Opponents am I Facing?

After the flop itself, the number of opponents is a key factor in determining whether you want to c-bet. A heads-up pot is the best situation for c-betting because you only have to get by one opponent, and it's likely that the flop missed him.

Facing two opponents is much more problematical. It's now much more likely that the flop helped someone. Hence, I like c-betting here only when my hand is strong or the flop appears to have helped me, like an ace-high flop when I led from early position. With three or more opponents, a c-bet isn't likely to take the hand down. So unless you have a strong holding, it's usually best to let the flop check around and reevaluate after the turn.

Am I In
or Out of Position?

Position is a two-way street in evaluating whether you should make a continuation bet or not. If you're out of position, it's more important to c-bet because you'd like to end the hand as quickly as possible and eliminate your positional disadvantage. If in position, your c-bet is more likely to work, but you have less need to c-bet because your positional advantage works for you throughout the hand.

The most general advice is that you're going to c-bet a little more out of position. Not only is winning the hand quickly a good result, but when out of position, it's likely you raised from early position rather than late position, and hence your opponents will credit you with a narrow range.

What Stage of the
Tournament are We In?

Many players overlook this factor, but it's very important. You should be most eager to make continuation bets in the middle stages of a tournament, roughly from the time the antes kick in to the time when many players start to show up with short stacks (Ms of 15 or less). In the middle of the tournament, your c-bets exert the most pressure. That's because stacks aren't so deep that players can call or float with impunity, but they aren't so short that players are looking to move all-in over the top of your c-bet.

In the early stages of the tournament, you want to c-bet for value a little more, and c-bet bluff a little less. In the later stages, when you're heads-up against a relatively short stack, you always want to factor his stack size into the calculation. *Should you c-bet or just move all-in?* If you c-bet and he moves all-in, what will you do? You should work out the answers to these question before making a continuation bet.

Example 4-2. You're reaching the late stage of a live tournament; about 100 players remain of an original 700. The blinds are 1,500 and 3,000, with a 300-chip ante producing a starting pot of 7,200 chips. You were dealt the

preflop in fourth position with a stack of 200,000, the early position players fold, you raised to 7,000, and only the big blind, with a stack of about 110,000, called. The pot is now 18,200 chips.

The flop is the

The big blind, a tight, competent player, checks. You've been very active for most of the day and your image is loose and aggressive. *Should you make a c-bet, check, or push all-in?*

We can quickly eliminate the all-in push as the worst of the three choices since you'll only be called by better hands. Since you're risking roughly 100,000 to try to pick up the 18,000 already out there, your opponent needs to fold about 75 percent of the time for this play to be profitable. (Note that if he calls and he has the best hand, you still have a few outs.) This play has merit with a pair of queens, but with just ace-high you need to look for something better.

So the choice is between c-betting and checking. If we step through our checklist, here's what we see:

1.   **Flop texture.** It's not the driest flop, but it's not bad for a c-bet since jack-ten is the only holding that gives a straight draw. A heart flush draw is also possible, and there's only one high card which is good.

2.   **Player image.** Your image is loose and aggressive, so he'll think you're capable of c-betting with absolutely nothing. He's tight, competent, and out of position, which would usually mean he was calling with something decent. But he was getting huge pot odds when he called, (14,200-to-4,000 or approximately 3.5-to-1), so his hand could be almost anything except complete junk. Hence, his wide range makes a c-bet look like a good option.

3.   **Position.** You're in position and can milk that asset and see another card if you want. Neutral for c-betting.

4.   **Stack sizes and tournament status.** At the start of the hand, your M was 28 and your opponent's was 15, and his low M should be a warning flag. This means it's important to consider his stack size carefully before you make any bets, and right now the pot is 18,200 chips. If you make a normal c-bet of about 60 percent of the pot, you'll be betting another 10,000. If he calls, the pot will be 38,000 and he'll have about 86,000 left. He won't be pot-committed at that point, but any further action will commit him. But if you make a c-bet of 10,000 and he wants to raise, expect his whole stack to go in.

(Making a normal raise will definitely commit him, so all-in becomes his only move.)

As we look back at this list, we can see that the first three factors are either neutral or slightly favorable for c-betting, but the stack size is a huge argument for checking. With just ace-high, you don't want to see an all-in response to your c-bet. But if his hand has value, he'll see that you could easily be betting with nothing, and he has a short stack that's on the verge of pot-commitment. Both considerations make an all-in move from him just a little too likely. Check and see what happens on the turn.

Example 4-3. You're early in the second day of a big tournament with a stack of 105,000. The blinds are 500 and 1,000, with a 125-chip ante producing a starting pot of 2,625 chips, so your M is 40, and you are currently second in chips at your table. While not having many good hands so far, you've won a couple of big pots when hitting the flop hard.

Preflop, you raised to 2,500 in third position with the A♥J♥ and were called only by the button with a stack of 75,000 and an M of almost 29. He's a loose-aggressive player who 3-bets a lot, and from what you've seen, most of his 3-bets are with pairs or ace-x hands. The pot is now 7,625 chips.

The flop is the K♠4♥3♣ and you act first. *Do you c-bet?*

Yes. This is an almost perfect position for a c-bet to take down the pot. The flop is dry and missed most of your opponent's range. As a bonus, you know that he likes to 3-bet a lot preflop, but here he didn't. This tells you that pairs and ace-x hands make up little of his range, so if he's not holding a king, your ace-high is probably best.

In addition, your image is good since you've won some big pots and many players are subconsciously reluctant to go against players who've been winning, regardless of their style. And since you're out of position and not many cards actually improve your hand, you're happy to take the pot down right now. Plus, both of your stacks are deep enough that stack sizes don't play a big role.

In short, almost every factor is working for you. Therefore, a c-bet is clearly your best option.

Example 4-4. It's late in the second day of a big tournament. The blinds are 4,000 and 8,000, with a 1,000-chip ante producing a starting pot of 21,000 chips. Preflop, you are in second position with a stack of 766,000 and an M of 36, are the chip leader at the table, and your image so far is moderately tight and aggressive.

You raise to 21,000 with the

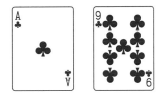

and are called by the player in the cutoff seat, an aggressive opponent with a stack of 450,000 and an M of 21. The flop is the

the pot is now 63,000 chips, and the action is on you. *C-bet or check?*

You have medium pair on a very dry flop which is not a bad hand. If your aggressive opponent called with a pocket pair, it's most likely lower than your nines. (Higher pairs could have 3-bet preflop.) If he called without a pair, he probably missed the flop. No draws are possible, so it's likely you have the best hand. Therefore, based on this information, a c-bet here would be a solid value bet.

Your opponent will also assess this flop as a good one for you to c-bet, whether you hit it or not. He should at least call with any pair as he's unlikely to give you credit for a real hand. He could also float with all sorts of hands using his position to try to win the pot after the flop.

He could also raise, and you should assess what to do in response to a raise before you c-bet. His raising range would consist mostly of monster hands and bluffs, but given the preflop action it's hard for him to have a monster. A set is unlikely because a pair of kings would probably have 3-bet preflop, and a set of nines requires the two case nines, leaving only a set of fives. In addition, two pair hands are all unlikely due to the nature of the board, and given his aggressive nature and the dry flop, it's likely that his raising range is mostly bluffs, so be prepared to call.

Putting all the pieces together, a c-bet of about 40,000 is a good play. So go ahead and bet.

Example 4-5. It's early in a major tournament. Blinds and antes are 300 and 600, with a 75-chip ante producing a starting pot of 1,575 chips. Preflop, the player in fourth position limped for 600. He's tight and fairly passive with a below-average stack of about 21,000. Your hand is the A♥K♠, you raised from the hijack seat to 2,300, your stack is a healthy 66,000, and your image is tight and aggressive. The big blind, who had just arrived at the table, calls, as does the original limper. The big blind's stack is about 50,000, and the pot is now 7,875 chips.

The flop is the 9♦8♠6♦ and the big blind and the limper check. *What should you do?*

Just check. This isn't a good spot for a c-bet. You're against two opponents and the flop was obviously a bad one for your range. Also, keep in mind that the original limper, although tight and passive, has seen you raise and the big blind call that raise, and still wants to play. The only hand that really fits this sequence is a medium-to-low pair, and several of those just became sets.

So take a free card. If an ace or a king come on the turn and the limper checks again, you're probably in good shape.

Example 4-6. It's nearing the end of the first day at a major event. Blinds are 500 and 1,000, with a 100-chip ante producing a starting pot of 2,400 chips. Your preflop stack was 100,000 with an M of 42, putting you in second place at the table.

It's folded to you in the cutoff seat, your hand is the K♦9♦, and you raise to 2,700. You've been active, and your image is aggressive and somewhat loose. The button and the small blind fold, but the big blind calls, making the pot 6,800 chips. The big blind, who is more aggressive and looser than you is also the biggest stack at the table with about 150,000.

The flop is the K♥T♠3♣ and the big blind checks. *Should you make a continuation bet?*

This is a good place to check. You have a hand (top pair, weak kicker) which has good value in a small pot. If you check and the big blind bets the turn, it's an easy call. But if you bet and get raised, your situation becomes very uncomfortable, with a big pot already and the chance of getting very big on the turn.

Hands with solid value and few scare cards are good candidates for checking rather than continuation betting. It's best to avoid big raises that force you to make tough decisions, but at the same time there aren't many cards that will radically change the value of your hand on the turn. (Here aces are the only scary card on the turn.) If you check, you can call a turn bet and get to the river with a small pot.

The Aggressive Check

There's one maneuver that falls under the category of "When not to continuation bet," but it's a special play that really deserves its own discussion. I call it the "Aggressive Check," and it's a form of slow-playing that's especially effective against aggressive players. So let's start with a concrete example and see how this play works.

You pick up a hand like the

in middle position and raise preflop. You get one caller, a loose-aggressive player who plays a lot of hands and isn't shy about betting, raising, and 3-betting. You go to the flop heads-up and out of position.

The flop is something like the

You have top pair, decent kicker and there are two high cards on board (high here meaning ten or better). Your opponent's range was presumably wide, and you should have the best hand almost all the time.

If you c-bet this flop, expect to take down the pot against a loose-aggressive player most of the time. He'll see the two high cards and fold all his medium and low pairs, various suited connectors, and most of his suited aces. He'll call only with hands that contain a queen or a jack, or something like ten-nine, giving him a straight draw.

On the other hand, if you check, the picture changes. Now he'll assume that either you have a monster, you've missed the flop entirely, or you have a jack or a weak queen and you're playing for pot control. In any case, the pot looks ripe for the taking and a loose-aggressive player will bet most of the time, and if you just call he'll probably bet the turn as well. Your check kept his entire range in the hand, giving you a chance to make a lot of money.

Two conditions make the Aggressive Check possible:

1. **Two high cards on board.** When you make top pair on a board with a single high card, a continuation bet will still generate a lot of action from weaker hands because they'll recognize a good c-betting flop. But a c-bet on a board with two high cards should fold out the weaker hands and only generate action from the stronger hands. So by checking, you indicate weakness and get to play a strong hand against his entire range.

2. **A loose-aggressive opponent.** The modern loose-aggressive player makes money by attacking hands where he doesn't think his opponent has a premium hand, and shying away from hands where the opponent sends a clear indication of strength. Failing to c-bet a flop with two high cards sends the message that you either (1) don't have anything or (2) you have second pair or a lower pair and you're trying to get to showdown cheaply. Either way, you've lifted a red flag that the pot is winnable with enough aggression, just what a loose-aggressive player likes to see.

Responding to Continuation Bets

Your opponent raised before the flop and you called. Now the flop comes and he throws out a continuation bet. *What now?*

Much of the answer to this question depends on whether you're in or out of position after the flop, and what you know about your opponent. Let's step through a series of cases and see how you should respond to a c-bet. In all these situations, we'll assume that you're in the early to middle stages of a tournament and stacks are relatively deep.

Case No. 1: Out of position with a solid value hand. When picking up a solid hand like top or second pair on the flop, you can't in general fold to a c-bet. Nowadays, many players will c-bet a large majority of the flops where they took the lead preflop, and since most flops miss most hands, your made hand will often be good.

You don't, however, need to be aggressive with your made hand, especially if you don't fear a lot of overcards that could hurt you. Out of position, my tendency is just to exercise some pot control and call a continuation bet, after which I can wait and see what he does on the turn.

Here's a typical example.

Example 4-7. It's early in a tournament with deep stacks all around. Blinds are 50 and 100. The player in third position raises to 250 and the button calls, and you don't yet know much about either player. You pick up the

in the big blind and call, and go to the flop with a pot of 800 chips.

The flop is the

You check to the raiser, he bets 550, and the button folds. *What do you do?*

Raising is certainly possible here with your top pair, top kicker, but if he reraises, you're in a difficult spot. You can't really lay your hand down, but if he does have an overpair or an eight, it's going to cost a lot of money early in the tournament.

My preference is for just calling and exercising pot control. A key point is that since an ace is in your hand, only one overcard, a king, hurts you. Otherwise, there are no possible draws and you can keep the pot manageable even if he continues betting. Notice that if he has something like a pair of tens, he only has two outs twice, and if he has a hand like king-queen or queen-jack, he only has three outs twice, and giving a free card risks little.

Here's a slight variation that shows when raising is better.

Example 4-8. Also early in a tournament with deep stacks and blinds of 50 and 100. This time you have the A♣T♣ in the big blind. The player in third position, who seems more aggressive than average but still not a madman, raises to 300 and the action folds around to you. The pot is 450 chips and it costs 200 to call, so you're getting 2.25-to-1, and with ace-ten suited, this is an easy call. The pot is now 650 chips, you're heads-up, and out of position.

The flop is the T♥9♥4♠ giving you top pair, top kicker. You check to the raiser who bets 400. *What's the right response?*

Unlike the previous example, the best play here is to raise and try to end the hand now. In the previous example, a king was the only overcard that could scare you. But in this hand, you wouldn't be happy to see a king, queen, or jack on the turn, all of which could give your opponent a higher pair. In addition, any heart could complete a flush, a king, queen, jack, eight, seven, or six could complete a straight, and even a nine could make trips. That's a huge number of scary turn cards, so it's important to make a move now while you're pretty sure you have the best hand. Raise to 1,000 and hope to take the pot down right now.

Case No. 2: Out of position with nothing. When you call preflop out of position and miss the flop, your default play is to check and fold to a c-bet. Floating (calling without a hand with the idea of taking the pot away on a later street) is too difficult when you have to act first. However, there are situations where bluffing at the pot makes sense. Here's an example.

Example 4-9. It's early in a tournament with deep stacks everywhere and blinds of 50 and 100. The player in fourth position, who seems somewhat tight, raises to 275. You call in the big blind with the A♣J♣ producing a pot of 600 chips.

The flop is the K♦6♣4♠. You check and your opponent bets 380. *What do you do?*

There is no really wrong answer here, although folding seems exceptionally tight. Just calling and seeing the turn is a completely reasonable play.

However, the play I like is raising to about 1,000. Dry king-high flops are prime flops for continuation betting because it's hard for anyone to hit them. Your opponent probably thinks you missed, and it's likely he missed as well. So rather than play the hand out of position, make a cheap check-raise bluff and try to win it now. If he reraises, your hand can hit the muck, and if he calls, you're done with the hand unless you hit something good on the turn.

Case No. 3: In position with a good hand. By "good hand" we're talking about anything from monsters down to middle pair. In position and facing a continuation bet, your default play is to just call. With very strong holdings, you're calling to keep your opponent in the hand. Ideally, you'd like him to improve on the turn to a hand that's still second-best. With merely good hands, like an overpair to the board or top pair of some sort, you're calling for several reasons:

1.   To keep his entire range in the hand.

2.   To under represent the strength of your hand.

3.   To allow him to fire a double-barrel bluff on the turn with a hand he would have folded to a raise on the flop.

While calling is the default play, you'll raise in some situations and try to end the hand right now. These situations usually arise when you have top pair or an overpair but you're vulnerable to overcards and cards that could complete draws. Here are two examples.

Example 4-10. Early in a big tournament, deep stacks all around, and the blinds are 100 and 200. The player in fourth position, who's been loose and aggressive since play began, raises to 575. You have the

call on the button, and the blinds fold. The pot is now 1,450 chips. The flop is the

The player in fourth position c-bets to 850. *What do you do?*

The best play is to just call. You have a good hand, top pair with second-best kicker. You're ahead of almost his entire range, and calling keeps all that range alive, and on the turn, you only have one overcard to worry about, an ace.

There's only a tiny chance of a straight draw on this board, but there are two clubs. So there's a small chance that you're giving your opponent a free card to hit a flush, but that's only a small chance and it shouldn't govern your play. The two clubs actually help you in an important way: your opponent may interpret your call as possibly representing a flush draw. When a non-club appears on the turn (which is likely), he'll probably think that his overall position is stronger and yours is weaker.

The final point is that he's an aggressive player which means the chance that he fires a second barrel on the turn is greater. Today's aggressive players look for clues that a bluff is a mistake, and by calling instead of raising, you're sending a message that a second barrel has a better chance of working.

Example 4-11. Same conditions as the previous examples, with most players having deep stacks, and the blinds are 150 and 300. The player in third position, who's about average on the loose/tight scale, raises to 750, you have the Q♠J♠ and call in the cutoff seat, and the remaining players fold. The pot is now 1,950 chips.

The flop is the J♥8♠7♦ and your opponent makes a c-bet of 1,200. *What should you do?*

Unlike the previous case, you should raise and attempt to win the pot right now. You have top pair with a decent kicker, but there are many cards that can arrive on the turn that will make you uncomfortable. Any ace or king could give your opponent an overpair; any heart could complete a flush; several medium and low cards could complete a straight. So by calling, you could face a very difficult decision on the next street. But raising will help simplify any future decision-making, and taking down the pot right now isn't a bad result either.

Case No. 4: In position with nothing. Just because you miss the flop doesn't mean you have to give up on the hand. Continuation bets are common in today's game, and since most hands miss most flops, many of these bets are simply bluffs. One way to counter the proliferation of c-bets is to just call in position, whether you hit the flop or not. This play is known as *floating*, and it's really just the flip side of continuation betting: a very cheap bluff. When the turn card comes, the attacker then has to decide if he wants to fire a second barrel (with nothing), or give up on the hand.

Floating isn't simply a bluff; it's also a necessary part of a good overall strategy. If you're mostly calling continuation bets with strong hands, you need to call at least once in a while with nothing to keep your calling range somewhat balanced. The best hands to float are those which are also best flops for c-betting, including:

1. Ace-high flops.

2. Dry flops with a single high card.

3. Paired flops.

Notice that these are flops where the c-bettor is most likely to be betting with nothing, so a float will have the best chance of winning the pot.

If you float the flop and your opponent then checks the turn, it's often a sign that he's given up on the hand, and you'll frequently win by just betting at that point. Another effective maneuver is the delayed float where you check the turn after he checks, then bet the river if he checks again. By passing up the chance to bet the turn, you give the impression of a solid value hand that's not too worried about the arrival of the river card.

If we compare floating to the alternative play of raising on the flop, we can see why it's a popular move. Whether you raise the flop or call the flop and bet after a check on the turn, you've invested almost the same amount of money in your bluff. But floating allowed you to invest that money with more information, namely that your opponent has checked the turn. But if he fires a second barrel, you can get away from the hand for just the cost of your flop call.

As you might expect, floating is most effective if you've established a tight image. The looser your image, the more a float will be seen by experienced players as a move rather than as a real hand.

Donk Betting

A donk bet is simply an initial bet on the flop into the preflop raiser. As an example, suppose that the preflop action is folded to the player in third position who raises. The action folds around to the big blind who calls. The flop comes and the big blind, instead of checking to the raiser, makes a bet.

The donk (short for "donkey") bet got its name because the play of checking to the raiser seemed so natural that only a weak player would make any other play. If you have a strong hand after the flop, check to the raiser and let him bet, after which you can raise. If you have a weak hand, check and hope your opponent checks behind. In this case, you haven't invested any money and perhaps you'll get to see a free card.

However, in today's game, the donk bet has become a legitimate play with its own complex overtones. If you're the preflop raiser and one of the blinds leads with a donk bet on the flop, you have to ask yourself a bunch of questions:

1. What kind of player am I up against?

2. Does this bet signify a strong hand, a weak made hand, a draw, or a total bluff?

3. If I call, do I want to call again on the turn if my hand doesn't improve?

4. Can I win the pot with a raise?

5. Does either of us have a short stack and does that enter into my decision?

If you call a preflop raise from the blinds, you get to make donk bets too. In this case, you'll need to ask the same questions, but from a different point of view. Let's start by looking at some general guidelines for making donk bets.

If you're facing a tight, straightforward player, the donk bet becomes a solid weapon, although one you want to be careful not to overuse. By donk betting, you've taken over the initiative in the hand, forcing your opponent to react to you rather than the other way around. Here are a few good situations for donk betting a straightforward player:

1. Boards with medium or low cards are good regardless of your hand strength because they connect well with your presumed calling range but will miss most of his raising range.

2. Hands where you have a mix of motley assets are good candidates for donk betting because your bet also functions as a semi-bluff. A typical case would be a hand where you had a medium-to-low pair, plus a gutshot straight draw and a backdoor flush draw. Your bet may win the pot right away, but you have a collection of outs if it doesn't.

3. Range balancing with donk bets against straightforward players is a minor consideration in tournaments because you won't be showing down enough hands to enable players to get a line on what you're doing. An occasional donk bet with a hand like a set or two pair is more than sufficient.

Against players who fit the profile of the young, loose, ultra-aggressive player, donk betting becomes more problematic. Loose-aggressive players will often counter these bets with a raise, which is good strategy on their part. After all, their preflop raise indicated strength, so continuing with another raise on the flop simply says "Yes, I have what I said I had." In addition, donk betting against a flop of medium cards now becomes less threatening since the opening range of a loose player will include many hands which hit that range, and this strategy with weak value hands is also less attractive since a raise will put you in an awkward situation.

A better strategy against loose-aggressive players is to donk bet less frequently, and with a mixture of strong hands, strong draws, and bluffs. You can easily fold the bluffs to a raise, while trapping with the strong hands. The draws are especially good if the stack sizes allow you to come over the top with an all-in reraise.

Example 4-12. It's early in a big tournament and all stacks are relatively deep, and the blinds are 100 and 200. You're in the big blind with the

The player in third position raises to 550. He's an older player and from the action you've seen so far, his style is tight and somewhat mechanical, and after raising preflop, he makes a continuation bet most of the time.

The action folds around to you and getting almost 2.5-to-1 odds, you call for 350 more producing a pot of 1,200 chips. The flop is the

You have a variety of assets on this flop: bottom pair plus a gutshot straight draw and a backdoor flush draw. This is a good spot to lead out with a donk bet of about 700, a little more than half the pot. With all middle cards, the flop is solidly within your calling range, while not likely to have helped your opponent if he raised with two high cards. If he calls, you have jacks, sevens, eights, and hearts on the flop to help your hand.

Most important, your bet will either end the hand (you'll fold if he raises) or give a much better idea of where you stand if he calls. But if you check and call a c-bet, you'll have the same amount invested but his range will not be narrowed at all. And on the turn, there will be a lot of cards you won't want to see, and you'll be out of position with no idea of where you stand in the hand.

Example 4-13. You're nearing the bubble in a big live tournament. The blinds are 3,000 and 6,000, with a 600 chip ante producing a starting pot of 13,800 chips. Everyone folds to the player in the cutoff with a stack of about 150,000. He's a tight, conservative player who's been playing cautiously for a while, obviously hoping to survive the bubble and get into the money. He raises to 14,000, which has been the standard raise this round, and the button and small blind fold.

You're in the big blind with the J♠9♠ and a stack of 380,000. You've been reasonably aggressive but not crazy during the bubble phase, and your stack has increased by about 100,000 over the last hour and a half. You elect to call, making a pot of 35,800 chips.

The flop comes the 8♣6♥5♠. *Should you check or make a donk bet?*

You have a few assets here: a gutshot straight draw, a backdoor flush draw, and two overcards. However, more important than your actual assets, is the situation at the table. Your opponent has an M of about 11, and he's been playing conservatively, trying to get into the money. Now, in late position, he's made a stab for the pot and we can confidently put him on one of two hands: either a high pair or two high cards. That's because a player who's trying to sneak into the money will almost never put 10 percent of his stack in the pot with something like a pair of sixes.

If that's his range, he's not happy with this flop. So if you bet, he's quite likely to fold everything but the high pairs, and a very tight player might even fold some of those in this spot, fearing that you've hit a set or two pair. If he raises, he has a high pair and is willing to go all the way. If he calls, his likely hand is a high pair but he's not yet ready to get all his money in. But what's important is that he'll be folding most of his range right now, so a bet should be profitable. Make a donk bet of about 20,000 and see what happens.

Example 4-14. You're in the money at a regular weekend tournament at your local casino. Blinds are 5,000 and 10,000, with a 1,000-chip ante producing a starting pot of 24,000 chips. The player in second position, with a stack of 700,000, raises to 25,000, and the action folds around to you in the big blind with a stack of 400,000. Your hand is the J♣T♣, you call another 15,000, and the pot is now 64,000 chips.

The flop is the 9♣8♣5♥. *What do you do?*

You started the hand with an M of 17 (40 big blinds) and flopped a straight flush draw, a huge hand under the circumstances. (If your opponent started with a pair of aces, you're about a 56-to-44 favorite.) At this stage of the tournament, be happy to get all your money in right here. So let's look at the best way to make this happen.

Suppose you check and your opponent bets 40,000, a reasonable continuation bet. The pot becomes 104,000 chips, and you have 385,000 left. You could check-raise all-in, but it's a big overbet and the strength of your hand will be clearly exposed, allowing your opponent to get away from all but his best hands with a loss of only 40,000.

Compare this result to what happens if you lead at the pot with a donk bet of 40,000. If your opponent now elects to raise to 100,000, the pot becomes 204,000 and the effective stack is now 345,000. Thus, you can now make a somewhat more than pot-sized bet by moving all-in. Not only is this a more efficient use of your chips, but if your opponent now folds, you've picked up 100,000 instead of 40,000.

In this case, the donk bet not only gives you a chance to win the hand right away, but it positions you better for the all-in move which your stack demands. And thinking ahead this way is a key strategy when your M drops below 15 or so.

Playing Against a Donk Bet

How you play against a donk bet should depend almost entirely on your assessment of the bettor. Different types of players use donk bets (if they make them at all) in different ways. Let's look at some player types and see what a donk bet represents.

1. **The weak straightforward player.** A donk bet from this player usually means middle or bottom pair. He won't bet a strong hand or a draw because he wants to trap with it, and he won't bluff with nothing because it's easier to throw the hand away. He's betting with a medium hand to "find out where he's at" before he invests too much money. The best response is a quick raise, which lets him know it's time to fold.

2. **The competent mid-level player.** A donk bet from this player is rare and usually means a drawing hand. With a strong hand out of position, the mid-level player will reliably check-raise rather than donk bet.

3. **The good, somewhat tight aggressive player.** For most players in this group, a donk bet usually means the kind of hands we've described earlier: draws and weakish made hands with a variety of outs. Pure bluffs and strong hands tend to be underrepresented in their donk bet ranges.

4. **The modern loose-aggressive player.** For today's loose-aggressive players, a donk bet is simply another weapon in their arsenal. They can donk bet with strong hands, drawing hands, weak made hands, and complete air. The best way to treat the situation is to forget that you were the preflop

aggressor and just consider the strength of your hand against their likely range and the fact that you will have position through the hand. If you have a made hand, call and see what happens on the turn. If you don't but the flop would appear to hit your range, float some of the time and see if you can take the pot away on the turn.

Example 4-15. It's relatively early in a big tournament, most stacks are deep, and the blinds are 200 and 400, with a 50-chip ante producing a starting pot of 1,050 chips. You're in the hijack seat with 45,000, pick up the

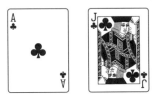

and the action folds to you. You've had a lot of playable hands over the last couple of levels and your image is probably loose. You raise to 1,000, the standard raise at this level for your table, the cutoff and button fold, and the small blind, with about 60,000, who has been the most aggressive player at the table for several hours, calls, and the big blind folds. The pot is now 2,850 chips.

The flop comes the

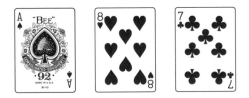

and the small blind leads for 1,800. *What do you do?*

Given what we know of the small blind's style, his range with this bet is wide. Since you raised from the hijack seat, he's probably putting you on a reasonably wide range as well, and thinks that this flop has missed almost all of your range, except the part that contains an ace.

You certainly can't fold, but calling is somewhat better than raising. By calling, you're keeping his entire range alive, and sketching out a range for yourself that includes weak aces, pairs below aces, and some straight draws, as well as some floats. That range is big enough to enable him to keep firing after almost all turn cards. Also notice that your actual holding is near the top of your calling range, so you need to be prepared to invest some money in the hand, and the situation is very +EV for you.

Example 4-16. You're at the end of the first day of a big tournament. Blinds are 400 and 800, with a 100-chip ante producing a starting pot of 2,100 chips.

You're in third position with the K♣J♣, your stack is 70,000, and your image has been tight, so you decide to make a slightly aggressive play and raise to 2,000. The button, who also has been on the tight side, calls the 2,000, leaving him with about 60,000. The small blind folds but the big blind calls, making the pot 7,300 chips. The big blind has just joined the table and you have no line on him. His stack now appears to be about 100,000, the second-biggest stack at the table.

The flop is the T♠8♠6♣. The big blind leads for 4,500. *What do you do?*

Although you haven't seen the big blind play a lot of hands, you do have a piece of information about him: he has a big stack at this point, which means he's more likely to be a loose aggressive player than a tight aggressive player. That's because loose players are more likely to accumulate chips quickly on the first day of play. It's not rock-solid evidence, but it's all you have, so make use of it.

Meanwhile you have a problem. The big blind was happy to lead into the pot despite facing two opponents who are probably unknown to him. You raised preflop from a relatively early position and the other called in position. The flop most likely missed your range, but it might have solidly connected with the caller's. Despite this information, the big blind was happy to lead out when he could have checked instead and waited to see the action. You have only a couple of overcards and a backdoor flush draw, while the big blind is showing strength and you don't yet know anything about the button. You could rationalize a call against just the big blind, but the presence of a third player behind you tips the scales. Under the circumstances, it's best to let this hand go. Stay patient and you'll have much better opportunities to get involved.

Playing Monster Hands on the Flop

For our purposes, a monster hand is any hand of two pair or better on the flop. These include two pair, trips, sets, and straights on the low end, and flushes, full houses, quads, and straight flushes on the high end.

When you flop a monster, you no longer have any question about whether or not you'll play the hand. It's extremely likely that your hand is the best at the table, and you have to play it. The key question becomes "On the flop, will I play this aggressively or will I slowplay?"

In general, this question has an easy answer. Your default should be to play the hand fast. If you can bet, bet. If you can raise, raise. This is the best default strategy for cash games, but it's even more correct in tournaments because of the limited time available to accumulate chips. The best hands for accumulating chips safely are the monster hands, and they don't come along often. So when you're lucky enough to get a big hand, put the whip to it and bet.

Most beginners and many weak players tend to slowplay big hands. They see poker as fundamentally a game of misdirection, and they love the idea of tricking their opponents by representing a small hand when they actually have a big one. And sometimes this approach will in fact work, and they'll win a big pot. But in my experience, the direct approach will work more often, and in the long run excessive slowplaying should cost you money.

To see why playing fast is usually better than playing slow, let's suppose you flop a monster in a tournament situation where the stacks are medium to deep. (Ms of 40 or more, or more than 60 big blinds for each player.) Let's see what happens in each of several situations:

1. **Your opponent has little or nothing.** Slowplaying might pick up a bet if your opponent decides to bluff at the pot at some point.

2. **Your opponent has a hand with some value, like a medium pair.** Slowplaying is unlikely to win much because the standard strategy for these hands is to check or call and try to get to showdown.

3. **Your opponent has a good hand, like an overpair or top pair, top kicker.** The two approaches often get the same result in this situation. Slowplaying certainly allows these hands to bet at the pot. A good player, however, won't want to create a huge pot, so they'll often bet the flop and check the turn, or vice-versa. If you lead out instead, they'll certainly call the flop and perhaps the turn as well, especially if you have any sort of loose-aggressive image.

4. **Your opponent has a big hand, but not as big as yours.** Here the advantage of playing fast becomes obvious. Your opponent will call your bets and may raise as well. Hence, you're likely to win his whole stack in this scenario.

5. **Your opponent has a draw that will win if it hits.** Playing the hand fast may win a small pot if the opponent gives up on the flop or turn, or doesn't hit his draw. Slowplaying may cost you your entire stack.

The conclusion for relatively deep-stack play is that slowplaying and betting aggressively often win about the same amount when your opponent doesn't have much, but the direct approach can win his entire stack when he has a pretty good hand. In addition, slowplaying also contains the risk of costing you your entire stack when he hits a draw.

But as stacks get shorter, the difference between the two approaches disappears. With shorter stacks, it only takes a couple of bets for a short stack to get pot-committed, so either approach will usually work.

Although playing big hands strongly should be your default approach, there are situations where slow-playing is preferable. Here are a few examples.

1. **You have a real monster.** Here we're not talking about two pair and sets but about the really big hands: full houses, quads, and straight flushes. These are hands that don't need to worry about being outdrawn, but they are also hands where it's unlikely for your opponent to have a hand on the flop. Imagine, for example, that you have a pair of nines and the flop is the 9♠7♠7♥. Right now you have a full house, but it's unlikely your opponent has anything more than an overpair or a draw. But by slowplaying, he may catch a hand that could cost him his whole stack on the river.

2. **You're up against a super-aggressive player.** Super-aggressive players play lots of hands preflop. After the flop, they'll try to win the hands where they missed the flop but perhaps their opponent did too. That requires betting at a lot of flops and turns as long as they think their opponent may be weak. So playing slowly allows a super-aggressive opponent to bet the hand for you, while playing strongly tells him you have something worthwhile and allows him to release a hand he might otherwise have played.

3. **You can't represent anything but a strong hand.** On a very dry flop, draws are impossible and two-pair hands are unlikely. And when you bet strongly on a dry flop, you're representing either a good hand or a bluff, while checking and calling represents a weak top pair or some sort of low to middle pair. Therefore, slowplaying these flops may win a bet or two that otherwise would not be available.

Example 4-17. It's early in a major tournament, the stacks are generally deep, and the blinds are 100 and 200. You pick up the

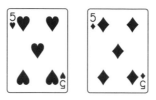

in the big blind. Your stack is 22,000 producing an M of 73 (110 big blinds). The first four players fold and the player in fifth position (19,000) limps for 200. The button, an aggressive player with 31,000 (the big stack at the table) raises to 850. The small blinds folds but you and the original limper call. The pot is now 2,650 chips.

The flop is the

giving you bottom set. *Should you check?*

The best play here is to check. Bottom set on the flop is very good for you, and the king or the ten might have hit either of the other two players. In addition, straight draws are unlikely, and the possibility of a club flush isn't big enough to alter your play, plus it's routine to check to the raiser and let him bet the hand. And since he's aggressive, you have even more incentive to make the normal play.

You check, as does the player in fifth position, and the button bets 1,800. *What's your response?*

You should call. With an aggressive player controlling the hand, there's no need to reveal your strength, and there's also the possibility that the middle player will make a move after you call.

You call 1,800 and the middle player folds. Assuming no club comes on the turn, your plan will be to check again and let the button fire a second barrel.

Example 4-18. Once again, it's early in a tournament with relatively deep stacks all around, and the blinds are 100 and 200. You're in the big blind with a stack of 24,000 and an M of 80 (120 big blinds). The player in third position, who seems a bit on the tight side, but not drastically so, with a stack of about 18,000, raises to 600, the player in the cutoff seat, who just arrived at the table, calls, and the button and small blind fold. The pot is now 1,500 chips. You hold the 7♠7♣, so you're being offered very nice odds and call another 400, making a 1,900 chip pot.

The flop is the A♥8♦7♦, giving you bottom set, and you're first to act. *Do you make a donk bet or check to the raiser?*

Checking to the raiser is standard and would not be a bad play. However, taking the lead with a donk bet is a real option. The difference between this and the previous example is the ace on the flop. In the old days, players played tight ranges and an ace on the flop was likely to hit someone's hand. In the modern game, ranges are wider and aces form a smaller part of the range, so an ace on the flop is more likely to miss. Hence, leading at the ace (with a donk bet) was an almost unknown strategy before, but now it's a play you'll sometimes see from an aggressive player. When the initial raiser doesn't have an ace or has a medium ace, he's now under some real pressure.

Here the raiser was a somewhat tight player in early position, so his range is probably narrower and aces will be a sizeable part of it. That's fine for you because you're just representing the ace. If the leader actually has an ace, he has to come along, as does the cutoff player. It's also possible that one of your opponents will stick in a raise, which is perfect for this strategy.

The other difference between this hand and the previous example is the more drawish nature of the board. In addition to the flush draw, there are two medium cards creating a variety of straight and gutshot straight draws. So your bet ensures that the draws get charged to play, which is always good. Lead out for about 1,200 and be prepared to reraise if either player raises.

Example 4-19. It's Day 2 of a big tournament and the table has a mixture of deep, medium, and short stacks. The blinds are 1,500 and 3,000, with a 300-chip ante, producing a starting pot of 7,200 chips. You're in the big blind with 220,000 (M = 31) and pick up the 6♣3♣. The player in fourth position (160,000) limps, as does the player in the cutoff seat (70,000). The small blind (300,000) also calls, and you check. Your image so far has been aggressive and a little tricky. The fourth position player and the small blind have both been aggressive, and the player in the cutoff seat has been tight and his stack has been dribbling away over the last couple of hours. The pot is now 19,200 chips.

The flop is the 4♦3♥3♠, the small blind checks, and you have flopped trips. *What do you do?*

This is a tough situation because of the number of players in the hand. You can lead out or check, and there are arguments to be made for either play. Let's list the merits and demerits and see which case seems stronger.

If you lead out, you're essentially saying to the table "I checked in the big blind with any two cards, and — lucky me — one of them was a trey, so now I have trips and you're dead meat." Alternatively, you might have nothing and realize that this flop creates a good chance to steal the hand. Your aggressive, tricky image helps here since your opponents may assume that the chance you're betting with air is better than the chance of actually holding a trey and electing to bet it. You should get a call from overpairs, and might get a bluff raise from someone who doesn't believe you. And with three players still in the hand, it's likely that at least someone else will go to the turn.

If you check and either of the two remaining players has an overpair, it's likely they'll take a stab at the pot. If no one has an overpair, it's possible someone with a couple of high suited cards might try to take down a pot that no one appears to want. The aggressive player in seat four might just bet anyway assuming the flop missed everyone and the hand is winnable. If either player does bet, you should plan on calling rather than raising. That's because raising marks your hand as either trips or a bluff, whereas calling could mean a lot of things, including a medium pair or a straight draw. *What's the better play?* There are reasonable arguments for both actions. My guiding principle with a big hand is, "When in doubt, bet out." If the hands are favorable, a bet begins the process of building a pot, while slowplaying too often just tries to win an extra bet. (And sometimes not even that.) In this situation, I'll bet 11,000.

Example 4-20. It's the third day of a big tournament. The money bubble is still a few hours away. The stacks range from moderately deep to very shallow. Blinds are now 3,000 and 6,000, with a 600-chip ante. The table is eight-handed producing a starting pot of 13,800 chips. You're in the big blind with a stack of 500,000, which is narrowly the biggest stack at the table.

The action folds around to the hijack seat who makes a minraise to 12,000. The typical raise at this level has been to 14,000, so this is a little unusual. His stack is about 400,000 and he's been active and aggressive. Action folds around to the small blind who calls for 9,000. His play hasn't been particularly tight or loose, and his stack after calling is about 150,000.

In the big blind, you have the

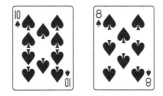

The pot is now 34,800 chips and it costs another 6,000 to call, so you have no choice. You call and the pot becomes 40,800 chips.

The flop is the

giving you bottom two pair on a wet flop, and the small blind checks. *What do you do?*

Unlike the previous examples, your play here is straightforward. You have two pair on a wet board, and while a big favorite to have the best hand right now, you need to try and win it immediately, as there are a lot of turn cards that you don't want to see. (Hearts, nines, and queens come immediately to mind.) So you need to bet, and it should be relatively large. I would make an almost pot-sized bet of 35,000.

Besides charging any draws a hefty price to call, the big bet simplifies your action in case of a raise from either player. If the hijack seat folds and the small blind raises, he'll need to raise all-in and you will then call. If the hijack raises to 80,000 or 90,000 and the small blind folds, you should move all-in yourself. Your hand is likely best and you still have outs even if has a made straight.

With a wet board and a big hand against a known aggressive player, it's important to recognize that you're committed to this pot as soon as the flop lands. In addition, a big flop bet gives you the best chance of winning right now and also enables you to make the all-in move against the aggressive player with the bigger stack.

Example 4-21. The bubble has passed and only a small number of players remain in a major tournament. Blinds are 7,500 and 15,000, with a 1,500-chip ante. This table is down to seven players, producing a starting pot of 33,000 chips. You're on the button with a stack of 300,000 and an M of 9 (22 big blinds).

The player under-the-gun, an aggressive player with a stack of 700,000, raises to 33,000. You have the K♦K♣ on the button and elect to call. Your image so far has been aggressive and you're hoping your image, combined with your relatively short stack, will let you make a play to double up. The big blind, another aggressive player, calls as well. The pot is now 117,000 and you have 267,000 left in your stack.

The flop is the K♠Q♣5♦. Both your opponents check. *What do you do?*

A final group of situations where slowplaying is preferred to betting with a monster are those where someone in the hand is on the verge of getting all their chips committed to the pot. In this hand, that someone is you. Notice your M was 9 when the hand began and now your stack is just a little bigger than twice the pot. And as long as you can get someone else to make a stab for the pot, your all-in move will be seen as equivalent to a call. But by betting after two checks, your only sensible bet is all-in because a smaller bet looks stronger since it commits you to the pot anyway.

Since there is no turn card that will make you consider folding, just check and see if one of the other two players will try to take down the pot. If an innocuous card comes on the turn and both players check again, just check to the river and give them one last chance. With top set, your goal should be to double your stack, not just pick up the existing pot.

Playing Drawing Hands on the Flop

Drawing hands on the flop are intrinsically difficult to play. A drawing hand typically has little or no value at the moment, but a single card on the turn can turn it into a monster. The dual nature of the hand means that many different betting lines will be possible, and choosing the right line will be difficult, especially when compared to most other hands. Your position, stack size, image, and number of opponents all play a role.

The standard line with a drawing hand is the semi-bluff: you bet or raise, and your move gives you a couple of ways to win. That is if your opponent can fold, or (if he calls) you hit your draw on the turn or the river.

The basic semi-bluff works well if you're in position, but less well when that's not the case. And when semi-bluffing, you'd ideally like to see both the turn and river cards for the price of one bet. So notice that when in position, you can bet the flop, and if your opponent calls he will often check on the turn, giving you the choice of seeing the river for free. But this doesn't work so well when out of position since you have to act first on the turn.

First, let's take a look at the different possible lines you can take with a drawing hand on the flop when you're in position and see what circumstances are typically the best for each line.

In Position Line No. 1: Opponent checks and you bet. This is your standard semi-bluff move. If you took the lead and bet your hand preflop, it appears to be a standard continuation bet and will sometimes win the hand right here, although not as often as formerly because players now are more willing to call continuation bets and see what happens on the turn. And if your bet is called, your opponent may check the turn giving you the option of seeing the river card without betting.

However, the stack sizes can affect the play. If the effective stack is an M of less than about 14 (or 35 big blinds if antes are in play), then moving all-in on the flop and getting maximum fold equity is a usually better choice than just making a normal bet. The all-in move assures that you can see both the turn and river cards, and also denies your opponent a chance to come over the top with an all-in bet.

Unfortunately, in this situation in today's tournaments, the all-in move will usually be interpreted as a semi-bluff. If your opponent has a made hand, expect to frequently get called, although not enough to make the move a negative equity play. If you actually have a monster rather than a draw, moving all-in is a great play and also balances your ranges.

In Position Line No. 2: Opponent checks and you check behind. This line allows you to see the turn card for free, which is usually a good deal. It's good for balancing your play a bit (you have some drawing hands in your checking range), but it's particularly good in two other situations.

1. If your opponent is loose-aggressive and prone to check-raising, he doesn't get that chance.

2. If you have a well-concealed straight draw, it can come on the turn and give your opponent no clue that he's facing a concealed monster.

Now let's take a look at the different possible lines you can take with a drawing hand on the flop when you're out of position and see what circumstances are typically the best for each line.

Out of Position Line No. 1: You check, opponent leads out, and you call. This option produces a cheap turn card and prevents you from being raised off the hand. It's useful against a modern loose-aggressive player who might be willing to put you to the test with a semi-bluff. It's also a more effective option with a straight draw than a flush draw because in hands with two of a suit on board even weak opponents will credit you with a possible flush draw. A straight draw, however, is more likely to be interpreted as a medium pair, which in turn greatly increases your implied odds when the hand hits.

Out of Position Line No. 2: You check, opponent leads out, and you raise. This is a strong play in two different situations. The first occurs when your M is about 15 or less. In this case, your raise will be all-in, garnering maximum fold equity while allowing you to see both the turn and river cards when called.

The second occurs with deep stacks. Since you'll be playing your monsters the same way, your raise will often result in a call from your opponent followed by a check on the turn (after your check). In this case, you'll see the river for free.

Out of Position Line No. 3: You check, opponent leads out, and you fold. If your opponent has a short stack, his bet will be all-in, and depending on the pot odds and the strength of your hand, it may be best to lay your draw down. Take a look at the first example below for some of the calculations involved.

The key ideas in choosing a betting line for a drawing hand is whether you have fold equity and whether your line will enable you to see both the turn and the river cards for the price of a single bet. If you don't have much fold equity or could get bet off the hand on the turn, a check or call will probably be the better play on the flop. However, in many cases, semi-bluffing will be a strong maneuver.

Example 4-22. You're just beyond the bubble in a major tournament. The blinds are 5,000 and 10,000, with a 1,000-chip ante, and with seven players at the table, this produces a starting pot of 22,000 chips. The action folds to you on the button and you raise to 25,000 with the

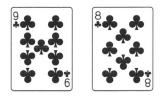

Your image over the last few hours has been loose and aggressive, and you picked up many uncontested pots during the bubble period.

The small blind calls the 20,000, leaving him about 100,000 behind and the big blind folds. The pot is now 67,000 chips. The small blind was tight during the bubble phase, only getting involved with premium hands.

The flop comes the

The small blind moves all-in. *Do you call or fold?*

The fun part of playing a drawing hand comes when you make a nice semi-bluff and watch your opponent squirm while he tries to figure out if you have a monster, a draw, or just air. The flip side of a drawing hand comes in a spot like this where you try to figure out if the price is right to call an all-in. Furthermore, a lot of these situations arise at the end of a tournament where the smallish stacks have no choice but to move in; your fold equity vanishes and you're left with nothing but pure pot odds.

The basic pot odds are easy to calculate. He bet 100,000, creating a 167,000 chip pot. Thus, you're getting odds of 167,000-to-100,000, or 1.67-to-1 to call. This means you need to win 37.5 percent of the time for your call to be correct.

$$0.375 = \frac{1}{1 + 1.67}$$

So is a straight draw good enough? That depends a bit on what he has. If you knew your straight draw would always win when it hit, and you had no other ways of winning, then your winning chances would be 31.5 percent.

$$0.315 = 1 - \left(\frac{39}{47}\right)\left(\frac{38}{46}\right)$$

where,

   39 is the number of cards on the turn that miss your hand,

   47 is the number of cards left in the deck on the turn,

   38 is the number of cards on the river that miss your hand, and

   46 is the number of cards left in the deck on the river.

(This, by the way, is a number worth memorizing. It's the chance that a hand with eight outs wins when the outs always win and there are no other ways of winning. The corresponding number for a flush draw with nine outs is 35 percent.)

So if the hand is just a question of whether or not you hit your straight, it's a pretty easy pass. But the reality is a little more complex. If he's moving all-in with a couple of overcards, for instance, then hitting a nine or an eight might be good enough to win. But if his overcards are ace-king, then we lose half of our straight outs since hitting a queen gives him a better straight than ours.

Let's use one of the hand simulation software apps to see what our winning chances are against some hands that he might actually have.

His Hand	Results	Our Winning Chances
3♥3♣	set	25.9%
J♥T♣	two pair	30.1%
A♣J♥	top pair	32.6%
A♣T♠	middle pair	32.6%
A♣K♥	overcards	32.2%
K♣Q♥	overcards	31.9%
A♣Q♥	overcards	41.9%
6♥6♣	underpair	52.7%

This table yields an interesting observation. For most of his possible hands, including two pair, top pair, middle pair, and overcards, our actually winning chances are within a couple of percent of the raw chance of winning with a pure straight draw. The exceptions are sets (where we can hit our straight but still lose if he hits a full house), underpairs (where we can win by hitting a nine or an eight), and one of the overcard combinations (where he only has a gutshot straight draw). The takeaway here is that if you're drawing to the low end of a straight, the odds of the straight draw are pretty close to your actual winning chances.

Since the small blind was a tight player and his stack wasn't critically low, there's no reason to believe that a large part of his range consisted of the hands where we're doing unusually well. Therefore, we should fold.

Example 4-23. You're into the second day at a major tournament and the bubble is on the horizon. Stacks at the table range from very short to very deep. Blinds are 2,000 and 4,000, with a 400-chip ante, producing a starting pot of 9,600 chips.

You're in the cutoff seat with a stack of 225,000 and an M of 23 (56 big blinds), and your image has been loose and aggressive. You pick up the A♠J♠ and raise to 10,000. The button, who started the hand with about 350,000 and whose image is similar to yours, 3-bets to 25,000. You realize that his range is wide and that your hand may be best at this point, so you call another 15,000. The pot is now 59,600 chips.

The flop is the T♣9♠8♠, giving you both a straight and a flush draw and you act first. *What's your play?*

While straight draws or flush draws depend on some fold equity to work as semi-bluffs, combination draws can be tremendously strong and often make you the favorite in the hand if it's played to the finish. Here you have a combination straight and flush draw with 15 outs (9 flush outs plus 6 additional straight outs). You also have two overcards which can provide some additional outs depending on your opponent's hand.

To see how strong a combination draw is, here's how you stand right now against some hands your opponent may have, assuming you get to see both the turn and river cards:

His Hand	Results	Your Winning Chances
A♥T♦	top pair	62.4%
A♥A♦	overpair	55.2%
7♦6♣	low straight	52.2%
9♣8♦	two pair	51.6%
9♥9♣	set	39.4%

As can be seen, you're a favorite against all these made hands except a set where you still have almost a 40 percent chance.

In such a good position, you should consider yourself committed to the hand at this point in the tournament. The only real question that remains is how to best get all your money in while also maximizing your fold equity.

Right now the pot is about 60,000 chips and the effective stack is 200,000, and since your stack is more than triple the pot, you can't push all-in to start. Such a big bet telegraphs your strength. Instead, there are two lines you can consider.

1. You lead out with a bet, he raises, and you move all-in.

2.   You check, he bets, and you move all-in.

Let's look at the first line and see if that works. The pot is now about 60,000 chips, so if you lead out with a bet it will be in the range of 40,000 to 50,000. So let's suppose you lead out for 40,000 producing a pot of 100,000 chips (and your remaining stack is just 160,000). A pot-sized raise on his part would require raising to 180,000 (40,000 to call your raise, making a pot of 140,000, and then another 140,000 for a pot-sized raise). Since that's more than your existing stack, he's going to move all-in if he wants to raise at all.

So the first line doesn't really work. When you bet he might fold or call, but if he raises, it will be all-in.

The second line, however, is just the first line in reverse. If you check and he bets, your all-in move will be a little less than a pot-sized raise, which is perfect. You'll extract the maximum fold equity, and you'll be a favorite against most of his calling hands.

The downside of Line No. 2 is that he may check behind. In this case, you get to draw for free, which isn't a bad result.

The quick lesson from this problem is that with a starting M in the 20 to 25 range (roughly 50 to 65 big blinds with antes in play) and a strong draw on the flop, the all-in check-raise will be your default maneuver when out of position.

Example 4-24. Now let's take a look at the previous hand again. This time we'll change your starting chip stack in the cutoff from 225,000 to 425,000. Your new M is about 44 (106 big blinds). The button once again has you easily covered, this time with 650,000. Your hand and all the rest of the preflop action is the same, so the pot is about 60,000 chips going to the flop, and your stack is now 400,000.

Once again, the flop is the T♣9♠8♠ and you have to decide between two lines: leading out or checking with the intent of check-raising. *With these stack sizes, which line looks better?*

Now you can lead out on the flop and still move all-in with a bet that's not quite a pot-sized bet. Here's how the math of leading and then raising looks:

1. The pot is 60,000 chips.

2. You lead out with a bet of 40,000 (two-thirds of the pot), making the pot 100,000 chips, and leaving you with 360,000.

3. The button raises to 140,000 and the pot is now 240,000 chips.

4. You now move all-in with your 360,000 stack. In effect, you have called his 100,000, creating a 340,000 pot, and raised 260,000, which is about 75 percent of the existing pot.

Also notice that with these stacks, the exact size of the bets and raises didn't matter much. You could have led off with a half-pot bet (30,000) and he could have made a smaller raise. In either case you would have moved all-in on the end without significantly overbetting the pot.

The dividing point for these two lines of play is an effective M of about 30 to 35. If the effective M is less than 30, you want to choose the check-raise option for your draw. If it's more than 35, leading out and moving all-in after a raise is a more efficient choice. For Ms between 30 and 35, the two plays have equivalent drawbacks; make your choice based on your sense of what will work best against this particular opponent.

Part Five
Playing the Turn

Playing the Turn

Introduction

After the flop but before the river, the gods placed the turn. And when the turn card arrives, you can see six of the seven cards that will eventually constitute your hand. Furthermore, with only one card to come, the leader is very likely to still be the leader after the river is dealt, and in many cases, the trailer is drawing dead. However, the leader can only rarely be sure of that.

Since the trailer has a smaller chance of catching up, value bets have higher equity than on the flop. This means if your opponent is drawing, he has only about half as much chance of making his draw as on the flop, and any reasonably-sized bet will deny him the proper odds for hitting his hand, and a player with a drawing hand will need to rely on implied odds to justify playing on.

In tournament play, issues of pot commitment need to be considered carefully. If the players began the hand with Ms in the 20 to 40 range and there was betting action both preflop and on the flop, a turn bet may be committing one or both players to the pot. The turn bet thus often functions as preparation for an all-in move on the river.

The turn card can also function as a *scare card*, something we haven't encountered yet in our discussion of preflop and flop play. A scare card is simply a card that has the potential of changing the likely leader in the hand. When a scare card appears, either player may be able to use it to their advantage.

The opposite of the scare card is the *non-scare card* which is a card that is unlikely to alter the status of the players. A typical example occurs when the top card on the flop pairs on the turn. If you had a lower pair than top pair on the flop, your status is the same. If you were ahead after the flop, you're still ahead, and if you were behind on the flop, you're still behind.

When to Bet the Turn

There are a lot of reasons for betting the turn. You can bet for value, can bet to protect your hand from a draw, can bet as a bluff, or can bet just because no one else seems to have any interest in the hand. These categories aren't mutually exclusive; sometimes a bet can contain elements of all these types. Let's take a look at the reasons for making some standard bets and consider one or two examples of each.

When to Make Standard Bets

Reason No. 1: Bet a strong hand for value. Making a value bet is the simplest case for betting the turn. You have a made hand ranging from a good pair to a monster and believe your hand is best right now. If you're right, your opponent has only one card left to turn the hand around. (Even if he has something like a combination straight and flush draw, he only has 15 outs and 31 misses.) So bet to get more money in the pot.

How big should your value bet be? In general, depending on the stack size, the relative strength of your hand, and your estimate of his hand, it should be somewhere between two-thirds and the whole pot. Let's take a look at how all these factors interact.

1. **The stack size is the key element.** If your hand is very strong and the stacks are not deep, then you should size your bet so that an all-in bet on the river isn't a massive overbet.

    Suppose, for instance, the turn card has come and you have a well-concealed straight on a rainbow board. The pot is 20,000 chips and the effective stack is about 90,000. Betting half the pot offers him reasonably attractive odds to call, and if he calls, you will go to the river with a 40,000 chip pot while the remaining effective stack is 80,000. So to put him all-in, you'll have to make a river bet of twice the pot. a pretty big overbet.

If you bet three-quarters of the pot on the turn (15,000) and he calls, the pot will be 50,000 chips and there will be 70,000 left to bet. Now an all-in move for 70,000 is only a small overbet, giving him a better chance to call. The important point is that a small increase in the size of your turn bet can make an all-in river move look less threatening.

2. **If your hand isn't a monster, then getting all the chips in on the river shouldn't be a major consideration.** Let's say you have two pair and think your opponent is likely to have top pair or a flush draw, but there's some chance he has you beaten with a set. In this case, a simple bet of half the pot or even a little less is more appropriate.

Example 5-1. Blinds are 300 and 600, with a 75-chip ante, for a starting pot of 1,575 chips. Your starting stack was 60,000, with an M of 38 (100 big blinds). You pick up the

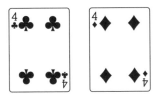

in third position and raise to 1,600, get called by the cutoff (starting stack of about 70,000), and the big blind (about 82,000). The pot is now 5,775 chips.

The flop is the

giving you bottom set. Your hand is probably best and well-disguised. The big blind checks, you make a continuation bet of 4,000, the cutoff calls, and the big blind folds. The pot is now 13,775 chips.

At this point, your opponent still has a wide range of hands. He could have a queen with a decent kicker (something from ace-queen down through queen-ten), a flush draw, a middle pair (jacks, tens, or nines), or a pair of eights. He could also have a pair below eights, although that's less likely, and there's some chance he's floating in position, and also a very small chance that he has a better set. Two pair are highly unlikely on this board, and only gutshot straight draws are possible.

The turn is the 3♣, a good card for you. If he has a hand like king-queen he'll think that there is still a good chance that it's best. So bet again to extract more value from the queens and to charge the flush draws.

In addition, notice that right now the pot is less than a quarter of your stack, and an even smaller percentage of his stack, so sizing your bet to set up a river all-in won't be possible. So a good bet size is 8,000 to 9,000, about two-thirds of the pot. If he holds a good queen, it'll be difficult for him to fold for that price. If his hand is a flush draw, he'll be able to convince himself that the remaining stacks are big enough to give him the implied odds to call.[8]

Note that checking with the idea of check-raising isn't a good move. The cutoff may decide to play pot control with a pair of queens, and if he has a flush draw, he may be happy to see a free card. So playing the hand straightforwardly gives you the best chance to pick up two bets rather than one.

Example 5-2. Blinds are 50 and 100, your starting stack is 21,000 producing an M of about 140 (210 big blinds). You pick up the 8♠4♣ in the big blind and expect to be folding your hand quickly.

---

[8] But two of his flush outs will pair the board and give you a full house. So his flush draw won't be as good as it appears.

However, the first three players fold and the player in fourth position limps, the cutoff and button also limp, the small blind folds, and you check and see a hand for free. The three other players all have starting stacks close to yours, and the pot is 450 chips.

The flop is the J♣8♦4♥. You've hit bottom two pair, a nice result after checking a junk hand, and lead for 350, a good play. Bottom two pair is a strong hand right now, but becomes increasingly vulnerable as the hand develops. Someone can easily hit a better two pair, or the board can pair on the turn or river and counterfeit your bottom pair. Checking with the idea of check-raising is also risky since most players will want something good to lead into three opponents, so the hand may just get checked around. The player in fourth position calls 350, the other two players fold, and the pot is now 1,150 chips.

The turn card is the K♦. This puts a flush draw and some possible straight draws on board, but otherwise it's all right. Although someone holding king-jack is now ahead, other possible hands like king-queen or king-ten now have a reason to call your turn bet, but these hands were unlikely to call the flop bet. You're still a big favorite to be in the lead, but it's important to bet again and a good bet size is 900 to 1,000, large enough to get good value from a king or one of the draws.

Example 5-3. Blinds are 150 and 300, with antes starting at the next level. Your stack is 14,000, producing an M of 31 (47 big blinds). You pick up the 7♥6♥ under-the-gun and raise to 800. Raising suited connectors in early position, even low ones, is a good move for a tight player. Your opponents will put you on a tight range of high pairs and Broadway cards, and when you connect with a flop of medium and low cards your hand will be well disguised. Everyone folds except the big blind who calls with a stack of about 17,000 and an M of around 38 (57 big blinds). The pot is now 1,750 chips.

The flop comes the J♣7♦4♦ and the big blind checks. Although you only have middle pair, it's important to bet. You probably have the best hand and a lot of cards can arrive on the turn that won't make you happy — aces, kings, queens, tens, and diamonds.

You bet 1,200 and the big blind calls, making the pot 4,150 chips. The turn card is the 6♠, a good card which gives you a well-disguised two pair. Once more the big blind checks and again, you have a clear value bet. His most likely holding is a jack with a decent kicker, a medium pair of tens, nines, or eights, or a flush draw. Betting charges the flush draw to see another card, which is good, and it also extracts some value from the pairs. If he has a hand like queen-jack suited, he'll think that your range includes a lot of overcards or medium pairs, and there's still a reasonable chance that his hand is good. Value bets like this are simply the bread and butter of solid tournament play.

Reason No. 2: Bet with a medium-strength hand which is likely to be best. It's sometimes the case you have a hand which is not particularly strong, but the betting action so far indicates that your opponent's range probably hasn't connected with the board. Usually these are hands where you have a medium to low pair, and the board consists of a single high card and some low cards, perhaps with a pair arriving on the turn. In these cases, you need to bet.

The bet serves a double function, both for value and protection. If you've analyzed the situation properly and are ahead, your bet is a value bet regardless of how weak your hand really is. But if your holding is something like a medium to low pair, a lot of cards could come on the river that you wouldn't like, so chasing your opponent out of the hand (at this stage) is a good thing.

Example 5-4. Blinds are 100 and 200. You have the

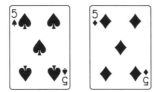

in the big blind, and a stack of 24,000 producing an M of 80 (120 big blinds). The action folds around to the player in the cutoff seat whose stack is a little smaller than yours and who raises to 550. The button and the small blind fold, and you call. The pot is now 1,200 chips.

The flop is the

a dry rainbow flop. You check and your opponent, somewhat surprisingly, checks behind indicating that your pair is likely best at this point.

The turn is the 7♦. Rather than check, you elect to lead for 600. If your hand was best on the flop, then pairing the board didn't hurt you, and since your opponent raised from late position, his range should be wide. That is, only a small part of his range are pairs or queen-x type hands. So by betting, you'll protect yourself from losing on the river (if he folds), or charge him for drawing to what are probably six outs.

The bet serves one additional function, as a blocking bet. If in fact your opponent is sitting on a queen with a mediocre kicker or a medium pair, your bet may set the price for the turn and prevent him from putting you on the defensive with a larger bet. Taking the initiative may also save you money on the river if he elects to play for pot control. All in all, that's a lot to accomplish with a single half-pot bet.

Your opponent folds.

Example 5-5. Blinds are 500 and 1,000, with a 100-chip ante producing a starting pot of 2,400 chips. You have the 8♠8♣ on the button with a stack of 95,000 and an M of about 40 (95 big blinds). The action folds to the loose, strong, aggressive player in third position whose stack is about 14,000, and who raises to 2,500. Everyone folded around and you call with your medium pair and position. The small blind folds but the big blind, with a stack of about 90,000, calls. The pot is now 8,900 chips.

The flop is the J♥7♦3♠, and you have position plus second pair. The big blind checks and the initial raiser bets 4,800, slightly over half the pot.

Notice that this is an ideal flop for continuation betting, with no straight or flush draws. It's likely the raiser would have bet this flop with his entire range even if he wasn't an aggressive player. As is, your pair is ahead of most of his range and calling is correct. This you do and the big blind folds. The pot is now 18,500 chips.

The turn is the J♠, a non-scare card, and your opponent checks. If you were ahead after the flop, that's still the case, and if behind after the flop, that hasn't changed either. However, with one more jack now accounted for, it's a little less likely that you're behind.

The combination of the arrival of the jack and your opponent's check is a favorable sign. With his wide preflop range, it's most likely that his bet on the flop was a continuation bet bluff and the jack on the turn doesn't allow him to represent anything extra; had an ace, king, or queen arrived, he could have fired another barrel, figuring that he could take the pot if you had a hand like a pair below jacks. Loose-aggressive players need to be good at tempering their aggression when the hand doesn't go well.

Your best move now is to bet. If your analysis is correct, your hand beats your opponent's and you're betting for both value and protection. A lot of cards can come on the river that you won't like and hardly any cards help you, so bet to win the pot now. Also note that a big bet isn't necessary because the board is dry and the chance of a backdoor flush draw is pretty low. You bet 7,000 and your opponent folds.

Reason No. 3: If you could have made a continuation bet on the flop but didn't, make a delayed c-bet now. You shouldn't make continuation bets on every flop because you usually need to keep your opponents guessing about your strategy and your hand. When you don't make a continuation bet on the flop, your range needs to be a mixture of value hands and hands that missed entirely, so your opponents can't assume that failure to bet means you don't have anything.

And when you have something and don't bet the flop and it is checked around, frequently, but not always, bet the turn. You need to get value from your hand at some point, and since the check-bet sequence under represents your hand, you're more likely to get called by a weaker hand on the turn.

Checking the flop and betting the turn is called a delayed c-bet, and it serves both as a pot control move and a balancing move. It's a useful addition to your repertoire; beginners and intermediates don't use it enough.

Example 5-6. Blinds are 200 and 400, with a 50-chip ante producing a starting pot of 1,050 chips. You're in third position with the K♣Q♦, your stack is 48,000, with an M of 46 (120 big blinds), the first two players fold, and you raise to 1,000. Your image at this point is tight-aggressive.

Everyone folds to the cutoff who calls. He's fairly loose but not particularly aggressive, with a stack of 32,000. The button and the small blind fold, and the big blind, with a stack of about 38,000, calls. He's tighter than you but also on the aggressive side. The pot is now 3,650 chips.

The flop is the Q♣8♠2♦ giving you top pair with a good kicker on a very dry board, and the big blind checks. You could certainly make a continuation bet here, but since the board is very dry and only one card (an ace) can scare you on the turn, there's little harm in checking, and with your top pair hand, you're not particularly interested in creating a big pot. Also, the standard line would be to bet the flop and check the turn, but sometimes reversing the check and the bet is a good balancing play.

You check and the player in the cutoff seat checks as well. The turn is the 3♣ and the big blind checks again.

At this point it's time to bet. You've underrepresented your hand with the flop check, so it's likely that your bet here will not be interpreted as a strong queen. If either opponent has a weak queen or an underpair, you should get a call and may get a call on the river as well.

You bet 1,800. Both the cutoff and the big blind fold.

Reason No. 4: Bet when you hit your draw and it is not disguised. On the flop, when you're drawing to a flush or an obvious straight, and you hit your hand on the turn, you need to bet. Attempting to be clever by checking runs into two problems:

1. With the possibility of an obviously strong hand on board, your opponents are likely to check and take a free card.

2. If a cooler card arrives on the river, like a fourth flush card, your river bet may not get any callers.

The best way to make money in this situation is to make a decent bet on the turn which can pay off in a number of ways:

1. If someone else has a value hand, they may think you're bluffing or are making a semi-bluff, and pay off at least one street.

2. If they're drawing, they may call.

3. If they just made a weaker flush or straight, they'll certainly call this bet and may call a river bet as well.

If none of these situations apply, then you probably don't have a way to make money on this hand, so you might as well take it down now.

Example 5-7. Blinds are 750 and 1,500, with a 100-chip ante for a starting pot of 3,150 chips. The table has been playing fairly tight with just a couple of loose-aggressive players in the mix. You pick up the A♠T♠ under-the-gun and your stack is 220,000 for an M of 70 (147 big blinds). You're the biggest stack at the table and your image is a little loose but very aggressive. You raise to 3,600 and the players in the hijack and the button seats call. Their stacks are 120,000 and 90,000 respectively. The hijack player has been tight and somewhat passive while the button player seems about average for the table. The pot is now almost 14,000 chips.

The flop is the Q♠J♣3♠. It's a good flop for you with the nut flush draw and a gutshot straight draw, plus an overcard. You bet 9,000, and both opponents call. The pot is now 41,000 chips.

The turn is the 9♠ and you've hit the nut flush. So go ahead and bet since it's the right play. You want to extract as much value from this great hand as possible, and if you check, there's no guarantee that either of your opponents will take the lead. But if you lead with a bet of something like 15,000, a number of good things may happen:

1. Someone holding the K♠ might move all-in as a semi-bluff.

2. Someone with the K♠ or J♠ may call with their flush draw.

3. Someone holding king-ten or ten-eight might call or raise with their straight.

4. Someone with a queen might call with top pair.

5. Someone with two pair will call.

6. Someone with a non-nut flush might move all-in to prevent you from drawing out if you have the A♠ or K♠ with a non-spade.

That's not an exhaustive list, but the lesson is that there are lots of hands that might call on this board, and two opponents, either of whom could make that call. If you wait and check, the big danger is that both opponents may check, after which another spade on the river might kill all your action. So avoid this train wreck with a good bet now.

Reason No. 5: Bet to set up an all-in on the river. If your hand is strong enough to warrant getting all the chips in the middle, consider whether you can size your turn bet so that a river push is not a massive overbet. If the effective stack is about 2.5 times the current pot or less, there's no problem; any reasonable bet will allow an all-in move on the river that's not out of line. In the same way, if the effective stack is six times the current pot or more, you can't get all the money in without either the turn or river bet looking suspiciously large.

The area that requires careful thinking is when the effective stack is three, four, or five times the current pot. Here are three examples illustrating proper bet sizing.

Example 5-8. The Effective stack is three times the current pot. Let's say that after the flop betting, the pot is 10,000 chips and the effective stack is 30,000. Here's what the pot and effective stack look like after four differently-sized bets on the turn, followed by a call:

Turn bet	Pot on the River	Effective Stack
3,300 = ⅓ pot	16,600	26,700
5,000 = ½ pot	20,000	25,000
7,500 = ¾ pot	25,000	22,500
10,000 = pot	30,000	20,000

The only real error is the small turn bet of one-third of the pot. It leaves an effective stack which is about 60 percent bigger than the pot, and any of the other bet sizes avoid this problem. The optimal bet is probably the half-pot bet which offers the opponent good immediate odds while still producing a river all-in move which isn't a massive overbet.

Example 5-9. The effective stack is four times the current pot. Again, we'll assume that after the flop the pot contains 10,000 chips, but now the effective stack is 40,000. Here's the new chart showing how things look on the river for turn bets of different sizes:

Turn Bet	Pot on the River	Effective Stack
3,300 = ⅓ pot	16,600	36,700
5,000 = ½ pot	20,000	35,000
7,500 = ¾ pot	25,000	32,500
10,000 = pot	30,000	30,000

Note that when the effective stack is four times the pot, a pot-sized turn bet leaves exactly a pot-sized river bet (a factoid that's useful to remember and saves some mental work at the table.)

In this case, both the half-pot and the one-third pot bet are too small, leaving big all-in overbets on the river. But both the three-fourths and the full pot bet work with the three-fourths pot bet probably working best in practice since it appears a little less threatening than a full pot bet, but at the same time it's not so small that it looks like a trap.

Example 5-10. The effective stack is five times the current pot. Here the pot remains at 10,000 chips but the effective stack is now much larger, approximately 50,000. Here's our new chart:

Turn Bet	Pot on the River	Effective Stack
3,300 = ⅓ pot	16,600	46,700
5,000 = ½ pot	20,000	45,000
7,500 = ¾ pot	25,000	42,500
10,000 = pot	30,000	40,000

Now only the full pot bet on the turn works, leaving an all-in move on the river that's slightly larger than the pot. All other bet sizes are too small.

Our first five reasons covered most cases of betting for value on the turn. Now let's look at bluffing on the turn.

When to Double-Barrel

Double-barreling refers to a very specific (but important) sequence:

1. You raised preflop.

2. You missed the flop (or ended up with a weak made hand such as an underpair), made a continuation bet, and got called.

3. You missed the turn and now have either nothing or a weak hand.

Betting under these circumstances is known as 'firing a double barrel.' You're representing a big hand, like a set or two pair, with the goal of picking up the pot from anyone who doesn't have a premium hand and doesn't want to face what may be a big bet on the river.

In the modern game, double-barreling is more common than it used to be. Players make continuation bets on the flop more often and with weaker hands, which leads to more calling and floating with weaker hands, which in turn creates more pots where neither player has much by the turn. At that point, double-barreling becomes a potentially profitable maneuver.

However, double-barreling can easily be overdone. But there are conditions that make it more likely to be successful, as well as conditions that indicate it's time to fold your tent and move on to the next hand. Let's start by looking at when double-barreling may be favorable.

Favorable Condition No. 1: Later is better. The closer to the money bubble, the more likely that a double-barrel bluff will succeed.

In the early stages of a deep-stack tournament, calling a turn bet might represent no more than 2 to 3 percent of your stack. That's not much of a risk considering that the bubble is far, far away and you're not likely to get there without taking a few chances. So why not take one now?

Once half the players have been eliminated, however, the risk calculus changes. Since the blinds have been rising much faster than stacks have been growing, calling a turn bet might represent 10 percent or more of your stack. At the same time, your chance of getting in the money has roughly doubled. Put these two points together and players are much less likely to contest a double-barrel without a solid hand. And of course, as we approach the bubble, this tendency gets even greater.

The moral: don't overdo the double-barrel bluffs early when the blinds are small. But make them a bigger part of your game as you get deeper into the tournament.

Favorable Condition No. 2: When a scare card hits or when your opponent is tight and passive. Firing at a tight-passive opponent should be fairly obvious at any stage, and using scare cards well is a key part of successful double-barreling.

A *scare card* is simply a card that threatens to change the leader in a hand. Suppose you hold the

in your hand and the flop is the

giving you top pair with the third-best kicker, and after betting the flop and getting a call, there's good reason to believe that you're on top in this hand.

Now suppose the A♥ hits the turn. If your opponent called with an ace, he now has top pair and your queens are relegated to second pair. The ace constitutes a scare card.

A king is also a scare card, but it's not as scary because players generally have more aces in their range than kings. A spade is also a scare card, potentially giving your opponent a flush.

Let's say you raised preflop with a pair of sevens and got one caller. The flop was again the Q♣8♠4♠, you made a continuation bet, and your opponent called. If the A♥ comes on the turn, it's a good situation to double-barrel.

Your opponent may have a middle pair between jacks and eights, and figured there was a good chance you didn't have a queen. But once the ace arrives, he now has to worry that you might have an ace or a queen. So a second barrel here will make a lot of players lay down their middle pair; it's now too likely they're beaten.

Not all overcards are scare cards. If the flop came the 9♥8♥7♥ and a couple of players stuck around, the arrival of the A♣ isn't going to scare anyone. The flop was scary enough all by itself, and the arrival of a random ace is unlikely to change anyone's perception of the hand.

Example 5-11. Suppose your preflop raising range includes pairs from any position and a lot of Broadway cards. You pick up a pair of fours in early position and raise, getting a call from the button, a good and moderately aggressive player.

Now this flop hits: 7♥6♣3♦. You still have your pair and in addition a gutshot straight draw. Is this a good time for a continuation bet? It's actually a difficult situation with some arguments in both directions. You probably have the best hand, and a continuation bet may pick up the pot right here. (If you make a continuation bet and get raised, you have to call since your hand is too good to fold.) On the other hand, the only possible scare card on the turn is an ace, so there's little danger in checking in an attempt to keep the pot small, and calling if your opponent bets. I look at this and similar situations as a 60-to-40 proposition: make a continuation bet 60 percent of the time, check the remaining 40 percent.

Example 5-12. We'll use the same preflop situation as the last example. You raise with a pair of fours in early position and get a call from the same player on the button.

This time a different flop hits: J♥9♦2♥. And on this flop a continuation bet is a clearer play. What's the difference? First, it better connects with his perception of your range since you could easily have a pair of jacks with a good kicker, a set of jacks or nines, or a straight draw, and a continuation bet establishes the premise that the flop helped you. In addition, a lot of scare cards can come on the turn, including a heart, an ace, king, queen, or ten, and they'll all look threatening to a player who called with a jack, a nine, or some medium to low pair.

A continuation bet on this flop also allows a lot of threatening double-barrels on the turn in addition to the possibility of winning the pot by immediately representing strength. So pay attention to scare card potential and your continuation bets should be more profitable.

Favorable Condition No. 3: The board fits what you should have. After a preflop raise, your opponents will (perhaps subconsciously) take into account both style and position and put you on a range of hands. Their perceived range will probably be a subset of your real range, and perhaps a very small subset. When a moderately tight player raises from early position, for instance, most players at the table will think his likely holdings are the following:

1. Unpaired Broadway cards, plus ace-king and ace-queen.

2. Medium pairs.

3. High pairs.

They'll put unpaired Broadway cards plus ace-king and ace-queen first because there are lots of them. They'll put high pairs at the bottom because only aces, kings, and queens count as high pairs and there are only a few of these. Medium pairs go in the middle because the exact number of hands that count as medium pairs is a little fuzzy — Are sevens a medium pair? How about sixes? — and in any case, there are more of these than high pairs.

So if the flop seems to fit your perceived range, they'll respect your continuation bet, and frequently respect your second barrel even more. Here's an example.

Example 5-13. It's the middle stage of a tournament, a few levels before the bubble. Blinds are 500 and 1,000, with a 100-chip ante, and you're in second position with a stack of 120,000 and an M of 50 (120 big blinds). Although your style is moderately loose, circumstances have kept you out of a lot of hands so your current image is tight. You pick up the

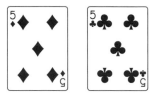

and the under-the-gun player folds. You'll raise small pairs from early position, but it's unlikely that anyone at the table knows this for sure, so 2,700 goes into the pot.

The action folds to the player in the cutoff seat, someone who's a little tight and not especially aggressive, who calls. His stack is about 85,000, above average for the table. The button and the big blinds fold, the pot is now 7,800 chips, and the flop is the

The flop has, of course, completely missed your hand. However, you can't open with a pair of fives in early position if the plan is to give up when you don't flop a set or hit a straight draw. Those flops are just bonuses. So be prepared to fight for and win some pots that don't connect with your hand. Here's a perfect example.

This dry flop probably missed your opponent. In addition, the king connected with some of the hands you're supposed to have. So play it that way. That is, assume you started with ace-king or king-queen and play the hand accordingly. The fact that your image is tight just makes your story all the more credible.

You bet 4,200 and the player in the cutoff seat calls. The pot is now 16,200 chips and the turn is the Q♦.

A queen doesn't help your pair of fives, but this is no time to be squeamish. If your opponent called with any sort of medium to low pair, the queen is another high card that he didn't want to see. So this a good double-barreling opportunity.

You bet 7,000, a perfect bet if you actually have what you're representing — two pair or top pair, top kicker, or perhaps even ace-queen. Your story is compelling and completely consistent, and the player in the cutoff should frequently fold.

When *Not* to Double-Barrel

You raised preflop, got called, missed the flop, made a continuation bet, and got called again. Now the turn has come and you still don't have much. We've just looked at a few cases where double-barreling was a good bet. Now let's examine these conditions where double-barreling is at least questionable and at worst clearly bad.

Unfavorable Condition No. 1: Early in the tournament is problematic. Late in the tournament many players are mostly concerned with making the money and bluffing can often push them off a hand. But early in the tournament they are just playing poker and trying to find out what their opponents are like, and early tournament thinking looks more like this:

1. You bet before the flop. *So what?*

2. You made a continuation bet. *Big deal.*

3. You fired another barrel on the turn. *Hey, who does this guy think he is, Phil Ivey? I got a pair, pal. I ain't going nowhere.*

Therefore, early in a tournament is a good time to pass on some of the marginal double-barreling situations. Furthermore, cultivating a somewhat tight image can pay off later when the pots are much bigger.

Unfavorable Condition No. 2: When the turn pairs the top flop card. This is an especially good time to shut down if your continuation bet was a bluff. If your opponent called with some variety of top pair, he obviously isn't going away. If he called with something else, his situation didn't get worse and the likelihood that he's facing top pair just went down a lot. Pairing the top card on the turn is an extreme example of a no-scare card.

Unfavorable Condition No. 3: When the turn card is inconsistent with your story. Let's say you have a fairly tight image and raise preflop in early position with the J♥9♥ and the flop is the 6♣5♠4♦. You make a continuation bet in the hope that the flop completely misses your opponent, but he calls, and a 2♥ arrives on the turn. If you fire again, the only story you're telling that's consistent with this board is an initial raise with a low pair that's turned into a set or a straight. Odds are your opponent won't find this credible.

Unfavorable Condition No. 4: When a non-scare card arrives. Non-scare cards are low cards that don't fill any flush or straight draws, or any card that pairs the board. Random low cards obviously don't fit in any narrative you were trying to tell. We covered the problem with pairing the top flop card in Unfavorable Condition No. 2. A turn card that pairs one of the other board cards simply makes it less likely that you flopped a set. But if you didn't flop a set, how much of your range included a particular low card? Not very much.

Unfavorable Condition No. 5: When the turn fits your opponent's story. Suppose you raise from early position preflop with the A♦K♦, get a late-position caller, and the flop is the T♣9♠9♥. You make a continuation bet, he calls, and the turn is the 8♥. Since you raised preflop from early position, your opponent is expecting you to have a range of mostly high cards.

Therefore, this turn shouldn't help. But his calling range included lots of medium cards and medium pairs, and his call on the flop indicated that the flop connected with his hand in some way. So unless he's floating, anything that connected with the flop would be helped by the arrival of the 8♥. It's a turn card that fits his story, not your story. Move on to the next hand.

Unfavorable Condition No. 6: Don't bluff a calling station. If your opponent is a calling station, don't try multi-street bluffs under any circumstances. They won't work. By bluffing, you're actually playing into his one strength. Just give up and move on.

When to Bluff the Turn

In the last section, we looked at double-barreling, which is a special case of bluffing the turn: firing a bluff after you had already made a continuation bet on the flop. However, that's not the only kind of bluff possible. The turn offers a number of good bluffing opportunities even if you checked the flop. Let's look at a few of them.

Bluffing Opportunity No. 1: If your opponent made a continuation bet on the flop and then checked the turn, bet big hands and bluff with air. A common mistake of tight players is to consistently make a continuation bet on the flop, then bet if they actually have a hand but check the turn if they were bluffing. It's a huge leak in their game since most flops miss most players. Against such a player, float the flop with a lot of different hands, then bet the turn after a check, whether you have anything or not.

Of course, this play requires position, and it's another illustration of just why position is so important. If you're out of position and the turn action is check-check, you can often make a move on the river, but the leverage of a turn bet followed by a big river bet isn't there. In addition, to avoid being obvious and totally unbalanced, bet the turn with your big hands as well.

Example 5-14. The blinds are 600 and 1,200, with a 150-chip ante, the table is eight-handed, producing a starting pot of 3,000 chips, and about two-thirds of the field still remains in the tournament. The tight and not particularly strong player in second position raises to 3,600, and his stack is about 60,000 for an M of 20 (50 big blinds). He doesn't play a lot of hands, and you can reliably put him on a narrow range which includes medium but not small pairs.

The action folds to you on the button with the

Your stack is 130,000 with an M of 43 (108 big blinds), and your image is loose and aggressive, but not crazy. You elect to call and try to use your positional advantage and superior skill after the flop. The button and blinds fold and the pot is now 10,200 chips.

The flop is the

The preflop raiser bets 5,100, exactly half the pot. With two overcards and a flop that missed most of his range, you elect to call. The pot is now 20,400 chips.

The turn is the A♠. Your opponent now checks.

This is a great time to bet and take the pot away. Tight players with narrow ranges don't often check when an ace arrives. Since the ace usually helps their hand and their range is narrow in early position, they generally bet if an ace appears and it helps them.

Look at it this way. If your opponent was holding ace-king, ace-queen, or even ace-jack, he liked his hand preflop but didn't like the flop at all. But he bet (the flop) because it gave him a chance to win, and was unhappy when you called.

Now an ace arrives and he actually has a hand, but not a monster. Most players with top pair would bet here. But he didn't, instead, he checked. Conclusion: Your opponent probably doesn't have one of these holdings. Perhaps he has a hand like yours or even a medium pair, and the ace is a genuine scare card, matching a bunch of hands that he fears. So it's time to bet.

You bet and he folds.

This is a bread and butter maneuver against tight but unimaginative players. Use it to your advantage.

Bluffing Opportunity No. 2: Bet to take down a pot no one wants. Sometimes no one will make a move at the pot. Two or three players get involved preflop, no one bets the flop, and then it's checked to you on the turn. It's possible everyone has a hand that they're slow-playing until the river, but that's not a likely scenario. Much more probable, no one has anything, and the first player to bet will win the pot. So make sure that person is you.

Example 5-15. It's early in the tournament and the blinds are 150 and 300. The action is folded to the fourth player with 23,000 who raises to 750. The next two players fold, you call on the button with the 3♥3♣ and a stack of 21,000, the small blind folds, but the big blind calls with 17,000. The pot is now 2,400 chips.

The flop is the Q♦T♠4♣, everyone checks, and the turn is the 2♣. The big blind and the preflop raiser check again and now it's your turn.

Neither of your opponents has made a move for the pot and some players have a tendency to assume (especially when they don't have much of a hand) that their opponents are laying a deep trap, sitting on a monster and just waiting to pounce once you stick your head up. That's possible, but some other explanations are more likely. Let's run through some variations and see why.

1. It's unlikely that anyone has a set or two pair. With a hand that good, why let two streets go by without building a pot in the hopes of maybe winning one bet on the river? This is especially true when two medium high cards appear (even though there is no two flush).

2. It's also unlikely that anyone flopped a queen; a top pair hand would have bet by now just to protect itself.

3. There's a possibility that someone has a ten and is playing pot control because of the overcard. Still, you have only two

opponents, and the chance that one was dealt a playable ten is well under 50 percent.

4. Then there's the most likely explanation; no one has anything, or they have a hand like yours and don't like the overcards on board.

You should bet and try to take this pot. *How big should a bet be?* With a 2,400-chip pot, I'd bet something like 950, around 35 to 40 percent of the pot. It looks like a carefully calculated amount, as though you first slow-played a monster and are now trying to trap someone into calling. In fact, of course, you're just trying to take down the pot for as low a price as possible.

Also, when betting into two opponents rather than one, you'll get a little extra credit for having a real hand, which slightly increases the equity of your bet. Every little bit helps.

When to Raise the Turn

Let's say you're in position and an opponent bets the turn. (He may or may not have bet on the flop.) *When do you want to raise?*

It's easy to say "Raise if you have a big hand," and that's often (but not always) true. However, instead of just calling for pot control, there are also cases where you'll raise even with a hand of medium strength. Let's take a look at a few situations where raising the turn is a strong play.

Situation No. 1: You have a big hand and want to set up an all-in on the river. The most common scenario for raising the turn comes when you have a very strong hand and, because of the stack sizes, you're perfectly happy to eventually get all the chips in the pot. Your goal is to make this happen without chasing away a hand that has some chance of calling your river bet. Let's look at a couple of examples.

Example 5-16. It's a big tournament and about two-thirds of the field has been eliminated. The blinds are 800 and 1,600, with a 200-chip ante. There are now eight players at your table producing a starting pot of 4,000 chips. The player in second position, with a stack of 80,000 and an M of 20 (50 big blinds), raises to 4,200. He's been fairly tight so far, but he's aggressive when holding a hand.

The action folds to you on the button. You hold the

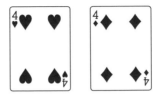

and your stack is 100,000 with an M of 25 (63 big blinds). You call, the blinds fold, and you go to the flop with a pot of 12,400 chips.

The flop is the

giving you bottom set. Your opponent makes a smallish continuation bet of 4,400 which is just over one-third of the pot.

Continuation bets on an ace-high flop are pretty routine, so by itself the bet doesn't say much about his hand. Consider the possibilities:

1. He could have raised with a good ace (but not a weak ace since he raised from second position and we think he's pretty tight.)

2. He could have raised with KK, QQ, JJ or TT, in which case he's not happy to see the ace.

3. He might have raised with ten-nine or nine-eight, or maybe a couple of other nines. He could also have raised with a couple of Broadway cards, or a medium pair below nines.

4. And of course there's the worst-case scenario — he could have raised with a pair of aces or nines, and you're crushed.

In all cases except the last one, it makes sense for him to bet and represent the ace; that may be enough to take down the hand. If he has a set, he still wants to bet because raising from early position and then checking is very suspicious and your range should contain an ace a high percentage of the time.

The last possibility, where he has a better set, needs to be disregarded. The stacks are relatively short, and there's no possibility that you'll reason this out before all your chips are in the middle. So forget about this possibility and concentrate on how to win the most money in the much more likely scenarios.

First, the right way to start is by calling rather than raising. A raise shows real strength and should chase away most holdings that don't contain an ace. A call, on the other hand, makes a statement more like *"I know your bet represents an ace, but everybody c-bets in this position, so maybe you have something, but I have something too, and maybe my something is better than your something."* Of course, there's no guarantee that a call will get more money from his non-aces, but it's a start.

You call 4,400 and the pot is now 21,200 chips. The turn is the Q♠ and your opponent bets 5,100, about one-quarter of the pot.

This second small bet by the early position player suggests he's trying to show some strength at minimum cost and perhaps buy a pot that's up for grabs. Since you're pot-committed, now is the time to check out the stacks and the pot and figure out what sort of raise (if any) will let all the chips get in on the river.

If you call, the pot becomes 31,400 chips. Each player has contributed 13,700, so his remaining stack is about 66,000 and yours is about 86,000, making his the effective stack. But if you call now and then push all-in on the river after a check, your push will be about twice the current pot. That's a pretty big bet and he'll be able to get away from most of his range. Therefore, it's probably best to raise something now which allows a better push on the river. Let's look at a couple of raise sizes and see what happens.

1. **Minimum Raise.** You make a more or less minimum raise to 11,000 and he calls. Now the pot is about 52,000 and his stack is about 56,000. An all-in move on the river is just over a pot-sized bet.

2. **Slightly Larger than Minimum Raise.** You make a slightly larger than minimum raise to 15,000 and he calls. Now the pot is about 60,000 and his stack is about 52,000. An all-in move is now just a little less than the pot.

3. **Reasonable Size Raise.** You make a reasonable raise to 20,000 and he calls. Now the pot is about 70,000 and his stack is about 47,000. An all-in move is now about 65 percent of the pot.

So what's the best raise size among these three choices?

At first glance, it's a tough problem. A small raise makes the call on the turn easier but it also makes the call on the river harder. A large bet reverses the problem, making the river call easier but the turn call harder. However, the decision gets easier if we consider a couple of other points.

1. A second spade just arrived on the turn which opens a couple of possibilities. He might now have a flush draw, making his turn call a little easier. Ideally, he might be holding the A♠K♠ or the A♠Q♠, in which case he could believe that he has the best hand, plus a draw to the nuts.

2. Even without a flush draw, he'll know that we could have a flush draw and our bet is a semi-bluff, giving him a good reason to call. A larger bet on our part is more in keeping with a semi-bluff.

3. Whichever bet size we pick, the river bet will be much larger. Therefore we want to make that the easier bet to call.

Put all these pieces together and a larger turn bet and a smaller river bet appears best. Thus, the reasonable size raise is the better option.

Situation No. 2: Raise the turn when you have the nuts or something close to it. This scenario is pretty simple. You have a really strong hand, either the nuts or close to the nuts. The stacks are deep, so the previous situation doesn't really apply. Your opponent bets the turn. — he may have bet the flop as well. — you should raise.

This may seem obvious but a surprising number of players will just call on the turn hoping their opponent will bet the river as well, after which they will spring the trap and raise. This variation appeals to those for whom the chief delight of poker is surprising their opponent with a clever play. And that's a treat, of course, and I like it as well as the next guy. But what I prefer even more is winning the maximum amount of money in a hand. For that goal, raising the nuts is best. Let's see why.

When you have a very strong hand, your opponent can have one of several types of hands. Let's estimate what happens with each possible type.

1. **Your opponent has nothing and he's just fired a double-barrel bluff.** If you raise, he'll fold. Just calling, on the other hand, allows him to check and fold to your river bet. There's also a small possibility he'll fire a third barrel on the river, in which case you'll raise and pick up that bet. So calling is slightly better because it allows a small chance of picking up an additional bet.

2. **Your opponent has a hand of medium strength, like middle or top pair.** In most cases, your opponent would be better off checking for pot control after betting the flop. However, our assumption is that he did bet the turn and now the results are similar to No. 1 above. So if you raise now, he'll probably fold. Call, and he'll likely check the river. And when you bet on the river, he'll usually fold because your betting pattern looks strong — call, call, then bet. As before, calling is somewhat better because you will sometimes pick up an extra bet.

3. **Your opponent has a very good hand, but not as good as yours.** Raise the turn and he'll probably call. He doesn't have

the nuts and you've shown real strength, so he has to be a little worried. But not many players will lay down a very strong hand on the turn to your first show of strength. If a draw is possible, he'll realize that you may be semi-bluffing, and that will help keep him in the hand. On the river, he'll check and then be a big favorite to call your river bet.

If you just call the turn, the river can go a number of ways. He might check and call, hoping to pick off some bluffs. But he might bet since you've shown no strength yet, and if there is a bet, and you raise, he might call your raise.

So raising gets a big edge here. If he's not willing to bet all the way with the hand, raising will pick up a turn bet and perhaps a much larger river bet as well. If he's willing to bet through the river, raising the turn eases the way to getting all the money in on the end.

4. **Your opponent has the nuts.** No difference here. All the money goes in whatever you do on the turn.

Looking at all the cases, it's easy to see that raising the turn comes out ahead. Calling gives you a small chance of winning another bet when he has no hand or a medium-strength hand. Raising gives a good chance of winning a much larger river bet, or even his whole stack when he has a pretty good hand. Furthermore, raising is especially good with a draw on board since you're charging him to see a card when he has a draw, and when he doesn't, he has to consider that you may be semi-bluffing.

Situation No. 3: After floating the flop you still have a bluffing hand. The logic here goes as follows. Your opponent raises preflop and you call with something. The flop comes and you miss completely, or end up with a weak holding like a small pair or a gutshot straight draw. Your opponent makes a continuation bet and you think he's an aggressive player who bets a high percentage of flops. So you call with the intention of taking the pot away on the turn.

On the turn, you'll bet if your opponent just checks. But if this is an aggressive player, he often won't check. Instead, he'll fire a second barrel even without a hand, and a raise on your part will sometimes take the pot down.

Prudently applied, this strategy can be effective, and here are a few guidelines to help you make this play at the right time.

1. Your opponent needs to be aggressive enough to fire a second barrel as a bluff. Don't try this move against tight players.

2. This move works best on dry boards. If an obvious draw is present, your move will look like a semi-bluff to a lot of players, who will then finally call to see if the river card fills the draw.

3. The move is a little more effective if your opponent has made a small turn bet. Many players fear that small bets are traps, but they're more often attempts to take down pots cheaply.

4. This is a move for the middle or late stages of a tournament, not the early stages. As players are eliminated and the bubble gets closer, they are less willing to jeopardize their tournament life, so the move will now work more often. (The early stages are better spent paying attention and gathering information for middle and late-stage bluffs.)

Situation No. 4: His turn bet is most likely a semi-bluff. If you have a value hand and your opponent takes the lead on a board where draws are his most likely holding, then raise to protect your hand and deny your opponent good drawing odds. This is an especially good play if your opponent is aggressive. The probability that he has a semi-bluff will outweigh the chances that he actually has a hand better than yours.

Example 5-17. It's a big tournament, and about half the players have been eliminated at this point. Blinds are 800 and 1,600, with a 200-chip ante producing a starting pot of 4,200 chips. You're in third position with the A♠Q♠, your stack is 170,000 with an M of 40 (106 big blinds), you haven't played many hands since you sat down so your image is tight, and your stack is the second-biggest at the table.

The first two players fold. You raise to 4,100 and everyone folds to the somewhat tight and passive player on the button, who calls. His stack is 100,000 with an M of 24 (63 big blinds). The big blind calls as well. He's been loose and very aggressive, and his stack is about 310,000 with an M of 74. The pot is now 14,900 chips.

The flop is the 9♣8♣4♠, the big blind checks, and you've flopped a backdoor flush draw and two overcards. It's not a huge hand, but might still be the best hand at the table, and you have position on the dangerous player in the big blind. You make a continuation bet of 7,000, a little less than half the pot, the button folds, and the big blind calls. The pot grows to 28,900 chips.

The turn is the A♥ giving you top pair with a good kicker. The big blind leads for 11,000 and the action is on you.

This is a good spot to raise. You now have a solid value hand and your opponent is known to have a wide range and be very aggressive. He may believe that the arrival of the ace on the turn will allow him to chase away a lot of strong pairs (KK, QQ, JJ, TT) either with this bet or with a follow-up bet on the river. He may also be drawing to a straight or a flush and be semi-bluffing. So given his profile, the stack sizes, and the stage of the tournament, he may be bluffing figuring that you don't have a good enough hand to play a really big pot and jeopardize your substantial stack.

Given his wide range and aggressive nature, all that can be said is there are lots of scenarios where he wants you to go away and doesn't want to see a raise. Put another way, when playing really aggressive players, you have to take advantage of situations like this or else be slowly whittled away.

You raise to 40,000. He stews for a long while to let you know that his decision is agonizingly close, then folds.

When to Check the Turn

Of course, you're not always going to be betting or raising the turn. Often, simply checking is the best play. Sometimes checking exercises pot control; sometimes it can trap your opponent or induce a bluff; and sometimes checking is just a prelude to folding. Let's look at the major reasons for checking the turn, plus a few examples.

Reason to Check No. 1: Check for pot control. "Big hand, big pot. Small hand, small pot."

The most common reason for checking the turn is pot control. Suppose you have a hand like top pair or second pair, it's relatively early in the tournament, the stacks are deep, and you're not interested in playing a big pot (with this hand). If you bet the flop or someone else bet the flop and you called, you're content to skip this round of betting and see what happens on the river. The nature of no-limit hold 'em is that pots increase on a geometric basis as bets and raises are made. So shortening the hand by removing a betting round is how players control the pot sizes. (Note that checking the flop and betting the turn gets you to the same situation and is often an equally good sequence.)

Let's look at a couple of practical examples.

Example 5-18. It's the first level of a big tournament, blinds are 25 and 50, and you're in the big blind with 21,000 and an M of 280 (420 big blinds). The player in third position, whose stack is a little bigger than yours at about 23,000, and who's already played several pots and seems aggressive, raises to 150. The player in the cutoff seat, who you don't have a read on yet, and who has about 20,000, just calls. The button and small blind fold and you call with the

The pot is now 475 chips.
The flop is the

You check and the original raiser bets 250, the cutoff folds, and you call. The pot is now 975 chips.

Should you have raised on the flop? It's a play, but I prefer calling. You have a decent but not a great hand on a dry flop. If you raise and get reraised, you won't know where you stand and it's then probably best to throw your hand away. The downside of calling is that your hand is fairly transparent: your likely hands are either a pair of queens or a pocket pair between queens and eights, a pretty small set of possible hands. But the downside of raising is that the pot starts to get big and you're out of position with a good but not great hand. Both plays have downsides, but the downside of calling is a little more manageable. The turn is the 6♥ and the action is on you.

Again, the right play is to check. This is a classic pot control situation with a hand that's good enough to call a bet, especially from a very aggressive player, but where you'd be uncomfortable calling a big raise if you take the lead. Notice also that there are few scare cards on the river. Specifically, of the two overcards to the queen, you're only worried about an ace. If you have the better hand right now, your opponent most likely only has two or three outs.

The other reason for checking is your opponent. If he's as aggressive as you believe, a check may induce him to bluff the turn and perhaps the river as well. You make money against very aggressive players by giving as few clues as possible to the actual strength of your hand. They make double and triple barrel bluffs because those plays usually work! That is, very few opponents can take this kind of pressure with just a single pair in their hand. But by not being afraid to take a stand, their aggression turns into a liability.

You check and (to your surprise), your opponent checks behind. The pot remains at 975 chips.

His check is probably a sign that he can't beat a pair of queens and he's given up on the hand. If a blank comes on the river, your best move will be to make a small value bet, around 350, and see if he'll bite.

Example 5-19. It's the middle of the first day of a large tournament and most of the field is still in play. Blinds are 200 and 400, with a 50-chip ante producing a starting pot of 1,050 chips.

You're in fourth position with the Q♠T♠, your stack is 27,000 with an M of 26 (68 big blinds), about average at this table, and your image is fairly aggressive The first three players fold. You raise to 1,000, the hijack seat folds, but the cutoff calls. He's relatively new at the table but seems to be aggressive. However, his stack of 16,000 and an M of 15 is second smallest at the table. The button and the blinds fold and you go to the flop with a pot of 3,050 chips.

The flop is the Q♣J♠5♦. You could make a continuation bet but decide to check instead. It's a close call and there isn't any wrong play, but several factors influence your decision:

1.   Up to this point, you've been aggressive and have made a lot of c-bets, so this might be a good time to back off. With top pair, your hand will be at the top of whatever range your opponent assigns to you.

2. There are only two high cards whose arrival might be a little scary — aces and kings.

3. By checking, you keep your opponent's entire range alive. Since he's aggressive and probably won't credit you with checking top pair, he might get inspired to run a bluff.

He bets 1,400 and you call. The pot is now 5,850 chips. The turn is the 4♠ and again you decide to check. The turn card didn't change anything unless he happens to hold a pair of fours or five-four, which would be unlikely and unlucky although it now gives you a flush draw to go along with your top pair. Since your opponent was willing to take the lead, just continue the plan. At this point, your hand looks like a pair of jacks or some medium pair, and it's reasonable for him to think he could push you off those hands.

He bets 2,600, slightly less than half the pot. Again, you call, and the pot is now 10,050 chips.

On the river, your plan is to check and call if he bets no matter what card hits the board. Since you've underrepresented your hand on both the flop and the turn, he may bet the river with nothing. By keeping his entire range alive, you won't be able to interpret a bet by him as representing a value bet that beats your pair of queens.

One of the worst mistakes players make is to set a trap but then fold the river because their opponent's bet 'must' represent a really strong hand. So if you set a trap, be prepared to see it through.

Reason to Check No. 2: Check to allow your opponent to bluff the river with hands he would fold on the turn. When you have a strong hand like a set or trips, and your opponent has shown some interest in the pot, checking the turn can be a good play. The idea is that a bet on the turn might chase away most medium-strength hands, but a check, indicating some weakness, might be enough to let him either bluff the river or make what he thinks is a thin value bet.

This play can be made either in or out of position, but in position is better since it allows you to bet the river if he actually decides to check the river. A somewhat dry board is also helpful so that he can't have a lot of outs with the sort of hand you think he has.

Example 5-20. You're in a big tournament with about 40 percent of the field remaining. The blinds are 1,000 and 2,000, with a 200-chip ante producing a starting pot of 4,800 chips, and you're on the button with the J♣8♣, and a stack of 150,000 producing an M of 31 (75 big blinds).

After two folds, the player in third position, a standard tight-aggressive player with a stack of about 120,000 and an M of 25, raises to 4,800. The loose-aggressive player in the hijack seat, with about 100,000 with an M of 21, calls. This person has made some strange bluffs and you think he might be the weakest player at the table. You call with position, a reasonable hand, and 3-to-1 pot odds. The blinds fold and the pot is 14,400 chips.

The flop is the 8♥8♠5♠ and your trips are almost certainly the best hand. The player in third position checks. The player in the hijack seat bets 7,000 and you call, disguising your hand and hoping for a raise from the third player. However, he folds and you go to the turn with a pot of 28,400 chips.

The turn is the 3♣, which is unlikely to help your opponent's hand. He checks, and now it's worth giving some thought to what this player might actually have. Since he called a bet preflop and led into two players on the flop, his most likely holdings are a pocket pair, probably nines up through jacks, or two Broadway cards, possibly suited. Less likely are a pair of sevens or sixes, and still less likely is the case eight.

Given the stack sizes, a bet now threatens all his chips. If you bet, say, 16,000 and he calls, the pot will be 60,400 and he'll have about 70,000 left. With those sizes, the river action will be an all-in bet. So your opponent will have to decide, after you bet the turn, if he's willing to play for all his chips on the river. If we're right about his possible holdings, he'll probably fold most of that range to a bet now.

But if you check behind, the problem changes. Depending on the river card, most of his range will start to look better, with his tendency to bluff in spots, this player may decide that this is just the place to take the pot away. He might also think that his holding is good enough for a thin value bet. In either case, you're much more likely to win an extra bet with a check now.

Reasons to Check No. 3: A trap against a very aggressive player when you're holding a good hand. In judo, the key to success is using leverage to make your opponent's strength and weight work against him. A similar principle applies when you're matched against a very loose-aggressive player in tournament poker. A loose-aggressive player plays a lot of pots, often without much of a hand. He knows that most confrontations after the flop involve two marginal hands, and he's good at winning a lot of those pots. There aren't many players, after all, who want to invest half their stack in defending top pair, weak kicker.

In order to stay out of trouble, good aggressive players look for cues that you have a strong hand and not something marginal. Most of these cues are pretty simple. When you bet and raise, you're showing strength. When you check and call, you're showing weakness. And when you show weakness with a strong holding, you allow the loose-aggressive player to bet at pots where in fact you hold the upper hand. And as Layne Flack used to say, "Let the donkey do the work."

Example 5-21. It's early in the second day of a major tournament, and about 60 percent of the field still remains. Blinds are 800 and 1,600, with a 200-chip ante producing a starting pot of 4,200 chips. Action folds to a very loose and aggressive player in the fourth seat, with a stack of about 280,000, by far the biggest at the table, and an M of 67, who raises to 4,000. The action folds around to you in the small blind. You have the

and a decent stack of 100,000 with an M of 24 (62 big blinds). Your image is tight and straightforward.

You decide to slowplay and just call. If you hit the flop, your hand will be well disguised and potentially a big money-maker. Also notice that image here works in your favor, as an aggressive opponent will mostly not credit you with having ace-king in your range. So you call 3,200, the big blind calls as well, and the pot is 13,800 chips.

The flop is the

a dry flop. You have top pair, top kicker on a flop where no one is likely to have two pair. Of course, one of your opponents might have flopped a set, but that is also unlikely.

Consistent with your plan, you check, the big blind checks, and the aggressive player bets 5,500. It's a continuation bet of well under half the pot. Smallish continuation bets are consistent with an aggressive style. If his opponent has already decided to go away, there's no need for him to bet more. If his opponent has decided to stick around, there's also no need to risk more on what will mostly be a bluff.

You call, continuing to under represent your hand and the big blind folds. The pot is now 24,800 and the turn is the A♥.

This card is perfect for your purposes. Your call preflop and your check-call on the flop could be interpreted as a weak king or a medium pair that isn't convinced the king is good for your opponent. Consequently, the arrival of the ace should be very scary if you hold any of these hands, and your opponent could reasonably believe that a bet here will chase you off a lot of them. On the other hand, a bet on your part would be a giveaway for the sort of hand you're actually holding. You check and your opponent bets 9,500.

From your opponent's point of view, a bet of any size should be enough to chase you away, so the small bet is again perfectly logical. Now you can call or raise. *What's best?*

A raise gives away the trap, even more so than a bet would. It puts you on a strong ace, a two pair hand, or possibly a set. A call is also suspicious, but just might be interpreted as king-queen or king-jack, perhaps suited in hearts, and a call gives you a chance of making some more money on the river, while a raise will just chase away almost every hand that you're beating.

So after considerable thought you call, and the pot is now 43,800 chips. Also, the effective stack is about 80,000 chips.

You should now be prepared to check the river regardless of what hits since a bet of any kind is too likely to chase him away. The combination of your long pause on the turn followed by a call may convince him that you're sitting on a king and are willing to go away after just one more bet. It's also likely to be his only chance to win the hand.

Reason to Check No. 4: Check when a scare card hits and you have a decent hand. Suppose it's relatively early in the tournament. When you have a good hand on the flop but a dangerous card hits the turn, checking is usually best. We're talking about hands like top pair when an ace hits the board, or two pair or a set when a flush or straight draw appears to hit. The problem is that betting will mostly only fold out weaker hands that you're beating anyway, while keeping better hands in the pot. You may make this play later in the tournament as well for the same reason, but it's an even clearer play when the stacks are deep.

Example 5-22. It's early in a big tournament. The blinds are 50 and 100, you're in fourth position with a stack of 22,000 and an M of 147 (220 big blinds), the first three players fold, and you have the

You raise to 300, and the button and big blind call. Both have around 20,000, both seem to be tight players, and you haven't played enough in this level to have much of an image yet. The pot is now 950 chips.

The flop is the

giving you an overpair and some draws are possible. With the probable best hand and two opponents, you want to make a good-sized bet and chase at least one of them away. The big blind checks. You elect to make a continuation bet of 750, the button folds, but the big blind calls. The pot is now 2,450 chips, the turn is the A♣, and the big blind checks.

The best play here is to check behind. The big blind was getting good pot odds to call preflop. (The pot was 750 at that point and he needed to put in 200 to call, so he was getting 3.75-to-1.) He could have called with a lot of aces, especially suited aces. On the flop, he could easily have called with ace-queen, ace-jack, ace-ten, or A♦X♦. So a bet here won't chase away any aces and it won't get much action from hands that you're beating — check to keep the pot small and see what happens on the river. If the big blind checks again, make a half-pot bet for value. If the big blind bets the river with something like two-thirds of the pot, call because of the pot odds. Your hand looks weak because of the sequence of a c-bet and a check, so your opponent will be bluffing part of the time.

When Your
Opponent Raises the Turn

Let's suppose that you've taken the lead through a hand. You raised preflop and got called. You hit something on the flop, made a continuation bet, and got called again. Now the turn comes and you still have a hand with solid value, something like top pair or maybe an overpair but not a monster. Now you bet again and your opponent raises. (The same scenario applies if he checks the turn, you bet and he check-raises.) *What do you do?*

If your opponent is anything but a loose and very aggressive player, this betting sequence usually means a set (or better). He called preflop with a pair, flopped a set, called your c-bet in the hope you would bet again on the turn, and has now sprung his trap. If you can't beat a set, it's best to fold.

Like all poker rules, there are a few exceptions, although this rule has fewer than most.

1. If your opponent just lost a big hand and appears to be on tilt, don't assume he has a monster. In this case, it's more likely that he's steamed and raising something like top pair than that he has a really big hand.

2. If your opponent is a good loose-aggressive player, he probably understands that raising the turn and representing a set is a great bluff. In this case, you're in a tough spot because he'll also be raising with his monsters. The bigger his stack and the more aggressive he's been, the more likely this is either an outright bluff or a weak made hand with some outs. Use your common sense and proceed with caution.

If you have a tight image and haven't been especially active, this is a great bluffing move to employ when you're against a strong player and in position. It's most effective when the board is unpaired, not especially draw-heavy, and has at most one high card because you're representing a medium to low set.

Example 5-23. You're late in the first day at a major tournament and about 75 percent of the field still remains. Blinds are 200 and 400, with a 50-chip ante producing a starting pot of 1,050 chips. You pick up the

in second position and your stack is 32,000, with an M of 30 (80 big blinds). You've been active and your image is moderately aggressive.

The under-the-gun player folds, you raise to 1,100, and the player in fourth position calls. His stack is about 38,000 and he seems to be a moderately tight player. The action then folds around to the big blind who calls with 26,000 and an M of 25 (65 big blinds). He's also fairly tight, but you've noticed he'll defend his big blind with a lot of hands. The pot is now 3,950 chips, the flop is the

and the big blind checks.

The flop completely missed your hand but you decide that against two tight players it's reasonable to venture a continuation bet. You bet 2,000 but both your opponents call. That's not the result you wanted, but perhaps you're up against a spade draw and a medium pair. The pot is now 9,950 chips.

The turn is the Q♣. That's better and now you have top pair, top kicker, and the big blind checks once again. You're probably the only one helped by the turn, so you bet again, this time 5,500. The button folds, but the big blind raises to 11,000. Not what you wanted to see. *What to do?*

Unless your opponent is bluffing, he's representing a hand you probably can't beat. He called out of position preflop, but he likes to defend his blind and he was getting a great price (about 4.5-to-1) so his range is almost anything at this point. On the flop, however, he called out of position after you had bet and the button had called. That probably means he had at least a piece of the flop — maybe a pair, maybe a flush draw, maybe a pair and a flush draw, maybe a set. But on the turn, he raised after you bet again. Since you think he's a little tight, that raise pretty much eliminates the flush draw and the pairs, leaving the pair plus flush draw hands and the sets.

There's a little more evidence to be considered. He made a minimum raise, apparently fishing for a call, and he's put half his stack in the pot so far, and this isn't a play tight players make with just an underpair. Therefore, the evidence makes the sets more likely and the flush draw plus a pair a little less likely.

If you were up against a loose-aggressive player with a deep stack, you'd have a tough choice to make. But in this particular situation, it's best to fold. Every piece of evidence suggests he's sitting there with a set of tens, sixes, or treys. You've lost 8,000, but be glad to get away this cheaply.

Part Six

Playing the River

Playing the River

Introduction

When the stacks are deep, the river is the most important street in no-limit hold 'em and this fact puzzles many newcomers to no-limit. So why is the river more important than, say, the flop? There are three basic reasons, all of which work together.

First, the bets are much larger than on any other street. When bets are made in no-limit, the pot grows geometrically from street to street, and the cost of making an error grows along with the size of the pot. If you make a bad preflop move, like raising with a weak hand from early position, the actual cost of your mistake in terms of equity lost might only be between one and two big blinds. However, if there is betting action on the flop and turn, the cost of a bad error on the river might easily be 50 big blinds or more.

Second, there are no more cards to come after reaching the river. A player with the best hand who won't fold is 100 percent to win. And failure to bet a strong hand is therefore a much more serious error than on previous streets.

Last, more information is available than on any other street. You've seen your opponent take actions (sometimes multiple actions) before the flop, on the flop, and on the turn. With position, you've even seen your opponent act on the river. With that information, it's possible to narrow his starting range down to a fairly small set of hands. This means that whatever the skill difference between you and your opponent, the river gives you the ideal stage to use that edge.

Evaluating Your Hand

The first step in playing the river is evaluating your hand. This sounds simple enough, but it's actually a process that involves answering the four separate questions that follow, and all four are key in deciding the best strategy to use. By the way, a good player will mostly know the answers to these questions when he reaches the river. A newcomer may think about one or two of them, but will lose track of the big picture. Let's take each question in turn and see how the answers help you construct a river strategy.

Question No. 1: What do you have? This is really a two-part question — what's your actual hand, and given the betting action on all the streets, how strong is that hand likely to be? Given what has happened so far and your estimate of your opponent's range, you should be able to classify your hand into one of five categories:

1. The nuts, or close to it.

2. A strong hand but not the nuts.

3. A good hand given the action.

4. A hand with some value.

5. Busto.

With the nuts, your strategy is to get all your money in the center. With the second or the third nuts, your strategy will mostly be the same unless it's an obvious situation such as a four-flush on board. Since stacks tend not to be large in most stages of a tournament, it's unlikely that any action your opponent can take on the river will convince you to lay down a big hand. That is, the twin chance that your opponent is either bluffing or betting a merely good hand will be enough to keep you in the pot.

With a strong hand which isn't the nuts, you still want to bet for value. If your opponent raises, you'll have a tough decision to make. Raising, calling, or folding will all be possible depending on an analysis of the situation.

A merely good hand given the action so far usually requires what is known in the trade as a "thin value" bet. This is a bet that is likely to be profitable, even though you may only be a 60-to-40 favorite when called, and even though you're probably going to fold if raised.

A hand with some value might be a top pair or middle pair hand where you're willing to call and try to pick off a bluff, but betting isn't likely to be profitable. And a bust is a hand without even that much value; your only choices are bluffing or folding.

Question No. 2: What range can your opponent put you on? The average tournament player is pretty comfortable thinking about his opponent's range. "What does that bet mean?" "What could he have here?" Players who are serious about the game quickly train themselves to ask these questions, and that's good.

But an equally important question to ask is this: "Given what my opponent has seen, what does he think I have?" Asking this question is less natural simply because you *know* what you have, and it's harder to look at your bets through the eyes of someone who doesn't know your hand. But trying to see what your opponent sees is a necessary skill to develop, and will increase your hand-reading skills dramatically.

Question No. 3: Where is your actual hand in that range — top, bottom, or middle? Once you estimate the range your opponent assigns to your hand, see where your actual hand fits in that range.

If it is at the top of his range for you, then we say your hand has been *underrepped:* You've represented a hand that's weaker, perhaps much weaker, than what you actually hold. If you're first to act, you can bet with the expectation of being called. If your opponent acts first and bets, you at least need to call. Don't make the classic blunder of underrepping a hand, then being afraid to call on the end because your opponent bets and you convince yourself that he's ahead. So when underrepping a hand, you're trying to lure your opponent into betting. If he then bets, follow through and see what he's got.

If your hand is at the bottom of his range for you, then you've *overrepped* it. That is, he most likely thinks you have something better than what you actually have, and betting now turns your hand from a weak made hand into a bluff. Put another way, if you bet and get called, expect to lose, and if he raises, it's probably best to fold. Yes, bluffing might still be the best play under some circumstances, but generally, you'll be using your holding as a bluff-catcher.

A key point to keep in mind when evaluating your hand from your opponent's point of view is this: *When did you make your hand?* If you made a big hand on the turn or the river, it will be a little harder for your opponent to credit you with something strong than if you connected on the flop. (The obvious flush draw that connects on the river is of course an exception.) The better the player, the less likely this rule holds.

Question No. 4: How big is the pot? The last rule for evaluating hands on the river is to consider the pot size. The bigger the pot, the more likely that players have played the hand straightforwardly. The smaller the pot, the more likely that deceptive plays are involved. Also, and this is very important, the bigger the pot, the more important it becomes to just win what's out there. The smaller the pot, the more willing you are to slowplay to trap your opponent.

Playing a
Strong Hand on the River

Suppose you get to the river with a very strong hand — the nuts or something close to it. *How should you play it?*

Before you answer, consider one additional question. *Imagine that you make a pot-sized bet and your opponent then moves all-in. Will you call or fold?* If your answer is "My hand is too good, I'll have to call that bet," or "I'm pot-committed, I have to call," then treat your hand as if you had the nuts and play accordingly. If folding to an all-in seems a better choice, then you don't have a really strong hand. Instead, consider the advice in the next section on thin value betting. If, however, you're willing to go all the way with the hand, strategy gets pretty simple: bet and raise.

When first to act, you should almost always bet. Checking with the idea of getting a juicy check-raise is enticing, but runs the risk that your opponent may smell a rat and check behind, or just not have a hand that he feels is worth a bet on the river. But betting will often get a call from a player who thinks his hand is good enough to pick off a bluff, or who thinks that it has some value and just wants to see your cards. On the river, there will always be plenty of hands that won't bet but will call; betting gets money from them.

If you're in position and your opponent checks, bet your strong hands. If he bets and you're willing to go all the way, raise. If his bet is surprising in some way and you don't have the nuts, you can consider calling. In my experience, players tend to call too much and raise too little with very good non-nut hands. However, if you have some history with a player and feel strongly that he wouldn't bet the river without the nuts, (and such players do exist), then just call.

Example 6-1. It's the middle of the first day in a big live tournament. The blinds are 150 and 300, and antes kick in on the next level. You're in the cutoff seat at a full table with a stack of 28,000 and an M of 62 (93 big blinds). You've done well so far with the third-largest stack at the table, and your image is somewhat loose and aggressive.

On this hand, the action folds around and you look down to see the

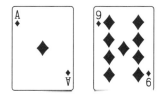

Both blinds have been somewhat tight, while the button is definitely loose, aggressive, and somewhat tricky. You decide your hand is worth a raise under the circumstances, so you raise to 800. The button calls and has about 20,000 remaining after the call, and the blinds fold. The pot is now 2,050 chips.

The flop comes the

You have bottom pair plus a backdoor flush draw on a dangerous board. You elect to take a pot-control line and check, and the button checks behind which seems a little surprising. The pot remains at 2,050 chips.

The turn is the 8♦. If the button has a ten, he just hit a straight, and you now have the nut flush draw to go with your pair. So betting half the pot as a semi-bluff seems reasonable. You bet 1,000 and your opponent raises to 3,000. The pot is now 6,050 chips and it costs 2,000 more to call. Your expressed odds are only 3-to-1, but you decide that if he has what he's representing (a straight) and you hit your flush, you'll win at least one more good-sized bet on the end. Thus you call. The pot is now 8,050 chips.

The river is the 2♦ and your flush has arrived, and the effective stack is about 17,000. *What's your play?*

You have the nuts, so your choices are to bet or check with the idea of check-raising. Note that if you check and he makes a normal-sized bet of 5,000 to 6,000, your check-raise will be all-in given the effective stack size.

But the default play in this case should be to bet. He actually has a wide range of possible hands that fit the betting action. Of these hands, however, very few are guaranteed to bet after a check, while most will call a bet, especially since only one flush card appeared on the flop. And to see the advantages of betting more clearly, let's run through some of your opponent's possible hands and see how they would react to both a bet and a check.

- **A weaker flush.** From your point of view, this is your opponent's optimal hand, particularly if he holds the K♦. Since the A♦ and Q♦ are accounted for, he could hold the K♦J♦, K♦T♦, or J♦T♦. The button would have called with all of these hands preflop, and could have raised any of them on the turn. The check on the flop might have been a little surprising, but we noted that he was tricky, so all of these hands are in his range. In addition, some of the lower suited connectors like the 7♦6♦ or the 6♦5♦ also fit the play.

  If you bet, all the flushes will at least call. No one, least of all a loose-aggressive opponent, will fold a flush at this stage of the tournament when getting 2-to-1 pot odds, and king-high flushes will probably move all-in.

  If you check, all the flushes will bet, and when you then move all-in, they have a problem. Those headed by the king will call, and those with low cards will mostly fold. And given how the hand has played out, I think it might be 50-50 that the jack-high flushes will call.

  Here's a little table that summarizes your profit when your opponent holds a flush:

Opponent's Hand	You Bet	You Check and Raise
He holds K-high flush	Stack	Stack
He holds J-high flush	1 bet	50% stack; 50% 1 bet
He holds low flush	1 bet	1 bet

The result is a slight profit for check and raising, which sometimes wins his stack when he holds a medium flush.

• **A straight.** A ten gives your opponent a straight, and there are a lot of hands containing a ten that might have called your preflop bet from the button, suited or unsuited: AT, KT, QT, JT, T9, or even T8, and of course a pair of tens might have called as well. The check behind on the flop doesn't quite fit, and most players would have bet with all these hands. But a tricky player might have decided it was worth setting a trap, especially if he actually flopped a straight. The 8♦ on the turn completed a straight if he didn't already have it, so the turn raise makes sense.

The arrival of the third diamond puts these hands in a quandary. If you bet, the straights can't raise because only a better hand should call. But the straights are too strong to fold, so they will call and you'll win your bet.

If you check, the straight has to decide whether to bet or not. You bet the turn and called his raise on a dangerous-looking board. Now a flush card hit and you're checking. This might be a trap with a flush, or you might have a ten and the pot will be split. Therefore, the prudent play for your opponent is to check behind. In that case, you win a bet when you lead and probably get nothing if you check. So in this variation, there's a big advantage to betting.

• **A set or two pair.** Given how dangerous the board is, all of these hands will check behind if you check. But if you bet, expect to get some calls. Again, betting yields a small edge.

- **A bluff.** On this board, anything from a pair on down constitutes a bluffing hand. If you bet, these hands will fold. If you check, it's unlikely that your opponent will try a bluff since he raised the turn (which would have been a bluff) and got called. Therefore, neither betting nor checking is likely to make any extra money here.

The net result is that check-raising shows a slight edge over betting if your opponent has a flush, but betting is a big winner if he has a straight, set, or two pair. The two plays are a wash if he has a weaker hand than that. However, the straights, sets, and two-pair hands are his most likely holdings given the betting action thus far, so leading out with a bet is the right idea. This result is typical for playing a very strong hand on the river — the gains from checking and trapping your opponent into making a bet he wouldn't have made otherwise are washed out by the lost bets if the hand is checked down and he would have called a bet.

Betting for Thin Value

We've just looked at value betting when you have a monster hand. It's a pleasant situation to be in, but mostly you'll reach the river without a monster hand. Often, you'll only have top or second pair, or maybe an overpair. Meanwhile, the board offers all sorts of scary possibilities for your opponent. He could have a set or two pair in any number of ways, or even a straight. Bet, and you could be walking right into a big raise.

Many players in this situation will elect to check the hand down, or check with the idea of calling a bet from their opponent to catch a bluff. Sometimes a check is the right play, but other times you can bet your modest-looking hand and be a favorite to pick up some extra chips if you've analyzed the situation properly.

There is a name for river bets with modest holdings: It's called *betting for thin value*, and it's a key part of maximizing your profit on the river. Thin value betting requires confidence above all — the confidence to trust that your analysis of the hand is correct and that your opponent is mostly going to show up with a hand you can beat. However, you'll lose a fair percentage of these bets, and that's why they call it thin value, after all. But you should win more than you lose, and that's enough to make the bet profitable.

To make good thin value bets, you need to know the answers to two questions:

1. Are my opponent's actions on the previous rounds of betting consistent with his having a better hand?

2. Have I overrepped my hand in the course of the betting?

If the answer to both questions is "no," then you have a hand that's a candidate for a value bet on the river.

It's also hard to say much about thin value betting without some examples, so let's look at a few hands and see when we can bet the river without a monster and when we need to back off.

Example 6-2. It's early in a big tournament. Blinds are 100 and 200, you're in the big blind with a stack of 25,000 and an M of 83 (125 big blinds). The aggressive player in third position, whose stack is about the same as yours, raises to 600, the somewhat tight player on the button, whose stack is about 22,000, calls, and the small blind folds. You have the

and make the call. The pot is now 1,900 chips.

The flop is the

giving you top pair and you check to the raiser. The third position player bets 1,050, the button folds, and you elect to keep the pot small and just call. The pot is now 4,000 chips.

The turn is the 6♣, unlikely to help your opponent's hand. You both check. The river is the 2♠ and you are first to act.

Your hand hasn't improved since the flop: it's still only top pair, good kicker. You could be losing to trip eights or various sets or even some overpairs. Nevertheless, you have a solid value bet because your opponent hasn't done anything that suggests he has a better hand. His half-pot bet on the flop looks like a straight continuation bet and may not mean anything. His check on the turn suggests that he either doesn't have anything or has something, but is playing pot control.

You, on the other hand, have underrepped your hand. Your flop call could be interpreted as any pair, and your check on the turn still indicates a weak hand. If he has something like a pair of tens or a weak queen, your bet is likely to get called.

If you bet and he raises, you have a problem. But your best estimate at this point should be that top pair, good kicker is best and could be called by many weaker hands.

You bet 2,400, your opponent calls, and he shows the

You take the pot.

Example 6-3. It's still the first day of a big tournament and the blinds are 200 and 400, with a 25-chip ante at an 8-handed table producing a starting pot of 800 chips. You're in the hijack seat with the K♠J♠ and a stack of 32,000 and an M of 40 (80 big blinds).

The first four players fold, you raise to 1,100, and the cutoff calls. He seems a little tight and not especially aggressive, and his stack is 22,000 after he calls. The button folds, the small blind, who you don't know much about and whose stack is 40,000, calls, and the big blind folds. The pot is now 3,900 chips.

The flop is the J♥9♣4♥ giving you top pair with a good kicker against two opponents, and the small blind checks. Although you're against two opponents, you do have top pair and there are some cards (aces and queens) that would be uncomfortable to see on the turn. So you make a continuation bet of 2,000. The cutoff calls and the small blind folds. The pot is now 7,900 chips.

The turn is the 9♦. This isn't a good card for you since a number of calling hands (A9, T9, 98) just made trips. You both check. The river is the 5♠ and you must act first.

As in the last hand, there's no evidence that your opponent holds a better hand than your top pair, second-best kicker. He called your continuation bet, indicating he had something, and he declined to bet when the nine paired on the turn, indicating the card didn't help his hand.

None of this is conclusive evidence of anything, but that's the nature of betting for thin value. He may be slowplaying a set of jacks or fours, or even quad nines. He might have jack-nine and be slowplaying a full house, or he might even have ace-jack and be controlling the pot. It's more likely, however, that he has a pair that you beat, or a straight draw that didn't hit. With thin value betting, you're just making a bet that you think will win the majority of the time that you are called (and only rarely raised). That's enough to show a handsome profit in the long run.

Note that since you've underrepped your hand with just a continuation bet on the flop and a check on the turn, there's a good chance that a weaker hand will pay your bet off. The key idea of thin value betting is that it's not enough to make a bet where you mostly have the better hand, there has to be a decent chance that when your bet is called, it's called by a weaker hand.

You bet 4,300. After some thought, your opponent calls and mucks a pair of tens.

In these first two examples, you had to act first on the river. If you have position on the river, your situation is even more favorable since you get one more crucial piece of information.

Example 6-4. It's late in the first day of a live tournament. Blinds are 300 and 600, with a 75-chip ante producing a starting pot of 1,575 chips. The player in third position, who seems fairly tight but likes to continuation bet whenever he opens in early position, opens for 1,600. His stack, after betting, looks like about 52,000. The action folds to you on the button and your stack is 60,000 chips (M = 38). You call with the K♠J♠, the small blind folds, and the big blind calls. He seems to be about average on the tight/aggressive scale, but he's been defending his big blind most of the time since antes kicked in. The pot is now 5,775 chips.

The flop is the K♥9♦6♣. The big blind checks and the preflop raiser now bets 3,100. You have top pair with a modest kicker and a player is still to act in the hand. You call and the big blind folds. The pot is now 11,975 chips.

The turn is the 3♣ which puts a flush draw on board and your opponent checks. Your top pair is likely good here and you bet 6,500, and your opponent calls. The pot is now 24,975 chips.

The river is the 4♣, putting the third flush card on board and completing some low straights. Your opponent checks again.

Your hand, top pair with a modest kicker, is even weaker than in our last couple of examples. Still, a bet is worth considering. The board has both potential flush and straight draws, and of course sets and two-pair hands are also possible. But your opponent checked the river, so it's unlikely he actually has any of these holdings. The stronger the hand, the more likely he wants to bet the river when first to act because there's too much danger that you'll check behind if he checks. The fact that he didn't bet the river forces you to downgrade his range dramatically. Consequently, his most likely holding is a pair from queens down through eights.

The only problem with betting is that you can't be sure that he'll call with a worse hand. If he has the hand you expect, let's say a pair of queens or a pair of tens, then he'll be worried that you have a pair of kings, but he also has to consider the possibility that you have a set, or even a flush. The low sets are unlikely since it's hard to believe that you called a flop bet against two opponents with a pair of treys or fours. The flush is also unlikely since it came via the back door route. But you could have a set of nines or sixes, and he has to add that to the possibility that you've got a king.

So should you bet? Before you do, consider this. Unlike the previous hands, here your betting so far perfectly represents your holding.

1.   With top pair you called a bet on the flop with two players still active in the hand. With an overpair or a set you might have raised, and with bottom pair or nothing you probably would have folded, but a call would be typical of anything from a pair of kings down to a pair of nines.

2.   With one player out and your opponent leading off with a check, you bet the turn. That's reasonable with top pair and no draws on board. You probably wouldn't have bet with a pair of queens, jacks, tens, or nines.

An intelligent opponent has to think that a pair of kings now represents the biggest part of your range, so the chance that you get paid off with a call isn't obviously bigger than the chance you get raised or beaten in a showdown. Therefore, in this case, I think the thin value from betting is indeed pretty thin, and I would be inclined to check the hand down without some sort of read that this particular opponent is likely to call with a lower pair.

Example 6-5. It's the opening level of a big tournament. Blinds are 50 and 100. Your stack is 25,000 (M = 167) and you have the

in third position. The first two players fold and you raise to 300. The action folds to the cutoff seat, who calls, the button folds, and both blinds call. All three players have stacks similar to yours and you don't know much about anyone at this point. The pot is now 1,200 chips.
     The flop is the

The blinds check. You bet 900, the cutoff and the small blind folds, but the big blind calls. The pot is now 3,000 chips.

The turn is the A♦. The big blind checks and you check behind for pot control and to get more information. The river is the 6♥, the big blind checks, and the action is on you.

Here you don't even have top pair, but this is still a spot for a good value bet. You weren't happy when the ace arrived on the turn because the big blind might have called the flop with several different aces. However, he has now passed on two chances to bet, so you have to conclude that the ace didn't help him and he's trying to get to showdown. (Remember, that he called the flop on a very dry board, indicating a hand of some sort.)

Can you get a call if you bet? If he has a jack, the answer is probably "yes." You didn't bet the turn when the ace arrived, so he has reason to think it didn't help you. If he has a pair between tens and eights he might also call to try and pick off a bluff or he might fold. Your continuation bet followed by a check has underrepped your hand, so there is value to be had if you size your river bet properly.

You bet 1,400, just under half the pot. Your opponent thinks for a long time and calls, showing the

You take the pot.

Checking the River

Betting the river is sometimes a good idea when you have a hand of some value, and there's a reasonable chance that a weaker hands can call and lose But you won't always bet the river. Sometimes you have to check instead, both in and out of position. There are a lot of possible reasons for checking the river, depending on the strength of your hand and the betting action so far. And here's a quick summary of the main reasons for checking.

1. Check with a hand with some value that can win a showdown or beat a bluff, but where weaker hands wouldn't call a bet.

2. Check strong hands when there are a lot of busted draws in your opponent's range and your check may induce him to bluff.

3. Check back in position when you have a hand like A-high that could still win a showdown.

4. Check when you have nothing but no bluff is believable.

Most checks will be with modest hands where the action up to that point has either accurately represented your hand or overrepped it. The fact that your opponent can narrow your range to something close to what you have makes betting unlikely to turn a profit.

When you have a strong hand, your default play should be to bet, and checking requires an unusual set of circumstances. Mostly, you need to believe there's a high probability he was on a draw and missed, and now your check on the river shows him that he might win the pot by bluffing. Players who miss draws are prone to this error, so wave a red flag and see if he charges.

Now let's look at a few examples where checking the river is a plausible option.

Example 6-6. It's the middle of the first day at a live tournament. Blinds are 150 and 300. You're in the hijack seat with the

Your stack is 23,000 and you've been reasonably aggressive so far. Everyone in front folds, you raise to 850, the cutoff and button fold, but the small blind, whose stack is 20,000, calls, and like you he's been somewhat aggressive, and the big blind folds. The pot is now 2,000 chips.

The flop is the

and the small blind checks. A-high flops are good flops for continuation betting against a player with a wide range, so you bet 1,100 and the big blind calls.

The turn is the J♣ and the small blind checks again. You now have a made hand, so your focus should be on getting to showdown where your pair of jacks may be the best hand, and you check behind. The river is the A♣ and the big blind checks again.

The appearance of the second ace makes it a little less likely that your opponent actually has an ace in his hand. If he has king-queen, he has a straight, but he checked both the turn and the river, so that's also not likely. If he had jack-ten, his bottom pair just got counterfeited, so you're now beating him with aces and jacks with a king kicker.

All in all, it's likely you have the best hand, and the only holding to really fear is trip aces. But if that's his hand, he should have led with a bet on river since your turn check indicates that he shouldn't assume you're going to bet the river. So going for a check-raise is a little optimistic on his part.

The problem with betting is that a lot of weaker hands will fold to a bet. A pair of tens, nines, or eights will all fold against this board since this opponent has to worry that you have an ace or a jack and just decided to check the turn through.

If you can't get a weaker hand to call, then don't bet. You'll only be paying off the occasional player who did slowplay an ace or a set. Check and see if your jacks are good.

You check and he turns over the T♣9♣. Your jacks are good.

Example 6-7. It's the middle stage of a big tournament. Blinds are 1,000 and 2,000, with a 250-chip ante producing a starting pot of 5,250 chips. The first three players fold. The fourth player, who's been aggressive and has shown a willingness to make some tricky plays, raises to 5,500 and now has a stack of about 150,000, (M = 29, 75 big blinds). The action folds around to you in the big blind with the A♠J♠ and a stack of 120,000 chips (M = 23, 60 big blinds). You call and the pot is now 14,250 chips.

The flop is the K♥J♣7♦, giving you middle pair, top kicker. Both you and your opponent check and the pot remains at 14,250 chips.

The turn is the 4♦. You check and your opponent bets 8,000. Given his aggressive history, you don't plan to lay down your hand just yet, so you call. The pot is now 30,250 chips.

The river is the 7♠. This card doesn't help any possible draws. If he bet the turn with a pair of sevens, he's now in the lead, but aside from that longshot, the river card didn't affect the hand.

Your best play is to check and call if he bets, as there are a couple of problems with leading:

1.   It's unlikely that a worse hand will call. If he holds something like queen-jack, he has to worry that you've been nursing a king or that your holding is exactly what you have, a jack

with a better kicker. If he holds a pair of tens, nines, or eights, he should fold because of the two overcards.

2. If you bet and he raises (probably with an all-in raise), you've put yourself in a tough spot. His range has now become very strong hands and bluffs. He's aggressive, so bluffing is a possibility, but you only have second pair and you're going to have to make a big decision, possibly for your tournament life. *Do you really want to call and risk getting knocked out of the tournament with second pair?*

Checking has one additional advantage. If he picked up a flush draw on the turn and bet as a semi-bluff, he might now be inclined to bluff the river. You, after all, haven't shown any great strength. You called preflop from the big blind, checked the flop, and called a bet on the turn. From his point of view, your most likely hands are second pair, a pair like tens, nines, or eights, or maybe a straight or flush draw that missed. A bluff on the river might well work.

You check and your opponent bets 22,000. You call and he shows the A♦T♦ for an overcard and a missed flush. The pot is yours.

Example 6-8. You're several levels into a live tournament. Blinds are 200 and 400, with a 50-chip ante producing a starting pot of 1,050 chips and the first three players fold. You have the A♦Q♦ in fourth position, your stack is 57,000 (M = 54, 142 big blinds), and you raise to 1,050 chips.

Action folds to the big blind with a stack of 42,000 (M = 40, 105 big blinds). He's normally somewhat tight, but has defended his big blind with a wide range. (A couple of levels ago you saw him show up with a straight when he defended seven-five offsuit against an early position raiser.) He calls and the pot is now 3,150 chips.

The flop is the 7♣5♥4♥, and the big blind checks. This isn't a great flop for continuation betting since it misses your perceived range and hits part of his range. (Notice that one advantage of defending a wide range in the big blind is the possibility of hitting a lot of flops.) You have ace-high and two overcards, so the best play is to check, which you do, and reevaluate on the turn. The pot remains at 3,150 chips.

The turn is the 3♠, putting a gutshot straight on board and the big blind checks again. You also check for the same reason as before.

The river is the 8♦. The big blind checks again.

If you had a hand like jack-ten or ten-nine, a bluff here would be a reasonable play. Your hand probably wouldn't win at showdown, and since your opponent has checked all three streets, a bluff has a reasonable chance of success.

However, with ace-high, the situation is completely different. Your hand can win a lot of showdowns against hands with two high cards, but if you bet and your opponent has any pair, he'll call because of the lack of action so far in the hand. In short, betting will chase away hands that you're already beating and lose more money to those hands that are ahead of you. Check your ace and see what happens.

You check and he shows the K♣J♣ and you scoop the pot. Another well played hand.

Bluffing the River

The default advice for bluffing the river in tournament play is pretty simple: don't do it. If you bluff the river in money play and your bluff fails, you can rebuy and continue. If you bluff the river in tournament play and your opponent calls, you can be crippled or out of the tournament altogether. That's a lot of equity to risk on a move where your true equity is hard to estimate.

Having said that, there are situations where bluffing the river makes sense and may be a high-equity play. Let's address a few of them.

Bluffing Situation No. 1: Bluffing at small pots can be a good play. Bluffing at a small pot is good for a couple of reasons: you're more likely to win, and you're less likely to be seriously hurt when you lose. When a pot is small, neither you nor your opponent has invested a lot of money, and, if he hasn't put much money in the pot, it's probably because he didn't have much of a hand. In that case, it's pretty easy for him to just fold and move on.

The other part of bluffing at a small pot is equally important. If the pot is small, your bluff will be a small amount of your stack, and if you get raised and fold, your position in the tournament won't be severely impacted.

Bluffing Situation No. 2: Bluff later in the tournament. As we go deeper and deeper into a tournament, players are increasingly conscious of finishing in the money, and they become more and more reluctant to call in marginal situations. Therefore, late in the tournament is the best time to execute a bluff, assuming you're telling a plausible story.

Early in a tournament, stacks are deep and players realize that their chances of doing well are still fairly slim. Consequently, bluffs carry less weight here and will get called more often.

Bluffing Situation No. 3: Avoid bluffing very strong or very weak players. Aim bluffs at mid-level players. Obviously this advice is only useful if you're strong enough to recognize the different player types.

Weak players hate to be bluffed out of pots and are likely to call if they have something. They want to see if they won the hand. (Note that in modern tournaments, these players are much more rare than they used to be. But there are still a few, and they mostly won't survive the first day of play in a big tournament.)

Strong players are good at analyzing the story you're telling and looking for pieces that don't fit. So bluffing a good player successfully is hard.

Example 6-9. It's early in a live tournament. The blinds are 100 and 200. The player in second position, with a stack of about 15,000, limps in for 200. The action folds around to the button whose stack is about 13,000, and who calls. Note that neither of these players seems particularly aggressive You have the T♥9♦ in the big blind and a stack of 16,000 and check. The pot is 600 chips.

The flop is the J♥6♣3♣ and all players check. The turn is the 3♦ and again everyone checks. The river is the 7♠ and the small blind checks. The action is now on you.

This is a common situation, especially early in tournaments. The board doesn't have any threatening cards, the pot is small, and no one seems to want it. Step up to the plate and see if you can take it down with a bluff.

How much should you bet? A half-pot bet seems a little too small since one of your opponents might decide to call with a low pair or an ace-high with 3-to-1 odds. Therefore, I'd bet something like three-quarters of the pot, which looks a little more like a real value bet. You bet 450 and both opponents fold.

Example 6-10. It's late in the second day of a big live tournament. About one-third of the field remains and 10 percent of the original field will make the money. The blinds are 1,800 and 3,600, with a 400-chip ante producing a starting pot of 9,000 chips. The first player folds and the older player, who has about 150,000 left, in second position raises to 10,000. He arrived at the table a little over an hour ago and has seemed pretty tight so far.

The action folds to the button, a loose aggressive player with a stack of about 190,000, who calls. You're in the small blind with the 8♠7♠ and a stack of 300,000. Your image is a little loose but very aggressive once you get involved in a hand, and you and the big blind call. He's new to the table and has about 80,000 left. The pot is now 43,600 chips.

The flop is the T♣9♦4♦. You flopped a straight draw and check, and the big blind also checks. The preflop raiser in second position bets 20,000, the button folds, you call, and the big blind folds. The pot is now 83,600 chips and the effective stack is about 130,000.

The turn is the A♥ and you check. The player in second position thinks for a bit and then checks.

The river is the K♠. *What do you do?*

The cards have been dealt and you now have a not-so-impressive 8-high. You won't win this hand at showdown so your choices are giving up or bluffing. If you decide to bluff, you also have to make a decision about how much to bet. As in a lot of poker situations, these aren't easy choices. Let's start by reviewing the hand and listing the factors for and against bluffing.

Our opponent hasn't been at the table long (an hour, we think), he's an older player, and he seems tight. Older players tend to be tight (there are exceptions), so let's put him on a tight preflop raising range. From second position, that range might look like

1.   All pairs from AA down through 99.

2.   AK and AQ.

That's a pretty tight range. If he's a little looser, it might include eights or even sevens, and maybe ace-jack and king-queen, especially suited.

The preflop raise got three callers, which was a high number for a raise at this stage of the tournament. The flop came the T♣9♦4♦, (with two diamonds), and the blinds both checked.

At this point, the original raiser made a continuation bet of 20,000, just under half the pot. All of the high pairs would have made this bet. Aces through jacks are overpairs to the board, and tens and nines just made sets.

What about ace-king and ace-queen? A weak player might make a continuation bet with these hands because he's seen two checks already and maybe betting is the only way to win. A better player would more likely check because he's against three opponents and missed the flop, and the board is connected enough to fit someone's hand. Since we don't have an opinion of how strong this tight player might be, let's say that ace-king and ace-queen became less likely holdings. After the continuation bet, two of the three opponents quit and only you remain.

The turn was the A♥, you checked and the tight player also checked. If we needed more evidence, we can pretty much eliminate ace-king and ace-queen at this point. With only one opponent and straight and flush draws still alive, we could expect a bet from the big aces, both for value and to prevent the draws from seeing a free card.

It's also unlikely that he started off with AA, TT, or 99 since all those hands now have sets and should be making at least a small value bet. Therefore, the most likely hands that fit this bet sequence are KK, QQ, and JJ, which bet the flop for value and then checked when an overcard hit.

The river was the K♠. If we've analyzed the hand correctly, he has one of three possible holdings. Two of those (queens and jacks) are facing two overcards and will fold to a decent-sized river bet. The other hand (kings) will probably move all-in. (If he fears we hold exactly queen-jack and just made a straight, he might only call.)

What should we do? The pot is 83,600 chips and although we don't, in general, want to bluff at big pots, this hand is an exception. Because we think he's a tight player, we were able to narrow his range dramatically, helped by a favorable sequence of cards. We think he has one of three possible hands, and if we bet, two of those hands will probably fold, while one will move all-in and win.[9]

So what's the right amount to bet? We don't want to bet too much since a too-big bet won't win any more money when he folds, but it will cost us more when he plays. At the same time, we don't want to bet too little because as we offer him better and better pot odds, at some point he will just shrug and call. If we bet half the pot, he'll be getting 3-to-1 on a call. That might be enough to chase him away, but it might not. At the same time, a pot-sized bet is offering him 2-to-1. and that's probably a bigger bet than we need. So betting something around two-thirds of the pot seems about right, which would call for a bet of about 55,000.

Are there any potential holes in this analysis? The one problem with this picture is our very fuzzy knowledge of our opponent. Our image of him is based on three components:

1. He's an older player.

2. He seems tight.

3. He's been at the table for an hour.

An hour isn't a long time to really get a handle on a player's tendencies. Depending on the speed of play in a live tournament, an hour represents somewhere between three and six rounds of the table, or between 25 and 50 hands. His "tightness" might be nothing more than a bad run of cards, or a willingness on his part to sit back a bit and get a sense of the table before getting involved.

---

[9] This implies that it's 2-to-1 in favor of folding if we bet. But it's actually better than that since there are only three combinations of kings left since the K♠ is on board as opposed to six combinations of both queens and jacks since no queen or jack is on board. Thus the odds of folding may be as high as 12-to-3 or 4-to-1.

On the other hand, this is a live tournament, and in these events you have to accumulate chips in a limited amount of time, which often requires making plays using limited observations. This opponent may turn out to be more devious than you're giving him credit for, but you have to make plays based on what you know at the moment. And given what you know right now, the bluff is a good play.

You bet 50,000. Your opponent thinks for a while and moves all-in.

Not what you wanted to see, but not every play you've reasoned out is going to work. Either he had a pair of kings or his check on the turn was a clever trap to set up a situation like this. Make a mental note that this player may be capable of more than just straightforward tight play, and fold.

When You Bet
and Your Opponent Raises

Sometimes you'll make what you think is a good value bet on the river, only to face a raise from your opponent. The raise tells you quite a bit about his hand. If he had a solid value hand, he could have called to see if his hand was good. But he didn't; instead he raised. This makes his range easy to assess, because it's completely polarized. Either he has a very strong hand or he's bluffing.

Responding properly to a raise really requires some solid knowledge about your opponent. Is he aggressive? Is he straightforward? Has he committed himself to the pot, or could he get away from the hand if you were to move all-in? Here are a few useful pieces of advice.

1. A tight, straightforward player rarely bluff-raises the river. This is true in the early part of the tournament, but it's even more true as the bubble approaches. When this sort of player raises on the river, he has something close to the nuts.

2. A weak player can bluff the river out of frustration or desperation. These sort of bluffs occur early in the tournament, often when an obvious draw misses. If you've assessed a player as weak and his play is consistent with a missed draw, be prepared to call some of these raises.

3. A strong, loose-aggressive player can raise as a bluff anytime he doesn't think you have a premium hand. Bluffing the river against players who can't call without a really good hand is one strategy that allows loose-aggressive players to accumulate a lot of chips. It can be overdone, but it's a powerful weapon and loose-aggressive players use it well.

Example 6-11. It's early in a live tournament and the blinds are 100 and 200. You're under-the-gun, pick up the

and your stack is 24,000 chips (M = 80, 120 big blinds). You raise to 600 and everyone folds to the cutoff, a loose, weak player who splashes around in a lot of pots, who calls. His stack has been whittled down to 12,000 from the 20,000 he had to start. The remaining players fold and the pot is now 1,500 chips.

The flop is the

you make a continuation bet of 800, and the cutoff calls. The pot grows to 3,100 chips.

The turn is the K♣. You check for deception and pot control, and your opponent also checks.

The river is the 4♦. You bet 1,300 and the cutoff raises to 4,000. *What do you do?*

Here's a good example of a favorable situation for calling a raise on the river. You have two pair, normally just a medium-strength value hand at this point. Your opponent's bet says he's sitting on trips or a full house. But he's a weak player who's lost a big part of his initial stack, and the betting up to now hasn't given any indication of a big hand. In addition, there were possible straight and flush draws on the flop which never arrived. Finally, his raise was suspiciously small for someone with a full house: The pot is now 8,400 chips and it costs you only 2,700 to call.

Getting better than 3-to-1 odds, you have to see what he's got. You call and he sheepishly shows the

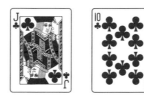

Your Opponent
Bets: Fold, Call, or Raise?

Up to now, we've mostly looked at hands where you took the lead on the river, either by betting a strong hand, betting for thin value, or bluffing. Now let's see what happens when someone else makes the first move.

Your opponent can take the lead in one of two ways: either by being first to act and leading out, or by betting after you've checked. For our purposes, we're going to lump these two cases together.

There's no easy formula for success. Facing a bet on the river is one of the most complex situations in no-limit hold 'em. You can fold, call, or raise, and assessing the best play depends on a host of factors:

1.   The pot odds.

2.   Your hand.

3.   What you think your opponent's range looks like.

4.   What he thinks your range looks like.

5.   His style and yours.

6.   The remaining stack sizes.

7.   The stage of the tournament.

8.   How the hand has played out.

These factors aren't arranged in order of importance because they're all important. Of course, in a given hand, some are more important than others, but determining the order of importance may require some keen hand analysis. Let's start with the simplest case, folding on the river.

Case No. 1: Folding the River

In a lot of hands, you just have to fold on the river. The simplest cases occur when you have nothing, can't represent much, and your opponent is betting. Here are a couple of typical examples.

1. You raised preflop with high cards, then made a continuation bet after you missed the flop, and your opponent called. The turn didn't help you and was checked around. The river card also didn't help, and now your opponent bets. Fold.

2. You played the hand with a draw, but the river was an obvious brick and your opponent bets. Fold. Trying to bluff after you miss a draw is a classic beginner's mistake. Avoid that blunder and save a lot of money.

More interesting problems occur when you have a hand with some value but folding is still a possibility. Here you're trying to balance the pot odds against the evidence that you're beaten. Take a look at the next example.

Example 6-12 It's near the end of the first day at a big live tournament and about 60 percent of the field still remains. The blinds are 300 and 600, with a 50-chip ante and the table is eight-handed producing a starting pot is 1,300 chips. Action folds to you in third position, your hand is the

and your stack is 45,000 with an M of 35. Your image at this point is a little tight, but certainly not nitty, you raise to 1,600 and the next two players fold.

The button, whose stack is about 31,000, calls. This player likes to see flops, but his post-flop play has been pretty solid and he's always had a reasonable hand at showdown. The blinds fold and the pot is now 4,500 chips.

The flop is the

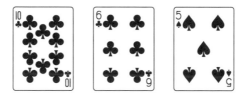

It's not a great flop for your hand, but there are some draws to guard against. So you make a good-sized continuation bet of 3,000 and your opponent calls. The pot is now 10,500 chips.

The turn is the A♣, giving you top pair, but the third club has arrived. This means that both betting and checking are reasonable, and you check for pot control. But the button bets 7,000 and you call producing a pot of 24,500 chips and an effective stack of about 20,000.

The river is the 4♦. You check and he moves all-in. *What do you do?*

You have top pair with a good kicker, but right now your opponent could have a set, a club flush, or even a straight. His betting is consistent with either hitting a set on the flop or making a flush on the turn. In addition, his image is that of a solid player whose post-flop betting isn't out of line.

After his all-in move, the pot is about 44,500 chips and it costs you 20,000 to call, producing pot odds of 2.2-to-1. Those are decent but not great odds. (A pot-sized bet on the river will always offer 2-to-1; you'll only get better odds when he made a small bet or had a short stack when he pushed.) And your image and play of the hand is consistent with the hand you actually have.

In short, there's no reason to believe your opponent is bluffing or is in any way out of line, and you're not being offered great odds to find out. Fold and move on to the next hand.

Case No. 2: Calling the River

Calling on the river doesn't mean it's likely you have the best hand. It means you have a hand with value that has some chance of either being the best hand or at least good enough to beat a bluff, and the pot odds you're being offered make calling an attractive proposition.

There are no hard and fast rules for making the decision to call. There are, however, a couple of indicators that point to a viable call:

1. The pot odds are very good.

2. You have underrepresented your real hand on one or more streets.

"Very good" pot odds vary from situation to situation. In my view, anything better than 3-to-1 certainly constitutes very good odds. As we saw before, 2-to-1 odds are just the odds offered by a pot-sized bet, and those odds are nothing special. That is, when trying to decide between folding and calling, you obviously believe you're an underdog in the hand. In that case, 2-to-1 odds only offer a sort of minimal compensation. Odds of 2.5-to-1 compensate for being a 71-to-29 underdog, and that's the first point where it feels like I'm being adequately compensated, and odds of 3-to-1 give me a much better feeling. Now it's only necessary to win one call in four to break even, and if the odds are better than 3-to-1, I'm comfortable calling as long as I'm not clearly beaten.

Under representing your hand is also a key idea because it should move into your opponent's betting range a group of hands that he thinks are value bets but which you are in fact beating. Depending on the play of the hand, that group may be large or small. However, when you're getting good pot odds that group doesn't need to be very big before you have a clear call.

Now let's look at a few hand examples where your choice is between folding and calling, and see how all these factors interact.

Example 6-13. It's late in the second level of a live tournament with the blinds at 50 and 100. The player in fourth position whose stack is 18,000 (M = 120, 180 big blinds), raises to 300, and so far he's been the most aggressive player at the table, both preflop and post-flop. Furthermore, from the hands that have been shown down, his preflop range is pretty wide. The action folds around to you in the cutoff with the

a stack of 16,000, and your image so far is tight. You elect to call, the button and the small blind fold, and the big blind calls. The pot is now 950 chips.

The flop is the

giving you top pair with the second-best kicker, and the big blind checks. The aggressive player bets 600, you call, and the big blind folds. The pot is now 2,150 chips.

The turn is the 2♣, a card unlikely to help your opponent. He bets 1,100. Your situation doesn't rate to have changed since the flop, so you call again. The pot is now 4,150 chips.

The river is the A♦ and your opponent bets 3,000. *What do you do?*

Your opponent raised preflop and then bet every street. If he were a tight player, you'd probably give him credit for a real hand and give up. But he's not a tight player. He's the most aggressive player at the table. So you can't go away without thinking the hand through carefully.

The combination of a wide preflop raising range and an aggressive post-flop style means he could have played a lot of hands this way: sets, straight draws, flush draws, overpairs, middle pairs, and overcards. In addition, you've somewhat underreped your hand. While your calling is consistent with your holding, it's also consistent with some weaker hands like middle pairs that probably wouldn't call this river bet.

The last item to consider are the pot odds. You're risking 3,000 to try to win the 7,150 that's in the pot now, so you're getting about 2.4-to-1. To break even when getting those odds, you need to win about 30 percent of the time. *Is that reasonable here?* I'd say yes.

Of course, it's possible your opponent has AK, AJ, or AT and has just hit his ace to take the lead. But it's also possible that he bet twice as a semi-bluff with a flush draw, and has now decided that the ace will be the scare card that chases you off the hand.

It's hard to make this call early in the tournament with a single pair, considering that you'll lose a big chunk of your chips if your opponent has what he's representing. But that's precisely what makes loose-aggressive players so dangerous. It's hard to call bets like this with so much on the line and a decent, but not huge hand. So here are three thoughts to keep in mind in these situations:

1.   You only need to win 30 percent of the time for your call to be correct.

2.   If you fold, your opponent will know he can push you off other hands down the road. Others at the table will pick up on this as well.

3.   You don't rate to finish in the money at any particular tournament. But you can increase your chances of finishing in the money by making good plays.

You call and your opponent shows the J♠T♠ for a missed flush draw.

Example 6-14. You're in a live tournament and about half the field has been knocked out. Blinds are 400 and 800, with a 100-chip ante producing a starting pot of 2,100 chips. The first two players fold and the third player, who seems tight and maybe a little weak, but by no means hopeless, and whose stack is 48,000 chips (M = 23, 60 big blinds), raises to 2,200. The players fold to you on the button. You have the Q♦9♦, a stack of 42,000 chips (M = 20), and your image is somewhat loose and aggressive, but you haven't gotten too far out of line.

You like the idea of playing a pot in position against this player, so you call and the blinds fold. The pot is now 6,300.

The flop is the K♠Q♥T♠ giving you second pair and a gutshot straight draw on a dangerous and connected board. Both you and your opponent check. Notice that although there are plenty of draws on this board, your hand isn't strong enough to bet. Your opponent has likely either missed entirely or has a strong hand.

The turn is the 7♣ and your opponent bets 4,800. This might be a strong hand betting for value, or it might be a hand that missed and now sees a chance to take the pot. You call and the pot is now 15,900 chips.

The river is the 3♦ and your opponent bets 14,000. *What do you do?*

At first, this example seems similar to the last one. You have a pair and your opponent is betting the river. He might be bluffing, and he might not. So can you justify a call as in the last hand?

In contrast to the last example, here you should fold. There are two factors that make this situation worse than before.

1. **Pot odds.** You have to put in 14,000 to win 29,900, giving you odds of 2.1-to-1. That's not as good as the 2.4-to-1 you were getting before, so be a bit quicker to fold.

2. **The betting sequence.** In the last hand, your opponent bet the flop, turn, and river, with relatively smaller bets on the flop and turn, and a larger bet on the river. That might look strong, but it's a not-uncommon sequence from a weaker player without much of a hand. A player bets the flop (perhaps as a semi-bluff), then bets the turn, then gets to the river, realizes he's put in a lot of chips and still doesn't have a hand, and makes a big bet to try to salvage the situation.

   Here we have a check on the flop, followed by big bets on the turn and river. The most likely explanation for this sequence is that the flop check was a trap with a big hand, hoping for a bet from you that never materialized, followed by two big catch-up bets on the turn and river. This sequence, in my experience, is much more dangerous than the bet-bet-bet sequence of the previous hand.

The combination of the poorer odds and the more dangerous betting pattern indicates this is a hand you need to let go. Instead, you call and your opponent turns over the A♠J♠ for the nuts.

Example 6-15. It's early in a live tournament and the blinds are 100 and 200. The first three players fold and the player in fourth position, whose stack seems to be about 22,000, raises to 550. He's been aggressive so far, but you think his judgment might be a little shaky. You call in the cutoff with the K♣J♣, your stack is 31,000 giving you an M of 103 (155 big blinds), and you've played a tight, solid, game thus far. The button and the small blind fold, but the big blind calls, making the pot 1,750 chips.

The flop is the K♥8♦4♣ and the first two players check. You have top pair with a decent kicker, and a back-door flush draw, and could certainly bet for value, but since only one overcard is possible (an ace), you elect to exercise a little pot control and check as well. The pot remains at 1,750 chips.

The turn is the 4♦, which shouldn't change the situation much. The big blind checks and the initial raiser now bets 1,100. Your top pair still looks good, so you call and the big blind folds. The pot is now 3,950 chips.

The river is the 3♠ and your opponent bets 2,000. *What do you do?*

You have to call 2,000 to win a pot of almost 6,000, so you're being offered almost exactly 3-to-1 odds. Those are big odds; you only need to win this situation one time in four to justify calling. When being offered 3-to-1 or better, your default response should be "I want to call. Can I justify folding?"

There are a lot of hands your opponent can hold that beat you. He could have ace-king, king-queen, or a set of eights, or even something like five-four or four-trey. But how many of those hands fit the betting we saw? Not too many, as it happens.

If he had a king with a good kicker, he would probably have made a continuation bet on the flop, especially against two opponents. If he flopped a set of eights, he might have bet, although checking would be more reasonable considering how dry the flop was.

What hands are most likely to raise preflop, check the flop, but bet the turn? Hands containing a four, like A4, 54, and 43, would have bet the turn but were unlikely to raise preflop. And the best candidates for this betting sequence are the A♦X♦ hands, which might have checked after missing the flop, but bet the turn when picking up a flush draw.

Of course, you can't be sure that he holds one of these hands, but when you're getting 3-to-1 on your call, certainty isn't required. A reasonable chance that he's fooling around should be sufficient.

You call and he turns over the A♦T♦.

Case No. 3: Raising the River

When your opponent bets the river, you won't always be calling or folding; sometimes you'll be raising. You don't need the nuts to raise, but without the nuts you need to think about what to do if he then reraises (which will often be an all-in move). Let's look at a few cases.

The simplest case is where you have the nuts, or a hand which, given your stack size, you're willing to take all the way. You raise, and if raising commits you to the pot, you go all-in. From that point on, whatever happens, happens.

A more interesting case occurs when you have a strong hand which isn't the nuts. You're willing to raise based on the action so far, but if a reraise comes you're going to have to fold. Most examples of this play involve having a weak flush or the idiot end of a straight, and it's a difficult move for many players to execute. They know they won't want to call if they get raised, and the idea of raising but then folding (on the river) seems, in the heat of battle, to be clearly wrong. So they just call, often missing a lot of potential value.

The last case for raising is as a complete bluff, but this is especially dangerous on the river after your opponent has already shown a lot of interest in the hand. I don't recommend it except in the most unusual circumstances.

Example 6-16. It's nearing the end of the first day at a live tournament and about 60 percent of the field remains. Blinds are 200 and 400, with a 50-chip ante producing a starting pot of 1,050 chips. There are two folds and the player in third position, whose stack is about 55,000 and who seems to be a somewhat tight player that's been running well, raises to 1,100. The cutoff, who's a little on the aggressive side, with a stack of 38,000, calls, and the button and small blind fold. You're in the big blind with the

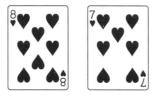

and a stack of 66,000 chips (M = 63, 165 big blinds), and your image is that of an aggressive player who likes to defend his big blind, and you call. The pot is now 3,950 chips.

The flop is the

giving you a flush draw. You check, the player in third position bets 2,000, the cutoff folds, and you then call. The pot is now 7,950 chips.

The turn is the 8♦ and you check. The player in third position bets 3,000 and you call. The pot is now 13,950.

The river is the 2♥ and you hit your flush. You could bet, but you think your opponent likes his hand and will stick in another bet on the river even though a potential flush has appeared. You check, he bets 6,000, and he has about 40,000 left.

Should you raise or just call? You have a weak flush, which beats all the hands he might have below a flush, but loses to several possible better flushes. So before you raise, ask these two questions:

1. Are there enough hands that I beat that would call if I raise?

2. What do I do if he reraises all-in?

Right now, your opponent's hands break down into a few possible categories:

1. Sets and two-pair.

2. Overpairs.

3. An unlikely straight (ten-nine).

4. Bluffs.

5. Flushes.

Meanwhile, your range (from your opponent's point of view) consists almost entirely of flushes and bluffs. If you had flopped a set of queens or jacks, would you really have checked the flop and turn with a board that offered straight and flush possibilities? Almost certainly not. With an overpair (aces or kings), you would probably have raised preflop.

A set of eights or the straight with ten-nine fit your betting pattern a little better, but these are unlikely and don't make up much of your range. If you're raising with a single pair, like ace-queen, you've simply turned your value hand into a bluff instead of calling to see if you're good.

In short, you're either bluffing or hit some sort of flush on the end and are now raising for value. In this case, all your opponent's hands below flushes are now bluff-catchers, and his high flushes are reraising hands.

So raising here is viable only if you think that he can call with some large chunk of his non-flush range. To make sure of that, your raise needs to be small enough so that the pot odds will make a call very attractive.

What sort of raise will work? Right now the pot is about 20,000. If you put in another 16,000 (6,000 to call and 10,000 to raise), your opponent will need to put in 10,000 to see a 36,000 pot, getting odds of 3.6-to-1. Those are good odds on the river, and hands like sets, two pairs, and overpairs will have to consider calling.

But if he reraises, you'll have to fold. He'll be putting in his whole stack, and only a flush headed by the ace or king can make that raise for value. There are players who can bluff off their whole stack on the river, but there aren't a lot of them, and you would need very strong evidence that he is such a player before calling that bet.

You raise another 10,000. He calls and shows the J♠J♦ for a set of jacks, and you take the pot.

Bet Sizing on the River

Bet sizing on the river tends to be a little trickier than on the flop and turn. On those earlier streets, bets of half the pot or a little less are not unusual. There's no need to bet more than required when making a continuation bet or when charging a drawing hand. But if you reach the river with a strong hand, the river bet will be your last chance to make money. In this case, you'd like to make a large bet. But if the pot is getting large relative to the stack sizes, you might want to make a bet that your opponent is comfortable calling, rather than one which commits him to the pot.

There are a lot of issues that affect the size of the bet on the river. Let's look at some of the factors you need to consider and develop a few guidelines for river bet sizing.

1. **Your default bet.** If you have a strong hand and the stacks are large relative to the pot, your default bet size should be in the range of 60 to 90 percent of the pot. Bets in this range offer your opponent odds between 2- and 3-to-1, which should be enough for a call if he has a hand and suspects that it's at least possible you're bluffing.

   Depending on the situation, you may have to make larger or smaller bets. But most river bets should fit nicely into this 60 to 90 percent range.

2. **Betting small.** If you have a good hand but the board is such that your opponent's range consists mostly of hands that will only call a small bet, then bet small. We gave a good example in the last section where a flush draw hit on the river. You needed to make a small enough bet so that one and two pair hands could consider calling.

   In general, don't make a bet smaller than about one-third of the pot. A bet this size offers your opponent 4-to-1 odds and there's no point in going smaller. A hand that won't be

389

intrigued by 4-to-1 odds probably won't be interested in 5- or 6-to-1 either.

3. **Betting large.** If you think your opponent has a strong hand but one which is still not as good as yours, overbet the pot or move all-in. This usually occurs when you have the nut flush or the nut straight but your opponent may have a weaker flush or a lower straight. It's difficult for players to lay these hands down in tournaments, so you need to charge as much as possible.

   A variation on this play occurs when both players are likely to be playing the board. In this case, a big bet is hard to call since your opponent will be calling just to split the pot.

4. **Blocking bet.** On the river, this is just a small bet that looks like a trap. Make a blocking bet with a weak made hand out of position hoping your opponent will just call and therefore limit the size of the river bet. By the way, blocking bets used to be a standard play but they don't work well in the modern game, except against a weak player. Good players will sense your intention and raise a small bet with both good hands and bluffs. Just checking is usually a more threatening play since it announces nothing and could be the prelude to a check-raise.

5. **Balancing bet sizes.** Some players advocate attempting to balance your bets on the river so your opponents can't draw any conclusions from your bet sizing. This is a valid strategy in live cash games where you might play the same group of opponents over and over again, but it's a superfluous finesse in tournaments. Most tables will be tables of strangers, not that many hands will go to the river, and many of those won't involve a showdown. In addition, your table may break up after just a few hours play, rendering any observations moot. Consequently, make the bet size that seems most likely to exploit what your opponents have.

Part Seven

The All-In Move

The All-In Move

Introduction

No-limit play differs from other forms of poker in that you can, when you want, bet or raise all the chips you have. It's a gripping move; you're potentially putting your tournament life on the line when you commit all your chips. Television loves the all-in. It's visual and dramatic, and it's not unusual to see whole episodes of the World Series coverage that consist of one all-in move after another.

Although moving all-in looks aggressive, the reality is usually a bit different. More often than not, the all-in is actually a desperation move, the only play available when the blinds get big and your stack gets short.

We're going to break this chapter into two distinct parts: moving all-in and calling an all-in. Moving all-in is mostly a short stack play. Calling an all-in requires combining a good estimate of your opponent's range along with the pot odds and the impact of winning or losing on your stack size. Both skills are crucial to being a good no-limit hold 'em tournament player.

Moving All-In

Moving all-in seems at first to be a violation of our basic rules of bet sizing. Most bets are some fraction of the current pot size. A small bet is about half the pot or less, while a big bet is between three-fourths and the whole pot. In normal play, where the stacks are relatively deep and plenty of play remains in the hand, bets larger than the current pot size are unusual and generally inefficient. A pot-sized bet is big enough to accomplish almost anything that a larger bet could accomplish.

However, things change as the stack sizes shrink relative to the blinds and antes. Now we have to look at the size of our bet or raise and compare it to the pot and what remains in our stack. Does our bet or raise leave us pot-committed? If our opponent calls or raises, is the pot so large compared to our stack that the pot odds alone compel us to stay in the hand?

If we are in a pot-committed situation, then we're usually better off moving all-in instead of making a normal bet of some fraction of the pot. Compared to a normal bet, an all-in move offers several advantages:

1. **Maximum fold equity.** By moving all-in instead of making a smaller bet, you maximize the chance that your opponent will fold.

2. **Zero fold equity for him.** By moving all-in you eliminate the chance your opponent could push you off the hand later.

3. **Minimum pot odds.** Your all-in bet gives your opponent the worst possible pot odds for a call.

4. **Maximum chance to hit your hand.** With a hand like ace-king preflop, you'd like to see all five cards to increase the chance of making a winning top-pair hand. But if you miss the flop, you'll find it hard to continue in the face of a big bet.

So by moving all-in preflop, you're guaranteed to see the turn and river cards.

5.   **Minimum information revealed.** If you move all-in preflop, your opponent gets the minimum possible information about your range of hands except that you like it well enough to push all your chips. You could have a big pair, a small pair, a couple of Broadway cards, or just suited connectors.

When are we pot-committed against a player with a bigger stack? As in most poker situations, the proper answer is "It depends." But here are a couple of good general guidelines:

1.   If you intend to play the hand and your stack is three times the current pot or less, then you're pot-committed.

2.   If you intend to play the hand with a stack that's three to five times the current pot, then you're in a bit of a gray area. While you can make a bet and still get away from the hand, moving all-in is an option you need to consider. The stronger your hand and the wider your opponent's range, the more likely you are to be pot-committed.

3.   If your stack is a little more than five times the current pot, you're not committed yet. But if you make a bet and get called, you probably will be. (The pot got larger and your stack shrunk.) Consider your options carefully.

Besides watching your own stack, of course, you also need to watch your opponent's. If his stack is smaller than yours and he is pot-committed, then so are you. Also, with a strong hand you have options: you can put him all-in yourself if you believe he might still call, or make a small bet and let him make the all-in move. And if your hand is good but not a monster, it's usually better to maximize fold equity by moving all-in first.

The Preflop All-In
Move and Push-Fold Tables

It's often the case in tournaments that your stack gets so small that moving all-in to open the pot becomes the best play. A good player will only get in this situation when he loses a big pot that's not quite big enough to knock him out of the tournament. Instead, he's left with a tiny M and faces the necessity of doubling up a few times to get back in the running. A weak or inexperienced player might reach this point by a long stretch of passive play which results in his stack being whittled down to almost nothing. (Good players understand how hard it is to come back from a near-death experience, and will make a bold move sooner rather than later.)

No matter how you reach that point, knowing how to play with a short stack is a key tournament skill. One tool that's been developed to help players is the *push-fold* table. A push-fold table is just a grid with a player's M listed in the rows on the left, and the number of opponents left to act in the columns across the top. The key assumption is that the pot is unopened and the action has folded around to you. Each cell of the table then lists the hands where moving all-in is a better choice than folding.

A typical cell in a push-fold table might look like this:

Five Players Left

M Value	Hands to Push All-In
5 < M <6	AA down through 44 AKs down through A9s AKo down through ATo KQs down through KTs

If you're sitting at a nine-player table, the first three players have folded, and you're fourth to act with an M between 5 and 6, the entry says that pushing is more profitable than folding if you hold a pair of aces down through fours, ace-nine suited or better, ace-ten offsuit or better, or king-queen suited, king-jack suited, or king-ten suited. (About 11 percent of all hands.)

These tables are computer-generated, based on several assumptions:

1. With what hands will your opponents call a push?

2. Are you in the money yet?

3. Are you almost at the bubble?

Push-fold tables are useful, but they have limitations which require some thought at the table.

1. While they tell you (based on the assumptions) if pushing is better than folding, they won't tell you if a normal raise is better than pushing.

2. They don't take the stacks of the players behind you into account.

Both these considerations are important. If your stack is in a gray area (with an M between 5 and 7) it may be the case that a normal raise of two-and-a-half or three times the big blind is just about as likely to win the pot as a shove. A normal raise also gives you a chance to assess your opponent's reaction before you commit. For instance, suppose the action is folded to you, you have a marginal pushing hand with an M of 6, and two of the remaining four players are tight. Their tightness means that a normal raise is more likely to win the hand, but it also means that if either one of them reraises, you have a chance to get away from a bad situation without having committed your tournament life.

In the same way, seeing either very large or very small stacks behind you means that those players will be more inclined to call an all-in. The big stacks won't be too damaged by calling and losing, while the small stacks will be desperate. However, if several stacks have Ms between 5 and 15, they're going to be reluctant to call an all-in without a premium hand. In the first case, you should be more inclined to make a normal raise, while in the second case, pushing becomes even more attractive.

With those caveats out of the way, let's look at pushing strategies for different levels of small Ms. And for the rest of this chapter, we'll assume that we're late in a big tournament but still a considerable distance from the bubble, and the blinds are 5,000 and 10,000, with antes totaling another 10,000 chips producing a starting pot of 25,000 chips.

M = 1 (2.5 Big Blinds)

If the starting pot is 25,000 chips and your stack is 25,000, your M is exactly 1 and your situation is *exactly* desperate. Moving all your chips in the pot is only enough for a smallish opening raise — 2.5 times the big blind. If you move in, anyone who calls is getting a healthy 2-to-1 on their money, and if by some chance the action folds around to the big blind, he'll be getting 3.3-to-1 on a call. In short, your all-in raise is highly likely to get called.

Despite the fact that you have very little steal equity, you need to move all-in with any two cards if the pot is not yet opened. In this case, your major asset is not your cards, but the fact that the pot is unopened, which means that unless you're under-the-gun, some number of people are already out of the hand. And the fewer the number of people that can potentially call you, the better your chances of surviving the hand. Remember, you only have enough chips to last one circuit of the table, and there's no guarantee that you will again see a hand that gets to you unopened.

When opening the pot with a small M, you actually have more fold equity than it might seem. Suppose the first three players fold and you open from fourth position. The player in fifth position looks down at the

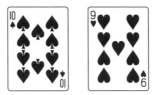

It's a hand that's easily worth a call if it ended the betting, but it doesn't. He has to worry about someone behind him waking up with a better hand and raising, so he may choose to fold and let someone else see what you have. If the action folds all the way around, the big blind should call with any two cards, but not everyone does what they're supposed to do.

M = 2 (5 Big Blinds)
or M = 3 (7.5 Big Blinds)

If the starting pot is 25,000 chips and you have 50,000 or 75,000, your M is a somewhat healthier 2 or 3, and the pressure on you is a little less. Even so, your best strategy is the same as before: move all-in with any two cards if the hand is folded around to you.

To the uninitiated, this looks like a desperation move, but it's really a sound play. Suppose, for example, you have 60,000, for an M of 2.4 (6 big blinds). If you make a 'normal' raise to 30,000, your stack shrinks to 30,000 and the pot grows to 55,000. If someone behind now puts you all-in by 3-betting to 60,000, the pot becomes 115,000 chips and it costs you 30,000 to call. You're getting pot odds of about 3.8-to-1, and no matter what hand you have and what reasonable estimate you put on his range, you're getting much more than the price you needed to call.

For a concrete example, suppose you raised to 30,000 with the

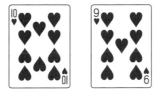

and the button put you all-in. Your best guess is that his range is something like this:

- All pairs: AA down through 22

- Suited aces: AK down through A8

- Unsuited aces: AK down through AT

- Broadway cards: KQ, KJ, QJ, suited and unsuited

That range comprises about 15 percent of all hands and dominates you pretty well. But your winning chances against that range are still about 38 percent, far above the 21 percent you would need to break even when getting 3.8-to-1 odds.

In short, your 'normal' 30,000 raise has already committed you to the pot, so you may as well push all-in. And compared to the situation where your M was only 1, your stack is large enough so that callers aren't getting great odds anymore, and you're going to win a lot of pots without opposition.

M = 4 (10 Big Blinds) or M = 5 (12.5 Big Blinds)

When your M reaches the range of 4 to 5, play starts to change significantly. It's no longer necessary to play every hand when the action folds around. You can afford to fold some unfavorable spots; in early position, you should actually be folding most of your hands. In middle position, you can play more hands, and in late position, you'll still be playing most of your hands.

What about the raise size? Is your stack large enough to make a normal-sized raise instead of an all-in?

The answer is no, although now it's a close call. While moving all-in is awkward because your bet is large compared to the pot, making a normal raise is also awkward because even a normal raise is a large chunk of your stack. For instance, suppose your stack is 100,000 (M = 4), everyone in front of you folds, and you decide to make a raise of 30,000 chips. That's a fine bet if it wins the pot.

But suppose an opponents moves all-in? Folding would now sacrifice 30 percent of your small stack. But if you're willing to call, then moving all-in to start was probably the better play, giving yourself the biggest possible fold equity.

So your strategy for these stack sizes is to move all-in when you want to play a hand and you're first in the pot, but to be selective about the hands to be played, depending on the number of players yet to act. And here's a table that will serve as a good guide for playable hands at these stack sizes, assuming you're sitting at a nine-handed table and no one has opened the pot.

Opening Hands for M = 4 or M = 5

Position	Players Left	Hands to Push	Hands Pushed (%)
Early	8, 7 or 6	AA - 88, AKs, AQs, AKo	5.0
Middle	4 or 5	AA - 55, AKs - ATs, AKo - AJo, KQs, KJs QJs, JTs, KQo	10.5
Cutoff	3	Any pair, AKs - A6s AKo - A8o, KQs - K8s, KQo - K9o, QJs - Q8s QJo - QTo, JTs - J9s, JTo	24
Button	2	Any pair, Any ace, Any king, Any queen or jack suited, QJo - Q6o T9s - T4s, T9o - T7o 98s - 96s, 98o - 97o 87s - 86s, 87o, 76s - 75s, 76o, 65s	60
Small Blind	1	Any two cards	100

Study this table and notice how quickly your range expands as the number of possible opponents starts to shrink. With six, seven, or eight players left to act, your range stays very tight. Most of your opponents will understand that a small stack forces you to be active, so you don't want to be caught in a situation where your hand is weak and a lot of players can take a shot at you. However, in the cutoff where only three players are left to act, you can expand your range to about a quarter of all hands. On the button with just the blinds to act, you're willing to push with 60 percent of all hands.

And if only the big blind is left, you can cheerfully push with your whole range. If he decides to call with his whole range (which very few players will do), you're in a breakeven situation. Otherwise, no matter what portion of his range he elects to call with, the combination of winning chances plus fold equity will allow you to show a theoretical profit.

If you examine our table carefully, note that we've assigned the same pushing range to all three seats in early position. Why not play a tighter range when under-the-gun? The argument for playing a tighter range is obvious: There are more players to act, so you'd like a stronger hand. But there's also an argument for being more aggressive in this position: In the next hand, you'll be in the big blind which is a negative equity situation. So before that happens, make a move to pick up some chips.

Good players have argued about this paradox for some time without reaching any definite conclusion, and computer simulations have consistently pointed to the need for a slightly tighter range under-the-gun. However, many players, myself included, have experimented with both plans of attack and found merit in the more aggressive approach. Proceed at your own risk.

M = 6 (15 Big Blinds) or M = 7 (17.5 Big Blinds)

When your M is between 6 and 7 in an unopened pot, you're in an awkward spot and no choice is really ideal. Let's look at an example and see just what's happening.

Example 7-1. Suppose the blinds and antes total 25,000 as in our previous discussions, but now you have a stack of 160,000 with an M of 6.4. You're at a nine-player table and the first two players fold. You have a holding which isn't a premium hand but which you'd like to play with a small stack — let's say you have the A♦J♦.

Plan A is just to move all-in, but in this case you're making a massive overbet of more than six times the current pot, a very inefficient bet. You're likely to chase away all the hands you beat, and get called mostly by hands that are beating you. Often you'll pick up the pot uncontested, but once in a while you'll go to the flop as an underdog, and sometimes a very big underdog. Hopefully you can do better than this.

Plan B is to simply make a normal raise. Let's say you raise to 25,000, or 2.5 times the big blind. Now the pot is 50,000 chips and we have 135,000 left in our stack. Sometimes this raise just wins the pot, and that's a fine result. You risked a little bit and took down a nice pot.

But suppose an aggressive player in late position with a stack of 800,000 wants to 3-bet. A normal-sized 3-bet would be to something like 65,000, but calling that 3-bet would commit you to the pot, and your opponent would know that, so he'd put you all-in instead. You'd have to call 135,000 to see a pot of 210,000, receiving 1.55-to-1 pot odds, and you would need to win about 40 percent of the time to justify calling this bet. If his range is loose enough, your ace-jack suited is good enough to call. But if he's 3-betting with a tight range, you don't have the price you need. It's not an ideal situation.

Another problem arises if a tight player just calls your initial raise. His call makes the pot 75,000 and leaves you with a stack of 135,000. Once again, if your plan is to continue with the hand, you're already pot-committed. If an ace or a jack flops, you'll have to get all the money in and see what happens. If you miss the flop and your opponent bets, it's time to fold, as a bluff can't be big enough to make him lay his hand down. With an M between 6 and 7, making a small raise preflop and then folding later isn't a disaster since it should only cost less than one-sixth of your stack. But it's certainly not a great result even if it's one you can afford.

As can be seen from the example, in this range of Ms, both approaches have drawbacks. Moving all-in is a big overbet, while making a normal raise leaves you in an awkward spot whether you're 3-bet or whether your opponent just calls. *So what's the right idea?*

In my opinion, the least bad alternative is making a normal raise. It avoids the big overbet which risks a lot to gain a little, and it gives a chance to take down the pot without resistance and build your stack. However, when you make a normal raise with this stack size, make sure to plan what to do if one of the players behind puts you all-in, and it's important to do this before your chips go into the pot, not afterwards. Proper planning prevents poor performance.

M = 8 (20 Big Blinds) or Larger

With an M of 8 or larger, you're no longer in a gray area. Now an all-in move is eight times the pot, a gigantic overbet. At the same time, a normal raise only commits one-eighth of your stack, so you can easily get away from the raise if circumstances demand it. Just make a normal raise, then play poker.

Moving
All-In After a 3-Bet

When a player with an M under 20 gets involved in a hand, a preflop all-in move is always on the table. In these situations, keep a careful eye on the pot and the stacks of both players. If a player has a stack that's less than three times the current pot, the next bet or raise should commit him to the pot if he continues with the hand. In this case, raising all-in will probably be better than just a simple raise.

There are many possible scenarios of preflop all-in moves after the initial raise has been made. Here's a basic example that illustrates many of the main points and shows how to analyze the choices.

Example 7-2. It's the end of the second day at a major tournament. The blinds are 8,000 and 16,000, with a 2,000-chip ante producing a starting pot of 40,000 chips at this 8-handed table. The action folds around to you in the hijack seat with 1.2 million and an M of 30 (75 big blinds). Your hand is the

and your table image is aggressive and moderately tight. You raise to 38,000.

The cutoff and button fold but the small blind 3-bets to 85,000. His starting stack was 540,000, with an M just under 14, and after his raise, he has about 455,000 left. You've been playing with this person for some time and he seems a bit tight but certainly capable of making moves. Also, in the hands you've watched, his judgment has been sound, and he's 3-bet before, but not to obvious excess.

The big blind folds and the action is back on you. *What do you do?*

The first point to notice is that your choices are folding, calling, and moving all-in. Raising without moving all-in doesn't make sense because a raise to something like 200,000 would leave him committed to the pot whether he just calls or puts you all-in.

Of the three choices, folding is certainly the weakest option. You have a good hand and the effective stack is short, so his range should be reasonably wide. What's more, after his raise, the pot is 155,000, and you only need another 47,000 chips to call. Those are enormous odds: 3.3-to-1. In addition, his smallish 3-bet has left him plenty of room to fold if you move all-in. You don't know if that was his intent or not, but it becomes another strong argument for playing the hand. So let's eliminate folding from our bundle of choices and focus on calling or moving all-in.

If you call, the pot is 202,000 and the small blind's stack is 455,000, and he will act first after the flop. If the small blind checks and you bet, he's not pot-committed and can just let the hand go. On the other hand, a flop bet by either player puts his opponent in a fold-or-all-in situation.

Given the huge pot odds you're being offered, you can call and play a simple and straightforward post-flop strategy:

1. If you hit your hand, try to get all the money in.

2. If you miss your hand and he bets, fold.

3. If you miss your hand and he checks, make a small continuation bet. If he raises, fold. If he calls, don't put any more money in unless you improve on the turn and no ace appeared on the flop.

This strategy should be enough to show a profit, and it also offers very low variance.

The alternative strategy is to move all-in now. This should fold out a lot of his weaker hands, but he'll call with the strongest hands in his range. To see how profitable this approach is, let's make a reasonable estimate of his calling range, then see how much of a profit you can show for various ranges which he might have 3-bet. We'll average all the information together and see whether the all-in move is likely to be better than a simple call.

First question: what's his calling range if you shove? He saw you raise from the hijack seat with four players left to act. Your image (we think) is tight-aggressive, and you have a relatively big stack. Consequently, he probably assesses your raising range as wide in this situation. In addition, we think he's capable of making moves, but not a wild man, so his 3-betting range won't be super-tight. It will have all his premium hands and some air as well.

Once you move all-in, your range shrinks in his eyes, but it still doesn't become super-tight. You have a big stack, enough to easily cover him, so he'll think there is some chance you're fooling around. Most players in his situation would certainly call with tens through aces, ace-king and ace-queen (5 percent of all hands). He might also call with nines and eights, and maybe ace-jack. He probably wouldn't call with king-queen, and certainly not with pairs below eights. Let's assign him a calling range of aces down through nines and ace-king down through ace-jack (6.3 percent of all hands).

We can use one of the hand simulation programs to see how often your

wins against that range in a showdown. Since you're seriously dominated by his calling range, you don't expect to do too well when he calls. In fact, you win about 35 percent of the time. Not too good. But you do win the existing pot when he folds, and you're getting odds when you shove.

Before you can see how well a shove works here, it's important to answer one more question: What percentage of hands were in your opponent's 3-betting range? We think he's a good player, capable of making moves, not just some rock 3-betting with the nuts. He saw you open the pot from the hijack and should believe you're aggressive, so put him on a range that's neither very tight nor very loose. Also, it's not necessary to know exactly what hands they are, you just need a good guess as to what percentage of hands he might have raised.

Let's say he might have 3-bet with 10 percent of his hands on the low side, and 15 percent on the high side. Now 15 percent is a pretty big 3-betting range, and the only reason you might be looking at a range this wide is because he made a small 3-bet which avoided pot-commitment and allows him to fold to a shove. This piece of evidence forces us to think that his range may be on the wide side, but it could also be a trap. However, we don't know this, so we'll go with the obvious assumption.

Let's start with the assumption of a 10 percent 3-betting range and see where the calculations lead us. Since we think he'll call with 6.3 percent of his hands, he'll fold the other 3.7 percent. We also know that if he calls, we'll win 35 percent (and lose 65 percent). Let's make a little chart and see how profitable a shove will be.

Case I: You shove, he folds (37 percent).

- You win the 202,000 in the current pot.

- Your expectation is 74,740.

$$74,740 = (0.37)(202,000)$$

Case II: You shove, he calls, you win (22 percent)

$$0.22 = (0.35)(0.63)$$

- You win the 202,000 in the pot plus another 455,000, the rest of his stack, for a total of 657,000 chips.

- Your expectation is 144,540.

$$144,540 = (0.22)(657,000)$$

Case III: You shove, he calls, you lose (41 percent)

$$0.41 = (0.65)(0.63)$$

- You lose the chips you shoved, 455,000.

- Your expectation is -186,550.

$$-186,550 = (0.41)(-455,000)$$

Thus, your net profit from a shove when his 3-betting range was 10 percent is 32,730.

$$32,730 = 74,740 + 144,540 - 186,550$$

If his 3-betting range was larger, he'll fold more of it and our shove will be more profitable. Now let's take a look at what happens if he was 3-betting with a 15 percent range instead of a 10 percent range. We'll make the same assumption as before if we 4-bet shove: He'll call with a 6.3 percent range and fold the rest of his hands. The breakdown looks like this:

- He 3-bets: 15 percent range

- We 4-bet shove, he calls: 6.3 percent range

● We 4-bet shove he folds: 8.7 percent of hands

In percentage terms, he's calling with 42 percent of his 3-betting hands and folding the other 58 percent. We're doing better than before, obviously, because we're folding out a larger percentage of his 3-betting range.

Assuming as before that we win 35 percent of the time when he calls our 3-bet, the percentage breakdown when we 4-bet shove becomes:

● 58 percent: We 4-bet shove, he folds

● 42 percent: We 4-bet shove, he calls

● 14.7 percent: We win (35 percent of 42 percent)

● 27.3 percent: We lose (65 percent of 42 percent)

Now we can calculate exactly what we win and lose in each of the three cases to see how profitable our shove is.

Case I: You shove, he folds (58 percent).

● You win the 202,000 in the current pot.

● Your expectation is 117,160.

$$117,160 = (0.58)(202,000)$$

Case II: You shove, he calls, you win (14.7 percent)

$$0.147 = (0.35)(0.42)$$

● You win the 202,000 in the pot plus another 455,000, the rest of his stack, for a total of 657,000 chips.

- Your expectation is 96,579.

$$96,579 = (0.147)(657,000)$$

Case III: You shove, he calls, you lose (27.3 percent)

$$0.273 = (0.65)(0.42)$$

- You lose the chips you shoved, 455,000.

- Your expectation is -124,215.

$$-124,215 = (0.273)(455,000)$$

Thus, your net profit from a shove when his 3-betting range was 15 percent is 89,524.

$$89,524 = 117,160 + 96,579 - 124,215$$

These two numbers give the boundary points for shoving: about 33,000 on the low side (if his 3-betting range was 10 percent) and about 90,000 on the high side (if his 3-betting range was 15 percent). Since we were looking at a pot of 202,000 chips to start, those are sizeable numbers. So shoving gives an equity of at least 15 percent of the existing pot, and possibly as much as 45 percent. As for calling, it's equity is difficult to exactly quantify, but it's not likely to be in this range, so shoving looks like the better play.

One final note. This was a long analysis and you can only see the hazy outline of this sort of thinking when you're actually playing a hand. But solving problems like this at home is great practice and the solution and key insights should stay with you, and good decisions during live play should also come much more easily.

Calling
Your Opponent's All-In

You don't always get to make the all-in move. Sometimes your opponents will move all-in and you have to respond.

When an opponent moves all-in, your decision usually boils down to two choices: fold or call. (If there are some players left to act and you have plenty of chips, there might be a third choice — raising to drive out some of the other players. But let's ignore that choice for the rest of this section and assume that folding or calling are the only options.)

Deciding whether to fold or call depends on four things:

1.   Your hand.

2.   The pot odds you're being offered.

3.   Your estimate of your opponent's range.

4.   How your hand fares against his range.

That may seem like a daunting list, but here's some good news: Nos. 1 and 2 are known to you, and No. 4 can be estimated from a table you'll see shortly. That leaves only No. 3, deducing your opponent's range, as a murky area. Even here, however, some common sense can simplify the problem.

When trying to pin down an opponent's range, keep these ideas in mind:

1.   **Has he been loose or tight?** Ideally, you'll have made a quick estimate of who might call and what their range might be. Loose aggressive players have wide ranges; if you raised with a good hand and your opponent shoved, you'll mostly be

calling if he's a loose player. Tight players have narrow ranges, and you'll need a pretty good hand to call.

2. **Look at his stack.** A player with a big stack can put you in with a fairly wide range. If his all-in raise is a third or more of his stack, expect his range to be tight.

3. **What has recently happened at the table?** If a player has been quiet for a while, expect his range to be tight. If he just lost a big pot, expect his range to be wide.

4. **What is your image?** If you have a tight image, a loose-aggressive player will come after you with a much wider range than usual, figuring that he has tremendous fold equity against you. A tight player will be less interested in your image than in the quality of his hand, so don't expect his range to be affected much.

Use as much information as you can gather to put a number on his range, then try to estimate how your actual hand is likely to do against that range.

Typically, an opponent who moves all-in with a dominating stack has one of the following ranges:

- 5 percent range (very tight): AA down through 99, AKs, AQs, AKo, AQo.

- 10 percent range (typical): AA down through 66, AKs down through A9s, AKo down through AJo, KQs, KJs, KQo.

- 15 percent range (loose): AA down through 44, AKs down through A5s, AKo down through A9o, KQs down through K9s, KQo, QJs, QTs, JTs.

- 20 percent range (very loose): All pairs, AKs down through A5s, AKo down through A9o, KQs down through K9s, KQo down through KTo, QJs, QTs, JTs, QJo, QTo, JTo.

One can argue about exactly what holdings should make up the edges of these different ranges, but it hardly has any affect on the calling or folding decisions for most hands.

The next table shows these four ranges across the top, and some typical hands with which you might have made your initial raise down the side. The values in the cells shows the winning chances of each hand against each range.

Winning Chances for
Various Hands Against Various Ranges

Hand	Opponent's Range			
	5 Percent	10 Percent	15 Percent	20 Percent
QQ	58%	65%	68%	71%
JJ	50%	59%	63%	66%
TT	44%	54%	59%	61%
99	40%	50%	54%	56%
88	36%	46%	51%	54%
33	34%	38%	40%	44%
AKs	51%	58%	61%	62%
AKo	49%	56%	59%	60%
AQs	39%	51%	56%	59%
AQo	36%	49%	54%	57%
ATs	32%	41%	48%	53%
A7s	30%	30%	40%	45%
A7o	26%	33%	37%	42%
KQo	29%	37%	41%	48%
QTs	32%	37%	39%	41%
JTs	34%	37%	39%	39%
87s	30%	34%	37%	38%
87o	26%	31%	33%	35%
73o	22%	26%	28%	29%

This is an incredibly important and useful table. If you're a player who plays a lot of tournaments, you need to spend the time to commit this table to memory, and you should be well rewarded for your efforts.

The left-hand column doesn't include all possible hands. But with a knowledge of certain key hands, you can easily extrapolate the information for any other holding you need. Pruning the table a bit makes memorizing it much easier.

A quick look at the table reveals some key insights:

• Getting 4-to-1 odds, you can call an all-in with any two cards. You need to win 20 percent of the time to break even at 4-to-1. Even seven-trey offsuit is 22 percent against the tightest range.

• Getting 3-to-1 odds, you can call with anything but complete junk. Those odds require a 25 percent winning chance, and any reasonable hand can win that often, even against a tight range.

• When getting 2-to-1 odds, you need 33 percent winning chances to call, and that requires you to exercise a little caution. And if there's a good chance that your opponent has a very tight range, then you need to be very selective: pairs eights or higher, AK and AQ will all work, but weaker hands are either dominated or a coin flip. However, if you think there's a good chance that he's moving in with a 10 or 15 percent range, then you can be much more liberal; any Broadway cards will work as well as suited connectors down to about eight-seven suited.

Note that absolute precision is not required. Your estimate of his range is necessarily a bit of a guess, so needing 33 percent and calling with a hand that's actually only 31 percent isn't a big mistake. The function of this table is to avoid gross blunders that are expensive.

Example 7-3. This first example is based on our earlier discussion of opening the pot with an M between 6 and 7. Suppose the blinds and antes total 25,000 and your initial stack is 160,000, so your M is just over 6. You have the

in fourth position, the first three players fold, you make an initial raise to 25,000, and action folds to the button whose stack is 800,000. He puts you all-in with a 3-bet of 160,000 and the blinds fold. The call will cost 135,000 to see a pot of 210,000 chips, and you're getting 1.55-to-1 odds, requiring about 40 percent winning chances.

Your image so far at the table has been moderately tight. You won a pot a little while ago and showed down the

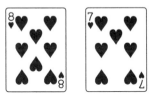

which had turned into a straight. The button has been a little more active than you but has always shown down solid cards.

This call will be for your tournament life. *What should you do?*

In a cash game, this could be a difficult decision, but using the table above lets us get to the essence of the problem fairly quickly. Your ace-jack suited falls between ace-queen suited and ace-ten suited, so you can extrapolate winning chances against the various ranges pretty easily. If he has a very tight range of about 5 percent, your winning chances are about 35 to 36 percent.

Against a 10 percent range you're doing much better, about 46 percent. Against the looser ranges, you're even better than that. Needing 40 percent to call, you can call his bet unless you think he's raising with a narrow range, in which case folding is better. Based on what you know, however, folding isn't really an option.

Consider the hand from your opponent's point of view:

1. You have a relatively short stack.

2. Your image isn't especially tight.

3. You raised from middle position.

Put all that together and you could be facing a fairly wide raising range. (Under the circumstances, the A♣J♣ is a pretty good hand.) Since you don't think he's an especially tight player either, you can't put him on a really tight range. So calling looks clear-cut.

Example 7-3. You're well into the money at a good-sized live tournament. The blinds are 15,000 and 30,000, with a 3,000-chip ante. There are eight players at the table producing a starting pot of 69,000 chips.

The table has been playing fairly loose, but nonetheless the action folds around to you in the cutoff. With a stack of 1.4 million and an M of 20 (47 big blinds), you look down at the 7♣5♥. Behind you the button (loose and aggressive) has about 800,000, the small blind (tight, passive) has 220,000, and the big blind (average aggressiveness) has about one million. Your own image is a little loose but not crazy and you decide to raise to 75,000.

The button folds but the small blind moves all-in for his last 220,000, and the big blind also folds. *What should you do?*

Step No. 1 is to calculate the pot odds. The pot was 69,000 chips to start. You bet 75,000 and the small blind added his last 220,000, making a pot of 364,000 chips, and you need to put in

145,000 to call. Your pot odds are 364-to-145, or almost exactly 2.5-to-1. Converting '2.5-to-1' to 'winning chances required to call' requires calculating and it comes to 28.6 percent.

$$0.286 = \frac{1}{1 + 2.5}$$

Step No. 2 is to think about his possible range of hands. He's a tight, passive player, so we first think that a tight, narrow range must be right. But his M was only 3 at the start of the hand (7 big blinds). While it's true that some tight, passive players will wait for premium pairs right to the bitter end, don't assume that's true for everyone. Today, even the fairly casual tournament player knows that you need to open up a bit when the end is nigh. That means you should put your opponent on a somewhat looser range, perhaps 10 or even 15 percent.

However, a further complication, is that he's moving all-in over the top of a player who has already opened the pot and shown some strength. Given the small size of his 3-bet, he should be pretty certain that he has little fold equity and his all-in will probably be called. This is an argument for a tighter range, so 10 percent is probably the most reasonable estimate here.

If we remember the bottom of our 10 percent range column, we notice that seven-trey offsuit has about a 26 percent winning chance. Our hand of 7♣5♥ should be a little higher than that, probably pretty close to the 28.6 percent we need. So our decision is basically a coin flip.

What should you do with a close decision? Call or fold? Some players like to engage in a little mental dialog at this point — something like this:

"I guess I gotta ask myself — do I feel lucky?"

"Sure you feel lucky, punk. You're in the money at a major tournament."

"That's right! I do feel lucky! I call."

My approach is a little more scientific. If the decision based on the actual odds seems to be a coin flip, I look to see how the presence or absence of this player will affect my chances in future hands. Would I rather play at the table with this fellow gone, or is it useful if he sticks around? Would a random player replacing him be better for the game?

In this case, I've got a tight, passive player sitting two seats to my left, and it's good to have a predictable, tight, not-very-strong player acting after me than someone who might move in from another table. So I'll fold and leave him sitting there.

There's one final consideration that affects the call/fold decision. When there are very few players left in the tournament, the prize jumps are getting larger, and your opponent is the one facing possible elimination because of a short stack, you should prefer calling rather than folding in close decisions. There's additional value to eliminating a player and guaranteeing a move up the prize scale.

Part Eight
Playing Styles

Playing Styles

Introduction

A *playing style* is just the sum total of a player's tendencies at the table. Does he like to raise a lot of hands from middle or late position? That's part of his style. Does he like to call in the big blind when getting good pot odds? That's also part of his style. Will he bluff the river once in a while, or do his river bets always indicate some sort of value? Will he limp preflop, or does he always come in with a raise? The answers to these and a lot of other questions constitute a player's distinct style.

With all the possible decisions to make in a poker hand, it might seem that there could be a huge number of possible styles. In fact, however, we can group players into just a handful. Poker decisions tend to be highly correlated: a player who can make big river bluffs will tend to play a lot of hands preflop, and he'll be betting and raising rather than limping or calling. Players who are comfortable limping preflop will tend to call with drawing hands rather than semi-bluff, and fold on the river without a made hand.

At any given time, one style will tend to dominate the tournament scene. Today, that style is the modern loose-aggressive style. It's based upon playing wide preflop ranges, betting and raising aggressively, accurate hand reading, and utilizing the power of fold equity to its fullest. Loose-aggressive players aim to dominate their tables in the early and middle levels, crushing the tight players and scooping all the chips in sight. In this section, we'll take a look at the different possible playing styles, discuss how the loose-aggressive style came to dominate tournament play, show how to play that style, and show finally how to play against that style.

An Outline
of Playing Styles

Complex games don't have simple solutions. If a game is sufficiently complex, it's unlikely that there will be just one effective way to play. It's much more likely that there will be several ways to play, all of which can be successful given a high level of skill. The history of chess reveals world champions who were great attackers, and others who were solid defenders. There were players who tried to follow the truth of a position wherever it led, and others who won by sucking the life out of their opponent's game. Many players and many styles, all of which could be deadly in the right hands.

No-limit hold 'em is hugely complex, but it differs from other complicated games in one key way: the essence of its strategy is *to conceal what you're doing from your opponent*. The harder it is for an opponent to figure out your hand, the more likely you are to win. A good poker style, therefore, has two components: play hands in a way that are likely to win the pot and likely to conceal your actual hand from an opponent until showdown.

This dual nature puts poker on a different plane from a game like chess. If you played chess with a grandmaster, he could tell you just what he intended to do and you still wouldn't be able to win. But in no-limit hold 'em, being able to narrow your opponent's range of hands down to a small number gives a huge advantage. If you think he's ahead, either fold or at least try to keep the pot small, while if you're in the lead, extracting more money is the way to go.

Four Basic Styles

We can assign most players to one of four basic styles:

1. Loose-passive.

2. Weak-tight.

3. Basic tight.

4. Loose-aggressive.

The first two styles, loose-passive and weak-tight, are really beginner's styles. Players who fit one of these styles probably just learned the rules of the game and started playing without bothering to read any books or join any of the video training sites available on the web. In the early days of the poker boom, tournaments were filled with players who fit in one of these categories, but now they're increasingly rare.

The loose-passive player thinks that poker is about showing down the winning hand. He'll play a lot of cards preflop, and after the flop hits, he wants to get to the river to see who wins. To a loose-passive player betting is sort of a nuisance. With a really big hand, he'll bet, but with second or third pair or a draw, he'll just call. You can't bluff a loose-passive player because he won't go away unless he has no hand. But you can value bet him whenever you have a strong holding, and he'll call you down to the end. If a loose-passive player appears at your table, count yourself lucky and see if you can collect a share of the money he leaves behind.

The other beginner that you'll occasionally see even today is the weak-tight player. His goal is to start with a good hand, hit the flop, and win a big pot on the river. However, things rarely turn out that way which makes poker a frustrating game. You can't bluff a weak-tight player much because he plays so few hands, and when he hits something decent on the flop, he's almost compelled to stick around.

But you can trap him, which is his fatal flaw. If a weak-tight player raises from early position, you know just what he has: a big pair, ace-king or ace-queen. That's it. If you pick up a medium suited connector in late position, just call. On the flop, you'll probably know where you stand, and if you hit the flop hard, you can win a huge pot. Weak-tight players go bust with a pair of aces or kings more than any other kind of player. It's a cruel game.

In the early days of the poker boom, tournament fields were full of variations on the loose-passive and weak-tight styles, which made those events easy pickings for good players. In today's game, you'll only occasionally see players like this sit down, and they usually won't last long. Your starting table is more likely to be some mix of the other two styles, the basic-tight player and the loose-aggressive player, and they're harder nuts to crack. Let's look at the basic-tight player first.

The Basic-Tight Style

Moving up a notch from the beginner's styles of the last section brings us to a style I call basic-tight. It's a conservative but effective style. A good basic-tight player can dominate a table of loose-passive and weak-tight players, while maintaining his stack and not taking lots of risk in the process. For someone starting as a beginner and looking to move up the ladder, basic-tight is a great style to play while learning the intricacies of planning and hand-reading.

Basic-tight, sometimes referred to as tight-aggressive, is essentially the style we taught in *Harrington on Hold 'em*. It's characterized by these main features:

1. Relatively narrow hand ranges, especially in early position.

2. Paying attention to pot odds and stack sizes when deciding to get involved.

3. Frequent continuation bets after taking the lead preflop.

4. Getting in big pots with big hands and keeping the pot small with small hands.

5. Using semi-bluffs with drawing hands.

6. Adjusting your style to the size of your M.

Basic-tight play imposes a structure on poker and lets you think within that structure in somewhat the same way that chess, bridge, and backgammon players think about moves in their games. Follow basic rules of thumb, operate with a plan, and constantly analyze your play and your opponent's to try to find optimal lines of attack.

Basic-tight play has a number of advantages over other styles, but its chief advantage is that it's easy to teach and relatively easy to apply. For someone coming to poker from other games, the basic-tight approach will seem natural and comfortable. With narrow ranges, you'll often have the best hand on the flop. You won't be faced with lots of difficult decisions about what to do with second- and third-pair hands. And the volatility of your game will be fairly low, and relatively quickly you'll be able to survive a long time in tournaments with a shot at making the money.

Since tournaments in the 2003-2006 period were filled with newcomers, most of whom played some variant of the loose-passive and weak-tight styles, basic-tight players did well in that environment, cashing frequently and sometimes making deep runs.

Weaknesses of the Basic-Tight Style

While the basic-tight style is easy to learn and can be an effective tool for the inexperienced player, it has several weaknesses which can be exploited. Against a veteran player, the basic-tight style is a relatively soft target. Here's a quick list of the problems a basic-tight player faces at a tough table:

1. **Ranges are too narrow.** The narrow ranges were a plus against the loose-passive player, but against a stronger player they don't offer enough deception. Flops of medium and low cards will generally miss the tight player's range entirely, while flops with high cards will generally hit pretty well. A good opponent can skip the high card flops and attack on the lower flops more or less regardless of his own holding.

2. **Top pair hands don't make much money.** The upside of playing mostly high pairs and Broadway cards is obvious — if a tight player makes a pair on the flop, it will often be top pair (or an overpair). The downside is a little less obvious — once other observant players at the table recognize the style,

they'll know that when a tight player is willing to get involved post-flop, he's probably got a hand like top pair. That makes the opponent's job pretty easy. They can stick around if they can beat top pair, and go away if they can't (and don't have a draw). After a while, the tight player's top pair hands won't make much money, and he'll be vulnerable to players looking to trap him with well-concealed sets or two pair hands.

3. **A tight player needs to be able to make big folds.** Another problem associated with narrow ranges is the need to sometimes make big folds on the turn and river. If the board shows one Broadway card and a tight player stays in the hand, his opponents can pretty accurately put him on something like top pair, good kicker. If they hold something better, they can make big value bets on the turn and river, and he'll need to let his hand go. A tight player who gets married to his top pair hands is in big trouble.

Countering the Basic-Tight Style

Once the basic-tight style became dominant in the period 2003-2006, creative players started looking for weaknesses in it that could be exploited. One weakness that stood out was the reraise (or 3-bet, as it became known) in response to a preflop raise.

At a table mostly full of basic-tight players, a raise from under-the-gun represents a narrow range — something like aces down through jacks or tens, along with ace-king and ace-queen, suited and unsuited, about 5 percent of all hands. Players would open the pot with wider and wider ranges as you moved around the table, and by the time action reached the button, you could expect to see a range that include low pairs, suited connectors, weaker Broadway cards, and even hands like the 9♥7♥ from the most aggressive players in the group. Even from a basic-tight player, a late position raise might represent a range of 20 to 30 percent of possible hands.

But suppose a basic-tight player raised from the cutoff seat and someone 3-bet from the button. What range is he representing? The traditional view at the time was that a reraise preflop represented a huge hand — aces, kings, maybe ace-king, maybe queens. Against the widest of these ranges — AA down through QQ and AK — queens was 40 percent to win, jacks was 36 percent, and ace-queen offsuit was only 24 percent. Against the narrowest range (AA and KK) even QQ was only 18 percent. Most players at that time would fold almost their entire range against a reraise, calling with QQ, JJ, and AK, and only re-reraising (4-betting) with AA and KK.

This approach, however, created a huge opportunity for profit. Knowing someone would raise a 20 percent range from the cutoff but only call or reraise a 3-bet with a 3 percent range, you could simply 3-bet any two cards and make money even if you later folded every hand where you met resistance.

This insight led to a surge of what was called *light 3-betting*. It began in the high-stakes online cash games in 2005 and 2006, then gradually percolated down the scale to the $2-$4 and $1-$2 online games. And by the time Black Friday rolled around (April 2011), you could find players 3-betting light in the 5¢-10¢ online games!

Light 3-betting quickly led to other adaptations as players realized what was happening and sought to avoid exploitations. Calling ranges widened so that simply 3-betting any two cards couldn't be a winning strategy. Light 4-betting also appeared, as players found that they in turn could exploit the light 3-bettors.

The 3-betting and 4-betting revolution eventually made its way to tournament play where it was potentially even more effective than in cash games. Tournament players were more concerned with survival than cash game players who could always buy back in if they lost their stack. This made aggressive 3-betting a more dangerous weapon in the deep stack and medium stack phases of a tournament since calling or 4-betting might quickly lead to an all-in move. It lost most of its value as the tournament moved to the short stack phase since at that point players would decide whether they were good enough to get all-in or not before they made their first raise, and a player who's already decided to play for his whole stack can't be intimidated.

The trend started by light 3-betting and 4-betting quickly led to the development of a very aggressive style of play which revolutionized tournament play during the period 2008-2011. Let's now look at that style in some detail and see how it affects good strategy in 2014 and beyond.

The Modern
Loose-Aggressive Style

Tournaments have always featured a mix of generally tight players and generally aggressive players. In the past, both strategies have been successful when combined with solid poker fundamentals and good hand-reading skills. However, today's loose-aggressive players have created a distinct style which is new, successful, and hard to combat.

The basic-tight player builds his strategy around good cards and good hands. Given his position at the table, if he picks up two good cards he's willing to play the hand; if not, he isn't. If he connects with the flop in some way, he's willing to keep playing. If not, he might toss in a continuation bet to see if no one else wants the pot, but otherwise, he's pretty much done with the hand.

The modern loose-aggressive player builds his strategy around good situations rather than good cards. If the situation looks good, he'll play a mediocre hand. If the situation is very good, he might play with any two cards. For the good loose-aggressive player, great cards are a bonus. He thinks he can win hands without them, but if he picks up a pair of aces, that's icing on the cake.

In the next two chapters, we'll take a look at this style, understand why it's so successful, and talk about how to combat this style when you encounter it at a tournament table.

The modern loose-aggressive style is built on four pillars:

1.   A reconsideration of chip value.

2.   Use of fold equity.

3.   Excellent hand-reading skills.

4.   Getting paid on your big hands.

Except for the first pillar, reconsidering chip value, none of these are new ideas. Good players have understood fold equity for a long time, no one has ever disputed the value of being a good hand-reader, and everyone wants to get paid on their big hands. But it's the combination of all four ideas that creates a distinctively new style that's particularly hard to counter at the table.

Loose-Aggressive Pillar No. 1: A reconsideration of chip value. The traditional view of chip value was derived from the Independent Chip Model which we discussed earlier. The more chips you had, the less each individual chip was worth. The fewer chips you had, the more each chip was worth. You could demonstrate this easily in simple cases. Suppose only three players remained in a tournament and three prizes remained to be paid. If one player had only a single chip and third prize was $1,000, his single chip was worth a tiny bit more than $1,000 because he's guaranteed to at least finish third. If the leader has 1,000,000 chips and first prize is $10,000, each of his chips is worth a little less than a penny apiece because all he can win is $10,000. The Independent Chip Model implies a certain level of conservative play because if a small stack contains very valuable chips, you probably don't want to jeopardize them to try to win chips of much less value.[10] [11]

---

[10] The idea that chips change value and the more you have the less each chip is worth was first demonstrated in the 1987 edition of *Gambling Theory and Other Topics* by Mason Malmuth. However, Malmuth also states that this concept is weak in the early and middle stages of a tournament, and only really comes into play towards the end of a tournament.

[11] Another way of putting this is that the penalty for losing a pot is less for the big stack than it is for the small stack. Thus, this implies, that a player holding a big stack can play looser than someone with a small stack.

In the early and middle stages of the tournament, however, other considerations come into play. Now a big stack is a big advantage because other players don't really want to get in a hand with you. So with a big stack, you can put pressure on them, but they can't put pressure on you, and one of the maxims of basic-tight play is that given a choice you want to attack the medium stacks while avoiding involvement with the big stacks (who can threaten you with elimination), and the small stacks (who can take a hand and move in.) It's good advice in general, but it implies that having a big stack is in itself a big edge. If the other players are trying to avoid you, exploit their reluctance to play by attacking.

The key insight that the new breed of players developed was that while the Independent Chip Model could make some useful predictions about strategy at the final table, it wasn't giving useful advice for how to play in the early stages of tournaments. What you needed for that stage was the Snowball Rolling Downhill Model. Play aggressively and keep gathering chips, and the more chips you have, the easier it becomes to gather still more chips.

Loose-Aggressive Pillar No. 2: Use of fold equity. Every time you make a bet or raise, you have some fold equity. Your opponent can simply give up and the pot is yours, sometimes even folding the best hand, and fold equity is a hugely important component of aggressive play. For instance, when playing wide preflop ranges, you're going to play a lot of hands and often find yourself on the flop with either nothing or with what's clearly the second-best hand. In those situations, fold equity becomes your best friend.

Betting and raising aggressively has another component which is sometimes overlooked: you're taking your opponents well outside their comfort zone. A key mantra for the basic-tight player is 'big hand big pot, small hand small pot.' When a basic-tight player flops top pair or second pair, he's not looking to get all his chips in the middle; he's looking to get to showdown cheaply and see if his hand is best. Your bets or raises force him to decide just how much of his stack he wants to risk on this hand.

Often the answer will be, "Not that much," and he'll throw the hand away rather than risk it on what (for him) is an outsized pot.

Your bets don't need to be big to collect your fold equity. Many players will have decided to give up on weaker hands when the flop comes, and even a minimum bet will allow them to fold. Put another way, the crucial idea to remember is that *most hands miss most flops*, so fold equity is usually lying around somewhere.

As a result of his persistent betting, the loose-aggressive player collects lots of small pots in the early stages of tournaments. In fact, when you're moved to a new table after a few hours of play, you can immediately spot the good loose-aggressive players: they're the ones with the big stacks of green ($25) and black ($100) chips from the blinds and antes they've vacuumed up with their frequent small bets. The basic-tight players are easy to spot as well: they're the ones constantly needing to break their $500 and $1,000 chips to post their blinds and antes.

Loose-Aggressive Pillar No. 3: Excellent hand reading skills. Everyone needs to read hands well, but it's a more important skill for the loose-aggressive player than for anyone else. Hand reading is certainly useful for the basic-tight player, but because he's playing narrow ranges, he mostly finds himself with a good hand that's probably best, or with a draw, or with nothing. His draws and his nothing hands are easy to play whether he can put you on a small range or not. The good hands do require some skill as he tries to figure out if he's really best or second-best, but overall this style requires less in the way of hand-reading skills.

However, for the loose-aggressive player, excellent hand-reading is his lifeblood. He plays a wide variety of hands and only occasionally will he connect well with the flop. The rest of the time he'll have hands like top pair, weak kicker, or middle pair, or bottom pair, or nothing at all. To make the loose-aggressive style work, he has to win with a lot of these hands, and that requires him to answer two questions:

1. Given my opponent's likely preflop range, does he have something?

2. Given what I know, can I move him off most of the hands he likely has?

And a player who can get the right answer to these questions quickly can be successful in this style. If not, a tighter style is a better choice. This, by the way, is why players aren't advised to try to start with a loose-aggressive style: if your hand-reading skills are not yet developed, the style places too many demands on you. The right idea is to start tight, become a good hand reader, then move to a loose-aggressive style if that suits you.

Loose-Aggressive Pillar No. 4: Getting paid on your big hands. This last pillar is the real payoff of the loose-aggressive style. Frequent betting not only picks up small pots, but effectively conceals your big hands. When you're betting and raising a lot, players will recognize that you can't always have the nuts. Eventually, they'll start calling or raising your 3-bets and sticking around after the flop with paired hands. But when you pick up aces or flop a set, they won't be able to separate your big hands from your frequent bluffs. That in turn leads to big payoffs, especially when the tournament reaches the middle stages and players have to decide quickly whether or not their hand is good enough to play for their stack.

The loose-aggressive style solves the biggest problem that the tight player faces. When the tight player picks up aces under-the-gun and raises, no one calls. When he hits a set and double-barrels the flop and turn, his opponents fold quickly. When he 3-bets preflop with kings, his opponent lays his hand down. The loose-aggressive player faces no such problem, giving him a shot at winning someone's stack when he actually hits the occasional monster hand.

Playing the Loose-Aggressive Style in the Four Stages of a Tournament

We can break a big tournament into roughly four different stages. The first is the early stage, roughly the first three to five levels of Day 1. In this stage, the blinds are small and the stacks are mostly all large and the antes haven't kicked in yet. Everyone is playing deep-stack poker.

Stage 2 comes after a few levels have been played and the antes kick in. The typical M at the table is now under 100, but mostly higher than 50 — roughly 100 to 200 big blinds. One or two players at each table have had some bad luck and are actually short-stacked.

Stage 3 comes seven or eight levels later. In most tournaments, this will be the end of Day 1 or the beginning of Day 2. (In the main event of the World Series of Poker, Stage 3 doesn't arrive until about the end of Day 2.) Now each table is a mixture of deep stacks (M greater than 60), medium stacks (M between 20 and 60) and short stacks (M between 1 and 20). This stage continues until the bubble bursts.

Stage 4 covers the period from the bursting of the bubble to the final table. Few, if any, deep stacks remain as the blinds and antes keep relentlessly advancing. Most players are pot-committed as soon as they get involved in a hand. The primary skills are now when to move all-in and when to call an all-in.

As can be seen, each stage poses different sorts of problems for loose-aggressive players, and their game needs to adapt to the requirements of the different phases of a tournament. Let's look at each stage and consider how, if at all, the loose-aggressive player needs to adjust.

Stage 1: Hanging Back

Stage 1 is interesting because the deep stacks allow a loose-aggressive player to play several different ways. One approach (which I favor) is to play somewhat tight for a level or two while you size up the table and try to figure out who's who and what's what. Sitting out a few more hands than usual enables you to really focus on your opponents, and any hand that goes to showdown should tell you something about the players involved. 'Somewhat tight' just means 'not very loose.' Fold hands like medium suited aces and weak Broadway cards in early position. Don't open up your ranges much until you're in middle or late position. You're trying to keep your mind clear, accumulate some knowledge about your opponents, and perhaps leave the impression that you're actually a pretty tight player who can be pushed around.

A different approach to Stage 1 is to be almost 'crazy-aggressive.' No one wants to pay a big entry fee and get knocked out at the starting gate, and all the weak players are still alive, so take advantage by 3-betting, 4-betting, 5-betting, and betting aggressively after the flop. This style can work spectacularly well if you actually hit a couple of big hands, and you will pick up lots of small to medium pots. The downside, obviously, comes when you run into an opponent who picks up a big hand. Not everyone who adopts this mindset can get away from a clearly bad situation.

A third approach is to just play the same hand ranges you would play in Stages 2 and 3: wide but not crazy-wide. I don't like this approach for two reasons:

1. It gives your opponents plenty of time to study your game plan.

2. It's harder to intimidate your opponents when the bets and raises are small in relation to their stacks.

Even for a naturally loose-aggressive player, I think the best approach is to dial back the aggression a bit in Stage 1 and focus on getting a clear read on your table.

By the way, no matter what style you're playing, unusual situations can appear even in Stage 1. Be prepared to take advantage. Here's an example of what can happen.

Example 8-1. It's a big live tournament, nearing the end of the third level. Blinds are now 150 and 300, and the antes won't kick in until the next level.

Everyone started with 20,000, and you've been whittled down to 15,000. Your M is now 33 (50 big blinds), not terribly low but nothing to brag about at this stage. You've played a fair number of hands and played them aggressively; the other players probably see you as a standard loose-aggressive player, but not crazy-loose.

You pick up the

in fourth position. The first three players fold and you raise to 800. The action folds around to the small blind who moves all-in for 9,000. On the previous hand, he lost more than half his stack when his pair of kings were busted by a pair of aces.

The big blind folds and the action is on you. *What is the right play?*

Start off by taking a deep breath and recognizing that you're facing a big decision here, one that will have a major impact on your tournament. Be prepared to spend a little time to think it through and get it right.

First, let's note that whatever his hand might be, your opponent didn't have to shove. His M was 20, so he could easily have made a normal 3-bet to about 2,000, and if you 4-bet him and he folded, he'd still be able to play for quite a while.

Let's look at the pot odds next. They're never great when you're facing a massive overbet, but you still need to keep them in mind. Your bet made the pot 1,250 chips, his raise brought it up to 10,250 chips, and you need 9,000 to call. You're getting 10,250-to-9,000, or about 7-to-6. (Actually 1.14-to-1.) And at those odds, you need about 47 percent winning chances to call.

That's no bargain, but you do have ace-king offsuit, which is not a bad hand.

Next question: What's his range? That's always a tricky question, but here it's especially difficult because his action doesn't really fit any range well. He's betting 9,000 to pick up the 1,250 chips already in the pot. In essence, he's laying over 7-to-1. The only hands that are objectively strong enough to make this bet are aces and kings. But those are the last hands he'd want to play that way because he should be looking to generate more action and build a bigger pot.

To solve this problem, we have to look at his mental state and see what he might be thinking, then assign a range based on each possibility. In doing so, we'll use a technique we introduced in "Part Two: Stacks, Blinds, Antes, and Ranges," constructing a *range of ranges*. Each range will have a probability based on what we think he might be thinking.

So what are the possibilities? Let's list a few.

1. He's steaming after a bad beat and has completely lost his grip. Hence, he decided to shove with any two cards. It happens. If he's playing any two cards, our ace-king offsuit is 65 percent to win. Easy call.

2. He's steaming but he hasn't completely lost his grip. He's upset and wants to take down a quick pot, but he's not shoving junk and he's not shoving aces or kings. His range look something like QQ down through 88, plus AK, AQ, and maybe AJ. Against that range, you're about 56 percent. A variation on this play would be a range that included all pairs QQ through 22, plus AK, AQ, AJ, and KQ. Against that range you're a little less than 55 percent. That's a nice result because it means that our assessment of exactly what range he's playing in this case can be pretty fuzzy without affecting our result much. Still an easy call.

3. He's not steamed at all, but he's picked up a genuinely big hand and he's decided to act like he's steaming, hoping to get

a call from a decent hand. His range here is probably AA, KK, QQ, and AK. Now your winning chances are about 39 percent. Big fold.

So we have three possibilities and three corresponding sets of ranges and winning chances. We don't know his actual mental state, but we're pretty sure our estimate covered all the bases. Now we just have to assign reasonable probabilities to each of the cases and see what happens.

The third possibility is unlikely, partly because there are so few premium hands, and partly because just one hand has occurred since his bad beat. If this is the real scenario, we've been pretty unlucky. I'd assign this variation no more than a 10 percent probability.

The first possibility is unlikely as well. I've seen people tilt badly, but tilting usually means impaired decision-making more than outright craziness. Given a choice between two plays that are both somewhat reasonable but where a clear-thinking player would quickly choose (A) over (B), the tilter finds a reason to pick (B). Let's put this variation in the 10 percent area as well. It's that high only because the bad beat just happened.

The second possibility is the most likely, and it fits the tilting scenario I just outlined. It's not a good play, but there is some misguided logic behind it, and mostly it will just take down the pot. If we're estimating the first and third at 10 percent each, then this variation must be 80 percent.

If we accept those three estimates, then we can quickly estimate our overall winning chances to be 54.4 percent.

$$0.544 = (0.10)(0.65) + (0.80)(0.55) + (0.10)(0.39)$$

where
>0.10, 0.80, and 0.10 are the probabilities that Possibility 1, 2, or 3 have occurred respectively, and
>0.65, 0.55, and 0.39 are the probabilities of winning given Possibility 1, 2, or 3 respectively.

And since we needed 47 percent winning chances to call, and this estimate puts us well over that number, we call.

Notice also that there's a pretty big margin of error here. If we bump Possibility No. 3 up to 30 percent and eliminate Possibility No. 1, we get the estimate of our overall winning chance to be 50.2 percent.

$$0.502 = (0.70)(0.55) + (0.30)(0.39)$$

This new calculation, with less reasonable estimates, is still a comfortable call, so we can be pretty happy with our original calling decision.

This particular scenario, (early in the tournament, you have a strong hand but not aces, someone sticks in a huge overbet), happens with some frequency. The old breed of players would habitually give up and rationalize that they were probably facing aces so it was okay to fold. It's hard to put up a lot of money to enter a tournament where you think you have a good chance to get in the money and then face a puzzling hand where you might lose most or all of your chips. Calling is hard and folding is easy, so most players will just fold and lose a few chips.

The new breed of players handles these situations much better. As a group, they understand that building a big stack early gives them good chances to push people around and pick up more chips later; to them, a situation like the example above represents an opportunity, not a threat — a chance to pick up a lot of chips quickly with the odds solidly in your favor.

Stage 2: Ramping Up

Stage 2 begins roughly when the antes check in, and the addition of antes changes the risk calculus dramatically. Suppose the blinds are 200 and 400, with no antes. A raise of 2.5 times the big blind means you're putting 1,000 in the pot to win the 600 chips already there. Put another way, you're betting 167 percent of the pot to win the 600 chips. But now suppose the blinds are

200 and 400, but each player has to ante 50. Now the starting pot (at a 9-player table) is 1,050 chips. At this point, a 2.5 times big blind raise is the same 1,000, but now you're betting 95 percent of the pot to win 1,050 chips, a much better deal for the raiser!

When antes appear, everyone at the table needs to get more aggressive, opening a wider range of hands and being willing to get involved in more pots, whether by calling, raising, or 3-betting. This advice applies to tight players as well as loose ones. Even if you think of yourself as a tight player, the tide of the game has changed and you have to swim with that tide, not fight against it. Your opponents will be opening with wider ranges, so calling with weaker hands is justified and 3-betting with more hands is also correct strategy.

When you think about increasing your aggression, you also want to think carefully about the size of the antes. In his excellent book *Every Hand Revealed*, Gus Hansen advises looking at the ratio between the small blind and the individual ante. In our example above, the small blind was 200 and each ante was 50, so the ratio was 4-to-1. That's a pretty average number in most tournament structures. If the ratio is smaller, it means the antes are bigger relative to the blinds, and you can be even more aggressive. If the ratio is larger, the antes are relatively smaller, and you can dial back your aggression a bit. Hansen's advice is a crucial insight and well worth applying whenever the level changes and the blinds and antes increase.

Another argument for increasing the aggression at this stage is that the weak players in the field are still hanging around, mostly clinging to smaller stacks and hoping to hang on until the bubble. They're more vulnerable to being exploited than in Stage 1 because it's less clear how to proceed, so their play oscillates between misplaced aggression preflop and passivity post-flop. In short, they're easy targets and you'll need to play some hands just to get a shot at relatively easy money.

Example 8-2. It's late in the first day of a large live tournament and the antes started two levels ago. Right now the blinds are 250 and 500, with a 50-chip ante, producing a starting pot of 1,200 chips. Your stack of 36,000 (M of 30), about average at the table, and you've been active so your image is loose-aggressive.

The player in third position, whose stack is 49,000 (M of 41), limps for 500. So far, he's been the weakest player at the table, limping repeatedly and refusing to value bet some good hands post-flop. He has, however, hit a lot of flops, which has compensated for his deficiencies.

The action folds around to you on the button and you have the

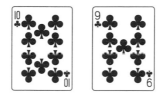

The blinds seem generally competent with the small blind being a little loose and the big blind a little tight.

You elect to raise to 1,800 and I like this play. You're coming after a weak player with position and a reasonable chance that you'll be heads-up on the flop. I'd make this play with a fairly wide range — pairs, suited aces, suited and unsuited Broadway cards, and medium suited connectors. I wouldn't make it with a larger range because you still need to worry about the blinds, either of who could see what was happening and stick in a 3-bet which would put a crimp in my plans. And despite the favorable situation versus the limper, you should still be folding hands like the Q♣8♠ or the 6♥5♥. Everyone has a line between appropriately aggressive and over-the-top, and that's mine. If your stack was even deeper, then you could stretch your range a little more, but an M of 30 (72 big blinds) isn't super-deep, so be a little cautious. The blinds fold, the limper calls, and the pot is now 4,800 chips.

The flop is the

That's a good flop. You've hit a flush draw and there are no high cards to connect with a Broadway hand. It's also unlikely your opponent connected with this flop, although he may have started with a pair and still feel good about his hand.

The weak player now checks. At this point, you're going to bet and try to take down the pot, but it's important to consider your bet sizing carefully. Here are some of your options:

1. **A big bet, 3,000 to 3,500.** Here you're making a pretty standard semi-bluff. You have a flush draw and two overcards to the board, so your hand is certainly strong enough for this bet. Your opponent will probably call with a medium or small pair or a flush draw. He'll call or raise with a seven. (It's very unlikely he has a big pair since he limped preflop and did not reraise.) And he'll probably fold everything else to a bet of this size. So you'll pick up a lot of small pots right now, but if he calls, you'll be behind, or up against another flush draw which is probably better than yours.

2. **A half-pot bet of 2,400.** This would be the standard bet size against a good player. Against this weak player, it will probably have the same effect as the big bet, folding out lots of hands that didn't connect while keeping his hands that did connect in the pot.

3. **A small bet of 2,000.** Against a weak player, this bet size makes a lot of sense. It's small enough to enable him to stick around with a lot of hands like overcards, suited aces, or

random suited junk because a weak player won't notice that he's not getting the right price to call with them. He just knows that the board probably missed you and it's a small bet, so he can play. If you can keep him involved with his whole range, you can win a lot of hands with a big bet on the turn.

With a made hand that was likely best, like a pair of jacks or tens, you would bet more, probably something in the range of 2,400 to 2,800. That bet size would represent a value bet to build the pot. The small bet better suits a drawing hand; you're setting a cheap price for the draw, keeping his range wide, and minimizing your loss if he comes over the top with a raise.

Against good players, it's dangerous to vary your bet size for different situations because they may be able to see what you're doing. Against weak players this isn't much of a worry because it's not likely they can put the whole picture together. You should worry about balancing ranges and bet sizes against good players; against weak players you have the luxury of playing as exploitatively as possible.

You bet 2,000 and he calls. The pot is now 8,800 chips and the effective stack is now 32,200. The turn is the K♠ and your opponent checks again.

Although technically you missed, this is a great card for you. (A queen would be a good card as well.) The high card makes it very hard for your opponent to call a bet with a medium or low pair. If he's been playing a suited ace, or something like queen-jack or queen-ten, it's also difficult for him to keep going; he hasn't hit his hand, and maybe facing a third bet from you. Does he really want to call off all his chips on the river with ace-high? Not too many players will.

Notice that an ace on the turn would be much worse for you. A big chunk of his range at this point are medium or low suited aces (and some unsuited aces as well), and you'd have no chance of moving him off a pair of aces.

The next question is how much to bet and in a spot like this, I like a bet of a little more than half the pot — 4,500 to 5,000.

That's probably enough to do the job while still leaving a lot of chips for a big river bet if necessary. It's hard for him to call without a real hand, and there are very few hands he can have at this point which fit the betting and can still call.

You bet 4,800. He thinks for a while and folds his hand.

This is a typical hand between a weak-tight player and a loose-aggressive player in the middle stages of a tournament. Let's assume that the tight player had his most likely hand, a pair of sixes or fives, and step back through the hand again, this time from the tight player's point of view.

The tight player picks up a low pair in third position. For argument's sake, let's give him the

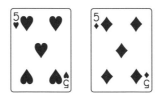

The first two players fold and he decides to limp which is his first mistake. The limp announces to his opponents that his most likely holding is either a medium or low pair, or suited connectors. He wants to see a flop, but because he doesn't have a premium hand he also wants to see a cheap flop, so he limps, hoping a few other players will limp behind him.

Either raising or folding is a better play. Raising disguises his hand and gives him at least a small chance of taking the pot down right now. Folding avoids trouble in a hand where he'll probably be out of position with a small pair and facing action from behind. Folding is also a prudent play which acknowledges that trying to play a low pair creates a situation that may be hard to handle. A man's got to know his limitations.

Action folds around to the button. It's a little unusual that the action got this far since any loose-aggressive player at the table would pick up on the limp from a tight player and realize they could raise with a wide range. However, each player would also have to contend with the threat from loose-aggressive players behind him, who could realize he was raising light and might 3-bet light with the additional advantage of position.

The button then reads the situation correctly and thinks his T♣9♣ is good enough to raise, especially with only the blinds left to act. Most, if not all, loose-aggressive players would agree with this, and in this spot, many would raise with very wide ranges.

The blinds don't attempt any sort of squeeze, so the action is back on the limper. The situation is now exactly what he tried to avoid: in order to stay in the hand, he has to invest even more chips, and without a set on the flop, he'll be out of position with no idea of what's happening.

At this point, reraising or folding is a better play than just calling. Reraising says to his opponent "Aha! I limped with aces or kings to lure you in, and now I'm springing my trap!" It's a play that might work. Loose-aggressive players have to be on the lookout for signs of real strength from tight players, and this move would certainly qualify. At the very least, it would take back the initiative and enable him to win the pot later if some high cards flop.

If he doesn't want to raise, folding at least gives him a cheap out for the hand. Without hitting a set on the flop, he's not likely to be able to win this hand out of position against a dangerous opponent. But he calls instead and we see a flop.

The flop of 7♣7♠4♣, although it lacks a five, is objectively pretty good for the tight player. If he's thinking in terms of ranges, his opponent is likely to have a wide range at this point and this flop misses most of it.

However, viewed another way, it's not so good. Since his preflop play (limp and call a raise) marked him as not having a high pair, his aggressive opponent can reasonably put him on one of three possible hands:

1. A couple of overcards.

2. A low pair.

3.   A fluke big hand or draw if he started with something like eight-seven suited or six-five suited.

When your opponent can narrow you down to a few alternatives, you're probably in trouble.

The tight player checks again. From his point of view, this is just a pot control move. He knows his hand might be best, and he'd like to check the hand down and find out.

The loose-aggressive player sees the check and realizes that the probability of a couple of overcards or a low pair has just gone up, while the probability of a big hand or draw has dropped a bit. He makes a small bet, figuring that a bunch of good things may happen:

1.   He might win the hand right now.

2.   If he's right about his opponent's holding, he's setting up bigger bets on the turn or river that will take the pot down.

3.   In the increasingly unlikely event that he's wrong about the hand and his opponent raises, he's cut his losses to a minimum.

4.   He knows that weaker players don't pay as much attention as they should to bet sizes, so he's not revealing much information with the small bet.

The tight player once again has to decide what to do. He wants to call and knows there's a good chance his pair is still the best hand. He also knows continuation bets are common and don't necessarily indicate a strong hand, and finally, he knows the bet is not large. Put another way, everything that he knows for sure adds up to a call. But the pot's getting bigger and he only has a pair of fives, something that does not make him happy. Still, it's too soon to fold, so he calls.

The K♠ arrives on the turn and the action is once again on the tight player. Again, our tight player is not happy. His opponent raised preflop and bet the flop. He might be bluffing, but he might also have a strong hand, and now a king arrives. The tight player's hand still hasn't improved, but a bunch of hands his opponent might have had, like ace-king and king-queen are now beating him. And of course, he might have had a high pair to start with. How much money does he want to risk in this pot with a pair of fives? He checks again.

The loose player still hasn't made anything, but he recognizes that his opponent, given how the hand has been bet, probably wasn't helped by the king. So he bets again. If his opponent is sitting on a low pair, which looks increasingly likely, this bet should win the pot.

Back to the tight player. He begins to count the pot and his stack. The pot is now 13,600 chips and it will cost him another 4,800 to call. He started the hand with 49,000, and if he calls, he will have invested 8,600 so far. In addition, the pot will be 18,400 chips going to the river, and he might have to face a river bet of 14,000 or so. Does he want to invest a third of his stack to see if a pair of fives holds up? Suppose he calls and the river is a queen or an ace. Will he call that bet? If not, should he call *this* one? Consequently, our tight player folds, and the loose-aggressive player takes down the pot.

We've spent a lot of time on this hand because it illustrates perfectly the dilemma of a tight player in the modern game. Apart perhaps from his opening limp, which is almost always a bad play, he made no bonehead blunders. He didn't even lose that much money, only 3,800 on a modest hand, and he can rationalize that much more could have been lost if he had called down to the end.

But from our vantage point, we know that he had the best hand all along. Still, we can't criticize him too much for not taking the hand any further. As far as he knew, he was no better than a coin toss to win, and he didn't want to risk a third of his stack on what might be a 50-50 event.

However, our loose-aggressive hero managed to increase his stack by 5,000, about 15 percent, without any hand at all. He just needed to bet and keep on betting, while watching to see if his opponent showed any confidence in his hand. Multiply this hand by hundreds or thousands of instances, and it's easy to see why money is flowing steadily from the tight players to the aggressive ones. The tight player needs a good hand to play; the aggressive player only needs a good situation. Good situations come up much more often than good hands.

For a loose-aggressive player, the goal in Stage 2 is not to bust your opponents (although there's nothing wrong with that), but to look for good situations and keep gathering chips. Contrary to the impression you might get from TV poker, most hands are not confrontations between quads and straight flushes, or even between sets and straights. Most flops miss most players, so most hands are battles between weak, weaker, and weakest. If you can use aggression to win two-thirds or three-fourths of these confrontations, you'll be able to chip up steadily, level by level.

Stage 3: On to the Bubble

I think of Stage 3 as starting when roughly 40 percent of the field remains, and continuing until the bubble bursts with about 10 percent of the field left. By now, the loose-aggressive players who were successful and a little lucky in Stage 2 have built imposing stacks. Each table might have one, two, or three of these players. The remaining seats are filled with surviving tight players of varying skills, plus some loose-aggressive players who were not as lucky during the Stage 2 action. The overall table is a nice mix of comfortable big stacks, cautious medium stacks, and desperate short stacks.

If anything, this stage favors the loose-aggressive players even more than Stage 2. And if you're a loose-aggressive player with a big stack, Stage 3 strategy looks like this:

1. **Play tight and avoid confrontations with the other big stacks.** Don't let your ego get involved with trying to decide who's really the biggest, baddest dude. The other big stacks are good players who have the resources to bounce you from

the tournament. Allowing that to happen at this stage is almost criminal because there is so much easy money to be made with little risk. Only get seriously involved with another big stack if you have a monster hand.

2. **Pick on the medium stacks without mercy.** The tight players with medium stacks are your prime target. They'll get involved in hands because they need to keep accumulating chips to stay afloat. However, they won't want to jeopardize their chances of cashing, so they can be pushed out of hands with aggressive betting. The closer you get to the bubble, the more aggressive you can be.

3. **Take the odds against the small stacks.** Small stacks (with Ms of 10 or less) can be pretty sure they won't survive to the bubble without taking some decisive action, so be prepared to see some all-in moves from this group. The typical move is an all-in 3-bet after the pot has been opened. Check the pot odds and use the techniques from the last chapter to see if a call is justified. One of the great benefits of building a big stack is the ability to make these calls when the odds are good without jeopardizing your stack, and calling these desperation moves is a good way to keep chipping up.

As you get close to the actual bubble, dealing with short stacks requires a little more caution. Once the finish line is in sight, they often become super-cautious, to the point that players start laying down kings or queens so as not to jeopardize their chances of cashing. When someone like that does play a hand, watch out!

Here's a good example of what can happen. I remember being near the bubble at the World Series of Poker a few years back. The fellow on my right had already mentioned this was his first World Series and he'd be ecstatic if he actually cashed. When we were about 20 players away from the bubble, he announced to nobody in particular that he wanted to cash so much that he wouldn't get involved with anything less than a pair of aces. Round after round of the table went by and he never played a hand. With three players left to go before the bubble, an aggressive player in middle position raised and this fellow, with an M of about 10, moved all-in. Everyone else folded and the original raiser contemplated his hand. He had plenty of chips and wasn't worried about being knocked out or even seriously damaged, — he just wanted to make the right play. Finally, after agonizing for a couple of minutes, he called and showed a pair of kings. My friend showed his aces and won the hand.

The raiser was getting a little less than 2-to-1 to call, and admitted after the hand that he just couldn't fold kings getting that price. But he should have, because what other hand could the novice have had? The odds against his having the other pair of kings was astronomical, and he wasn't making that play with queens, jacks, or ace-king with the bubble so tantalizingly close. Sometimes people *will* actually tell you their hand — you just have to listen.

Example 8-3. It's late in the second day of a major live tournament, and about 25 percent of the field remains. Blinds are 1,500 and 3,000, with a 300-chip ante producing a starting pot of 7,200 chips. Action folds around to the cutoff seat who raises to 6,500, just above the minimum. He's a marginally competent player who tends to be mostly tight, although he's shown down a couple of hands indicating a pretty wide range in late position. He's also able to make an aggressive move on occasion, especially if not too many chips are at risk. His stack was about 150,000 to start, for an M of about 21 (50 big blinds).

The button and the small blind fold and the action is on you in the big blind. Your stack is 240,000 with an M of 33 (80 big blinds) and your hand is the

So far you've been loose and aggressive, playing a lot of hands, and everyone at the table is aware of your style. You 3-bet to 16,000.

This is a typical move in a loose-aggressive player's repertoire. You're making this play for several reasons:

1. Your hand has some value and if it connects with the flop, you'll usually have a good and well-disguised hand. It's also not likely your somewhat tight opponent is playing cards that will connect with a low flop.

2. Your opponent can't ignore the possibility that you have the hand you're representing, a high pair or something like ace-king or ace-queen. Loose-aggressive players, like everyone else, occasionally do pick up very strong hands. If an ace or a king comes on the flop and your opponent is playing middle cards, he won't be happy.

3. You may take down the pot right now. As a loose-aggressive player, you don't usually have a lot of fold equity preflop, and if you've been at the same table for several hours and your opponents are reasonably observant (which of course is not always the case), they'll know you play wide ranges. Thus, they'll tend to stay in the hand with you and your fold equity will mostly come post-flop. Still, you might win the pot right here.

Your opponent calls and the pot is now 36,200 chips.
    The flop is the

giving you middle pair with a weak kicker. You act first and make a small bet of 12,000.

The small bet here has several functions. It might win the pot, of course, but that's more of a bonus than a goal. Comparing modern hold 'em to the hold 'em of a few years ago, fewer hands are decided preflop or on the flop, and more are decided on the turn and river. A small bet now gives you more freedom to maneuver later.

The small bet also looks like a trap. When your opponent goes over the hand in his head on the turn or river, he's going to ask "Why did my opponent make a 3-bet preflop and then a small flop bet? Maybe he hit a big hand and it's a trap! Arrrgh." The more ideas you can plant in his head, the more likely you are to get a fold on a later street.

The final reason for betting small goes back to an old principle of war and politics: If you want your opponent to retreat, give him an escape route. Barring a miracle turn or river card, we don't want this hand to go to a showdown, we want our opponent to give up. So betting small allows him to leave the hand cheaply, and dodges any pot-commitment situations, and we definitely don't want him to get pot-committed when we're holding a pair of sevens.

The player in the cutoff now raises to 27,000. Well, loose-aggressive players will see this sort of action fairly frequently. It generally doesn't mean great strength. If he had a set of tens or treys, would he be announcing his strength this early? Probably not. More likely he'd be calling in position and looking to trap on the turn. This raise is probably an attempt to end the hand now. He may have a small pair like us and realizes that his hand will be harder and harder to play on the turn and river, so he's showing some strength and trying to wrap things up now.

We don't want to let this happen, so you call. The pot is now 90,200 chips. And the effective stack is now about 107,000.

The turn is the K♣. That's a good card for you, partly because of your preflop 3-bet. It allows you to represent ace-king or king-queen, two hands which were plausibly in your preflop range and which have just made top pair.

Now it's time to take down the pot. Given the pot size and your opponent's stack, you only have one play, move all-in. Why such a big bet when we've been blathering on about the virtues of betting small? Right now our opponent isn't pot-committed. He can still walk away with about 70 percent of the stack he had when he started the hand. But if we make a small bet and get called, he'll be pot-committed, and that's the last thing we want. A big bet now is the logical consequence of our earlier small bets, and there are a lot of holdings in our range that would justify this bet. We could have a set, a big pair, ace-king, or king-queen. We could also have two clubs for a flush draw, or queen-jack or nine-eight for straight draws. We might even have a flush and a straight draw. Our bet says we have one of these hands, and our opponent will have to risk his tournament life to find out the truth.

This might look like a crazy play, but when you play a loose-aggressive style you have to make some plays like this. Even when your opponent thinks you may bluffing, he'll often find it difficult to call bets like this when he could just fold and play on with a decent stack.

You move all-in. He thinks for a while and folds.

Example 8-4. This is the same table as the previous example, a little later in the second day of a major live tournament. A little more than 20 percent of the field now remains, but a couple of hundred players still must be eliminated before the bubble pops. The blinds are 2,000 and 4,000, with a 400-chip ante, and the table now has eight players producing a starting pot of 9,200 chips.

The player under-the-gun raises to 8,500. His stack is about 300,000 with an M of 33 (75 big blinds). He's been aggressive throughout the day, so this under-the-gun raise doesn't necessarily indicate a tight range. A lot of aggressive players today actually like to use the under-the-gun spot as a good stealing location since players who don't know the latest nuances will credit them with a big hand.

The action folds around to you on the button. As noted before, you have a loose-aggressive image and everyone at the table knows that. Your stack now is about 350,000 with an M of

38 (87 big blinds), and you call with the A♦J♦. Also notice that this player has a stack that could really hurt you, so with your good position, there's no need to provoke a big confrontation yet.

The small blind folds and the big blind, with a stack of about 190,000 (with an M of 21), calls. He arrived at the table a short while ago and you don't know much about him. The pot is now 30,700 chips.

The flop is the Q♣7♦4♥.

The big blind checks and, somewhat surprisingly, the under-the-gun player checks as well. You make a small bet of 9,500.

Even though you missed the flop, this is a good bet. We discussed the small bet sizing in the last hand, and the same logic applies here. The bet takes the initiative and attempts to win the hand right now. If it doesn't win, you're showing strength and setting up other moves later in the hand. The big blind check-raises to 20,000 and the under-the-gun player folds.

Part of being a successful loose-aggressive player is being able to get away from a hand where your opponent is actually strong, rather than just having some sort of weak hand that you'll give up on the turn or river. Is that what's happening here? Is a fold necessary or can you still win this hand later?

While every situation has to be judged on its merits, there are some good rules of thumb that often apply. Here are a couple:

1. Small bets show weakness; big bets show strength.

2. Strength preflop or on the flop is less likely to be real than strength on the turn or river.

3. All-in or pot-committing moves are usually the real thing.

To see why these rules work well, let's go back inside the head of a tight player. He knows you're a loose-aggressive player and also knows you're sometimes playing junk and pushing him around. And he doesn't want to let that happen. But a tight player, like most everyone else, doesn't want to get knocked out of the tournament; in fact, there's a good chance he wants to stay in the tournament much more than you do. If you're a professional, this tournament is one in a long series of tournaments. But for the tight amateur, this might be his only tournament of the year. So his desire to stay alive is much greater than yours, and that fact informs all his decision-making.

1. If he makes a small bet, it means he wants to try to win the pot without risking much. If he doesn't want to risk much, he's not confident his hand is good. But if he bets a lot, he wants to win a big pot, so he thinks he has a strong hand.

2. Small bets on early streets are probably probe bets and he can make those bets without getting pot-committed. Big bets on the last two streets, after already putting money in the pot on the early streets, show that he's serious.

3. All-in bets speak for themselves. He has a hand and wants to double up.

So should you call this check-raise? A check-raise is a strong move, but it's a small raise and we're still on an early street. He might have a strong hand, but he also might be firing his one bullet to take down the pot. As a loose-aggressive player, you'll see a lot of these flop moves and you need to know how to react. Folding is not a mistake. However, you can call and use your position to get one more piece of information, his turn bet, before you make a final decision. The flop is very dry and would have missed a lot of hands in his range. He may be thinking, correctly, that it also missed a lot of hands in your range. So calling is the loose-aggressive play, but folding isn't unreasonable. You call and the pot is now 70,700 chips.

The turn card is the 3♣. That doesn't help you and it's unlikely to have helped him, so nothing much has changed. The big blind now checks.

If the big blind's hand was strong enough for a check-raise on the flop, then the arrival of the 3♣ shouldn't bother him. What's more likely is that the big blind was taking a stab at the pot with some sort of check-raise bluff and now doesn't want to put in any more money.

Should you bet? Probably not. If you bet and he raises, you'll need to throw your hand away. You do have outs (aces and jacks probably give you the best hand) so wait until the river comes and reevaluate. If you didn't have any outs, a bluff would be more reasonable. You check and the pot remains at 70,700 chips.

The river is the 6♣. The big blind bets 20,000 and the pot is now 90,700 chips. The big blind appears to have about 140,000 chips left.

That's a very small bet, less than one-third of the pot. Small bets like this on the river are rarely value bets or traps; most of the time they are blocking bets, designed to let the bettor see a showdown with a minimal investment. So it's likely that he has something and doesn't want to call a big bet and wants to find out if his hand is really best. His most likely holding on this board is a medium pair, say tens, nines, or eights. Those hands also pretty well fit his action so far: the preflop call in the big blind, the check-raise on the flop (he thought his hand was best and didn't want to see another high card) and his check on the turn when you wouldn't go away on the flop.

The best response to a blocking bet is usually a big raise. It's also your only chance to win the hand since if this analysis is right, an ace-high hand won't be good. And you need to make a substantial raise because that's exactly what your opponent is trying not to see.

You raise to 100,000. He thinks for a while and folds.

Your last bet actually fits a bunch of hands you could have been holding. If you started with two clubs, you hit a flush. If you started with a pair of fives, you made a straight. You might also have a set, or a pair of queens. Of course, he could have any of these hands too, but his betting indicates that he doesn't.

He won't always fold here. Sometimes he'll have been playing a strong hand deceptively, and sometimes he'll actually call with a small pair and put his tournament on the line. But most players will give this up and try to survive with a slightly smaller stack rather than make a stand.

Here's a key point to remember: When a player starts a hand with a low M (say 10 or less), he often decides before the hand starts that he's willing to go all the way if he picks up something promising like a medium pair or ace-queen or better. But when a player starts a hand with an M greater than 20 (as here), he hasn't made that determination yet. He's probably still thinking defensively, trying to make sure the betting doesn't get away from him. And all the betting in this hand indicates that's the case, making the big bet on the river such a high-percentage play.

Chipping up with bets and raises that apply a lot of pressure is a good way to keep building your stack. However, the real payoff for the loose-aggressive player comes when you pick up a genuinely big hand, but no one suspects. Here's a typical example.

Example 8-5. A little less than 20 percent of the field remains in a big live tournament. You're sitting at an eight-player table with blinds of 3,000 and 6,000, with a 600-chip ante producing a starting pot of 13,800 chips.

You're under-the-gun with a stack of 620,000 and an M of 45, and right now, you're the second-biggest stack at the table. You've been relentlessly aggressive for hours, picking on the medium stacks at the table, winning lots of pots, but engaging in very few showdowns. Most of the players at the table have been playing tight to varying degrees, and few have wanted to risk their stacks to see what you have.

You pick up the K♠K♣. You haven't actually seen a premium pair for quite a while, so this is a nice surprise. You raise to 14,000, just under 2.5 times the big blind which is at the high end of the standard opening raise at the table this round.

The action folds around to the cutoff seat, a somewhat tight player, who calls. You've taken several pots away from him with aggressive post-flop play, and you suspect that he has a pretty good hand. After calling, his stack seems to be about 300,000.

The button folds and the big blind, who is also a tight player, but who likes to take good pot odds, calls. He was looking at a pot of about 42,000 and it only cost him 8,000 to call, so he was getting better than 5-to-1. You assess he could have almost any reasonable hand. His stack is about 240,000 and the pot is now about 50,000 chips. The flop is the J♣7♦6♣ and the big blind checks.

You have a very strong hand, an overpair to the board. There are also flush and straight possibilities, so charging any possible drawing hand to play is good. However, the key idea is that when you play a loose-aggressive style you have to bet your strong hands. Your good opponents know you bet a lot and can't have the hands you're representing most of the time. So they just have to decide if their hand is good enough to take a stand against you. If it is, they'll play, and if it isn't, they won't. Here you should expect anyone with a pair or a draw to see at least one more street, and you need to make them pay for that. In addition, your bet will be interpreted as a standard continuation bet, which may or may not mean anything.

You bet 25,000, half the pot. On a dry board, you would bet a little less, but the presence of the draws encourages you to make a bigger bet. The player in the cutoff calls the 25,000 and the big blind folds. The pot is now 100,000 chips.

The turn is the K♥, a perfect card. Beside giving you the current nuts, it serves another purpose. On several occasions, you've picked up pots by betting scare cards on the turn. (See some of the previous examples in this chapter.) It's a standard technique of loose-aggressive players, and our opponent will probably have picked up on this by now. If he has a hand like ace-jack, he won't be especially worried about the appearance of an overcard. Your range is still wide in his eyes and he'll think he's beating most of it.

You should bet again partly because you'd probably do that even if the turn missed completely. *How much to bet?* The pot is 100,000 chips and the effective stack is 260,000. So a bet of 40,000 looks about right. It's not a big increase over your flop bet, so it might give an impression that you're trying to bluff without risking much. But it's also an amount that leaves him pot-committed if he wants to raise, making an all-in raise his only move besides calling. And if he just calls, an all-in bet on the river is just slightly larger than a pot-sized bet.

You bet 40,000, he moves all-in for his last 260,000, and you call. Your opponent shows the A♣J♠, the river is the 9♦, and your set of kings takes the pot and knocks him out.

If you play a loose-aggressive style, you'll see hands like this with some frequency. Your opponent was tired of shipping chips over and probably decided a while ago to make a stand with any decent hand. When you raised preflop and he saw ace-jack suited, he was happy to call. When he hit top pair on a not-too-wet flop, he was ready to get all his chips in.

Sometimes you'll hit a big hand on the flop and win the pot because no one has anything. But when you do have a big hand, you're much more likely to get paid off than a tight player.

Stage 4: The Endgame

The endgame arrives after the bubble has broken and the post-bubble phase of desperate all-ins by short stacks has also passed. At this point, perhaps 6 to 7 percent of the field remains alive. Hardly any truly deep stacks are in play; an M of 40 to 50 is very good, and much of the field has Ms of 15 or less.

In this stage, loose-aggressive play won't be nearly as effective as before. A lot of the field will decide to commit to the pot as soon as they pick up their cards and see something playable. Others will call to see a flop and then decide. Playing small ball to steal pots on the turn or river isn't especially effective because many contested pots will be decided earlier.

Consequently, the tight style actually does pretty well at this stage because many tight players are familiar with the push-fold game and can make good decisions about pushing or not. Many loose-aggressive players, on the other hand, recognize that their strength lies in hand reading and post-flop play, but don't make a study of push-fold theory. Unfortunately for the tight players, not many (of them) are still alive in the tournament, and the players with the biggest stacks are mostly those who played a loose-aggressive game earlier.

So if you played a loose-aggressive style and survived to the endgame with a decent stack, your goal now should be to tighten up and look for good spots. But don't become a nit, drop the weakest hands from your ranges and look for good odds on all-in moves from the short stacks. The chips accumulated in the early stages allow you to take advantage of desperate moves without jeopardizing your stack.

Countering
the Loose-Aggressive Style

Have we reached the end of poker evolution? Is the loose-aggressive style the ultimate poker style for tournament play which all players must copy to be successful?

In poker, there is no "ultimate style." The simple game that best models poker is the child's game of rock-paper-scissors. Each player conceals his hand behind his back and arranges his fingers in one of three ways: clenched fist (rock), palm out (paper), or two fingers extended (scissors). The players then show their hands. Paper wraps rock, rock breaks scissors, and scissors cut paper. If both players extend the same hand, the game is a tie and you play again.

There is no best hand in rock-paper-scissors. Each hand beats one hand, loses to another hand, and ties the third. A strategy based on always playing the same hand loses because if you know what your opponent is doing, you can pick a hand that beats him. Optimal play against another good player is to randomly pick one of the three choices, which guarantees you a tie against someone with the same strategy. Any other strategy can be exploited.

Although poker is light-years beyond rock-paper-scissors in terms of complexity, it's similar in terms of how strategies interact. If your opponent knows what you're doing, he can counter it with an exploitative strategy of his own. When he doesn't know what you're doing, his job is much more difficult.

So let's suppose you're an intelligent player who by nature is inclined to play a somewhat tight strategy. You're not a nit, but you're also not inclined to open under-the-gun with jack-nine suited. You think you have some decent hand-reading skills, but you're no Phil Ivey. You plunk your money down and enter the Main Event at the World Series of Poker. You suspect that when you sit down at the table, you'll see a bunch of good young loose-aggressive players, a couple of tight players like yourself, and a couple of weak players who may be hard to categorize. What's the right approach? What should you be trying to do to give yourself the best chance to go deep?

You can't simply play what we've categorized so far as a basic-tight style. That's a great style for beating weak, loose players, the sort of players we saw in large numbers in tournaments from 2003-2007. It's a style that's easy to understand and easy to teach, and it's a great style for grasping basic concepts like pot odds and pot control. But it's also an easy style to exploit, and the modern loose-aggressive style is the perfect style for exploiting the conservative tendencies of the basic-tight player.

To adapt to the modern game, you need to do what the loose-aggressive players did when confronting tight players: examine the weaknesses of the style, and exploit them. So let's start by looking at the loose-aggressive style again, but this time focusing on its particular weaknesses.

Weaknesses of the Loose-Aggressive Style

The loose-aggressive style is built on two key elements:

1. Play wide ranges.

2. Aggressive betting and good hand reading.

As we've seen, both of these ideas are powerful and effective against a standard basic-tight player, exploiting his unwillingness to get involved in a big pot without a big hand.

These techniques, however, can be turned into weaknesses by someone who understands what loose-aggressive players are doing. Let's reevaluate the pillars of the loose-aggressive style and see how you could turn the tables.

Pillar No. 1: Play wide ranges. By definition, loose-aggressive players play wide ranges. That's the essence of the style. When you play wide ranges, several good things happen. First, you see lots of flops, which greatly increases the number of big hands you'll see over the course of the tournament. Second, you become unpredictable. Your opponents eventually realize that your wide range of hands means you could connect with any flop and that, in turn, makes them cautious. When you bet on the flop, they start imagining all the big hands you could have — sets, two pair, straight draws — instead of what you're likely to have, which is often nothing.

Here's a good example to drive the point home. Suppose you're in the big blind with the

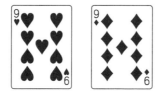

Action folds to the button, a loose-aggressive player. Based on what you've seen, you estimate that his range for a button raise is at least 50 percent of hands. He raises and you call. What are your winning chances after each of the following flops?

1. Flop A: 7♠6♠4♣

2. Flop B: K♥8♣2♠

3. Flop C: J♥6♠6♦

4. Flop D: A♣K♣4♥

All four of these flops missed your hand. (Nothing too surprising there.) Three of the flops contained overcards. One contained two overcards. But here are your actual chances postflop against the button's estimated 50 percent range:

1. Against Flop A: 66 percent

2. Against Flop B: 66 percent

3. Against Flop C: 63 percent

4. Against Flop D: 47 percent

You're a very small underdog against Flop D, and better than a 60 percent favorite against the other three. Those numbers might be surprising to a lot of players, but they make perfect sense. The upside of a wide range is that it could hit any flop pretty hard. But the downside of a wide range is that *it rates to miss any particular flop*. If you think about it, that should be pretty obvious. If a king flops, a wide range will have some kings in it. But it will have many more hands that don't contain a king.

The first lesson here is pretty clear. If you're playing a loose-aggressive player who plays wide preflop ranges and you hit a medium to high pair on the flop, you have a strong hand. If he bets the flop (and he will), you're going to have to call, and you'll probably have to call any turn card as well.

Basic-tight players get themselves into trouble in the hand reading process against a loose-aggressive player. They know intellectually that their opponent has a wide opening range, but as the hand goes on and more bets are made, they tend to make evaluations as though a tight player were betting. *"He raised preflop and then when a king appeared he bet the flop, and then he followed up with a bet on the turn! He's seen me call twice so he must at least have a pair of kings. My nines can't be any good!"*

A good loose-aggressive player can fire all three streets if he thinks that will make you lay down what you have. Be prepared.

Pillar No. 2: Aggressive betting and good hand reading. Betting and hand reading are really two sides of the same coin; neither works without the other. Aggressive betting scoops up the fold equity lying around the table, but without good hand reading skills an aggressive player walks into a lot of traps. Put another way, good hand reading without aggressive betting just leaves a lot of easy money on the table.

The loose-aggressive style hinges on the fact that most flops miss most hands. If you're a typical basic-tight player who needs solid values to call bets on multiple streets, then you'll be laying down many of those hands to aggressive betting.

But what happens when you actually hit a hand? The aggressive player needs to figure out when that happens, otherwise his profits built up from several hands of aggressive betting can evaporate when you actually have a monster and he doesn't realize it.

So how do they decide if their opponent has a big hand? Most loose-aggressive players look first at whether or not their opponent has put more money into the pot after the flop than required to stay in the hand. If the aggressive player bets the flop and gets called, the opponent has only invested the minimum to stick around. That action most likely indicates a medium pair, a weak top pair, a draw, or pot control with a good top pair. If the aggressive player bets the flop and gets raised, the opponent has shown he's interested in this hand and willing to put in some real money. The stronger the move and the later the street, the more certain the aggressive player can be that he's facing a big hand.

Loose-aggressive players don't have any incentive to fight over a hand where you've shown strength and they don't have much. Why pick on a hard target when the early part of a tournament offers so many easy opportunities for chipping up? Furthermore, their opponents are entitled to pick up a good hand once in a while. A more sensible plan is to let this hand go and try again later.

A move on the turn carries even more weight than a move on the flop. Let's say a loose-aggressive player makes a preflop raise and you call from the big blind. On the flop, you check, he bets, and you call. At this point, he probably thinks you have something but are not yet committed to the hand. A nondescript turn card comes, again you check, and again he bets, seeing a good chance to win the hand right now. You raise, and suddenly his calculus changes. Your hand now looks like you hit a set on the flop, slowplayed one street, then sprung your trap on the turn. Calling may put him in a position of facing an even bigger bet on the river, — better to let this go right now.

Against a tight player, the loose-aggressive player doesn't expect to see a lot of bluffs. Tight players know they should bluff, but they rarely do. In truth, bluffing isn't really in their nature. They like betting big hands where they're confident of winning, and the loose-aggressive player knows this. So he doesn't want to risk a lot of money on the off-chance that a tight player has uncharacteristically decided to bluff. For the aggressive player, poker is a numbers game. He'll win a high percentage of pots at a weak table; he doesn't need to try to win every pot.

So if you've established a table image as a basic-tight player, how can you exploit your image against a loose-aggressive player? The analysis above points the way. You need to do three changes to your natural game and we'll look at them one at a time.

Change No. 1: Bluff some weak hands. A tight table image can pay some enormous dividends if you know how to use it. Loose-aggressive players aren't expecting you to do much except play your hands straightforwardly. As a result, your bluffs have a much higher than normal chance of succeeding. Take a look at this hand.

Example 8-6. It's the third level of a live tournament. Blinds are 150 and 300, and the antes kick in next level. You're at an active table with several young loose-aggressive players and a few older players with various styles. You've played tight the first two levels and are pretty sure everyone has an image of you as a basic-tight player. You've 3-bet only once, at the end of the first level, when you picked up aces. Your opponent immediately folded.

After three folds, the player in fourth position raises to 700. He's an older player who's played a lot of hands, but not that aggressively, you think he's one of the two weakest players at the table, and his stack has drifted down to 16,000 — everyone started with 20,000. The player in fifth position, a loose and aggressive player whose stack is about 26,000, 3-bets to 1,700, and you believe him to be a good player. The player in the cutoff seat folds but another loose-aggressive player on the button 4-bets to 3,800. He's a strong player who reached the final table of this tournament the previous year.

The small blind folds. You're in the big blind with just over 20,000 and hold the

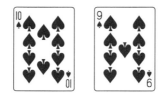

What do you do?

You could fold, of course, but a better play is to 5-bet to about 9,500. Risky? Crazy? Let's see. Imagine that you made this raise. Now put yourself in the position of each of your opponents and ask what your range looks like. You're a tight player. You haven't given much action through a few hours of play. Now you see a raise, a 3-bet, and a 4-bet in front of you and make a 5-bet that essentially commits you to the pot. *What hand does that?*

The answer is aces, and maybe kings, and that's it. And if someone actually has a pair of kings, it's much more likely that you have aces than the last two kings. Raising here is just an example of using your table image to make a high-percentage play. But if you had a loose-aggressive image, this play would just be a risky bluff. Your opponents might fold or they might not, but they wouldn't automatically credit you with aces or kings. But here they more or less have to.

If you make a play like this and everyone folds, try to look disappointed. And if someone asks you if you had aces, just smile ruefully and say "Yep."

Most players who play tight don't realize that the image they've created makes bluffing a lethal weapon. In general, tight players are tight because that's their nature. They like having solid values behind them; they don't like being out on a limb. When they invest, they look for stocks with solid earnings and good dividends; they're not looking for the next red-hot biotech or ultra-trendy restaurant chain, and in investing, that's not a big problem. A solid portfolio will do just fine over time. But in poker, it's a huge problem. They've created a money-making image but don't use it.

So if you're a naturally tight player, don't fall into this trap. Bluffing is a more powerful weapon for you than for anyone else at the table. Use it sensibly.

Change No. 2: Slowplay some strong hands. Slowplaying is a tool that tends to be overused by players with no experience or just a little experience. Slowplaying a hand is great if the goal is to trap your opponent for an extra bet. When you check/call a very strong hand instead of betting or raising, you show some weakness and this can result in picking up one extra bet somewhere down the road. But it's a disaster if you have a big hand and your opponent has a big hand but not one as big as yours. In that case, slowplaying may win an extra bet or two, but cost you a chance at his stack.

When you have a tight image and are matched in a hand against a loose-aggressive player, slowplaying takes on a whole new dimension. The loose-aggressive player is looking for pots that can be taken down because you're trying to get to showdown with a hand that's decent but not great. If he can sniff out those hands where you won't stand up to a double or triple barrel, he can steal another pot. Slowplaying sends him a signal that, yes indeed, you're not in love with your hand and will give it up if he can only apply enough pressure.

Slowplaying is mostly ineffective in tight, low stakes cash games because your opponent may not have a great hand and can't be trapped into leading out at the pot. He can play pot control just like you. But a loose-aggressive player in a modern tournament is a different creature. His mission is to chip up by taking pots from tight players like you. So slowplaying big hands now becomes effective.

Some hands and flops are much better for slowplaying than others. Suppose you have a tight image and raise preflop from second position with a pair of kings. A loose-aggressive player calls from the button. If the flop comes the

you can forget about slowplaying. You have the sort of hand he expects you to have, and a check on the flop won't induce him to put more money in the pot.

On the other hand, suppose you raise from second position with a pair of eights and the flop is the

This is a perfect situation to make a continuation bet on the flop and then shut down on the turn. Your set of eights is well concealed and this flop could easily have missed you. A loose-aggressive player will look at this flop and see an excellent opportunity to take down some chips. The only aggressive action you need to take here is a bet or raise on the river.

Change No. 3: Embrace volatility. If you're a solid basic-tight player, you probably don't like volatility. An ideal tournament would be one where you play good hands, hit flops, get called by loose bad players, and accumulate chips steadily, all the while avoiding big risks.

Once upon a time, when tournaments were full of bad players, this was almost an achievable dream. But not any more. Today's tournaments have fewer genuinely bad players, and many more good ones. Even worse, the good players are playing in a style designed to extract chips from tight players who can't adjust to the new game. So your chance of keeping up with the blinds and antes just by playing good, solid poker is slim.

Having said that, we've given you some weapons that will let you hold your own with aggressive players who read you as tight — pick good situations to bluff, and be prepared to slowplay big hands. But these weapons come with a big price tag: They make your results much more volatile. A big bluff, when it fails, may cost you a big part of your stack. A well-timed slowplay may let your opponent draw out, again costing you a chunk of your stack. The swings will get much larger, and you may find yourself wandering around the casino in the middle of the second level, wondering what happened.

To excel in modern tournaments, you're sometimes going to need to make plays with big swings to accumulate chips. Example 8-6, where we recommended making a 5-bet bluff preflop, is a good example. It's a great situation given your image and the styles of the players in the hand. It should work fairly often, earning you a lot of chips. But once in a while one of your opponents will actually hold aces himself, or someone will raise just to see what you'll do, and almost half your stack will be gone.

Some good plays are like that. The equity is real, but the swing will be huge. But to be successful, you need to be able to make these plays.

Example 8-7. It's late in the second day of a major tournament. The blinds are 2,000 and 4,000, with a 400 chip ante producing a starting pot of 9,600 chips. You've been at the same table all day and have had a good chance to observe your opponents, and they in turn have had a good look at you. It's a tough table with several good loose-aggressive players.

The action folds around to the button, a loose and very aggressive player who plays wide ranges and is relentless at trying to push players off hands when the situation looks right, raises to 9,000. His stack is about 300,000, with an M of 31. The small blind folds and the action is on you in the big blind.

Your hand is the

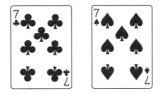

your stack is 150,000, and your M is approximately 16. So far today you've been somewhat tight, although certainly not a nit. You've caught a little more than your share of good hands, have managed to actually chip up a bit, and have been active in defending your big blind. *What's the best play with your sevens?* Folding is out of the question. The aggressive player's button range is probably something like 50 percent of all hands, and you're way ahead of that range, so your choice is between calling and 3-betting. But calling leaves you out of position with a hand that's likely to be facing overcards after the flop, and you're not getting the odds needed to call with the hope of flopping a set, so raising is better.

Now comes the real questions: How much do you raise? and what do you do if your opponent moves all-in? Both questions are important. When playing a loose-aggressive player and contemplating a reraise, you always need to know what to do if you get 4-bet. Loose-aggressive players 4-bet a lot in situations like this, and figuring out the play before it happens will let you make much better decisions.

Thus, a good 3-bet size here is about 30,000, a little more than three times his initial raise. That's bigger than a typical 3-bet, but not so big that it looks suspicious. It's also big enough that a 4-bet from him should be an all-in move. You raise to 30,000 and he moves all-in.

This is an easy call, but let's go through the numbers so the reasoning is clear. The pot is now 185,200 chips, and it costs you your last 124,000 to call. You're getting odds of almost exactly 3-to-2, meaning you need to have at least a 40 percent winning chances to call for profit. Here's how you're doing against subsets of the button's initial range:

Button's 4-Bet Range	Winning Chances for 77
5%	33%
10%	42%
20%	49%
30%	52%

Only if the button has a very tight 4-betting range will you not be getting the correct odds to call, and since he has plenty of reason to think you may fold, it's unlikely that his range is this tight. Remember, he sees you as a basically tight player who likes to take good pot odds and defend his blind. That means your defending range is wide, so there must be a good chance you'll fold to an all-in move. Therefore, he should be prepared to move all-in with a reasonably wide range. His logic is good, but your pair of sevens is near the top of your defending range.

You call his all-in and he shows the

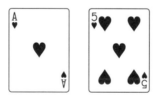

making you almost a 2-to-1 favorite. Your sevens hold up to win, increasing your stack to over 300,000.

Although this example may look simple, it's actually a difficult hand for a fundamentally tight player to play well. Most tight players would look down at the sevens and say something like "OK, I've got a small pair, it's an easy call. If I flop a set, maybe I can win a big pot." In fact, the pair of sevens give you a great opportunity to make a play against this specific opponent. If it doesn't work, you'll be out, but if it succeeds, and this should be the case more often than not, you'll be in great shape. Embrace volatility.

Example 8-8. It's early in the third day of a big live tournament. Blinds are 4,000 and 8,000, with an 800-chip ante producing a starting pot of 19,200. A little over 20 percent of the field remains and the players at your table are mostly loose and aggressive, but a couple of them seem to be tight and haven't been involved in too many pots.

You're in the cutoff with a stack of 300,000 and an M of about 16, the first five players fold, and you pick up the A♠T♠ and raise to 18,000, the standard opening raise at this level. Your image is fairly tight as you haven't seen many good hands or situations, and your stack has been whittled down from 350,000 at the start of the day.

The action folds around to the small blind, one of the most aggressive players, who calls. His stack seems to be about 550,000 after his call, and the big blind folds. The pot is now 51,200 chips.

The flop is the T♣T♦6♦ and the small blind checks.

With trips and an M of 16, you're going all the way with your hand no matter what appears on board. So your goal is to keep your loose-aggressive opponent in the hand and to try to build the pot at the same time.

Since you led preflop, a continuation bet is mandatory, and a continuation bet bluff is one bluff that tight players are comfortable making because it's cheap and non-committal. Furthermore, your opponent will be suspicious if you don't make one, so bet half the pot and see what happens.

You bet 26,000 and the small blind calls. The pot is now 103,200 chips and the effective stack is now 256,000. The turn is the 3♠ and the small blind now leads out for 30,000.

The flop action was predictable. He checked, you made a standard continuation bet, and he called. At this point he could have nothing or something, but in either case he'll try to win the pot.

The lead-out bet on the turn is a little unusual since he could have checked to see if you would show weakness by checking behind. Then he could lead out on the river with a big bet and expect to take the pot down. There are two possible explanations:

1. He doesn't have anything, doesn't think the turn helped you, and wants to take the pot down right now with a cheap bet before a high card or a diamond appears on the river.

2. He has something like a medium pair, thinks it's probably best, but he's giving you a chance to make a raise and tell him he's beaten.

What's the right response? A tight player who has nothing will mostly go away at this point, so just calling and indicating that you like your hand may be enough to prevent you from winning any more money on the river. If that's true, a small raise on your part actually makes sense. If your opponent has something like a pair of eights, he may be unwilling to fold to a small raise, thinking there's a decent chance you have something like two high cards. Furthermore, a small raise doesn't risk much and might be your best chance to build a big pot in case your opponent actually has a pair.

You raise to 65,000 and the small blind calls. The pot is now 233,000 chips and the effective stack is now 190,000. The river is the Q♥ and the small blind checks.

The check makes some sort of small or medium pair more likely since he didn't elect to bluff at the pot. In addition, your stack is smaller than the pot, so any reasonable smaller bet will be pot-committing anyway, and he knows that. Therefore, the best play is to move all-in. You're hoping he has some sort of pair and thinks you could have a smaller one. The small blind calls and shows the 9♥9♦ and you take the pot.

A potential weakness of some loose-aggressive players is that by playing many hands with wide ranges, they tend to assume everyone at the table is aware of their style and will play wide ranges against them. At a table of other loose-aggressive players, that's mostly true. But it then becomes difficult to pick up signals that your opponent actually has a good hand, after which it's easy to rationalize that any bet or raise is a bluff. After a long day at the table, they may make that assumption even against someone who isn't so loose. In this case, your opponent stuck with his pair of nines although your raise on the turn should have been a clear warning signal that something was afoot.

Example 8-9. It's near the end of the second day at a live tournament and you've been at this table for about two hours. Three players seem to be strong, loose-aggressive players, a couple are clearly tight players, and have dwindling stacks, and a couple of others are hard to categorize. A little less than 30 percent of the field remains and the field won't hit the bubble until the next day.

The blinds are 1,000 and 2,000, with a 200-chip ante producing a starting pot of 4,800 chips. You're second to act with a stack of 90,000 and an M of just under 19 (45 big blinds). The under-the-gun player folds and you look down to see the K♥K♦ and raise to 5,000.

Three players fold, but the player in the cutoff seat calls. He's one of the tight players and his stack is about 70,000. The button folds and the small blind, one of the aggressive players, calls, and his stack is about 240,000, the second-biggest stack at the table. The big blind folds and the pot going to the flop is 18,800 chips.

The flop is the 9♣8♦4♣ and the small blind checks. As a tight player, you'll be perceived having a narrow range from second position and people will expect you to have a high pair, perhaps aces down through nines, or two high cards. Also, a tight player who opened in early position will usually make a continuation bet with his entire range on a flop of medium or low cards, especially with flush and straight possibilities out there, and any other play would look suspicious. So you bet 11,000, just over half the pot.

The tight player in the cutoff folds, but the aggressive player in the small blind calls, and the pot is now 40,800 chips. From what you've seen, the small blind doesn't give up on hands easily if he sees a chance to win. Therefore, he could probably have anything at this point.

The turn is the K♠, giving you a set of kings, and the small blind checks. You check behind, the pot remains at 40,800 chips, and the effective stack is about 74,000.

The check after the king arrives is crucial for your plan because it establishes a compelling narrative. Suppose your hand was QQ, JJ, or TT. You would make a continuation bet on the flop with a strong hand, an overpair to the board, hoping to build a pot. Now the king arrives and you'd be afraid the overcard may give your opponent a bigger pair, so you would switch into pot control mode and check, and your goal in this scenario would be to get to a cheap showdown and see if your hand was good. With aces, the king wouldn't be a concern and you could keep betting. If you had ace-king, the king would actually give you a hand and let you bet for value. But the check on the turn sells the idea that your most likely range now is queens through tens.

The river is the A♣, a perfect card for you. If you in fact held QQ, JJ, or TT, you're now looking at two overcards to your pair and feeling sick. The small blind pushes all-in.

Although it's possible he has a higher set or a flush, you must call. From his point of view, your most likely hands are QQ, JJ, and TT. He could beat you with a flush, a set, an ace, a king, or even two pair. As far as he's concerned, there's no way a tight player can call this bet. You call, he shows a pair of sixes, you take down the pot and increase your stack to almost 190,000.

From the small blind's perspective, the hand told an obvious story.

1. You raised in early position with a hand like jacks. He called with his small pair and would prefer to be in position with his pair but he figured could outplay you from any seat.

2. You had an overpair to the flop so you made a combination continuation bet and value bet. He called because he knew the flop didn't help you and thought he could represent something later.

3. A king came on the turn and he checked. You shut down, obviously to play pot control, and that's what tight players do. And when you checked, he recognized the pot control move and figured a river bet would probably take the pot if it were big enough.

4. The river A♣ should have made your position untenable, and he could now represent a lot of hands that crushed you. So he moved all-in expecting a quick fold.

About ten years ago, Layne Flack described a style for combating the aggressive play of that day. He called it the "donkey approach," and it involved just doing the opposite of what a tight, rational analysis would dictate at any point. The turn check in the previous hand is a good example. Since a key part of successful loose-aggressive play is first-rate hand reading, the "opposite" approach creates some real problems, especially if your opponent doesn't think you're capable of anything particularly subtle. (On *Seinfeld*, George Costanza discovered a similar approach — just do the opposite of what you naturally do — was the key to successful dating.)

Glossary

Poker has always had its own terminology, and the growth of online poker as well as poker forums has added even more terms to the traditional lingo. Here is a useful collection of terms, phrases, and examples that will help you navigate the world of tournament poker talk.

3-bet: The first pre-flop reraise.

Example: Pre-flop, the under-the-gun player raises and the player in middle position folds. The cutoff reraises and this reraise is called a 3-bet. Historically, 3-bets were rare and indicated a very strong hand, often aces or kings. In modern no-limit hold 'em, 3-bets are more common and are often an attempt to push a tight player off a good but not exceptionally strong hand. This type of move is also known as '3-betting light.'

4-bet: The second pre-flop reraise.

Example: Pre-flop, the under-the-gun player raises and the player in middle position folds. The cutoff reraises (a 3-bet) and the button and the blinds fold. If the under-the-gun player now raises again, his reraise is called a 4-bet. (Had the button or one of the blinds made the second preflop reraise, this is also called a 4-bet.)

5-bet: The third pre-flop reraise. If the effective stacks are about 100 big blinds, a 5-bet will often be an all-in move.

ABC poker: The most straightforward style of playing poker in which you bet your good hands, check your medium-strength hands, and fold your weak hands. You do not make plays which do not reflect the true strength of your hand, and if your opponent makes a large bet or raise, you assume they have the hand they represent. This strategy is close to optimal against tables of weak, loose, passive players who play too many hands and stick around too long. But it's a losing strategy against a table containing several aggressive players who can exploit this style ruthlessly.

aggressive: A player who prefers to bet and raise rather than just check and call. Aggressive players are more successful than *passive* players because their betting action gives them two ways to win: their opponents can fold, or they can show down the best hand.

air: A hand with no value which almost certainly can't win at showdown. Players with air after the flop have a choice of folding or trying a bluff to win the pot.

all-in: Moving all your chips to the center of the table with a bet or raise. The player is then said to be all-in. Betting or raising all your chips is also known as *pushing, shoving,* or *jamming*. In a tournament, a player who is all-in will be knocked out of the tournament if he loses the hand.

ante: A fixed amount that each player puts in the pot before a hand begins. Antes are uncommon in hold 'em cash games. In tournaments, antes will usually begin after the first few blind levels have been played. While antes vary from tournament to tournament, it's not uncommon for the sum of all the antes to approximately equal the big blind. In addition, antes have a significant effect on strategy since the larger pots encourage players to play more aggressively.

backdoor flush: A flush made by hitting flush cards on both the turn and river.
Example: Your hold cards are the 4♦ and 3♦. The flop comes the A♦Q♠T♣, giving you three cards to a diamond flush, also known as a *backdoor flush draw*. If the turn and the river are both diamonds, you would have made a *backdoor flush*. Not only will hitting the flush will most

likely give you the winning hand, it will also be well concealed and may be very profitable.

balanced range: A range of hands roughly balanced between powerful hands, medium-strength hands, and bluffs. A player with a balanced range is hard to play against because they could be holding almost any sort of hand. The contrast to a balanced range is a *polarized range*.

bet: The first player who puts money into the pot on a given round is said to make a *bet*. He will win the pot unless a later player *calls* his bet (puts an equal amount into the pot) or *raises* his bet (puts more money into the pot).

betting pattern: Handling situations with certain persistent patterns of bets, raises, and calls. For example, a tight, conservative player who picks up a hand like ace-king or ace-queen might raise preflop, make a continuation bet on the flop whether he hits his hand or not, then bet the turn if he has a high pair or check the turn if he doesn't. This particular pattern is easy to exploit: call the flop with anything, then bet the turn if the leader checks. A good player will vary his betting patterns to remain difficult to read while a weak player will stick to stereotyped patterns, rendering himself easy to read.

big blind: In hold 'em, the big blind is the second player to the left of the dealer, also known as the button. After the small blind makes a compulsory bet to start the game, the big blind then makes a compulsory raise of twice the small blind's bet. These two compulsory bets then become the starting pot as long as no *antes* are required.

After the small blind and big blind make their compulsory bets, the other players act in turn, starting with the player to the left of the big blind, who is said to be *under-the-gun*. Every other player has the option to call the big blind's bet, raise the big blind's bet, or fold. If some players call but no one raises, the big blind has an option of checking and seeing a flop, or raising himself. If he chooses not to raise, he is said to be *checking his option.*

blocking bet: A bet made on the turn or river with the intention of heading off a larger bet from your opponent. For instance, if you have a medium-strength hand on the river, you might be willing to invest a small amount to see if your hand is best, but if your opponent makes a big bet, you intend to fold. Making a small bet and showing some strength could have the effect of making your opponent call, fearing you have a really big hand. In this way, your bet serves the purpose of 'setting the price' for the river and blocking your opponent's intentions.

bluff: A bet made with a weak hand designed to chase your opponent out of the pot. Players mix appropriate numbers of bluffs along with their value bets to achieve a balanced strategy that is difficult for their opponents to categorize.

bluff catcher: A hand which has some value but which can really only beat a bluff.
 Example: Your hand is the A♣J♠. The board has come the J♥T♥9♣4♣2♥, and your opponent makes a big bet on the river. You have top pair, top kicker, but with the straight and flush draws on board, your opponent's bet is representing a big hand. Thus, your top pair is now only a bluff catcher, not a value hand.

board: In hold'em, the board consists of the common cards in the center of the table — the flop, turn, and river cards. If a player's best five-card hand doesn't use his hole cards, he is said to be *playing the board.*

bottom set: A set made by using the lowest card on the flop. If a player holds a pair of deuces in his hand and the flop comes the A♦J♣2♠, he has made 'bottom set,' the lowest possible set on that board.

brick: A card on the turn or river that doesn't help your hand in any way.

bubble: In a tournament, the period just before all remaining players qualify for a cash prize. The last player to be eliminated before the money is known as the *bubble boy*. Many players play too tight during the bubble period, hoping to get in the money. This offers a great opportunity for aggressive players to attack freely and pick up chips.

burn card: A card discarded by the dealer from the deck before a live card is dealt. In each street of a live hold 'em game, the dealer puts one card in the muck before dealing the three cards of the flop, or the single card of the turn or river. These dead cards are known as the burn cards.

button: The player to the right of the small blind who acts last on each betting round from the flop on. The button is the seat with the maximum positional advantage in each hand.

buy-in: The amount of money you need to put down to enter a tournament or a cash game. In tournaments, the buy-in is a fixed amount, ranging from $50 or less for a small, one-day tournament at a casino to $10,000 for the Main Event at the World Series of Poker. (Some specialized events with limited eligibility have charged even more than this.)

In cash games, the buy-in is a range of amounts which you can tailor to your bankroll or preferences. A casino spreading a $1-$2 no-limit hold 'em table, for instance, might allow buy-ins between $50 and $300, corresponding to a range of 25 to 150 big blinds. The poker room manager can tell you what ranges of buy-ins are allowed for the game you're interested in.

call: A player makes a call when he matches the amount of money that has been put into the pot so far in the betting round. By calling, he remains in the hand and retains his equity in the pot. Unlike a bet or a raise, a call makes no effort to win the pot at that point.

calling station: A player who will call every street post-flop with a made but very marginal hand, such as second or third pair. Calling stations are targets for relentless value betting with a good hand, but they cannot be bluffed.

check: In hold 'em, if no one has made a bet, a player can elect to check (putting no money in the pot) rather than bet. The player stays in the hand and can call or raise if another player opens the betting. Checking is only possible in a post-flop betting round. Before the flop, the small and big blind have made forced bets to open the betting, so no checking is possible.

Example: Three players remain in the hand after the flop. The first player elects to check, as does the second player. If the third player also checks, the hand is said to be 'checked around,' the betting action is concluded, and the turn card is dealt. If the third player opens the action with a bet, the first player has the option of calling, raising, or folding. The second player then has the same options.

check back: Checking after your opponent has started the betting by checking to you. Checking back is both a way of disguising your hand (if it's strong) or of exercising pot control (if you have a medium-strength hand that doesn't want a large pot.)

check in the dark: Checking before the flop cards are dealt. The player who is first to act on the flop in a live game can announce "checking dark" before the flop cards appear. In this case, he's required to check and the action passes to the next player in turn. There is no advantage to the announcement, but it's routine for players who act first to check to the player with a positional advantage, so the cost of a dark check is little or nothing. The dark checker retains the right to make a check-raise if a bet is made by one of the other players. Players can also check dark on the turn and/or river.

check-raise: A raise on the flop, turn, or river after first checking the hand. A good check-raise with a strong hand can often win an extra bet from an aggressive player who will attack any sign of weakness.

check-shove: A shove on the flop, turn, or river after first checking the hand. Like the check-raise, the check-shove is done with the idea of picking up an extra bet from an unsuspecting player who will bet when he sees a sign of weakness. But it can also be done as an attempt to make the bettor fold. It's mostly a tournament move from a player with a short stack. In a cash game, the move is unusual because with large stacks, a shove becomes a huge overbet.

chip utility: The relative value of chips in tournament play. Accumulating a given number of chips is more valuable to a small stack than a large stack because they represent a greater percentage increase in the stack. Thus the utility of a single chip is larger in a smaller stack.

cold-call: A pre-flop call of a raise from a player who hasn't yet put any money into the pot, as opposed to a call from the blinds, or a call of a limp.

combo draw: A drawing hand which is both a straight draw and a flush draw.
Example: You hold the Q♠J♠ and the board is the K♠T♦2♠. You have an open-ended straight draw (K-Q-J-T) as well as a flush draw in spades. The flush draw gives you nine outs, while the straight draw gives you an additional six

outs, for a total of 15 outs. (You don't pick up eight outs with the straight draw since you already counted the A♠ and the 9♠ as cards that give you a flush draw.) A combo draw with 15 outs makes you the overall favorite against a hand like top pair (with two cards to come).

connected flop: A flop whose cards are all close together, with two of the same suit. Connected flops are dangerous since they create possible flush and straight draws.

Example: You pick up the A♦A♥ under-the-gun and raise, get two callers in late position, and the flop is the J♠T♠9♦. This flop is highly connected with many possible straight draws, and a flush draw for anyone holding two spades. In addition, anyone who called with a medium pair has now made a set. Your aces are extremely vulnerable and difficult to play in this situation.

continuation bet: A bet made on the flop after a player has taken the lead by raising preflop. On average, good players will make continuation bets on 60 to 70 percent of their flops.

counterfeiting: A situation in hold 'em where your hand is devalued by the appearance of the turn or river card.

Example: Your hole cards are the 4♦4♠. The flop is the Q♣Q♦6♠. At this moment, your hand is two pair: queens and fours with a six kicker. Now suppose the turn card is the 6♥. The appearance of the second six on board has rendered your pair of fours worthless. Your best possible hand is still two pair (queens and sixes), but to make it you have to play the board. Your fours are said to have been *counterfeited*.

cutoff (CO): The player who acts just before the button.

deep stack: A stack which is more than about 150 big blinds. Deep stacks offer high implied odds which allow players to play more hands.

delayed c-bet: A continuation bet made on the turn rather than the flop. Normally, a player who takes the lead in the preflop betting will make a continuation bet on the flop, whether he has hit his hand or not. Since he showed strength preflop, his continuation bet carries more weight than a bet from a player who didn't show strength preflop. If the leader has a modest hand after the flop, he may elect to check the flop and make a bet on the turn instead, which is known as a delayed continuation bet. The effect of delaying the bet is to control the pot size by taking a betting round out of play. It's also a way of disguising betting patterns so that the player becomes less predictable.

disguised hand: A strong hand which is hard to read from the board. For example, if the board is the K♣Q♦8♠5♣4♥ and you hold the 7♦6♦, you have the nuts (the only possible straight), but your hand is extremely well disguised. A player holding a set of kings, for instance, will probably lose his entire stack because he has the second nuts and the chance that you hold seven-six is very unlikely.

domination: A situation where two players hold the same high card, but one player has a higher kicker. The player with the lower kicker is said to be dominated.
  Example: Before the flop, two players go all-in. When they expose their cards, one player shows ace-king and the other shows ace-queen. The queen is dominated by the king. In order to win, the trailer has to hit one of the three remaining queens in the deck or make an unlikely hand such as a straight. The player with the ace-king is more than a 70 percent favorite to win the hand.

donk bet: A lead-off bet on the flop made by a player who didn't take the betting lead preflop.
  Example: Preflop, the under-the-gun player makes a standard opening raise and everyone folds but the big blind, who calls. After the flop, the big blind acts first and rather

than checking to see what the under-the-gun player does, instead leads with a bet. Donk bets are generally considered a mark of a weak player, but can be a tool in the hands of a good player.

double barrel: A bluff where you miss the flop but make a continuation bet, get called, and then make another bet on the turn.

double belly buster: A straight draw in which the player has a chance of hitting two different inside straight draws.

Example: You hold the J♣T♣ and the flop is the A♦Q♥8♠. Putting the board together with your hand gives A-Q-J-T-8, and you can make an inside straight if a king comes, and a different inside straight if a nine comes. The two different draws make your holding equivalent to an open-ended straight draw.

dry board: A flop which does not offer any possible draws. For example, on a flop like the K♥8♦2♣, no one can have a straight or flush draw.

early position: In a nine-handed hold 'em game, the first two players to act after the blinds (the under-the-gun player and the player to his left) are said to be in early position. They act first preflop, and unless the blinds join in, they will act first on the post-flop betting rounds. Early position is a disadvantage because you have to act before your opponent, thus giving him more information than you have.

effective stack: The smaller of two stacks that are involved in a hand. The players base their decisions on the size of the smaller, effective stack since that represents all the chips that can be won or lost in the hand.

Example: In a $1-$2 no-limit hold 'em cash game, the player under-the-gun, with a stack of only $30, raises to $6. You are on the button with a pair of deuces and a much larger stack. If you call and only the two of you see the flop, the effective stack would then be $24, the amount your opponent has left since he has the smaller stack.

equity: See *expected value.*

expected value (EV): The exact value of a particular action in a hand. Expected value can be positive (+EV) or negative (-EV) depending on whether a particular action will make money or lose money in the long run.

Fancy Play Syndrome (FPS): Describes a player who likes to make clever exotic plays when simple plays would make more money.

Fill up: To hit a card that makes a big hand, like a straight, flush, or full house.

final table: The last table of players in a tournament. In tournament play, the starting field is spread among as many tables as necessary to accommodate the field. With 900 entries, for instance, the casino would need 100 tables to house the entire field at nine players per table. As players are eliminated, tables are gradually broken up to let the remaining players play at full tables if possible. When the field has been reduced to just nine players, the players sit at the final table, and remain there until a winner emerges. In the Main Event of the *World Series of Poker*, the final table is currently known as the *November Nine*.

fish: A very weak player. Fish typically call a lot, pay no attention to their opponent's possible hands, and lose lots of money quickly.

fit or fold: An excessively conservative style where a player will fold on the flop unless he makes a good hand (medium pair or better) or has a strong draw. Fit or fold players rarely, if ever, bluff.

flat call: Just calling a bet rather than folding or raising. A flat call may indicate strength since the caller has made no effort to bluff his opponent off the hand.

float: Call a continuation bet with nothing with the aim of taking the pot away with a bluff on the turn. Floating is effective against players who routinely make many continuation bets.

flop: In hold 'em, the first three community cards. When playing hold 'em, each player is dealt two cards, called the *hole cards*. The deal is followed by a round of betting, called the pre-flop betting. When that round concludes, the dealer discards one card from the top of the deck (the *burn* card), then deals three common cards in the middle of the table, called the *flop*. Another round of betting then follows. Action after the flop has appeared is known as *post-flop* play.

flop a set: A situation where one of the flop cards matches a pair in your hand, giving you three of a kind.
    Example: You call a preflop bet with the 4♦4♣. The flop is the A♠K♣4♥. You now have a set of fours which is almost certainly the best hand at the table.

flop texture: The character of the flop. A flop will favor some types of hands and not others. Deciding what hands will fit well with a given flop texture and whether your opponent is likely to have those hands is a key poker skill. *Dry flops*, *wet flops*, *paired flops*, and *rainbow flops* are all examples of flop textures that will drive the flop betting.

flush draw: A hand with four cards of a suit which will become a flush if a fifth card of the suit appears.
    Example: in no-limit hold 'em, a player's hole cards are the A♦K♦. The flop is the 8♦7♦4♠. The two diamonds in his

hand plus the two diamonds on the flop give him a flush draw. Any diamond on the turn or river will complete the *nut flush*, giving him a very strong hand. (His chance of actually hitting the flush, if he stays in the hand until the end, is about 35 percent.) Many players will bet aggressively with a flush draw since they can win the hand in two ways: Their opponent may fold, fearing they have a strong made hand, or they might actually hit their flush, giving them a monster hand.

fold equity (FE): Part of the equity of a bet that results when the opponent folds, giving you the pot. All bet/hand combinations contain two kinds of equity: fold equity and showdown equity. A bet can make the opponent fold now or on a later street, without ever having to reveal the hand. A hand can have showdown equity as well, which is its ability to win when the hand goes to showdown. Put the two equities together and you have the total equity for the hand.

free card: A card on the turn or river that didn't have to be 'paid for' by making or calling a bet.

Example: Preflop, a player in early position makes a raise and you call in late position with the 9♦8♦. The flop is the K♣T♦7♥, giving you an open-ended straight draw. The early position player bets. You raise with your drawing hand and your opponent calls. The turn is the 7♦, which doesn't help your straight, but your opponent checks and you check back, enabling you to see the river card for free. Your raise on the flop enabled you to get a free card on the turn.

freezeout: A tournament format with a single chance to enter. If you enter and lose all your chips, you're knocked out and can't get back in.

grinder: An online player in cash games or tournaments who tries to make a living by playing an enormous number of hours each day, and keeping multiple tables going at the same time.

gutshot: An inside straight which can be filled by only one card. *Example:* You hold the T♦8♦ and the flop comes the A♥J♥7♣ giving you a gutshot straight draw. The J-T-8-7 can only be filled by hitting exactly a nine. A gutshot straight draw can give you a playable hand if you have other ways of winning, like a small pair or overcards.

hand reading: The art of reducing your opponent's hand range from a large number of hands to a small number by making logical deductions from his actions. The answers to questions like "What hands would he have raised preflop from his position?" and "Which of those hands would have checked and called on the flop?" enable a player to gradually whittle down his opponents possibilities to a small, manageable number of hands.

heads-up (HU): A poker game involving only two players. All tournaments, except super satellites, end with a heads-up showdown.

hijack seat: The seat two to the right of the dealer button. The hijack has worse position than the *button* or the *cutoff* seat, but better position than earlier seats at the table.

hyper-LAG: A player even more aggressive than a loose-aggressive (LAG) player. Hyper-LAGs will play a wider range of hands, bet more, raise more, and shove more than LAG players. Hyper-LAGs are sometimes able to accumulate huge stacks of chips in the early stages of tournaments, but suffer later when players are compelled to defend their shorter stacks.

image: How someone is perceived at the table. A player who has been involved in many pots, betting and raising actively, is said to have an aggressive image. A player who mainly sits on the sidelines, rarely raising and mostly checking or calling, will have a passive image.

When playing poker, it's essential to understand the images of the other players, as this will give you clues about their hands and how you should play against them. When a player who has been tight and passive enters the pot with a solid raise, it's safe to assume they have a premium hand. When a loose, aggressive player enters with a raise, he could have a wide range of possible hands.

While it's important to know your opponent's image, it's equally important to be aware of your own image. When you understand how you appear to your opponents, how they will interpret your play should also become apparent, as well as what moves you can make.

implied odds: Money which you might win in the future as a result of making a particular play. For instance, when you call a bet to draw to a flush, the value of your call is based partly on the immediate odds being offered by the pot, and partly on whatever money you might be able to win if you hit your flush. That future money makes up your implied odds.

Independent Chip Model (ICM): A mathematical model which allows you to make statements about the value of a stack in tournament play. ICM is especially useful in Sit 'n Go's where it allows you to calculate the optimal strategy for making and calling all-ins when only a few players remain and only a few places get paid. Its use in larger multi-table tournaments is more problematic since the model assumes that stacks of different sizes are equally likely to accumulate or lose chips on future hands; there is plenty of evidence, however, that larger stacks accumulate chips more easily.

information bet: A bet made to get information about the strength of your hand by gauging your opponent's response. Also known as betting "to see where you stand." Such bets are often mistakes.

in position (IP): A player who acts after his opponent acts. Being in position is a serious advantage, and can be a decisive factor in deciding whether to enter a hand at all.

isolation play: A play made when a weak player is in the hand with the intention of causing other players at the table to fold, usually leaving you one-on-one in position with the weak player.

Example: Preflop, a weak player in the third seat limps into the pot. You know from past history that this player tends to limp with a wide variety of weak hands. Acting next, you make a big raise which should have the effect of chasing the remaining players out of the pot unless they have a big hand, leaving you isolated and in position against the weak player.

jam: Move all-in. Synonyms are *shove* and *push.*

kicker: An unpaired card which completes a hand. In some cases, the kicker will play and may determine who actually wins the hand.

Example: In a no-limit hold 'em tournament you have the A♣K♦ and your opponent has the 9♥9♠. Before the flop, you push all-in and your opponent calls. The flop is the Q♥Q♠9♦. Your opponent has flopped a *full house,* nines full of queens, while you have just a pair of queens.

You're preparing to take the walk of shame out of the tournament hall. The turn is the Q♦. You improve to a hand of three queens while your opponent improves to a better full house, queens full of nines. The river is the Q♣.

Amazingly, this card lets you win the hand. Both you and your opponent now have four queens, but your fifth card, the kicker, is the A♣, whereas your opponent's fifth card is any of the nines. (It doesn't matter if he uses the nine on board or one of the nines in his hand.) Your best five card hand, Q-Q-Q-Q-A, beats his best hand, Q-Q-Q-Q-9, because of the better kicker.

LAG: See *loose-aggressive*.

late position: The cutoff and button seats at a nine-handed hold 'em table. A player in late position will act last or next to last on the flop and later streets. Acting last is a big advantage in hold 'em since you act with more information than the other players.

lead: To make the first bet in a hand post-flop.

leak: A persistent type of error in one's play which allows equity to slip away. Plugging leaks is a goal of improving players.

leveling war: A series of raises between two players with weak hands, each of whom is trying to bluff the other out of the pot by representing progressively stronger hands.

light: A bet or raise made with a weaker than normal hand.
> *Example:* Your opponent raises preflop from middle position. On the button, you make a 3-bet with the 9♠8♠. This is too weak a hand to make a 3-bet for value; you are said to be 3-betting *light*.

limp: Calling the big blind preflop, but not raising. Players who subsequently call are also known as limpers.

line: A player's betting sequence post-flop.
> *Example:* A player holds the A♥K♥ pre-flop and raises, getting one call from the big blind. The flop is the K♣Q♣4♠. The big blind checks, the player bets, and his opponent calls. The turn is the 5♦.
>
> The big blind checks, and the player checks as well with the intention of keeping the pot size small and making a *value bet* on the river if the big blind checks again. The betting sequence of bet-check-bet is known as a line. In most hands, many lines are possible, and each one gives a different impression of what the player may hold. After a hand, good

players will often analyze their line, trying to determine if a different line would have yielded a better result.

line balancing: Making sure that your various betting lines are properly balanced between strong hands, medium hands, and bluffs. Failure to balance your lines can result in exploitation by observant opponents.

Example: After leading preflop, a player makes continuation bets on the flop with all his strong hands, all his medium hands, and a few hands where he misses the flop altogether. He believes that his opponents won't be able to tell what he has when he bets. While true, his approach means that when he doesn't bet, he has a weak hand. An opponent can then bet with anything after the leader checks, certain that he'll win the pot. The leader's attempt to balance his betting line has resulted in a totally unbalanced checking line.

line check: A posthumous discussion of the line chosen by a player when playing a hand. Discussing your lines with friends and mentors is one of the best ways of improving your game.

locksmith: A very tight player who only wants to play premium hands and who only gets a lot of money in the pot with a very big hand, usually a set or better. (See also *nit.*) Locksmiths are easy to play against because they rarely, if ever, bluff, and you almost always have a pretty clear idea of what they have.

loose: A player who likes to be involved in the action and tends to play a wide variety of hands in different situations. A loose player who likes to bet and raise with a lot of hands is known as *loose-aggressive*; a loose player who simply likes to see a lot of flops, but tends to check and call instead of betting is known as *loose-passive*. The opposite of a loose player is a *tight* player.

loose-aggressive (LAG): A player who enters a lot of pots but usually plays them aggressively by raising rather than calling. He likes to take control of the pots he enters.

loose-passive (LP): A player who enters a lot of pots, but generally by calling instead of raising. He will typically continue after the flop with weak hands. (See *calling station*.) This is a losing style of play at almost any stake.

M: In tournament play, the ratio of a player's stack to the current starting pot size. The M ratio gives the number of rounds a player could play before the blinds and antes consume his whole stack. The concept was first developed by the brilliant backgammon and poker pro Paul Magriel, and was named after him. The ratio helps determine what level of aggression is optimal and what hands are playable and not playable.

Example: Late in a tournament, the blinds and antes are 2,000 and 4,000, with a 500-chip ante and there are eight players at the table. (The small blind is 2,000, the big blind is 4,000, and each player antes 500 per hand.) If your stack is 200,000, what is your M?

Answer: With eight players anteing 500 apiece, the antes total 4,000 per hand. Added to the blinds, we have a starting pot of 10,000. Dividing a stack of 200,000 by blinds and antes of 10,000, gives an M of 20.

made hand: A post-flop hand that already has some value, like a high pair or better. Contrast a made hand with a drawing hand, which still has to hit something good to have any value, or a trash hand, which has no value.

metagame: That part of poker which goes beyond the play of individual hands to the aspect of what you know about the other players and what they know about you, and how this knowledge should factor into your evaluation of the current hand. The better the players, the more the metagame should factor into your decision-making.

middle position: At a full no-limit hold 'em table of nine players, the third, fourth, and fifth players to act preflop. The first two players to act are said to be in early position, while the sixth and seventh players are in late position. (The blinds are the last players to act preflop but the first players to act on subsequent rounds.)

Middle position players can bet more aggressively preflop because they have a good chance of being in position after the flop. The late position players, however, can be the most aggressive because they are almost certain to be in position after the flop.

min-raise: The minimum raise possible at that stage of the hand. Preflop, a min-raise is a raise of twice the big blind. Post-flop, the minimum bet is the size of the big blind, and a min-raise would be twice the size of the current bet.

Example: In a $1-$2 no-limit hold 'em cash game, the first player to act after the blinds are posted has three options: he can call for $2; he can make the minimum raise, which would be to $4; or he can raise to any amount larger than $4, up to the size of his entire stack.

monotone: A flop with all three cards of the same suit. For example, a flop of the Q♠T♠4♠ is a montone flop in spades. Anyone holding a spade in their hand now has a flush draw. Anyone holding two spades has a made flush. Because it's so easy to make a flush on a monotone flop, anyone who doesn't have flush possibilities will usually bet cautiously.

monster: A huge hand which is almost certain to win the pot. On an unpaired board, straights and flushes are monsters. On a paired board, full houses and four of a kinds are the monsters.

muck: The discard pile. A player tossing his hand away is said to muck his hand, or throw his cards into the muck.

multiway pot: A pot with three or more players post-flop.

nit: An extremely tight and conservative player who needs to have a good hand before entering a pot, and who will rarely, if ever, bluff. A nit's ultra-conservative style makes him easy to read, and thus he doesn't pose a real threat to a strong player. However, at a table of loose, weak, highly aggressive players, the nit's style is close to optimal and he can expect to be a solid winner.

nut flush: A flush headed by the highest flush card not on board, usually an ace which can't be beaten by any other flush.
  Example: You hold the A♥J♥, and the board is K♥8♥7♣3♦2♥. You have a heart flush headed by the ace, which beats any other player with two hearts in his hand.

nuts: In hold 'em, the best possible hand given the board. Being able to determine whether or not your hand is the nuts is an important skill for the beginning hold 'em player.
  Example: After the river card is dealt, the board is the Q♣J♣7♠9♣7♦. *What is the nuts?*
  Answer: Holding the K♣T♣ is the nuts, giving you a king-high straight flush. The second nuts (second-best possible hand) is the T♣8♣, giving you a queen-high straight flush. The third nuts is the 7♥7♠, giving you four of a kind. Note that on a paired board, four of a kind will always be a possibility.

nut peddling: Playing only strong hands preflop, then raising only when those hands become very powerful post-flop, making hands like two pair, sets, or better. *Nits* and *rocks* play this way. It's a low-variance style and somewhat effective at a table of weak players. Against good opponents, it's relatively ineffective since it's a predictable style.

one gapper: A hand with two cards separated by one rank, such as the J♠9♠. One-gappers are useful for making straights, although not quite as good as connectors like the J♠T♠. The one-gapper needs a specific card (here a ten) to have straight potential, while the connector can build a straight on either end.

open ended straight draw (OESD): A hand with four consecutive cards to a straight, needing only one card on either end to complete a straight.

Example: In hold 'em, your hole cards are the J♠9♣. The flop is the A♥T♠8♥. You now have the J-T-9-8, a straight draw open at both ends. Either a queen or a seven on the turn or the river will complete your straight.

Since there are four queens and four sevens left in the deck, and 47 unseen cards in total, your chance of hitting the straight on the turn is $\frac{8}{47}$, or about 17 percent.

open raise: A pre-flop raise after all the players in front of you have folded.

opposite player: A player who consistently plays his hands in a way opposite to their true strength.

out: A card which will give you the winning hand if it hits. If you have the A♥K♥ in your hand and the flop comes the J♣T♥4♥, any heart on the turn will give you the nut flush and any queen which is not the Q♥ will give you the nut straight. You have nine outs from the hearts and three more outs from the queens, for a total of 12 "sure" outs. In addition, an ace or a king might give you a winning pair, for six more possible outs.

out of position (OOP): A player who acts first in a betting round. Being out of position is a disadvantage because the first player to act gives information to subsequent players, who can use that information to make better decisions.

over the top: To make a raise over a bet or raise.
Example: Player A bets, player B raises, and Player C then makes yet another raise. We say that Player C came *over the top* of Player B.

overbet: A bet larger than the current pot.
Example: After the pre-flop betting in a no-limit hold 'em game, the pot stands at $100. The flop is dealt and the first player to act checks. The second player now bets $150. Since this bet is larger than the pot, it constitutes an *overbet*.

overpair: On the flop, a pocket pair higher than any of the board cards.

paired board: In hold 'em, a board with at least one pair showing
Example: After the river card is dealt, the board looks like this: K♣4♥2♠2♣9♦. The two deuces make this a paired board which are especially dangerous since *full houses* and *quads* are now possible hands. The presence of a pair on board will often make players cautious and slow down the betting.

passive: A player who tends to check and call rather than bet and raise. Passive players have trouble being successful because they mostly need to win by showing down the best hand, which can be difficult. An *active* player is more focused on betting and raising, which allows him to win pots when his opponent folds.

playing the board: When a player's best five-card hand in hold 'em consists of the board cards, he is said to be *playing the board*.
Example: A player's hole cards are the 2♣2♦ and the board is the Q♣ Q♠T♦T♥4♠. His hand is two pair, queens and tens, with a four kicker. Although his deuces make a pair, they don't play because the pairs on board are of higher rank.

Also notice that neither deuce can be used as a kicker because the four on board is a higher rank.

playing fast: Betting or raising aggressively on every street of the hand. This way of playing gets a lot of money in the pot quickly, and will usually force medium-strength or drawing hands to fold.

playing position: Making bets and raises when a player has good position. It's a big advantage to have position in a hand, but some players are too timid to make good use of their potential positional advantage. A player who knows how to play position is constantly using his advantage to take down pots or put extra pressure on his opponents.

pocket pair: In hold 'em, two hole cards of the same rank. For example, a player dealt the 6♥6♣ as his hole cards has a pocket pair of sixes. Pocket pairs are very strong in hold 'em, and a player can expect to be dealt a pocket pair about once every 17 hands. A pair of aces in the hole is sometimes referred to as 'pocket rockets.'

polarized range: A range that consists only of very strong hands and bluffs. On the river, a player will often call with their medium-strength hands while betting or raising with their very strong hands (for value) and some of their trash hands (as a bluff). Players who exclusively call and raise like this are said to have *polarized ranges,* and this style can also be used by the initial bettor. A polarized range isn't necessarily a worse strategy than a balanced range; much depends on the history between the players.

position: A player who acts after his opponent is said to "have position on him."
   Example: In no-limit hold 'em, you are sitting on the button. Before the flop, the player under-the-gun raises, the players between you and him fold, you elect to call, the small

blind folds, and the big blind calls. After the flop, the big blind will act first, followed by the player under-the-gun, followed by you. Since your opponents both have to act before you do, you have position on them. Since poker is a game of incomplete information, having position is a significant advantage in the hand. On each betting round, you will have more information than your opponents when you act, which will translate into better decision-making.

pot-committed: Having so few chips in your stack relative to the size of the pot that any all-in move by your opponent will require a call because of the favorable pot odds that are being offered. If making a normal-sized bet will leave you or your opponent pot-committed, then an all-in move is likely preferable.

pot control: Making plays to limit the size of the pot with a good but not great hand.
  Example: On the flop, a player makes a hand like top pair, good kicker. He bets and his opponent calls. The turn does not improve his hand and he elects to check. Although his hand is reasonably strong, the possibility that his opponent may be trapping makes him unwilling to create a big pot with this hand. Instead, he prefers to keep the pot somewhat small and perhaps make one final bet on the river if his opponent has not shown strength. It's an important concept, although passive players will take the idea to extremes.

pot odds: The money odds offered by the pot if you call a bet. For example, if the pot contains $20 and it costs you $5 to call, the pot odds are 4-to-1.

pot-sized bet (PSB): A bet that's the size of the pot. If someone has acted and bet in front of you, a pot-sized raise will be the amount required to call the first bet, plus the size of the pot at that point.

Example: The pot is $40 and your opponent bets $30. A pot-sized raise on your part would be $30 (to call his bet) plus $40+$30+$30, (the size of the pot at that point), or an additional $100, for a total of $130.

pre-flop: The first betting round in hold 'em after the two hole cards are dealt but before the three flop cards are dealt.

probe bet: In no-limit hold 'em, a small post-flop bet made with the intention of either winning the pot without much risk or getting some information on how well you're doing in the hand. In the modern game, probe bets are less common than they used to be since opponents correctly interpret them as showing weakness and respond by attacking with a big raise.

protect your hand: Make a post-flop bet which forces your opponent to pay more money for the chance of hitting his drawing hand.

Example: You raise preflop with a pair of aces, are called by one player, and the flop comes the K♠8♣7♣. Your pair of aces are likely still good, but with two clubs and two connected cards on board, your opponent could have a flush draw or any of several possible straight draws. A bet here prevents your opponent from getting a free card to beat you, and is thus said to 'protect your hand.'

pulling the trigger: Making a big bluff after some thought.

push: Move all-in. Synonyms are *shove* or *jam*.

ragged board: A dry board that offers little chance of connecting with any of the players.

Example: In a no-limit hold 'em cash game, the under-the-gun player raises and gets two calls from players in late position. The flop is the 9♠4♣2♥. This ragged board is unlikely to connect with anyone unless someone was holding a small pair and just made a set.

rags: Low cards which probably don't help the hand of either player.
Example: In a no-limit hold 'em cash game, the player under-the-gun raises and gets 3-bet by the button. The under-the-gun player then calls. The flop comes the A♥4♣2♦. This flop might be described as 'ace-rag-rag' since the four and deuce are unlikely to help either player given the preflop betting.

rainbow: A flop containing cards from three different suits. The K♣T♦4♠ fkop, for instance, is a rainbow flop. Notice that it doesn't allow anyone to make a flush unless two more flush cards come on the turn and the river.

raise: A bet which is larger than any previous bet or raise on this betting round. A raise takes control of the pot; anyone who wishes to stay must at least match the size of your raise with a call, or else fold.

In live poker, you need to make sure that your raising action is clear, and beginners sometimes run into trouble here. Suppose that after the flop, your opponent opens the betting with a $30 bet and you wish to raise to $100. If you pick up a $100 chip, announce 'Raise to $100' or something similar, and put the chip into the pot, you're all right as your action is clear. But if you simply put the $100 chip into the pot and say nothing, your action could be interpreted as a call of his bet (in which case you're waiting for the dealer to give you $70 in change) instead of a raise. The rules require the dealer in this case to interpret your move as a call.

Suppose instead that you moved four $25 chips into the pot and said nothing. In this case, the dealer will interpret your action as a raise to $100 since your action makes no sense if you wished to call. You can protect yourself and avoid confusion in live games by always announcing your action before you make it.

raise for value: To make a raise because you believe you have the best hand, and you have a chance to either make weaker hands fold or extract more money from them.

range: The set of hands with which a player might have played as he did. For instance, if a very tight player raises under-the-gun in no-limit hold 'em, we might decide that his range is probably a high pair (aces down through tens) or ace-king or ace-queen. During the play of the hand, good players try to assign a range of hands to their opponent and then narrow the range as more information becomes available. In some cases, it's possible to narrow the opponent's range to a single hand, although this is rare.

range war: A description of the thinking process of modern poker in which players try to assign a range to their opponents, then see how that range connects with the flop. At the same time, they try to assess what sort of range they appear to present to their opponents, to see how they might be viewed by the other players.

raw winning probability: The probability that you can win a hand if the board was dealt out to the river with no further betting.

rebuy tournament: A tournament structure in which players who are knocked out can reenter by paying another entry fee which may be the same or less than the original entry fee. A rebuy tournament might allow multiple rebuys by the same player, or limit the rebuys to only one. The period of time in which rebuys are allowed is known as the *rebuy period*. In online tournaments, the rebuy period is often 60 to 90 minutes. In live tournaments, the rebuy period may last for an entire day. A tournament in which no rebuys are permitted is called a *freezeout*.

reverse implied odds: Being in a position where your opponent is getting implied odds from you. If you have a hand with little chance to improve, you may expect to lose money, on average, if the hand is played down to the river.

river: In hold 'em, the last (fifth) card dealt to the board, and the round of betting that follows.

satellite: A tournament run with the intention of awarding one or more players an entry fee to a larger tournament. A *single-table satellite* usually pays a single entry fee to the winner. A *mega satellite* will award multiple entry fees to the highest-finishing players.

    Example: The entry fee for the Main Event of the World Series of Poker is $10,000. Prior to the Main Event, the organizers will run single-table satellites with a $1,050 entry fee. As soon as 10 players sign up, a table will start. The winner will get his $10,000 entry fee paid, while $500 will go to the organizers.

satellite qualifier: A player who qualifies for a major online or live tournament through a satellite process. Tournaments with many satellites are particularly attractive to strong players since satellite winners are generally weaker than the average player. During the first day of play, strong players try to identify the satellite qualifiers and attack them with aggressive play.

scare card: A card on the turn or river that has the potential to give someone a strong hand.

    Example: In a no-limit hold 'em cash game, you hold a pair of sixes on the button. A player in early position raises, you call with your pair, and the flop comes the T♣4♦2♦. The player in early position makes a continuation bet of two-thirds of the pot, you call since you have a pair, and the board is unlikely to have helped your opponent's hand. If he raised preflop with hands like ace-king, ace-queen, or ace-jack, your pair gives you the best hand.

The turn card, however, is the A♠, a genuine *scare* card. If he has one of those aces, he now has the best hand. While he could have a hand like king-queen or queen-jack, the ace is threatening enough that you're going to fold if he bets again. Of course, if the leader doesn't have an ace in his hand, then the turn ace is a scare card for him as well, and may stop him from betting.

semi-bluff: A post-flop bet or raise with a hand, usually a drawing hand, that probably needs to improve to win the pot, and which has outs to become the best hand.

set: In hold 'em, three of a kind, with one of the cards being on the board and the other two in the player's hand.

Example: You hold the T♥T♠ and the flop is the Q♣T♦2♥. You have a set of tens.

Example: You hold the T♥9♠ and the flop is the Q♣T♦T♠. In this case, your hand is also three tens, but here we say you have *trip* tens, not a set.

short stack: A stack of chips fewer than about 20 big blinds. In a tournament, some players will be reduced to short stacks as the tournament grinds on. For instance, if the blinds in a tournament have risen to 1,000 and 2,000, you have only 15,000, and other players at the table have 100,000 or more, you will be considered a short stack even though you may have many more chips than at the start of the tournament. A good player with a short stack will adopt a very specific strategy to survive, generally moving *all-in* as soon as he picks up a decent hand.

shove: An all-in move. Synonyms are *push* and *jam*.

showdown equity: The value of a hand at showdown. The value of a hand is made up of two parts: *fold equity*, which is the value of being able to make your opponent lay down his hand, and *showdown equity*, which is the value of being able to win when the cards are finally shown down after the river.

Sit 'n Go: A tournament with no specified starting time. Online sites or casinos will maintain a signup list for sit 'n go tournaments, and as soon as the required number of players sign up, the tournament will start. Sit 'n go's are usually single table tournaments, but multi-table versions are possible, especially at online sites.

slowplaying: Playing a strong hand in a deceptive manner by checking and calling rather than betting and raising. Good players know to slowplay some of the time; bad players tend to slowplay either too much or not at all.

small ball: A style of play that involves making small bets and raises rather than large ones, putting pressure on the opponent and gaining information at small cost.

small blind: In hold 'em, the small blind is the first player to the left of the dealer, or *button*. To start the hand, the small blind makes a compulsory *bet*. When the stakes of a game are listed, the size of the small blind is the first number given. For example, if in the first round of a tournament the blinds are 50 and 100, the small blind's compulsory bet is 50 for each hand. If the small blind remains in the hand, he will be first to act on each betting round after the *flop*.

smooth call: A call of a bet or raise on the flop. A smooth call sometimes indicates great strength since the caller hasn't made any effort to bluff his opponent off his hand, but is content to simply see the next card.

speculative hand: A hand that is unlikely to make the best hand on the flop, but which is well-concealed and can win a big pot if it does manage to hit. Typical speculative hands are small pairs, suited connectors, and suited one- or two-gappers.
Example: Your opponent leads out preflop and you call with the 9♠7♠. In most cases, you will have to throw this hand away after the flop. But if the flop comes the 8♣6♦5♥, you have made the nut straight, and your opponent, if he has a high pair, is unlikely to give you much credit for a hand.

split pot: When two or more players make equivalent five-card hands, the result is a split pot, with the money divided equally between the players. Because of the large number of common cards, split pots are more common in hold 'em than in other poker games. In determining a split, the suits of cards do not matter; only the rank is important. If necessary, all five cards may be used to see which hand outranks the other.

squeeze play: A preflop maneuver which puts pressure on an initial raiser through the threat of others acting behind him, thus 'squeezing' him between the others.
Example: In the preflop betting, Player A opens the pot, Player B, with a speculative hand, calls, and Player C now makes a large raise. Player A is caught in a vise. He may feel he has a good enough hand to call Player C, but what about Player B who (as far as he knows) may be trapping with a big hand. In these circumstances, Player A might fold the best hand.

stack size: The number of chips in your stack. A big stack typically has 100 or more big blinds and a small stack has 20 to 25 big blinds or less. Stacks in between are known as medium stacks.

steal: Winning a pot with a *bluff.*

straight draw: A hand with four cards to a straight which will become a straight if the fifth card appears of the needed rank. Straight draws come in several forms. An *open-ended straight dra*w is a hand like 9-8-7-6 where the player can hit a straight by hitting either a five or a ten on the next card. A *gutshot straight draw* is a hand like 9-8-6-5 where the player needs exactly a seven to make his straight. A *double-gutter* is a hand like Q-T-9-8-6 where either a jack or a seven will complete the straight.

street: Another name (now somewhat obsolete) for the betting rounds in hold 'em. The flop is sometimes called "Third Street," the turn is called "Fourth Street," and the river is called "Fifth Street." In a book published in 2002, *Positively Fifth Street* (a play on an old Dylan standard), Jim McManus described his journey to the final table of the World Series of Poker in 2000.

string bet: A type of illegal betting motion. To make a legal bet, you need to move your betting chips into the pot in one smooth motion. (To be clear, you can also announce 'bet' and give the amount of the bet, although this isn't required.) A string bet occurs when you move some chips into the pot, then go back to your stack and move some more chips into the pot. This could give you an advantage by allowing you to see your opponent's reaction before deciding how many chips to commit. String bets are not allowed in cash games or tournaments, although you'll frequently see them in TV or film dramas. (Hero: I see your $200 — *moves chips into the pot — long pause —* and I raise you $200 more! — *moves more chips into the pot.*)

suck bet: A small bet which offers tempting pot odds, made with the idea of luring you into the pot with the worst hand.

suited connector: Two cards, such as the T♠9♠ which are next to each other in rank and of the same suit. Suited connectors are a speculative hand and often have to be thrown away when they miss the flop. However, they can make well-concealed big hands, and are frequently played aggressively by good players as a way of balancing their range.

TAG: See *tight-aggressive.*

table bully: A player who dominates the table by betting and raising a lot, winning most of his hands before they get to showdown. A table bully inspires fear in his opponents, and eventually forces them to take a stand with inferior hands.

tank: Thinking a long time about a difficult play. "He went in the tank and finally threw his hand away."

tell: In live poker, a physical mannerism that gives away a player's hand strength.
   Example: 'Strong means weak, weak means strong.' Beginners in live poker often try to act in a way opposite to the true strength of their hand. Once spotted, this tell makes their actions easy to interpret.

thin value: A value bet on the river made by a modest hand, usually with the help of accurate hand reading.
   Example: You hold a pair of jacks. The flop was the T♦6♣2♠, the turn was the K♣, and the river was the 2♥. A bet on the river with your jacks would constitute a thin value bet since a king or a deuce in your opponent's hand has you beaten. However, your reading of the betting has convinced you that your opponent is unlikely to have either of these cards.

tight: A player who likes to play only good cards and tends to play only a small range of hands. A tight player who likes to bet and raise with a lot of the hands that he plays is known as *tight-aggressive*; a tight player who mostly just checks and calls instead of betting is known as *tight-passive*. The opposite of a tight player is a *loose* player.

tight-aggressive (TAG): A style of play where you play relatively few hands but you play them aggressively, either by betting or raising instead of calling or checking. Most good players are some variation of this type.

tight-passive: A player who plays only a few hands but who plays them cautiously, checking and calling instead of betting and raising. A tight-passive player can be chased off most hands with small bluffs, but if he calls a bet, he'll have some sort of hand and won't be easy to chase away.

tilt: Losing control of your emotions after a big loss or a bad beat. In these situations, a player is said to "go on tilt," and will often lose lots of money as he attempts to get back to even. Good players generally have excellent control of their emotions and avoid this situation.

top pair: In hold 'em, top pair means one of your hole cards matches the highest card on board.
  Example: Your hole cards are the K♠Q♦ and the flop is the Q♥T♣4♠. You have top pair (queens) with a good kicker (your king). Someone who had a ten in their hand would have middle pair, and a player with a four would have bottom pair.

top set: A set which uses the highest-ranked card on board.
  Example: You hold the K♥K♦ and the flop is the K♠Q♣T♦. You now have the top set of kings.

trash: A worthless hand. Hands like T♦3♣, 7♥2♠, or 9♥4♦ are considered trash hands in no-limit hold 'em, and sensible players fold them preflop unless they have some very good reason for thinking they can steal the pot by betting. *Synonym*: garbage.

triple barrel: A bluff which is an extension of a double-barrel in which you make a third and final bluff on the river.

trips: In hold 'em, three of a kind formed by a pair on the board and a matching card in the player's hand.
>*Example:* A player holds the K♣Q♣ and the flop comes the Q♦Q♠4♠. The player now has three of a kind, queens. If he held two queens in his hand with one queen on board, he would have a *set* of queens.

turn: In hold 'em, the card (and betting round) that immediately follows the flop betting, and the turn is the last betting round before the river. In limit hold 'em, the betting limit doubles on the turn.

two gapper: A hand with two cards separated by two ranks, such as the J♠8♠. Two-gappers have some potential to make straights, although their potential isn't quite as good as connectors like J♠T♠ or one-gappers like J♠9♠. The two-gapper needs two specific cards (here a ten and a nine) to have straight potential, while the connector can easily build a straight on either end and the one-gapper only needs a single interior card.

two pair: A hand consisting of two pairs plus a kicker. Two pair beat any one pair or lower hand, and lose to any three of a kind or higher hand. If two players both have a two pair hand, the rank of the higher pair in each hand determines the winner. If the highest pair in each hand is the same, the rank of the second pair determines the winner. If both pairs in each hand are the same, the rank of the *kicker* determines the winner.
>*Example:* In hold 'em, Player A's hole cards are the K♥9♠, while player B's cards are the K♣7♠. After the river, the board is the K♦T♥T♠8♥2♦. Player A's hand is K-K-T-T-9 (using the 9 from his hand as the kicker). Player B's hand

is K-K-T-T-8 (using the 8 from the board as his kicker). Player A wins because he has a higher kicker.

two-tone: A flop which contains two cards of one suit and another card of a different suit.

Example: A flop like the T♦8♦4♥ is a two-tone flop, with two diamonds and one heart. Anyone holding two diamonds in their hand on this flop now has a flush draw.

underpair: On the flop, a pocket pair lower than any of the board cards.

under-the-gun: The player sitting to the left of the big blind. After the big blind makes a mandatory raise pre-flop, the under-the-gun player is the first to act. Because so many players are left to act behind him and he'll probably be out of position post-flop, the under-the-gun player will generally have a strong hand when he opens the betting.

value bet: A bet made to get more money into the pot with the belief that you currently have the better hand. A *thin value bet* occurs when your hand is not particularly strong, but from the betting (or lack of) you think your opponent will call with an even weaker hand.

Example: In no-limit hold 'em, you hold the K♣Q♠ pre-flop. All fold to you on the button, you raise, and the big blind calls.

The flop is the Q♥T♦8♥ and the big blind checks. With top pair and a good kicker, you make a *continuation bet*, and he calls. The turn is the 4♠.

Again, the big blind checks. Since it's unlikely that the 4♠ hit your opponent's hand, you bet again, and he calls again. The river is the 2♣.

The big blind checks for a third time. You still only have top pair, but your opponent has given no indication that he has a better hand. Therefore, a bet here would be a value bet on your part since it's reasonable to assume that your hand is still good at this point, and your opponent may be willing to call with a hand like a pair of tens.

valuetown: A happy destination where value bets are paid off by weaker hands. Also known as "valuetowning" or "taking your opponent to valuetown."

variance: The inherent variability of poker results. Players who are inadequately bankrolled for the stakes they are playing can be destroyed by variance, and it can be high in no-limit hold 'em. Also, loose-aggressive styles have more variance than tight-aggressive styles.

weak-tight: A player who plays a tight range, but who mostly checks and calls rather than bets and raises. Another name for a *tight-passive* player.

wet board: A board with many flush and straight possibilities. An example would be a flop like the T♥9♥8♥. Players may have hit a flush or straight already, or they could easily have a very strong draw.

window: The first flop card visible to the players. When the dealer deals the flop, he first burns one card, then pulls off three cards and places them in a stack face down on the table. He then turns over the stack. The first card now visible is said to be "in the window."

World Series of Poker: The world championship of poker, held each year in Las Vegas during June and July. The World Series is actually a series of tournaments in different formats, culminating in the Main Event, a no-limit hold 'em tournament with a $10,000 buy-in. The Main Event is played over 12 days in July, whittling a field of many thousands of participants down to a final table of nine players, the 'November Nine,' who then meet in November to play until a winner is determined.

Index

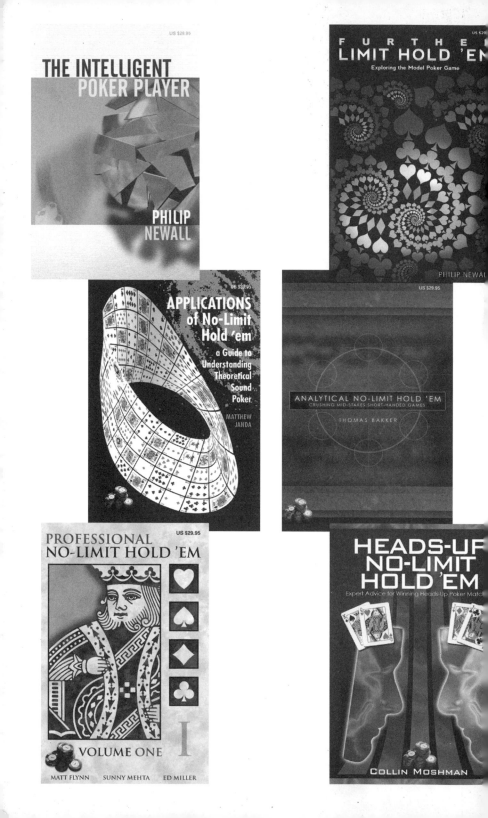